Young Writ[er's]
Thesaurus

D0596491

BAKER & TAYLOR

Young Writer's
Thesaurus

McDougal, Littell & Company

Evanston, Illinois

New York   Dallas   Sacramento   Columbia, SC

ISBN 0-8123-6212-8 (soft-cover)
ISBN 0-8123-6205-5 (hardbound)

Copyright © 1990 by McDougal, Littell & Company
Box 1667, Evanston, Illinois 60204
All rights reserved. Printed in the United States of America

Previously published in 1988 by Nelson Canada as
Young Canada Thesaurus
Originally published in 1986 by The Jacaranda Press as
The Macquarie Junior Thesaurus

R01048 57743

Some words entered in this thesaurus may have been derived from
trademarks. However, the presence or absence of this indication
of derivation should not be regarded as affecting the legal
status of any trademark.

94 95 96 97 98 99 / 10 9 8 7

Contents

Preface

The *Young Writer's Thesaurus* is designed for students in grades four through eight, although some will find it useful sooner and many will want to use it even in secondary school.

We have written the entries and arranged them on each page in a way that is clear and simple, and have omitted the abbreviations and codes that can be baffling and distracting to a young reader. This means that the thesaurus is ideally suited for teaching children what thesauri do and how they can be useful. Young readers will be able to progress naturally to more adult thesauri in their own time, secure in the knowledge that they understand how a thesaurus works and what sort of information it is likely to contain.

Since people use thesauri to find alternatives to the easy or well-used words they already know, our policy has been to include hard words at the expense of those easy ones that a young reader wouldn't bother to look up. Interesting colloquial words, legal and more formal words, but above all, words having the same or nearly the same meaning as others in the language have been chosen to form groups covering a large range of concepts.

Words that are very closely related such as *nice, pleasant, enjoyable, lovely, acceptable,* and *welcome* as well as words that are more loosely related such as *lesson, lecture, seminar, class,* and *course* have been grouped together, each under a **keyword** that reflects the overall meaning of the whole group. These keywords appear in alphabetical order in the thesaurus and each has its part of speech and definition and an illustrative sentence to show how it is used. Its **related words** are arranged under it in an order that has been carefully considered. Words most similar to the keyword come first, followed by words that may be less similar in meaning or usage. Instead of just listing those related words, we have provided definitions and comments as to meaning and usage. For each related word we have also provided an illustrative sentence that gives the student a context for the word.

Each group of related words is confined to five or six words, as any more would be too much for the young reader to consider at once. Each group covers only one particular meaning of the words. Thus, a word might be used several times in the thesaurus, but in a different sense each time.

At the end of a group of related words, there are cross-references to similar and contrasting keywords.

The *Young Writer's Thesaurus* also includes several appendixes, which feature lists of words that pertain to various areas of the curriculum, such as science and social studies.

The thesaurus concludes with an index of all the words in the book. The index allows the student to locate a target word quickly, even if that word isn't a keyword.

The students this book is written for are in the first stages of learning to write. Many of them are eager readers who are exposed to new words every day. They want to add these words to their vocabularies and experiment with them in their writing. The thesaurus, like a dictionary, supports such experimentation. It is an accessible reference book that will guide the students' efforts. But we hope that the thesaurus will become more than a reference; we hope that it might be used creatively as well. For example, we encourage students to open the book while brainstorming story ideas, or to talk about interesting words as they browse through the pages together.

The *Young Writer's Thesaurus* has been a challenge and a pleasure to compile. We hope that students find it a useful and stimulating resource.

What is a thesaurus?

Have you ever been stuck for a word and felt very annoyed because you knew it was lurking somewhere but you just couldn't bring it to mind? Well, Peter Mark Roget often had just this problem, so he wrote down lists of similar words for his own use over the years. He was a doctor and often lectured to students at the Manchester Medical School in England, so he needed to use just the right words to express his meaning. In 1849, when Roget was 70, he began to put these lists in order so that they could be published. He called this treasure chest of words his "thesaurus."

Roget put together in the same group all the words and phrases that expressed a particular idea. For example, in a group called *force* in a thesaurus you might find *power*, *strength*, *might*, *muscle*, and *vigor*. These five words refer to some aspects of the idea of *force* but they are not the same as it and so they do not define it. Roget did not want his book to be like a dictionary, with definitions of every word. Rather, he wanted to gather in each group the words you might think of when a particular topic is being discussed. They are related to one another by being in the same area of meaning but they do not necessarily mean exactly the same thing.

Roget's thesaurus was so useful to people trying to write letters, essays, speeches, and so on, that it was very, very successful. Twenty-eight editions were published in Peter Roget's lifetime.

Other publishers brought out their own versions. Some have just been called *Thesaurus*, while others were called *Roget's Thesaurus* even though they didn't come directly from Roget himself. Gradually, the word "thesaurus" has ceased to refer to one book and is now defined in dictionaries as a "book of words arranged in groups that have a similar meaning."

The Young Writer's Thesaurus

The *Young Writer's Thesaurus* is arranged in three sections — the word groups, the appendixes, and the index.

Word Groups

In the first section you will find over 940 word groups. Each group consists of five or six words or phrases that are closely related to one another. There is also some information about what each word means and how it can be used. This will help you make your writing and conversation more interesting and precise and also expand your vocabulary.

On pages x and xi you will find instructions that tell you how to use the thesaurus.

Appendixes

The middle section consists of useful lists of words related to particular topics. These include U.S. wildlife and geography, space, transportation, computer terms, and many others.

Index

The back section is the index. This is a list of all the keywords and related words in the thesaurus, arranged in alphabetical order. You can use the index to look up any word in the thesaurus to find which word group it is in and which page it is on.

On page 490 there are instructions telling you how to use the index.

What's in a word?

Maggie and Rob had never been away from Maryland before. When they arrived in St. Louis, they sent a postcard to their grandparents describing the journey.

"It was really *exciting*, but a bit scary to *soar* so high above the *land*. I realized that our *aircraft* was *zooming* further and further from our *home*. Never fear, the meals were *terrific*," wrote Maggie.

"Well, I had a *great* time *flying* over here. I couldn't see the *ground* from the plane as it was too cloudy. The food was *delicious*. I knew we were traveling far from our *birthplace*," wrote Rob.

These two children managed to describe the same incident and never used the same words. There is a wealth of meaning in each word in the English language. It is very important to learn to use words so well that you know which is the right one to express exactly what you mean.

Try browsing through this thesaurus and you will certainly come to appreciate the value of words. You will meet some words that are old friends and some that are new and exciting. You will want to have a dictionary to help you as well — a dictionary and a thesaurus go hand in hand.

Guide to the thesaurus

Look at the sample word groups on the opposite page. They have been marked with directions that will help you find your way through the thesaurus.

Keyword

This word gives you an idea of the overall meaning of the word group. It will usually be a word you already know. For example, the keyword **fine** tells you that this is the group to look at if you want to find other words that express the idea "with the sun shining, or without rain."

Definition

Only one meaning of the keyword is given. You can see that this is where a thesaurus is different from a dictionary, in which all the meanings of a word are listed next to that word. In the first sample, **fine** has been used with the group of words that mean "with the sun shining." Now look at the second sample. **Fine** has been used here too, with another meaning, "good."

Related words

These words are related in meaning to the keyword and also to each other. You may prefer to use one of these because it expresses your idea more precisely, or is a more interesting or unusual word than the keyword. The information following each related word will help you decide which one to use.

What the word means

This is another definition. It explains the similarities and differences between the related word and the keyword. With this information you will be able to choose a word with precisely the meaning you want.

Word use

This tells you if the word is a legal word, a formal word, or one you would use in everyday language.

Illustrative sentence

This is just one example we have thought of to show you how to use the word. You can probably think of many more examples yourself.

Cross-references

Similar words are other keywords that are like the words in this group. For example, **excellent** is the keyword of a group consisting of these words: *outstanding, fantastic, terrific, sensational, exceptional*. You can see that they have been put into their own group, separate from **good**, because they have a different shade of meaning.

Contrasting words are keywords that are unlike the words in this group. For example, **dreary** is the keyword of a group consisting of these words: *dismal, depressing, cheerless, bleak, gray*. All of these express an idea that contrasts with **fine**.

keyword •————— **fine** *adjective* ————————————————————• **part of speech**

definition — • with the sun shining, or without rain. *I'm enjoying the*
telling you *fine weather that we are having at the moment.*
what the
word means

sunny **Sunny** means having plenty of sunshine.
It was a lovely sunny day before the clouds
came over.

balmy **Balmy** means fine or pleasant. *In the*
balmy spring weather they were often
outdoors.

related •————— **mild** **Mild** can mean not cold, severe, or
word — extreme. *Why don't we go for a walk tonight*
related *since the temperature is so mild?*
in meaning
to the **fair** **Fair** can mean bright and free from clouds
keyword as the sky can be. The forecast was for fair ——• **illustrative**
weather all weekend. **sentence**

temperate **Temperate** can mean having a moderate
temperature or climate. *We've had a*
temperate October with very little frost.

contrasting words: **wintry, cloudy, dreary**

good *adjective*

of a high standard or worthy of praise. *This is a good*
piece of work.

satisfactory Satisfactory means good enough to meet ——• **what the**
your requirements. *He gave a satisfactory* **word**
answer. **means**

fine **Fine** can mean very good or of a high
quality. *He's a fine musician.*

commendable **Commendable** means worthy of praise.
They held a party for Donna to thank her
for her commendable work.

all right **All right** means **satisfactory**. *She did an*
all right job for us in very demanding
circumstances.

Cross- **neat** **Neat** means **fine** or pleasing. It is more ——• **word**
references — suited to everyday language. *That was a* **use —**
other *neat party last night!* **telling you**
helpful **when to**
keywords similar words: **great, excellent, nice, best** **use the**
that you •————— contrasting words: **bad, nasty** **word**
can look up

xi

abduct *verb*

to take someone away by force. *The terrorists **abducted** the politician as he was walking to his car.*

kidnap	To **kidnap** means to abduct someone and hold them prisoner until a ransom is paid, or some other condition is met. *Some criminals kidnapped the millionaire's child.*
spirit away	To **spirit away** means to take someone away in secret. *The story began with the children being spirited away to a magical land.*
poach	To **poach** can mean to take animals or fish from someone's property without permission. *Our chickens keep disappearing, so we think someone must be poaching them.*
rustle	To **rustle** can mean to steal cattle or horses. *The outlaw rustled livestock from nearby ranches.*

similar words: **capture, steal**

abrupt *adjective*

rude and quick-tempered. *He gave an **abrupt** answer.*

short	**Short** can mean rudely brief in your way of speaking. *The bus driver was very short with me when I asked the time.*
curt	**Curt** means rudely brief in your speech or manners. It is very similar to **short**. *His curt reply hurt me.*
brusque	**Brusque** means abrupt and impolite. *His brusque manner upset me.*
terse	**Terse** means using few words, often in an impolite way. *Her terse comment showed plainly what she meant.*
blunt	**Blunt** can mean plain and direct in your way of speaking. *They gave a blunt refusal to our request.*

similar words: **rude**
contrasting words: **talkative, polite**

1

abundant *adjective*

more than enough. *The cafeteria had an **abundant** supply of paper cups.*

ample
> **Ample** means more than enough in size or amount. *There was ample space for us all to fit in the car.*

plentiful
> **Plentiful** means great in amount or number. *The coach always had a plentiful supply of bandages at the football games in case anyone was injured.*

bountiful
> **Bountiful** can mean generous in number or amount. *The rains produced a bountiful harvest.*

copious
> **Copious** means large in quantity. *We took copious notes during the lesson because our teacher was reviewing the semester's work before the exam.*

prolific
> **Prolific** means producing plentifully. *We have a prolific apple tree in the backyard and always have enough apples for our family and friends.*

---

similar words: **numerous, sufficient**
contrasting words: **scant, insufficient**

---

accidental *adjective*

happening unexpectedly or by accident. *Don't get angry with her for breaking the window, because it was purely **accidental**.*

chance
> **Chance** means not due to any known reason. *I came across this valuable old vase during a chance visit to an auction sale.*

coincidental
> **Coincidental** means happening at the same time by accident or **chance**. *It was coincidental that we both went to the movies yesterday.*

random
> **Random** means not following a pattern or method. *The winning lottery ticket was drawn at random.*

haphazard
> **Haphazard** means not planned, or happening by **chance**. *He made many errors because he worked in such a haphazard way.*

fluky
> **Fluky** means obtained by accidental advantage or a stroke of good luck rather than by skill, especially in relation to sports. It is more suited to everyday language. *The fluky goal was scored when the puck bounced off a skate.*

---

contrasting words: **deliberate**

---

acclaim *verb*

to praise someone with sounds of approval. *The crowd **acclaimed** the champion with shouts and clapping.*

applaud	To **applaud** means to praise someone or express approval of them, especially by clapping your hands or calling out. *The audience applauded the singer at the end of her song.*
clap	To **clap** means to show approval or enjoyment of someone or something by striking your hands together. *They clapped for the funny clown after he had performed some clever tricks.*
cheer	To **cheer** means to greet someone with shouts of approval. *We cheered the winner as she crossed the finish line.*
toast	To **toast** means to express your approval of someone by having a special drink in their honor. *We toasted the new president of the club.*
honor	To **honor** means to show your admiration and respect for someone or something. *The Royal Swedish Academy honored the great scientist by awarding her the Nobel Prize.*

similar words: **praise**
contrasting words: **scold**

accompany *verb*

to go or be with someone. *I am going to **accompany** my parents on their overseas trip.*

escort	To **escort** means to go along with someone as a mark of respect or to guard them. *The police escorted the prime minister back to the hotel.*
chaperone	To **chaperone** means to accompany to make sure someone behaves properly. *The teachers will chaperone the students at the school dance.*
associate with	To **associate with** means to spend time with someone. *She only associates with girls in her own class.*
hang around with	To **hang around with** means to spend your spare time with someone. This is more suited to everyday language. *She hangs around with the girls on the baseball team.*

accomplish *verb*

to carry something out successfully. *Congratulations! You have **accomplished** a difficult task.*

achieve	To **achieve** can mean to accomplish something or bring it to a successful end. *You will have to work hard to achieve your ambition to be a musician.*
attain	To **attain** means to reach or complete something by trying hard. *He attained his goal of improving his French.*
fulfill	To **fulfill** means to carry something out. *He fulfilled his promise to repay the debt.*
carry through	To **carry through** means to finish or complete something. *She carried her plan through with great courage and determination.*
bring off	To **bring off** is an informal way of saying to accomplish. *The escape was dangerous but they managed to bring it off.*

accuse *verb*

to blame someone openly for doing something wrong. *He **accused** the girl of cheating on the test.*

denounce	To **denounce** means to speak out against something or someone. *The leader of the revolution denounced the traitors.*
frame	To **frame** can mean to make someone seem to be guilty of something. *I didn't do it, Your Honor; he framed me.*
allege	To **allege** means to declare something without having proof of it. This is rather a formal word. *The shopkeeper didn't see the girl steal the book but he alleges it.*
charge	To **charge** means to accuse or blame someone for something. This can be a legal word. *The police charged the motorist with speeding.*
book	To **book** can mean to record someone's name in order to accuse them of doing something wrong. *If you break the law again I'll have to book you.*

similar words: **fault**	
contrasting words: **forgive**	

achievement *noun*

something you gain by hard work. *They praised him for his **achievement** in completing the marathon.*

accomplishment An **accomplishment** is something you achieve through hard work. It is similar to achievement. *Winning the cup two years in a row was a great accomplishment.*

effort An **effort** is something done by trying. *The teacher thought my project was a good effort.*

success A **success** is a very good result. *Our team had a great success in the chess competition.*

feat A **feat** is something you do using great skill, strength, or courage. *It was a great feat to climb to the top of Mount Everest.*

contrasting words: **failure**

actual *adjective*

existing in fact. *This is the **actual** route used by the early explorers.*

real **Real** means true or actual. *We have a real Swiss cuckoo clock at home.*

concrete **Concrete** can mean existing as an actual thing, not just an idea. *The sports club Kate formed for blind children like herself was a concrete example of her courage.*

tangible **Tangible** means able to be touched or felt. *Mr. Williams gave the sports club a large donation as tangible proof of his support.*

material **Material** means existing in a form you can touch. *The bankrupt company's material goods were sold at an auction.*

physical **Physical** can mean having to do with **material** things in the world rather than spiritual things. *We need money to buy things for our physical needs.*

similar words: **true**
contrasting words: **shadowy, imaginary**

add   *verb*

to join something onto something else in order to increase it in size or number. *Add another bead onto the necklace to make it longer.*

supplement	To **supplement** something means to add to it. *She supplements her allowance by babysitting.*
throw in	To **throw in** means to add something as an extra. *The baker threw in an extra cookie with our purchase.*
append	To **append** means to join or add as an extra part. *We appended the check to the letter.*
tack on	To **tack on** means to add something onto something else. *The sentence appears to be tacked onto the end of the paragraph.*
attach	To **attach** means to fasten or join something to something else. *We attached the trailer to the car.*

similar words: **enlarge, insert**
contrasting words: **subtract, remove**

admit   *verb*

to agree that something is true. *I admitted that I had broken the vase.*

concede	To **concede** means to admit that something is true. *You may as well concede that you were riding the bike too fast.*
confess	To **confess** means to own up to something you have done. *I confessed that I had not listened when she told me to be careful.*
blurt out	To **blurt out** means to tell something suddenly or without thinking. *I meant to keep it a secret but then I blurted it out.*
acknowledge	To **acknowledge** means to say that you realize something is true. *I acknowledged that it was kind of her to forgive my carelessness.*
unburden	To **unburden** can mean to ease yourself or your mind by telling or confessing something. *I felt better after I unburdened myself and told her what I had done.*

similar words: **reveal**
contrasting words: **hide**

adult   *adjective*

grown-up or fully developed. *The **adult** birds are quite a different color from their young.*

mature

Mature means adult or fully developed. *The mature oak tree was tall and leafy.*

full-grown

Full-grown is so similar to **mature** you can usually use either. *When the moose is full-grown it will have a large set of antlers.*

in your prime

In your prime means **mature** and in the best time of your life. *The woman was in her prime as a runner and was winning all her races.*

seasoned

Seasoned means **mature** and good at something through long experience. *The seasoned sailor knew a storm was coming from the clouds and the wind.*

contrasting words: **young**

advance   *verb*

to move or go forward. *She **advanced** to the front of the room.*

progress

To **progress** can mean to advance or move forward. *The parade progressed slowly down the road.*

make headway

To **make headway** means to progress or move forward. *The car made little headway in the heavy rain.*

proceed

To **proceed** means to move or go forward, especially after stopping. *We drove carefully over the gravel road because the sign said "Proceed with caution".*

push on

To **push on** means to continue or go forward, usually with difficulty. *The weary travelers pushed on from one town to the next.*

forge ahead

To **forge ahead** means to move forward with great effort. *The explorers forged ahead through the thick bush.*

contrasting words: **reverse, leave**

7

advise   *verb*

to tell someone what you think should be done. *The doctor **advised** his patient to get more exercise.*

guide   To **guide** can mean to advise, lead, or direct someone in the way you think they should go. *His mother guided him in his decision to stay in school.*

suggest   To **suggest** means to put forward the idea of doing anything. *My tennis coach suggested that I practice my backhand.*

propose   To **propose** means to put forward or **suggest** something. *She proposed a good method of raising money.*

recommend   To **recommend** means to **suggest** something as being good or worthwhile. *The librarian recommended this book to me.*

advocate   To **advocate** means to speak in favor of something. *Our dentist advocates brushing your teeth after every meal.*

similar words: **warn**

adviser   *noun*

someone who tells you what you should do. *She is a very wise **adviser**, so I usually do what she suggests.*

guide   A **guide** is someone whose suggestions and advice you usually follow. *I let my conscience be my guide when I'm not sure what to do.*

mentor   A **mentor** is an adviser who is very wise and whom you trust. *When I need advice I talk to my aunt and uncle, who have been my mentors for many years.*

counselor   A **counselor** is a person who is specially trained to help people solve problems or difficulties. *The school counselor helped me to decide what I should do.*

guru   A **guru** is a wise and powerful teacher or **guide**. *Many people listened to the guru and tried to do everything he taught them.*

similar words: **teacher**

aggressive *adjective*

likely to attack others. *He is only **aggressive** if you tease him.*

combative **Combative** means ready or eager to fight. *Comics are full of combative superheroes who battle villains.*

belligerent **Belligerent** means angry and wanting to fight. *Her belligerent behavior toward her friends surprised us.*

pugnacious **Pugnacious** means likely to quarrel or fight. *He is so pugnacious that the others have stopped trying to be friends with him.*

hostile **Hostile** means acting like an enemy. *Their hostile reply to our invitation upset us.*

similar words: **argumentative, warlike**
contrasting words: **submissive**

agile *adjective*

lively and active. *The **agile** gymnast did the most difficult exercises with ease.*

athletic **Athletic** means physically active and strong. *Our runners are very athletic, which is why our school won the cross-country race.*

sprightly **Sprightly** means lively and merry. *He played a sprightly tune on the recorder.*

nimble **Nimble** means able to move quickly and easily. *Her nimble fingers made playing the piano look easy.*

spry **Spry** means **nimble** or active. *He is not as spry as he was when he was younger.*

light on one's feet **Light on one's feet** can mean agile or **nimble**. *The squirrel was light on its feet and avoided the car.*

contrasting words: **clumsy**

agree   *verb*

to say yes or to have the same opinion as someone else. *I **agreed** to his plan.*

concur	To **concur** means to agree with something. *I concur with your decision.*
assent	To **assent** means to agree to something. *They assented to our request for more money.*
see eye to eye	To **see eye to eye** means to have the same opinion as someone else. It is more suited to everyday language. *My sister and I see eye to eye on which TV programs we like to watch.*
shake hands	To **shake hands** can mean to clasp hands with someone as a sign that you agree about something. *I wanted to buy the car so we shook hands on the deal.*

contrasting words: **disagree, argue**

agreeable   *adjective*

pleasing or to your liking. *She is a very **agreeable** person to be with.*

good-natured	**Good-natured** means having a pleasant nature and being easy to get along with. *He's so good-natured everyone wants to be on his team.*
likable	**Likable** means easy to like. *The new girl was very likable and fitted into the class easily.*
amiable	**Amiable** means agreeable and friendly. *I telephoned my friend and we had an amiable conversation.*
charming	**Charming** means having the ability to please and attract people. *He is a charming boy and is sure to be popular.*

similar words: **nice, friendly**
contrasting words: **nasty**

alert   *adjective*

watching things carefully and quick to react. *The guards were **alert** to any danger.*

watchful
Watchful means alert or careful to notice what is going on. *She was always watchful when her children were swimming.*

observant
Observant means alert or quick to notice things. *The observant girl noticed where the cookies were kept.*

attentive
Attentive means watching carefully. *Only the most attentive people saw how the trick was done.*

awake
Awake can mean alert or ready for anything that might happen. *They were awake to the danger of riding a bike in city traffic.*

similar words: **inquisitive, wary**
contrasting words: **dreamy**

allow   *verb*

to let someone do something. *Will your parents **allow** you to come?*

permit
To **permit** is so similar to allow that you can usually use either. *The law does not permit you to leave school before you are fourteen.*

authorize
To **authorize** means to agree or **consent** to something officially. *The principal has authorized this excursion.*

license
To **license** means to give official permission to someone. *She is licensed to drive the school bus.*

tolerate
To **tolerate** means to allow something, although not very willingly. *I will tolerate the cat's presence in the house, but I'm not happy about it.*

consent
To **consent** means to give permission. *The teacher consented to my request for a drink of water.*

similar words: **approve**
contrasting words: **refuse, prevent, ban**

ancestor   *noun*

someone related to you who lived long ago. *What country did your* **ancestors** *come from?*

forebear	**Forebear** is so similar to **ancestor** that you can usually use either. *Our forebears came to the United States in search of a better life.*
forefather	**Forefather** is so similar to **ancestor** and **forebear** that you can usually use any of them. *Some of our forefathers mapped unexplored areas of this country.*
antecedents	**Antecedents** can be your line of ancestors. *Horse trainers think that it is important to know the antecedents of a thoroughbred horse.*
predecessor	A **predecessor** is someone who has gone before you, especially in a job or position. *Our new principal is younger than her predecessor.*

contrasting words: **offspring**

anger   *noun*

a strong feeling of annoyance caused by thinking that something wrong has been done to you. *He could not control his* **anger** *when he saw the broken window.*

wrath	**Wrath** is anger or revenge. It is a rather old-fashioned word. *When I'm naughty, I bring upon myself the wrath of my parents.*
ire	**Ire** is very similar to **anger** and **wrath**. Like **wrath**, it is a rather old-fashioned word. *My ire increased as the next-door neighbor's party became noisier and noisier.*
rage	**Rage** is violent anger. *When the bully was in a rage everyone was frightened.*
fury	**Fury** is a violent feeling, especially one of anger. It is very similar to **rage**. *He smashed the door in his fury.*
temper	**Temper** can be an angry or resentful mood. *She's often in a temper when she's had a bad day.*

anger *verb*

to make someone or something annoyed or violent. *When the visitors teased the monkeys it **angered** the zookeeper.*

incense   To **incense** means to make someone angry. It is a more formal word than **anger**. *The accused man's lawyer incensed the judge with her interruptions.*

enrage   To **enrage** means to make someone very angry. *His rude manner enraged the teacher.*

infuriate   To **infuriate** is so similar to **enrage** you can usually use either word. *The workers infuriated their boss when they refused to work overtime.*

drive someone up the wall   To **drive someone up the wall** means to annoy someone very much. This is more suited to everyday language. *That noise you are making is really driving me up the wall.*

similar words: **irritate, annoy**
contrasting words: **pacify**

angry *adjective*

very annoyed because you think that something wrong has been done to you. *She gave me an **angry** look when I was rude to her.*

offended   **Offended** means feeling displeased or hurt. *They were offended when their friend ignored them.*

irate   **Irate** means very angry. *The customer was irate when he wasn't served in his turn.*

furious   **Furious** means extremely angry. *She was so furious that she began to shout.*

infuriated   **Infuriated** means very angry. *My parents were infuriated when a careless driver ran into their new car.*

livid   **Livid** means almost uncontrollably angry. It is similar to **furious**. *He was livid when we told him we had scratched his car.*

similar words: **grumpy, annoyed**
contrasting words: **glad, happy, joyful**

annoy *verb*

to irritate someone or make them cranky. *Very loud music **annoys** me.*

aggravate To **aggravate** can mean to annoy or provoke someone. *Don't aggravate the teacher by shuffling your feet.*

exasperate To **exasperate** means to annoy someone very much. *Kevin exasperated us with his stubbornness.*

hassle To **hassle** means to worry or annoy someone. It is more suited to everyday language. *Don't hassle me when I'm tired.*

pester To **pester** means to annoy or trouble someone. *Blackflies pestered us when we went camping in May.*

get on someone's nerves To **get on someone's nerves** means to irritate or annoy someone. It is more suited to everyday language. *He gets on my nerves when he complains all the time.*

similar words: **irritate, upset**
contrasting words: **please**

annoyed *adjective*

irritated or made cross. *The **annoyed** customer demanded a replacement for the faulty toaster.*

indignant **Indignant** means annoyed about something that you think is unfair. *I arrived on time, so I was indignant when I was accused of being late.*

cranky **Cranky** means bad-tempered or cross. *Dennis was really cranky when his car had a flat tire.*

vexed **Vexed** means annoyed or irritated. It is a rather old-fashioned word. *Grandma said she was vexed by the store manager's rudeness.*

fed up **Fed up** means annoyed with or tired of something. This is more suited to everyday language. *We were fed up with camping after a week of rain.*

similar words: **grumpy, angry, dissatisfied**
contrasting words: **glad**

annoying   *adjective*

likely to make you cranky or angry. *This rain is so **annoying**, because I wanted to go to the beach.*

irritating	**Irritating** means causing anger or impatience. *"Your irritating chatter will have to stop," their teacher said.*
exasperating	**Exasperating** means very annoying. *It is exasperating when you can't think of the exact word you want to use.*
trying	**Trying** means annoying or **irritating**. *The way he keeps talking about himself is very trying.*
infuriating	**Infuriating** means causing very great anger. *My little brother's constant interruptions were infuriating.*
maddening	**Maddening** is so similar to **infuriating** you can usually choose either word. *It's maddening! — I'm sure I put my book on my desk but now I can't find it.*

contrasting words: **nice**

answer   *verb*

to acknowledge a question, request, letter, and so on, using actions or spoken or written words. *She **answered** the question with a shake of her head.*

respond	To **respond** means to answer, using actions or words. *People responded generously to the fundraising campaign.*
reply	To **reply** means to give an answer or response. *Did you reply to the letter?*
retort	To **retort** means to give a quick or sharp answer. *When I said that she was late, she retorted by saying that I was lucky she had come at all.*
react	To **react** means to act in answer to something. *We all react to danger in different ways.*
return	To **return** can mean to answer or **retort**. *He returned her greeting with a friendly smile.*

contrasting words: **question, ask**

apathetic   *adjective*

having no feelings for, or interest in, things that other people find interesting or exciting. *The people passing by seemed to be **apathetic** about the demonstration.*

indifferent	**Indifferent** means showing no interest or concern. *He was indifferent to my pain.*
halfhearted	**Halfhearted** means not showing much willingness or interest. *He made a halfhearted attempt to join in the party.*
lukewarm	**Lukewarm** means not very enthusiastic. *The proposal to erect a statue of the mayor received a lukewarm response at the council meeting.*
passive	**Passive** means letting things happen without taking any action yourself. *He would not be a good leader because he is too passive.*

similar words: **lethargic**
contrasting words: **enthusiastic**

appear   *verb*

to become visible. *The sun **appeared** over the horizon.*

come	To **come** can mean to appear. *There's something wrong with the TV— the picture comes and goes.*
emerge	To **emerge** means to come out into view. *She emerged from behind the trees.*
loom	To **loom** means to appear, often in a large or frightening form. *The man suddenly loomed in front of me out of the shadows.*
show up	To **show up** means to appear or be seen, often unexpectedly. *I was glad that my library book showed up when I tidied my room.*
materialize	To **materialize** means to appear in a physical shape. *Her figure materialized out of the mist.*

contrasting words: **disappear**

appearance   *noun*

the way something or someone looks or seems on the outside. *Her severe hairstyle gives her a fierce **appearance**.*

aspect

Aspect is the way a thing appears or seems. *The lush aspect of the countryside greeted us at every turn in the road.*

air

Air can be the way something looks or seems. It is very similar to **appearance** and **aspect**. *The businesswoman has an air of success.*

complexion

Complexion can be very similar to **appearance** and **aspect**. It can usually be used in the same way. *A fresh coat of yellow paint gave the room a completely different complexion.*

presence

Presence can mean your personal appearance or your way of doing things. *The rock star had the strong presence of a great performer.*

similar words: **manner**

approve   *verb*

to like something and agree to it. *We **approved** the idea of having a vacation on the farm.*

endorse

To **endorse** means to approve of or to support something. *Do you endorse the cutting down of trees in the rain forest?*

sanction

To **sanction** means to give approval or support to something. This is rather a formal word. *The principal sanctioned our plan to hold a car wash to raise money.*

advocate

To **advocate** means to speak favorably about something. *In my speech I advocated peace not war.*

bless

To **bless** means to approve something and to wish it every success. *He blessed our decision.*

hold with

To **hold with** is to approve of or agree with something. *I don't hold with the new rule.*

similar words: **praise, allow**
contrasting words: **disapprove of, fault**

argue *verb*

to disagree. *We **argued** about what color car we should buy.*

quarrel	To **quarrel** can mean to argue angrily. *We quarreled over who would have the first ride.*
squabble	To **squabble** means to argue angrily, but usually for a short time, about something unimportant. *Children often squabble during card games.*
have it out	To **have it out** means to argue until an issue is settled. *I'm not happy with Arvinder's plan, so the two of us will have it out at the meeting.*
clash	To **clash** can mean to disagree angrily about something you consider to be very important. *They clashed over what school the children should go to.*
conflict	To **conflict** means to disagree or be in opposition to one another. It is similar to **clash**. *Our ideas conflict about that because we are so different.*

similar words: **disagree**
contrasting words: **agree, cooperate**

argument *noun*

a disagreement. *We had an **argument** about who had won the race.*

quarrel	A **quarrel** is an angry argument. *You don't have to have a quarrel every time you disagree.*
dispute	A **dispute** is an argument or **quarrel**. *They had a dispute over who was the better singer.*
difference	A **difference** can mean a disagreement or **quarrel**, especially between two people who usually get along well. *I had a difference with Sara about what to do on Saturday.*
controversy	A **controversy** is an argument or a difference of opinion. *There has been a public controversy over where the new airport should be built.*
altercation	An **altercation** is an angry **dispute** or disagreement. *They had an altercation over who was to blame for the traffic accident.*

similar words: **conflict**

argumentative *adjective*

liking to argue. *Some people are **argumentative** if they are criticized.*

quarrelsome	**Quarrelsome** means likely to quarrel easily. *The children were quarrelsome because they were bored.*
cantankerous	**Cantankerous** means bad-tempered and likely to pick a fight. *The clerk was tired and in a cantankerous mood.*
contentious	**Contentious** can mean **quarrelsome** and fond of arguing. *A contentious person like her will fight about anything.*
contrary	**Contrary** can mean always disagreeing or purposely taking the opposite view. *He is sure to be contrary no matter what we suggest.*

similar words: **defiant, aggressive**
contrasting words: **submissive**

arrange *verb*

to put something in order. *She **arranged** the books on the shelf so that she could find them easily.*

group	To **group** means to gather things or people together because they are thought to be connected in some way. *The teacher grouped the students according to age for the track and field events.*
sort	To **sort** means to arrange according to type or kind. *We sorted the washing into piles for each member of the family.*
grade	To **grade** means to arrange according to a stage or step on a scale of positions, quality, or value. *Eggs are graded and priced according to their size.*
classify	To **classify** means to arrange according to quality or likeness. *This book classifies plants into different groups according to where they come from.*
file	To **file** can mean to put or arrange something in a file. *The librarian filed all the index cards so that we could find them easily.*

similar words: **list**
contrasting words: **disorganize**

ask   *verb*

to put a question to someone. *I'll **ask** my father to help me with this problem when he gets home.*

request	To **request** means to ask for something in a formal way. *The lawyer went to the judge to request a hearing.*
beg	To **beg** means to ask someone for something in a humble way. *I beg you to forgive me.*
implore	To **implore** means to ask someone for something in an earnest or urgent way. *Don't go, I implore you!*
entreat	To **entreat** means to **implore**. These two words are so similar you can often choose either of them. *We entreat you to help us escape.*
beseech	To **beseech** means to ask anxiously for something. *I beseeched him for news of the missing fishing boats.*

similar words: **demand**
contrasting words: **answer**

assemble   *verb*

to come together. *We **assembled** in the playground before going on the field trip.*

gather	To **gather** is so similar to assemble that you can usually use either. *A crowd gathered to watch the parade.*
meet	To **meet** means to come together for discussions or a shared activity. *The club meets at 9 o'clock every Friday in the community hall.*
congregate	To **congregate** means to come together in very large numbers. *A huge crowd congregated to see the fireworks.*
turn out	To **turn out** means to come along. *All her friends turned out for her wedding.*
rally	To **rally** means to come together for a common cause or purpose. *The people rallied behind their leader.*

associate *noun*

someone who is connected with you and shares your interests. *My father's accountant is a business **associate**.*

partner	A **partner** is someone who takes part in something with you. *You should always go skin diving with a partner.*
colleague	A **colleague** is someone who does the same sort of work as you. *People can learn a lot by talking to their colleagues.*
collaborator	A **collaborator** is someone who works with you on a special task or job. *The two friends were collaborators in writing a play.*
comrade	A **comrade** is a very close friend. *My father and my uncle have been comrades since being in the army together.*

similar words: **friend, helper**

astonished *adjective*

filled with sudden and great wonder. *We were **astonished** when we saw how red the sunset was.*

surprised	**Surprised** means filled with a feeling of shock or wonder at something unexpected or very unusual. *I was surprised by the party my parents gave for me.*
amazed	**Amazed** means filled with astonishment. *I was amazed that I had managed to complete the walkathon.*
astounded	**Astounded** means completely overcome with astonishment. *We were astounded when we discovered gold on our land.*
flabbergasted	**Flabbergasted** means shocked or greatly astonished. *I was flabbergasted when I won first prize.*
stunned	**Stunned** means astonished and very shocked. *News of the president's death stunned the world.*

astonishing   *adjective*

causing great surprise or wonder. *It was **astonishing** to see the slow tortoise beat the hare.*

amazing   **Amazing** means causing surprise and astonishment. *It was an amazing finish to the race.*

astounding   **Astounding** means causing complete surprise. *Those dinosaur bones are an astounding size.*

remarkable   **Remarkable** means very unusual and worthy of notice. *This is a remarkable story and should be published.*

staggering   **Staggering** means causing shock and wonder. *Soon everyone had heard the staggering news that the tortoise had beaten the hare.*

stupendous   **Stupendous** means astonishingly good. *The hero's stupendous feat would be remembered for a long, long time.*

similar words: **wonderful**

attack   *noun*

the use of force or weapons against a person or group of people. *The soldiers loaded their rifles for the **attack**.*

assault   An **assault** is a violent attack. *They made an assault on the enemy city.*

onslaught   An **onslaught** is a fierce rush or attack. *The sudden onslaught left many people wounded.*

ambush   An **ambush** is a sudden attack from a hidden place. *Our enemy's ambush caught us by surprise.*

blitz   A **blitz** is a sudden attack. *The people ran to the air-raid shelter for cover during the blitz.*

foray   A **foray** is a raid or attack in order to steal something. *We made a foray into the enemy's camp in the hope of capturing some hostages.*

contrasting words: **defense**

attack   *verb*

to use force or weapons against a person or group of people. *They **attacked** the enemy with all their strength.*

assault To **assault** means to attack someone or something violently. *The thugs assaulted the old man, and he had to be taken to the hospital.*

charge To **charge** means to attack someone or something by rushing violently at them. *The bull charged us and we just managed to escape in time.*

raid To **raid** means to attack someone or something suddenly. *We raided the other camp and stole all their sleeping bags.*

mug To **mug** means to attack and rob someone. *Someone might mug you if you walk through that park by yourself at night.*

beat up To **beat up** means to attack someone and hurt them. This is more suited to everyday language. *She told the bully not to beat up her brother.*

contrasting words: **protect**

attempt   *noun*

a try to complete or do something. *This will be our final **attempt** to reach the top of the mountain.*

effort An **effort** is a serious attempt. *Our effort to reach the top took all of our strength.*

endeavor An **endeavor** is a try or an attempt to do something that is worthwhile. *We knew our endeavors had been worthwhile when we finally reached the peak.*

crack A **crack** can be an attempt that may not be successful. It is more suited to everyday language. *After I tried to take the lid off, he had a crack at it.*

stab A **stab** is an attempt that hasn't much chance of succeeding. It is more suited to everyday language. *Can you make a stab at the answer?*

attempt   *verb*

to make an effort to do something. *I will **attempt** the yacht race next year.*

try	To **try** means to make an effort or attempt to do something. *It seems easy until you try it.*
undertake	To **undertake** means to attempt or say that you will do something. *I will undertake the job tomorrow.*
tackle	To **tackle** means to take on and struggle with something or someone. *Let's tackle the problem together.*
attack	To **attack** can mean to go to work on something strongly. *We shall have to attack the next difficult task now.*
work toward	To **work toward** means to make an effort to achieve something. *We have to work toward a fair solution to the argument.*

attract   *verb*

to make someone pay attention or come near, especially by being interesting or pleasing. *The new television show **attracted** the whole family.*

draw	To **draw** can be so similar to attract that you can usually use either. *Her cries drew me to the scene of the accident.*
lure	To **lure** means to attract or tempt someone by seeming to be very pleasant or exciting. *The TV advertisement lured me to buy the toy.*
magnetize	To **magnetize** can mean to attract someone so strongly that their whole attention is taken up. *The bright display of fireworks magnetized us.*
pull in	To **pull in** can mean to attract or **draw** someone, usually a large group of people. It is more suited to everyday language. *The final hockey game pulled in the biggest crowd.*

similar words: **charm**
contrasting words: **repel**

attractive   *adjective*

pleasing or appealing. *Going to the beach instead of studying is an **attractive** idea.*

magnetic	**Magnetic** can mean strongly attractive. *The new host of the TV show had a magnetic personality.*
irresistible	**Irresistible** means not able to be resisted or withstood. *The chocolate cake in the fridge was so irresistible that I had to have some.*
tempting	**Tempting** means inviting or enticing. *The clear, blue water of the lake looked very tempting on such a hot day.*
seductive	**Seductive** means enticing or captivating. *I love to sit in that chair because the cushions are soft and seductive.*
charismatic	**Charismatic** means having special personal qualities that give someone influence over a large number of people. *The charismatic leader had a large following.*

avoid   *verb*

to keep away from something or someone. *We went another way to **avoid** the traffic jam.*

miss	To **miss** can mean to avoid or fail to attend something. *I missed that film because I thought it would be boring.*
evade	To **evade** means to avoid doing or taking notice of something. *He manages to evade the school rules.*
elude	To **elude** means to avoid in a clever way someone who is looking for you. *The robber eluded the police.*
shirk	To **shirk** means to avoid doing a job or a duty. *They were very clever at shirking the hard work.*
steer clear of	To **steer clear of** means to avoid something or someone very carefully. *We steered clear of the deepest part of the river.*

contrasting words: **seek**

bad *adjective*

nasty or unpleasant. *There's a **bad** smell coming from that factory.*

atrocious
Atrocious means very bad or lacking in taste. *My parents would not tolerate such atrocious behaviour.*

abominable
Abominable means hateful or disgusting. *Slavery was an abominable practice.*

abysmal
Abysmal means so bad that it could not be worse. *This abysmal rain is ruining our weekend.*

monstrous
Monstrous means frightful or shocking. *The monstrous creatures on the advertisement for the movie discouraged us from going.*

rotten
Rotten means bad or dishonest. It is more suited to everyday language. *It was a rotten trick to sell him a bike that was broken.*

similar words: **nasty, pathetic**
contrasting words: **nice, good**

ball *noun*

something with a round or roundish shape, like the toy that you can bounce or kick, catch, or hit in games. *Throw me the **ball**.*

sphere
A **sphere** is something completely round in shape. *The potter formed the clay into a sphere before placing it on the wheel.*

globe
A **globe** is anything shaped like a ball, particularly a round map of the world. *Turn the globe around so that we can see Australia.*

orb
An **orb** is a ball-shaped object. It is used in poetry to mean a planet, the sun, or the moon. *The sun is the orb of the day.*

globule
A **globule** is a very small ball-shaped object, especially a drop of liquid. *Globules of sweat ran down his forehead.*

ban *verb*

to forbid something. *Our teacher **banned** chewing gum from the classroom.*

bar
To **bar** can mean to forbid or prevent something or someone. *They barred that particular glue from being sold to children.*

outlaw
To **outlaw** means to forbid something by law. *The government has outlawed the dumping of toxic wastes.*

censor
To **censor** means to prevent someone from seeing, hearing, or reading things that are considered objectionable for any reason. *The Board censored the film because it was too violent.*

disqualify
To **disqualify** can mean to prevent someone from getting something, or make them unsuitable to receive certain rights, or something similar. *The swimmer was disqualified for crossing into the next lane.*

boycott
To **boycott** can mean to stop buying or using something, as a means of frightening or forcing someone. *We boycotted the new detergent in an effort to stop the manufacturer from polluting the river.*

similar words: **prevent, exclude**
contrasting words: **allow**

bandit *noun*

an armed robber. *A gang of **bandits** broke into the bank.*

highwayman
A **highwayman** was someone who held up travelers on highways and robbed them, usually on horseback. *People traveling from town to town in England in the olden days were afraid of highwaymen.*

brigand
A **brigand** is a robber who lives with a gang of other robbers in hidden mountain or forest areas. *Beware of brigands when you get to that lonely mountain road.*

pirate
A **pirate** is someone who attacks and robs ships at sea. *The captain kept a lookout for pirates.*

buccaneer
A **buccaneer** is a more old-fashioned word for a **pirate**. *There are many exciting stories about buccaneers who lived long ago.*

similar words: **thief, criminal**

bare *adjective*

having no covering. *I like to feel the warm sun on my **bare** skin.*

exposed	**Exposed** can mean uncovered or bare, especially something that should be or is usually covered. *When the mountain climber lost his gloves his exposed hands became icy cold.*
naked	**Naked** means having no clothes on. *The naked baby chuckled as she splashed in the bath.*
nude	**Nude** means unclothed, **naked,** or without your usual clothes or coverings. *In the art gallery there were paintings of nude people that showed the beauty of the human body.*
bald	**Bald** means not covered with hair, or any other natural growth. *Dad always wears a hat in the garden to keep the sun off his bald head.*

bay *noun*

a sheltered part of the sea or a lake formed by a curve in its shore. *The sailing boats were anchored in the **bay.***

bight	A **bight** is a bend or curve in the shore of the sea. *The boat took shelter in a bight to avoid the worst of the storm.*
gulf	A **gulf** is a part of an ocean that is partly bounded by land. *The Gulf of St. Lawrence is a large gulf at the mouth of the St. Lawrence River.*
inlet	An **inlet** is a small narrow bay. *The smugglers rowed to an uncharted inlet from their ship moored in the harbor.*
cove	A **cove** is a small bay or **inlet.** *There was room for just a few cottages along the shore of the cove.*
estuary	An **estuary** is the mouth or lower part of a river that is affected by the tides. *The launch had to wait for high tide before it could cross the sandbar at the estuary.*

similar words: **lake**

beat   *verb*

to hit something or someone again and again. *The drummer **beat** out a steady rhythm.*

smack	To **smack** means to hit or slap. *The whale smacked the water with its gigantic tail.*
punch	To **punch** means to strike someone or something with your fist. *The karate teacher punched a board and broke it.*
thump	To **thump** means to strike someone heavily. *He thumped me excitedly on the back when I won the race.*
hammer	To **hammer** can mean to hit something forcefully over and over again. *She hammered the nail into the wood.*
bang	To **bang** is to hit or beat something noisily. *The children banged the pieces of wood together in time with the music.*

similar words: **hit**

beautiful   *adjective*

pleasing and enjoyable to hear, look at, touch, or smell. *The choir sang a **beautiful** song at the wedding.*

lovely	**Lovely** is so similar to beautiful that you can usually choose to use either. *My friend has a lovely face.*
exquisite	**Exquisite** means finely and delicately beautiful. *The bride's veil was made of exquisite lace.*
gorgeous	**Gorgeous** means richly beautiful, especially in coloring. *The peacock spread his gorgeous tail.*
stunning	**Stunning** means beautiful in a way that surprises you or captures your attention. It is more suited to everyday language. *It was such a stunning dress that everyone in the room turned to look at her.*

similar words: **pretty**
contrasting words: **ugly**

befriend   *verb*

to aid or be friendly toward someone. *She **befriended** the new boy at school because he didn't know anyone.*

defend To **defend** can mean to support someone or something by speaking on their behalf. *He defended me when they said I was a bully.*

champion To **champion** can mean to **defend** or fight for someone. *"I'll champion your cause," said the politician.*

stand by To **stand by** can mean to help or support someone loyally. *Friends should stand by each other in times of need.*

stick up for To **stick up for** means to **defend** or support someone. *Thanks for sticking up for me when the others started disagreeing with what I'd said.*

side with To **side with** means to be on the side of a person or a group of people in support of a particular issue. *He always sided with his friend in an argument.*

similar words: **help**

begin   *verb*

to take the first step in something. *Please **begin** work now.*

start To **start** is so similar to begin that you can usually use either. *I am going to start my project tonight.*

commence To **commence** is so similar to **begin** and **start** that you can usually use any of them. *The builders have commenced the additions to our house.*

embark on To **embark on** means to begin something that is going to be long or important. *He is embarking on a new job tomorrow.*

set about To **set about** means to begin doing or **start** preparing something. *I will set about cooking dinner.*

open To **open** means to begin or **start** something. *We opened the meeting with the singing of "America the Beautiful."*

similar words: **initiate, start**
contrasting words: **finish, stop**

behave *verb*

to act in a particular way. *Please don't **behave** badly when the visitors are here.*

conduct yourself   To **conduct yourself** means to behave in a certain way. *He conducted himself well even though his brother teased him.*

carry yourself   To **carry yourself** means to behave, walk, or stand in a particular way. *Everyone else was shouting but she carried herself calmly.*

perform   To **perform** means to behave. *The car performed well on our holiday.*

acquit yourself   To **acquit yourself** means to show what you can do in a particular activity. *He will acquit himself well in the debate.*

behavior *noun*

the way someone or something acts, especially in a particular situation. *The scientist studied how people's **behavior** changes when they are not allowed to sleep.*

conduct   **Conduct** is someone's behavior, especially toward other people. *The students' conduct was good and they worked together happily.*

deportment   **Deportment** is the way someone acts. It is a rather formal word. *The government official was expected to be polite in his deportment.*

demeanor   **Demeanor** is someone's **conduct** and appearance. It is a rather formal word. *Peggy's cheerful demeanor made us feel welcome.*

manners   **Manners** are the ways that someone behaves toward others. *We were told to watch our manners and be courteous to the babysitter.*

believable *adjective*

likely to be true or able to be believed in. *Your story is strange but* **believable***.*

credible	**Credible** is so similar to believable that you can usually use either. *I thought what happened in that film was quite credible.*
plausible	**Plausible** means seeming to be true or reasonable. *She had a plausible excuse.*
probable	**Probable** means likely to be true. *The witness gave a probable account of the accident.*
possible	**Possible** means maybe true, although there may be knowledge to the contrary. *It is possible that ghosts exist.*
conceivable	**Conceivable** means able to be imagined, although maybe unlikely. *It is conceivable that the rumor is true.*

similar words: **possible, likely**
contrasting words: **unbelievable, impossible**

believe *verb*

to think that something is right or true. *I don't* **believe** *your story.*

accept	To **accept** can mean to believe something to be true. *I accept that what you say really happened.*
trust	To **trust** means to believe or have confidence in something. *I trust what you tell me.*
take for granted	To **take for granted** can mean to believe something without questioning it. *I take it for granted that she really committed the crime.*
assume	To **assume** means to believe something without proof. *I assume you're the cause of this.*

similar words: **think**
contrasting words: **doubt**

bend *verb*

to turn something in a particular direction. *She **bent** the wire into the shape of a hook and pulled her ring from the drain.*

flex
To **flex** means to bend something, especially a part of your body. *You have to flex your spine when you lean over and touch your toes.*

deflect
To **deflect** means to bend or turn something aside. *I tried to hit the ball straight but the tree deflected it and it bounced into the creek.*

curl
To **curl** means to bend something into a curved or twisted shape. *I like the way you have curled your hair.*

curve
To **curve** means to bend something into a rounded shape. *The carpenter curved strips of wood to make the arms of the chair.*

loop
To **loop** means to bend something into an oval or circular shape. *You can make a knot if you loop the rope around twice and pull the end through.*

---

similar words: **turn**

---

best *adjective*

higher than the rest in quality or importance. *She is the **best** runner on our team.*

star
Star means the most brilliant or well-known. *She is our star runner.*

top
Top can mean the most excellent. *He is the top student in the class.*

leading
Leading means the most important or chief. *She is the leading dancer in the ballet company.*

head
Head can mean being in the position of leadership. It is similar to **leading**. *You had better ask the head librarian.*

principal
Principal means highest in position or importance. It is similar to both **leading** and **head**. *He is the principal actor in the film.*

---

similar words: **excellent, good, great, superior, main**

33

betray *verb*

to be unfaithful or disloyal to someone. *The spy **betrayed** her country.*

double-cross To **double-cross** means to betray someone by promising one thing and doing another. *She said she would keep my secret but she double-crossed me.*

sell out To **sell out** means to betray someone. This is more suited to everyday language. *He would sell out his friends if he thought he could get himself out of trouble.*

report To **report** can mean to complain or give information about someone or something. *We reported our noisy neighbors to the police.*

rat on To **rat on** means to betray someone by revealing information that should have been kept secret. It is more suited to everyday language. *They asked her to rat on me, but she wouldn't say anything.*

similar words: **blab**

big *adjective*

great in size or amount. *We made a **big** cake so that everyone could have a piece.*

large **Large** means of more than the usual size, amount, or extent. *An elephant is a large animal.*

bulky **Bulky** means **large** and awkward to manage because of its size and shape. *It was difficult to hide the bulky present.*

substantial **Substantial** means very great in size or amount. *The treasure hunters found a substantial fortune hidden away.*

generous **Generous** can mean big or bigger than you needed or expected. *Our neighbors gave us generous helpings of ice cream and chocolate sauce.*

ample **Ample** can mean large or well filled out. *She gets an ample allowance from her parents.*

similar words: **huge**
contrasting words: **small**

blab   *verb*

to tell or reveal a secret. *She was angry when I **blabbed** the name of her boyfriend to everyone.*

let slip	To **let slip** means to say or reveal something without meaning to. *You just let slip all the information about my secret experiments.*
let out	To **let out** can mean to tell a secret, or something similar. *Don't let out the details of our surprise party.*
give away	To **give away** can mean to let a secret be known. *Do not give away our hiding place to the others.*
let on	To **let on** can mean to **give away** a secret without meaning to. *Don't let on you know about your surprise party.*

similar words: **reveal, betray**

black   *adjective*

without any color or brightness. *He wore **black** socks to match his suit.*

dark	**Dark** can mean giving out very little light. *Her dark hair matched her dark clothes.*
pitch-black	**Pitch-black** means very black or **dark**. *The pitch-black clouds loomed on the horizon.*
inky	**Inky** means as black as ink. *He disappeared completely into the inky shadows.*
jet-black	**Jet-black** means of a deep, glossy black color, like the shiny coal of the same name. *He groomed the horse until its jet-black coat shone in the sun.*
ebony	**Ebony** means black, like the valuable wood of the same name. *The deer stared at me with its large, ebony eyes.*

block *verb*

to be in the way of someone or something. *The accident **blocked** the traffic.*

obstruct
: To **obstruct** means to block or close off something. *A landslide obstructed the road.*

barricade
: To **barricade** means to block or defend something with a barrier or a wall that has usually been built in a hurry. *The protesters barricaded themselves in the building and wouldn't let anyone in.*

blockade
: To **blockade** means to **close** a port, harbor, and so on, using ships or soldiers to stop supplies going in or out. *The enemy ships blockaded our main port and food became very scarce.*

bar
: To **bar** means to stop or prevent someone or something. *The guards barred them from entering the building.*

close
: To **close** can mean to block something off. *Heavy snow closed the road.*

---

similar words: **prevent, hinder**
contrasting words: **further**

---

blue *adjective*

having the color of a clear sky. *We searched anxiously for signs of rain clouds in the **blue** sky.*

azure
: **Azure** means having a sky-blue color. *I'm going to use that azure glaze on my pot.*

navy
: **Navy** means having a very dark blue color. *I used a navy pencil–crayon to color the ocean in my drawing.*

aqua
: **Aqua** means having a light blue-green color. *Boats bobbed up and down on the aqua sea.*

sapphire
: **Sapphire** means having a deep blue color. *As evening approached, the lake took on a sapphire hue.*

boast   *verb*

to speak with too much pride about your own affairs. *He **boasted** about winning the tennis tournament.*

brag	To **brag** is so similar to boast that you can usually use either. *A good sport doesn't brag about winning.*
crow	To **crow** can mean to boast or talk loudly of any success or victory you may have. *They wouldn't stop crowing about the way their team won the debate.*
bluster	To **bluster** means to speak or act in a noisy, boasting, or bullying manner. *To the dismay of his guests, the general blustered on and on about his military career.*
blow your own horn	To **blow your own horn** means to praise or say that you admire yourself. This is more suited to everyday language. *She isn't interested in what I do because she's too busy blowing her own horn.*
talk big	To **talk big** means to speak in a boastful way so that people think you are important. This is more suited to everyday language. *He talks big but he doesn't do very much.*

boil   *verb*

to cook something by heating it in a bubbling liquid. *We **boiled** the potatoes in the saucepan.*

poach	To **poach** means to cook something in a liquid that is just below boiling point. *Poach the eggs while I make the toast.*
coddle	To **coddle** means to cook something very slowly in water. *I coddled the eggs so they would still be soft and runny.*
simmer	To **simmer** means to cook something slowly in a liquid that has only a few bubbles rising. *Put all the ingredients for the soup in a big saucepan and simmer them gently for two hours.*
stew	To **stew** means to cook something slowly in a gently boiling liquid. *I stewed some apples in a little bit of water to eat with ice cream for dessert.*
braise	To **braise** means to fry something quickly in a pan, then **stew** it gently in a covered pot. *I love the delicious gravy you get when you braise chops with lots of onions and tomatoes.*

bold *adjective*

willing to take risks or face danger. *Jamie was the only one of us **bold** enough to say we were given too much work.*

fresh	**Fresh** can mean not showing respect, especially in the way you speak to someone. *Don't get fresh with me!*
pert	**Pert** means bold or impudent. *I don't like your pert way of speaking.*
saucy	**Saucy** means quite bold and rude. It is more suited to everyday language. *That's a saucy answer to give your mother.*
brazen	**Brazen** means without shame. *His brazen behavior embarrassed us all.*
forward	**Forward** means behaving boldly in order to make people notice you. *She was so forward in front of the visitors that her parents sent her from the room.*

similar words: **rude, unashamed, brave**
contrasting words: **shy, polite**

book *noun*

a number of pages bound together inside a cover, for writing in or for reading. *We borrow **books** from the library each week.*

manual	A **manual** is a book that tells you how to do or use something. *We looked at the manual to see how to fix the car.*
textbook	A **textbook** is a book setting out the information for a course of study in a subject. *We had two textbooks for science.*
anthology	An **anthology** is a collection of poems, plays, or short stories by various authors or from various books. *We studied several of the poems in the anthology at school.*
volume	A **volume** is a book, especially one of a series. *There were twenty volumes of the encyclopedia.*
diary	A **diary** is a book in which you write down daily events or thoughts. *I kept a diary while we were on vacation.*

similar words: **publication**

bored   *adjective*

feeling dull or tired because you aren't interested in what you are doing. *It rained all afternoon and the children complained that they were **bored**.*

blasé
    Blasé means so used to doing exciting things that they no longer interest or excite you. *I've been to the zoo so many times that I'm blasé about going again.*

tired of
    Tired of means bored with or no longer interested in something. *We are tired of playing Monopoly.*

sick of
    Sick of means very bored with or feeling that you have had enough of something. *I'm sick of my job.*

fed up
    Fed up means very bored, annoyed, or frustrated with something. *I'm fed up with having nothing to do all day.*

---

contrasting words: **excited**

---

boring   *adjective*

uninteresting or wearying. *This book is so **boring** that I don't think I'll finish it.*

dull
    Dull can be so similar to boring that you can usually use either. *The characters in the play are all very dull.*

tedious
    Tedious means long and boring. *The hero often makes tedious speeches about being well-behaved.*

stale
    Stale can mean uninteresting because it has been used so many times before. *The author has used a stale plot in his novel.*

monotonous
    Monotonous means boring because it is always exactly the same. *The announcer had a monotonous voice.*

humdrum
    Humdrum means boring because it is ordinary and doesn't change. It is similar to **monotonous**. *I'm going to try to change my humdrum life by finding an interesting hobby.*

---

contrasting words: **exciting**

---

boss   *noun*

someone who employs and directs people in their work. *Our **boss** is very fair and makes sure no one is overworked.*

supervisor   A **supervisor** is someone who directs or watches over people who are working. *The supervisor at the exam told the students to stop writing.*

superior   A **superior** is someone who is higher in rank or position than you. *My superiors were pleased with the report I gave them.*

overseer   An **overseer** is someone who supervises or is in charge of a group of workers. *The overseer told the new farmhands what to do.*

chief   A **chief** is the head person in a group. *We elected her as the chief of the committee to talk to the manager about our complaints.*

head   A **head** is someone who is in charge of a group or department. *The head of each group had to give a speech.*

similar words: **manager**

bossy   *adjective*

wanting to order other people about. *The little girl was **bossy** when she played with younger children.*

overbearing   **Overbearing** means bossy, arrogant, and expecting other people to do as you say. *I dislike her overbearing way of taking over our games.*

imperious   **Imperious** means **overbearing** or ruling over people in a severe and bossy way. *We didn't enjoy the tour because the imperious guide ordered us around.*

autocratic   **Autocratic** means ruling without caring about, or regard for, other people. *"What an autocratic king he is," groaned his subjects.*

dictatorial   **Dictatorial** means **overbearing**, or tending to order other people around. *The manager's dictatorial manner made him unpopular.*

authoritarian   **Authoritarian** means acting without considering people's freedom. *His parents were very authoritarian and wouldn't let him watch TV.*

similar words: **tyrannical**
contrasting words: **submissive**

bottom   *noun*

the lowest or deepest part of something. *I signed the letter at the **bottom** of the page.*

floor
The **floor** is the lowest flat part of a room or other space. *The floor of the cave was quite dry.*

foot
The **foot** can be the bottom part. *We camped in the valley at the foot of the mountain.*

base
The **base** is the bottom part of anything that gives support. *We stood at the base of the huge tree and gazed upward.*

bed
The **bed** can be the bottom or ground underneath a body of water. *The shipwreck was sunk in the mud of the ocean bed.*

contrasting words: **top**

brave   *adjective*

ready to face danger or pain whether you are afraid or not. *The **brave** shopkeeper showed no fear of the armed robber.*

courageous
Courageous means able to do or face something you find frightening. It is similar to brave. *The courageous girl swam across the flooded river to get help.*

fearless
Fearless means not feeling fear even in dangerous situations. *The fearless lion tamer put his head between the lion's jaws.*

bold
Bold means without fear, or ready to take risks. It is similar to **fearless**. *His bold deed was admired by everyone.*

heroic
Heroic means brave or acting in the daring way a hero does. *The heroic firefighter carried the child from the burning house.*

valiant
Valiant means brave or showing great courage. *Her valiant efforts saved her friend's life.*

similar words: **bold**
contrasting words: **fearful, frightened**

break   *noun*

a gap or open space in something. *The cattle got out through the **break** in the fence.*

split
: A **split** is a long narrow break or division in something. *My jeans were so tight I got a split in them when I bent over.*

crack
: A **crack** is a slight opening. *There was a crack in the cup and the tea leaked out.*

fissure
: A **fissure** is a long narrow break, usually in something hard or solid. *There was a deep fissure in the ground after the earthquake.*

rift
: A **rift** is a long narrow opening made by something breaking or dividing. *The violent explosion caused a rift to appear in the earth.*

crevice
: A **crevice** is a **crack** or cleft that forms an opening in something. *I quickly pushed the secret map through the crevice in the rock to hide it.*

similar words: **cut, hole**

brief   *adjective*

using few words. *There was a **brief** report of the accident in the newspaper.*

short
: **Short** can mean fairly brief or not as long as usual. *I had a short letter from my friend.*

concise
: **Concise** means using few words to tell a lot. *She gave a concise account of what had happened.*

abridged
: **Abridged** means made briefer by leaving out some parts. *I enjoyed the abridged version of the novel and then went on to read the complete edition.*

condensed
: **Condensed** means expressed in fewer words than before. *I haven't much time to listen, so give me a condensed version of what happened.*

contrasting words: **lengthy**

bright   *adjective*

giving out a strong light. *He drew a picture of a **bright** sun and a pale moon.*

light
Light means not dark. *My bedroom is always light because it has wide windows.*

illuminated
Illuminated means having been lit up. *The city buildings were illuminated at night during the festival.*

brilliant
Brilliant can mean shining with a bright light. *They enjoyed the display of brilliant fireworks.*

dazzling
Dazzling can mean shining with a light that almost blinds you. *Drivers should not look at the headlights of other cars because they are too dazzling.*

glaring
Glaring can mean being so bright that it is uncomfortable to look at. *She sheltered her eyes from the glaring sunlight.*

similar words: **shining**
contrasting words: **dark**

broad-minded   *adjective*

able to accept other people's ideas and ways. *When you start to meet different sorts of people you learn to be **broad-minded** and enjoy the things that are different about them.*

liberal
Liberal means broad-minded or able to accept a wide range of ideas. *His liberal views are a result of his desire to be fair to people with different ideas.*

tolerant
Tolerant means showing or having respect for, or patience with, other people's opinions or ways of doing things. *I try to be tolerant of her untidiness even though we have to share a room.*

indulgent
Indulgent means willing to give in to the wishes or feelings of others. *He is an indulgent father in most things but he insists on obedience.*

permissive
Permissive means allowing people freedom to do as they wish, especially in moral matters. *Helen can stay out late because her parents are permissive.*

similar words: **unconventional**
contrasting words: **strict, narrow-minded**

broke *adjective*

out of money. This word is more suited to everyday language. *I can't pay you back till next week because I'm **broke**.*

impecunious   **Impecunious** means not having any money. This is rather a formal word. *The impecunious young man gambled his last dollar at the races.*

destitute   **Destitute** means not having any money or the belongings that are necessary for everyday living. *The whole family was destitute after the fire destroyed their home.*

ruined   **Ruined** can mean having lost everything you own. *Many people were ruined by the disastrous floods.*

bankrupt   **Bankrupt** means unable to pay the money you owe to other people. *She was bankrupt after her business failed.*

insolvent   **Insolvent** means having more debts than you can pay. It is very similar to **bankrupt**. *Because he was insolvent he could pay only half of what he owed people.*

similar words: **poor**
contrasting words: **wealthy**

brown *adjective*

having the color of earth. *I want to ride that **brown** horse over there.*

beige   **Beige** means having a very light brown color, like natural wool. *The beige drapes blended well with the woodwork.*

fawn   **Fawn** means having a pale yellowish-brown color. *Gently I stroked the soft, fawn coat of the young Jersey calf.*

tan   **Tan** means having a yellowish-brown color. *I rubbed and polished the tan leather saddle until it shone like new.*

brunette   **Brunette** means having a rich dark brown color. *All their children have brunette hair.*

sepia   **Sepia** means having a dark brown color, like that used in drawing or photography, especially in very old photographs. *My great-grandmother has a sepia photograph of her wedding day.*

build *verb*

to make something by joining parts together. *The little girl **built** a tower with the blocks.*

construct	To **construct** is so similar to build that you can usually use either. *She constructed a bookshelf with the wood.*
erect	To **erect** means to build something up. *They have erected a house on the block next to our place.*
put up	To **put up** is so similar to **erect** that you can usually use either. *My mother put up a fence at the back of our house.*
shape	To **shape** means to give definite form, shape, or character to something. *The potter carefully shaped his pots.*
fashion	To **fashion** means to form something. *The carpenter fashioned a doll out of the piece of wood.*

similar words: **make**

bungle *verb*

to do something badly. *She **bungled** the whole job.*

botch	To **botch** means to spoil or bungle something. *He botched the cake by using too much sugar.*
fumble	To **fumble** means to handle something clumsily. *The receiver fumbled the ball and dropped it.*
muff	To **muff** means to miss or bungle something. It is more suited to everyday language. *I muffed my chance of being on the team when I dropped the ball.*
mess up	To **mess up** means to make a confused jumble of something. This is more suited to everyday language. *He was angry when his little brother messed up his stamp collection.*
fluff	To **fluff** means to fail to do something properly. This is more suited to everyday language. *The actor fluffed his lines.*

busy *adjective*

fully occupied. *My mother was **busy** painting my bedroom.*

active   **Active** means continuously busy. *My grandfather leads an active life even though he is eighty.*

hardworking   **Hardworking** means always willing to work hard. *He does well in his job because he is hardworking.*

industrious   **Industrious** can mean willing to work hard. It is very similar to **hardworking.** *She is an industrious student.*

hectic   **Hectic** can mean full of activity and confusion. *We had a hectic weekend packing for the movers.*

---

similar words: **energetic**
contrasting words: **lazy, lethargic**

---

buy *verb*

to get something by paying money. *I am saving up to **buy** a new bike.*

purchase   To **purchase** is so similar to buy that you can usually use either. *We purchased the radio with our own money.*

rent   To **rent** means to pay money regularly for the use of something, usually a place to live in. *We are renting a house near the school.*

lease   To **lease** means to enter an agreement to use something for a definite period of time in exchange for money. It is very similar to **rent**. *We decided it was cheaper to lease a car than to buy one.*

redeem   To **redeem** can mean to get back something by paying. *Thank goodness I managed to redeem the watch that I pawned.*

---

similar words: **get**
contrasting words: **sell**

---

buyer *noun*

someone who buys or pays money for something. *I am a regular **buyer** of that magazine.*

purchaser	A **purchaser** is so similar to a buyer that you can usually use either. *The purchaser of our old house loves it.*
customer	A **customer** is someone who buys goods from another person. *The shopkeeper was anxious to please his customer.*
shopper	A **shopper** is someone who is visiting a shop with the intention of looking for and buying something. *The shopper didn't see anything she liked, so she went to another store.*
patron	A **patron** is someone who regularly spends money at a shop, hotel, theater, and so on. *The local cinema has a lot of patrons on Sundays.*
consumer	A **consumer** is someone who buys and uses goods or services. *Advertising encourages consumers to buy more.*

contrasting words: **seller**

calculate *verb*

to work out something using mathematics. *He took out his ruler and **calculated** the area of the square.*

compute	To **compute** means to calculate or work out something using mathematics. *She computed the time it would take for light to reach Earth from the Sun.*
figure	To **figure** means to work out or calculate something. *I figure the cost to be $150, and if we save hard we can buy the bike by June.*
derive	To **derive** means to get the answer to a problem by working it out. *I derived the answer by adding the numbers together.*
reckon	To **reckon** means to calculate or count something up. *How much do you reckon I owe you?*

similar words: **count, measure**

callous *adjective*

showing no concern for someone else's feelings. *It was* **callous** *of them not to visit their lonely grandmother.*

hardhearted	**Hardhearted** means having no kind feelings toward others. *The hardhearted landlord refused to allow the tenants any more time to pay the rent.*
unfeeling	**Unfeeling** is so similar to **hardhearted** that you can usually use either. *"Too bad," was the supervisor's unfeeling reply.*
insensitive	**Insensitive** can mean lacking in feeling but not necessarily meaning to be cruel. *The insensitive coach yelled at the team for losing.*
stony	**Stony** can mean refusing to be moved by kind feelings. *I begged her for help but she had a stony heart.*
cold-blooded	**Cold-blooded** can mean having no feelings, especially of pity. It usually describes a more callous person or action than **hardhearted** or **unfeeling**. *The cold-blooded murderer shot the shopkeeper.*

similar words: **cruel**
contrasting words: **kind**

calm *adjective*

not getting excited or upset. *He always stays* **calm** *when there is trouble.*

cool	**Cool** means calm or not excited. *She was quite cool although everyone else was shouting.*
poised	**Poised** means calm, confident, and self-possessed. *Some people remain poised even in uncomfortable situations.*
relaxed	**Relaxed** means feeling at ease and unworried. *You will be able to think better if you are relaxed.*
placid	**Placid** means calm and peaceful. *Mary is a placid person and isn't upset by little things.*
composed	**Composed** means feeling calm in your body and mind. *I know you are upset now, but after a good sleep you may feel more composed.*

similar words: **peaceful**
contrasting words: **excited, upset, frightened, nervous**

cancel   *verb*

to put an end to the operation or effectiveness of something. *I wish we could cancel all the school rules and make new ones.*

dissolve — To **dissolve** can mean to bring something to an end. *The principal dissolved the meeting when no agreement could be reached.*

break off — To **break off** can mean to put a stop to something. *I decided to break off our friendship.*

abolish — To **abolish** means to put an end to something altogether. *A law was passed to abolish slavery.*

annul — To **annul** means to put an end to something, such as a law or a marriage. *The Supreme Court annulled the law.*

repeal — To **repeal** means to put an end to something legally and officially. It is similar to **abolish**. *The government repealed the tax on books.*

similar words: **finish**
contrasting words: **initiate, start**

capture   *verb*

to take someone or something by force. *The soldiers captured the village.*

arrest — To **arrest** means to take someone prisoner. *The police officer arrested the thief.*

apprehend — To **apprehend** means to take someone or something into keeping. *The police apprehended the burglar as he ran down the road.*

trap — To **trap** means to catch birds or small animals in a snare or to catch someone by surprise. *We trapped the bully who stole our toys.*

pick up — To **pick up** can mean to capture someone you are looking for, especially a criminal. *They picked up the escaped convict as he tried to flee across the border.*

hijack — To **hijack** means to seize something, using threats or violence. *The terrorists hijacked the plane and forced the pilot to fly to another country.*

similar words: **grab, abduct**
contrasting words: **free**

careful   *adjective*

putting time and effort into your work. *She is a **careful** writer.*

diligent   **Diligent** means paying careful and unceasing attention to what you
are doing. *The diligent worker was promoted to superintendent.*

conscientious   **Conscientious** means being particularly careful and thorough in
what you have to do. *The conscientious student kept good notes.*

attentive   **Attentive** means paying careful attention to someone. *The attentive
pupils learned a lot from the teacher's diagrams on the board.*

fussy   **Fussy** means being very careful in what you are doing, sometimes in
an irritating way. *He was such a fussy worker that he was the last one
to finish.*

similar words: **thorough**
contrasting words: **careless**

careless   *adjective*

done without taking enough care or paying enough attention. *His **careless** driving
caused the accident.*

thoughtless   **Thoughtless** means doing or saying something without thinking
carefully about it. *Her thoughtless remark hurt his feelings.*

casual   **Casual** can mean doing something without giving it enough thought.
His casual attitude to his work caused him to fail.

lax   **Lax** means careless or not strict. *The teacher was lax in keeping
discipline in the class.*

negligent   **Negligent** means not paying any attention to what you should be
doing. *He was negligent in carrying out his duties.*

irresponsible   **Irresponsible** means not careful or reliable, sometimes in a
dangerous way. *The lifeguard's irresponsible behavior alarmed us.*

contrasting words: **careful**

carry *verb*

to take something from one place to another. *The ship **carried** its cargo across the sea.*

transport	To **transport** is very similar to carry. *We hired a truck to transport our furniture to our new house.*
transfer	To **transfer** means to carry or move something from one place to another. *A helicopter transferred the sailors from their sinking ship to the rescue boat.*
convey	To **convey** means to carry something from one place to another. *A bus conveyed the passengers from the airport into town.*
deliver	To **deliver** means to carry something and hand it over to someone else. *A courier delivers the merchandise to each store.*
run	To **run** can mean to carry or **transport** someone to a particular place. *If you're ready now, I'll run you to school.*

similar words: **send**

catch *verb*

to capture something, especially after a chase. *The police **caught** the thief by forcing his car off the road.*

trap	To **trap** means to catch an animal in a device made for this purpose. *They trapped the foxes and then decided to let them go.*
snare	To **snare** means to catch birds and small animals with a device usually consisting of a noose. *The ranger caught the poacher who had snared the pheasants.*
ambush	To **ambush** means to attack something or someone after lying in wait in a hidden place. *The outlaws ambushed the stagecoach and robbed the passengers.*
waylay	To **waylay** means to lie in wait for someone or something, especially in order to attack, rob, or capture them. *They waylaid him outside his house and kidnapped him.*
take by surprise	To **take by surprise** can mean to come upon something or someone suddenly and when they least expect it. *The crocodile watched the zebra drinking at the river and took the animal by surprise when it surfaced nearby.*

cause *verb*

to bring something about or to make it happen. *Her forgetfulness* **caused** *a lot of trouble for us all.*

provoke	To **provoke** can mean to cause something or to stir it up. *His constant teasing provoked an angry response.*
induce	To **induce** can mean to cause something or to bring it on. *This drug induces sleep.*
produce	To **produce** can mean to bring something into being. *The rich soil produced good crops for the farmers.*
inspire	To **inspire** can mean to **produce** or awaken a feeling or thought in someone. *Her happy and kind nature inspires love in all her friends.*
evoke	To **evoke** means to **produce** something or to give rise to it. *The soft music evoked a feeling of calm.*

center *noun*

the middle and most important part of something. *There are many stores in the* **center** *of the city.*

hub	A **hub** can be a busy or important center. *The main street was the hub of activity in the town.*
heart	The **heart** can be the most important part, especially of an argument or situation. *We got straight to the heart of the matter and found out what the problem really was.*
core	The **core** can be the central, middle, or main part of anything. *The core of this lesson is that everyone is equal.*
nucleus	The **nucleus** can be the central and most important part or thing around which other parts are grouped. *The drummer was the nucleus of the new rock band.*
focus	The **focus** can be the main point of interest or attraction. *The new girl in the class was the focus of attention.*

similar words: **inside**
contrasting words: **outskirts**

change   *verb*

to make something different. *Darren **changed** his story so it would have a happy ending.*

alter
To **alter** means to make something different in some way. *They altered their plans so I could come too.*

adapt
To **adapt** means to change something to make it better suited to your needs. *We adapted the play so everyone could have a part in it.*

vary
To **vary** means to **alter** something a little bit. *I varied my lunch today by bringing a banana instead of an apple.*

convert
To **convert** can mean to change something completely. *With a wave of her wand the fairy godmother converted the pumpkin into a glass carriage.*

transform
To **transform** means to change the form or appearance of something. *New wheels and some bright red paint transformed the old go-cart.*

---

contrasting words: **keep**

---

charm   *verb*

to attract, win over, or delight someone. *She **charmed** me with her sense of humor.*

fascinate
To **fascinate** means to attract and hold the interest of someone completely. *She fascinated us with her stories.*

entice
To **entice** means to attract or tempt someone, especially by promising money, enjoyment, or some other gain. *The luscious cakes in the window enticed us into the shop.*

beguile
To **beguile** means to attract or enchant someone. *The kitten beguiled them by jumping into a box and peeking over the top.*

bewitch
To **bewitch** means to charm someone as if under a spell. *The wonderful music and dancing bewitched the audience.*

mesmerize
To **mesmerize** means to hold the attention of someone completely. *The beauty of the scenery mesmerized us.*

---

similar words: **attract**
contrasting words: **repel**

---

cheap *adjective*

of low price. *You can buy **cheap** fruit at roadside stands.*

inexpensive   **Inexpensive** means not costing very much money. *We want to stay at an inexpensive hotel.*

reduced   **Reduced** means being of lower price than usual. *The furniture was reduced because there had been a fire.*

discount   **Discount** can mean selling things at a cheaper price than usual. *We bought a washing machine at a discount store.*

no-frills   **No-frills** means being cheap because you don't pay for any luxuries. *We traveled second class and stayed at cheap hotels on our no-frills vacation.*

dirt-cheap   **Dirt-cheap** means very **inexpensive**. It is more suited to everyday language. *The bicycle was dirt-cheap.*

---

contrasting words: **expensive**

---

cheat *verb*

to take something belonging to someone else dishonestly or by tricking them. *He **cheated** me out of all this week's pocket money.*

swindle   To **swindle** means to cheat someone out of something, especially money. *The dishonest businessman swindled his client out of nearly all her savings.*

defraud   To **defraud** means to cheat or deceive someone so as to get their money, property, and so on. It is usually used in more formal language. *The dishonest manager defrauded the store of its profits.*

fleece   To **fleece** means to cheat someone out of all or nearly all of something. It is usually used in less formal language. *They fleeced him of every cent he had.*

rip off   To **rip off** means to cheat someone by making them pay too much for something. It is only used in everyday language. *She ripped us off by charging us $10 for that junk.*

---

similar words: **trick, deceive**

---

chew *verb*

to bite and crush food with your teeth. *Babies must have their food mashed because they cannot **chew** it.*

munch	To **munch** means to chew something noisily. *The cows were munching grass.*
chomp	To **chomp** means to chew noisily. It is similar to **munch**. *Don't chomp your food when you eat.*
nibble	To **nibble** means to chew or bite in little bits. *She nibbled her biscuit.*
gnaw	To **gnaw** means to wear something away by biting it again and again. *The mouse gnawed through the bag and ate the bread inside.*
masticate	To **masticate** means to chew in order to digest. It is a more formal word than **chew**. *He always masticates his food thoroughly.*

similar words: **eat**

chic *adjective*

attractive and stylish. *Your hair is very **chic**.*

elegant	**Elegant** means graceful or stylish. *The limousine was the most elegant car I have ever seen.*
smart	**Smart** can mean neat and keeping up with the latest fashion. *That's a smart new suit you have.*
dapper	**Dapper** means very neat and **smart** in a slightly showy way. *He's very dapper in his spotless white shirt and new bow tie.*
fashionable	**Fashionable** means in keeping with the style of clothes and appearance that most people think is attractive. *A beaver hat was once considered very fashionable.*
spiffy	**Spiffy** can mean very **smart** and stylish. It is more suited to everyday language. *I bought some spiffy new clothes for the dance.*

contrasting words: **old-fashioned**

choice *noun*

something or someone you have chosen or picked out from a number of things or people. *The blue one is my* **choice**.

selection
A **selection** can be a thing or things chosen carefully. *Bring your selection to the cashier.*

option
An **option** is something you have chosen or that you may choose. *What are my options in this situation?*

preference
A **preference** is something that you choose or like better than another. *My preference is to travel there by plane.*

alternative
An **alternative** is one of two or more choices. *We had to decide on one out of a whole list of exciting alternatives.*

elective
An **elective** is a course or subject that is not required but that you can choose to do. *I chose art as my elective.*

choose *verb*

to settle on something or someone above all the others in a group. ***Choose** a number between one and ten.*

select
To **select** means to choose something or someone carefully. *Have you selected a record yet?*

pick
To **pick** means to choose or **select** something from among a number of things. *Pick your favorite color.*

take
To **take** can mean to choose something from more than one alternative. *We lost our way after we took the wrong road.*

decide
To **decide** can mean to choose between various alternatives. *I decided that the sensible thing to do was to go to the party.*

fix
To **fix** can mean to settle on or determine. *I've fixed the price now and it's not too high and not too low.*

similar words: **prefer**

city   *noun*

a large or important town. *Thousands of people work in the many offices and factories in the city.*

metropolis	A **metropolis** is a large important city. *Denver is the biggest metropolis in the Rocky Mountains.*
capital	A **capital** is the main city of a country, province, or state and is where the government is situated. *Washington, D.C., is the capital of the United States.*
suburb	A **suburb** is a district of a city with its own shopping center, school, and so on. *We live in a suburb of Cleveland.*
town	A **town** is a large place with many people living in it. *We go into town to buy our supplies.*
concrete jungle	The **concrete jungle** means the city. It is an expression used to show that you think some things about cities are unpleasant, such as crowding and tall buildings. *My parents say they want to leave the concrete jungle when they retire and live in the country.*

contrasting words: **country (2)**

civic   *adjective*

having to do with a city, or the people who live in it. *The municipal buildings are usually in the civic center.*

urban	**Urban** means having to do with a city or town, or living in that city or town. *Most of the urban population works in offices and factories.*
metropolitan	**Metropolitan** means having to do with a very large city, or the people who live in it. *The metropolitan area spread for miles.*
suburban	**Suburban** means having to do with or living in an area that is often quite far from the city center. *There are many large suburban shopping centers surrounding the city.*
citified	**Citified** means having the habits or fashions of people used to living in a city. *People have become very citified as our town has grown.*

contrasting words: **country**

clean *adjective*

not having any dirt or stains. *We wore **clean** clothes to the party.*

spotless **Spotless** means free from stains, marks, spots, or any other similar blemishes. *Everything in the home was spotless.*

immaculate **Immaculate** means free from spots or stains. *Your uniform must be immaculate.*

hygienic **Hygienic** means clean and free from dirt and germs. *We are taught to be hygienic and always wash our hands before meals.*

spick-and-span **Spick-and-span** means clean and neat. This is more suited to everyday language. *I want your room spick-and-span before you go out.*

pure **Pure** can mean clean and **spotless**. *She has a lovely, pure complexion.*

contrasting words: **dirty**

clean *verb*

to remove the dirt from something or someone. *She **cleaned** her shoes.*

wash To **wash** means to wet and rub someone or something, usually with soap or detergent, in order to remove the dirt. *He washed his face and hands before dinner.*

scrub To **scrub** means to rub someone or something hard with a brush, soap, and water in order to remove the dirt. *He had to scrub his nails because they were filthy.*

cleanse To **cleanse** means to make something clean and pure. *We cleanse our skin every night.*

sterilize To **sterilize** means to destroy the germs in something, often by boiling it. *We need to sterilize our drinking water.*

mop up To **mop up** means to clean or wipe up dirt and so on with a mop or something similar. *Mop up the paint you spilled!*

contrasting words: **dirty, spoil**

clear   *adjective*

easily understood. *Give us some **clear** examples.*

plain   **Plain** can mean clear to your mind. *It's plain that you don't really want to come.*

obvious   **Obvious** means so clear that no explanation or thought is needed. *The answer to this question is obvious.*

evident   **Evident** can mean quite clear to your understanding. *It's evident you don't know what you're talking about.*

straightforward   **Straightforward** can mean not difficult or complicated. *I would rather you gave me a straightforward explanation.*

explicit   **Explicit** can mean fully set out or expressed in a clear way. *This bike comes with a booklet of explicit instructions.*

> similar words: **obvious**
> contrasting words: **confusing, vague**

clerk   *noun*

someone who works in an office and maintains files and accounts. *The **clerk** was asked to put the letter in the files.*

secretary   A **secretary** is someone who assists another person, usually by typing or writing letters and keeping files. *When I called my mother at work, her secretary answered the telephone.*

bookkeeper   A **bookkeeper** is someone who keeps records of a business's financial transactions. *The company asked its bookkeeper how much money was spent in April.*

agent   An **agent** is someone who has been given authority to act for another person. *I am Mr. Singh's agent, so I will sign the document.*

subordinate   A **subordinate** is someone who takes instructions from someone with a higher rank. *She appreciated her subordinate's work and gave him a promotion.*

> similar words: **helper**

clever *adjective*

good at thinking or learning quickly. *The **clever** girl found her way out of the maze in a minute.*

intelligent	**Intelligent** means having good mental ability. *He is an intelligent boy who succeeds in whatever he does.*
brainy	**Brainy** means having the ability to learn and understand easily. It is a less formal word than **clever** or **intelligent**. *She is so brainy she remembers everything she reads.*
smart	**Smart** means clever or **intelligent**. *Our dog is smart and has learned to open doors.*
bright	**Bright** can mean good at learning and understanding. *My friend is bright and explains problems I don't understand.*
brilliant	**Brilliant** can mean very, very **intelligent**. *Our most brilliant pupil won a scholarship when he went to the university.*

similar words: **shrewd, sensible**
contrasting words: **silly**

climb *verb*

to move up something. *The firefighter **climbed** the ladder.*

ascend	To **ascend** is so similar to climb that you can usually use either. *Jack and Jill ascended the hill.*
mount	To **mount** means to go up something. *I heard my mother begin to mount the stairs.*
scale	To **scale** means to climb up or over something, as if you were using a ladder. *She scaled the wall.*
clamber up	To **clamber up** can mean to climb something with difficulty, using both feet and hands. *As they clambered up the steep path that led to the castle, they nearly fell several times.*
shinny up	To **shinny up** means to climb something by holding fast with your hands or arms and your legs and pulling yourself up. *The boy shinnied up the apple tree.*

contrasting words: **descend, fall**

cloth   *noun*

a substance formed by weaving, knitting, or pressing fibers like wool, hair, silk, or cotton together. *The factory made many different kinds of* **cloth** *and sold them to the shops.*

fabric	**Fabric** is any woven, knitted, or felted cloth. *I bought some cotton fabric to make a sundress. The nursery animal mobiles were made of felt fabric.*
material	**Material** is cloth that has been or is capable of being woven. *The curtain material has a pretty floral pattern.*
textile	A **textile** is any woven cloth. *Silk, wool, and cotton are natural textiles. Nylon is a synthetic textile that is used to make parachutes.*
stuff	**Stuff** can be cloth or **fabric**. This word is not often used these days. *The pioneer woman bought some strong, woolen stuff to make clothes for her family.*

clothing   *noun*

the articles or garments that you wear on your body. *I always wear old* **clothing** *when I work in the garden.*

apparel	**Apparel** is clothing, especially the type worn on the outside. It is a rather formal word. *This shop specializes in wedding apparel.*
attire	**Attire** is clothing for a special occasion, usually rather rich or splendid. *The guests at the opening night of the play wore formal attire.*
dress	**Dress** can mean a particular style of clothing. *Susan did a project on the dress of the Middle Ages.*
garb	**Garb** is clothing of a particular style, especially if it shows your job or hobby or is rather eye-catching. *The doctor put on her garb before entering the operating room.*
wardrobe	Your **wardrobe** is your entire supply of clothing. *I've grown so much since last year that I need a whole new summer wardrobe.*

cloudy *adjective*

not sunny because of clouds. *The sky has been **cloudy** for days.*

overcast   **Overcast** is so similar to cloudy that you can usually use either. *Unfortunately, the sky was overcast the day of our picnic.*

dull   **Dull** can mean cloudy and gray. *A dull day with a lot of rain is forecast for tomorrow.*

misty   **Misty** means not bright or sunny because of a covering or cloud of mist. *The mornings are often misty in the mountains.*

foggy   **Foggy** means dark because of fog. *The motorists turned on their headlights because it was foggy.*

hazy   **Hazy** means not clear because of a thin mist or cloud of dust. *You can't see much of the view today because it is too hazy.*

similar words: **dreary**
contrasting words: **fine**

club *noun*

a group of people organized together to share a particular interest, sport, or hobby. *We started a chess **club** at school.*

association   An **association** is a group of people organized for a common purpose. It is similar to club. *My father belongs to an association of stamp collectors.*

assembly   An **assembly** can be a group of people gathered together for the same purpose. *The labor secretary made a speech to the assembly of workers.*

union   A **union** is a group of workers joined together to represent their own interests. *The union asked the managers of the company for higher wages.*

lobby   A **lobby** is a group of people who try to get public and political support for a particular cause. *She is the leader of the lobby for more government funding for schools.*

similar words: **group**

clumsy   *adjective*

unskillful in the way you move about or do things. *The **clumsy** girl knocked the vase over.*

awkward	**Awkward** means clumsy or not graceful. *The actor's awkward movements on stage spoiled the play.*
gangling	**Gangling** means tall and thin and moving awkwardly. *The gangling colt had difficulty running.*
all thumbs	**All thumbs** means not being skillful with your hands. *I was all thumbs when I tried to knit.*
accident-prone	**Accident-prone** means likely to have a lot of accidents. *Little children are very accident-prone and should be closely watched.*
heavy-handed	**Heavy-handed** means awkward and clumsy. *Without practice your piano playing becomes heavy-handed.*

similar words: **incompetent**
contrasting words: **agile, competent, skillful**

coat   *verb*

to cover something with a substance. ***Coat** the chicken with bread crumbs before you cook it.*

spread	To **spread** can mean to cover something with a layer. *Don't spread the bread too thickly with butter.*
daub	To **daub** means to coat something with a soft or sticky substance. *They daubed mud all over the clean wall.*
smear	To **smear** can mean to rub or **spread** something with grease, oil, paint, or dirt. *We smeared our faces and hands with charcoal so no one would see us in the dark.*
plaster	To **plaster** can mean to cover something thickly, as if with plaster. *She plastered the bread slices with butter.*
pave	To **pave** means to cover a road, path, or something similar with stones, tiles, bricks, or concrete to make a flat hard surface to walk on. *We paved the area around the pool with blue tiles.*

coating *noun*

a covering of some substance spread over a surface. *I put a **coating** of batter on the fish before frying it.*

veneer A **veneer** is a thin layer of wood or other material used to cover the surface underneath. *The walnut veneer on the pine table made it more attractive.*

skin A **skin** can be a surface layer. *I peeled the skin off the apple.*

crust A **crust** can be a hard outer surface. *We could walk on the crust of the snow without sinking.*

glaze A **glaze** is a smooth shiny coating or surface. *The potter put a beautiful blue glaze on his vase.*

film A **film** can be a thin layer or coating. *A film of oil covered the water where the boat had sunk.*

coil *noun*

a loop or series of loops twisting around. *We tied the end of the rope into a **coil** and threw it to the attendant on the dock.*

loop A **loop** is a round or oval shape twisted in a piece of ribbon, string, or something similar. *Make a loop with the string big enough to fit around the bundle of pencils.*

spiral A **spiral** is a curve or series of curves winding around away from a center. *The staircase went up in a spiral, twisting around and around to the very top of the tower.*

curl A **curl** can be something that has a spiral or curved shape. *The waves made huge curls in the ocean.*

twist A **twist** is something that is curved or bent around. *The bus crawled through all the twists in the road.*

cold   *adjective*

having or feeling a lack of warmth. *It's a very **cold** night. My feet are **cold**.*

nippy	**Nippy** means very chilly or cold. *In the late afternoon the breeze at the beach can be nippy.*
freezing	**Freezing** means extremely cold. *I'd better wear a coat in this freezing weather.*
frigid	**Frigid** can mean very cold in temperature. *The frigid temperature in Antarctica makes life difficult for the scientists who work there.*
sharp	**Sharp** can mean very cold or piercing. *The sharp wind blew right through our jackets.*
icy	**Icy** means cold like ice. *Let me rub your icy hands.*
frosty	**Frosty** means very cold or freezing. *We wore our scarves because it was such a frosty day.*

similar words: **wintry**
contrasting words: **hot**

color   *verb*

to put color onto something. *The dawn **colored** the sky with beautiful shades of pink.*

dye	To **dye** means to change the color of something. *I dyed my old white curtains a pretty blue.*
tint	To **tint** means to color something slightly. *The cook tinted the icing on the cake a pale blue.*
stain	To **stain** means to color something made of wood with a liquid that soaks into it. *He stained his pine desk to show the grain of the wood.*
paint	To **paint** means to cover something with a liquid coloring substance. *We are going to paint my bedroom.*
highlight	To **highlight** means to color something so that it stands out against the background. *The artist highlighted the flowers in her painting.*

colorful *adjective*

having many colors. *The opening of the Olympic Games was a **colorful** sight.*

bright

Bright means being strong, clear, and easy to see. *The artist used bright blue to paint the sea.*

vivid

Vivid means dazzling or very **bright**. *The vivid colors of the city lights delighted the children.*

rich

Rich can mean having fine, wonderful colors. *The rich velvet cloak looked lovely over her evening dress.*

garish

Garish means being brightly colored in an unattractive or unusual way. *The clown's garish suit made us all laugh.*

similar words: **gaudy**
contrasting words: **colorless, drab**

colorless *adjective*

lacking in color. *A shower of rain brought the **colorless** desert to life.*

pale

Pale means whitish or not having much color. *His face was pale with fright.*

pastel

Pastel means having soft **pale** colors. *Pastel colors suit most fair people.*

neutral

Neutral can mean having no particular color that stands out. *Everything about her appearance was neutral.*

faded

Faded means having lost its color. *The faded curtains made the room look shabby.*

bleached

Bleached means having had the color taken out. *The shirt had been washed so often it was bleached.*

contrasting words: **colorful**

combine   *verb*

to mix or put things together. *The conductor **combined** the two choirs for the concert.*

assemble	To **assemble** means to bring or put things together to make a whole. *We painted the model plane after we assembled the parts.*
blend	To **blend** means to mix things together so that they can't be separated. *You can blend flour and water to make glue.*
fuse	To **fuse** means to join two things together by melting them. *The machine fused the two metals by heating them.*
merge	To **merge** means to unite or bring two or more things together. *The police officer merged the two lines of traffic.*
amalgamate	To **amalgamate** means to join two or more things together so as to make one. It is very similar to **merge**. *The board of directors decided to amalgamate the two companies.*

similar words: **mix, join**
contrasting words: **separate**

come   *verb*

to get to a place you have been moving toward. *We will **come** to see your house in the morning.*

arrive	To **arrive** means to come to the end of a journey. *We set out early and arrived at dawn.*
reach	To **reach** means to get to or **arrive** at. *We were very glad when we reached home after our long journey.*
turn up	To **turn up** means to come or **arrive**. *She turned up late at the party.*
show up	To **show up** can mean to **arrive**. It is more suited to everyday language. *We all thought he wasn't coming but he finally showed up.*

similar words: **land**
contrasting words: **leave**

comfort *noun*

a lessening of sadness and worry. *I gained great **comfort** from her visits when I was in the hospital.*

consolation   **Consolation** can mean comfort or cheer in your distress. *Her optimism when I was sick was a great consolation.*

solace   **Solace** means comfort in a time of sorrow or trouble. *The two sisters found solace by being together when their parents were so ill.*

relief   **Relief** means freedom from pain, unhappiness, or worry. *What a relief to see them again!*

ease   **Ease** is freedom from any problem, discomfort, or pain. *He lived a life of ease after he won first prize in the lottery.*

similar words: **pity**

comfort *verb*

to cheer someone up or make them feel less sad or worried. *He **comforted** the baby by cuddling her.*

soothe   To **soothe** means to calm or comfort someone. *The soft music soothed me.*

ease   To **ease** means to give someone relief or comfort. *The news that the doctor was coming eased her mind.*

relieve   To **relieve** means to make someone free from pain, unhappiness, or worry. *The news that they were safe relieved us.*

alleviate   To **alleviate** means to make something easier to bear. *Talking to my parents alleviated my worry.*

lighten   To **lighten** can mean to make something less hard to bear. *Getting a new dog lightened Peter's sadness at losing his pet.*

similar words: **pacify**
contrasting words: **upset**

comment *noun*

a short note or statement that gives an opinion or explanation. *The reporters asked the mayor if he would make a **comment**.*

remark A **remark** is a brief expression of your opinion. It is usually spoken. *Have you got any remarks to make about my suggestion?*

observation An **observation** is a comment made about something you have noticed, usually not of great importance. *I said that the room looked a little messy, but it was only an observation.*

interjection An **interjection** is a comment made to interrupt a conversation or a speech. *I will stop speaking if there are any more interjections.*

exclamation An **exclamation** is something said or cried out suddenly in pleasure or fright. *She gave an exclamation of surprise when she opened his present.*

commotion *noun*

a wild or noisy disturbance. *There was a great **commotion** on the playground when two dogs started fighting.*

fuss A **fuss** can be a noise or disturbance. *Everyone made a fuss because the bus was late again.*

hullabaloo A **hullabaloo** is a loud, noisy disturbance. *She made a great hullabaloo when she won the contest.*

tumult A **tumult** is a noisy, violent disturbance or uproar, often made by a huge crowd. *A tumult of cheering burst from the hundreds of waiting fans.*

turmoil A **turmoil** means a commotion or a condition of wild disorder. *The house was in a turmoil when we were packing to leave.*

riot A **riot** is a disturbance of the peace by a group of people. *When the two rival gangs met there was a riot in the street.*

similar words: **noise**

compete *verb*

to set yourself against one or more people to gain or win something. *Ben and James **competed** for the running trophy.*

race	To **race** means to compete with someone in a contest of speed. *The drivers raced around the track.*
run	To **run** means to compete or take part in a race. *We ran against each other in the relay race.*
vie	To **vie** means to compete against or try to beat someone. *The girls vied with each other in games.*
contest	To **contest** means to compete with or struggle against someone. *The rivals contested with each other for his friendship.*

contrasting words: **cooperate**

competent *adjective*

good at doing a particular thing. *She is a **competent** driver.*

able	**Able** means having enough skill to do a particular job. *She is a very able pianist.*
capable	**Capable** means knowing the right way to do something and doing it well. It is very similar to **competent**. *He is a capable cook.*
expert	**Expert** means having a lot of special skill or knowledge. *She is an expert pilot.*
proficient	**Proficient** means skilled or **expert**. *He is a proficient nurse.*
good at	**Good at** means being able to do something well. It is less formal than **capable**. *She is good at playing baseball.*

similar words: **experienced, skillful**
contrasting words: **incompetent, inexperienced, clumsy**

competition   *noun*

a contest or a situation in which you try to do better than anyone else. *Jan won first prize in a poetry* **competition**.

game	A **game** is a competition with set rules. *Let's have a game of marbles.*
match	A **match** is an official competition. *The tennis match was very exciting.*
race	A **race** is any kind of competition that is always a test of speed. *We had a race to the end of the street.*
championship	A **championship** is a contest between the best in any sport or game. *The two teams fought for the championship.*
tournament	A **tournament** is a contest with a number of players. *The golf tournament was postponed due to rain.*

complain   *verb*

to tell about your troubles, illnesses, pains, or any of the things you are not satisfied with. *However much I try to please them, they always complain.*

grumble	To **grumble** means to complain crankily, usually in a low voice. *He grumbled about the dirty fingermarks on his book.*
whine	To **whine** can mean to complain in an annoying, high-pitched voice. *That child is always whining at his mother.*
nag	To **nag** can mean to keep on complaining or finding fault. *My brother nags me when I am late.*
gripe	To **gripe** means to complain continually and bad-temperedly. It is more suited to everyday language. *Please stop griping about how cold the weather is.*
protest	To **protest** means to complain about or object to something. *I protested that the cost of the shirt was too high.*

complicated *adjective*

having many related or entangled parts. *This material has a **complicated** pattern.*

elaborate	**Elaborate** means having great detail. *We worked out an elaborate plan.*
intricate	**Intricate** means having fine details or puzzlingly entangled parts. *We had to follow an intricate maze of paths.*
complex	**Complex** means difficult and complicated. *The problem was too complex for us to solve.*
involved	**Involved** means lengthy and going into great detail. *The witness gave an involved reply to the lawyer's simple question.*
convoluted	**Convoluted** means twisted, complicated, and difficult to understand. *He gave a convoluted answer when I invited him to dinner and I didn't know if he was coming or not.*

contrasting words: **easy**

compose *verb*

to create literature or music. *Would you please help me **compose** this limerick?*

write	To **write** can mean to create or produce something using words, musical notes, or other symbols. *I hope to write a novel one day.*
draft	To **draft** can mean to **write** or draw the outline or plan of something. *I still have a lot of work to do on my essay because I have only drafted it.*
pen	To **pen** means to **write** down something using a pen, usually a song or poem. This word is not often used as it can sound rather pompous. *Can you pen a few lines to go with this catchy little tune?*
dash off	To **dash off** can mean to **write** something in a hurry. *I must remember to dash off a note to my teacher.*
set down	To **set down** can mean to put something down in writing. *I must set down my memories of our overseas trip before I forget them.*

conceited   *adjective*

too proud of yourself and your own importance and abilities. *Carla was so* **conceited** *she thought she could do everything better than anyone else.*

vain
Vain means too proud of yourself in any way. *The vain man was always boasting about his important job.*

narcissistic
Narcissistic means loving yourself too much, especially your appearance. *He was so narcissistic he kept looking in his mirror.*

egotistic
Egotistic means always thinking and talking about yourself. *The egotistic boy told us all about his vacation but didn't ask about ours.*

stuck-up
Stuck-up means thinking your are better than everyone else. It is more suited to everyday language. *If you are stuck-up you will not have many friends.*

big-headed
Big-headed means conceited or **vain**. *I hope winning this award will not make you big-headed.*

similar words: **proud, pompous**
contrasting words: **humble**

concentrate   *verb*

to fix your mind on something. *If you* **concentrate**, *you'll solve the problem.*

focus on
To **focus on** means to concentrate or center your thoughts on something. *Focus on solving this puzzle.*

consider
To **consider** can mean to think carefully or direct your thoughts toward one particular thing. *Please don't rush me, because I need to consider before I reply.*

take notice of
To **take notice of** means to pay attention to something or someone with interest. *You should take notice of her advice.*

attend to
To **attend to** means to give something or someone your full attention. *Attend to your work!*

mind
To **mind** can mean to pay close attention, especially to what you are doing or to what is happening around you. *Mind that you don't trip.*

similar words: **ponder**
contrasting words: **daydream**

concert *noun*

a public presentation by musicians or other performers. *The audience applauded when the choir came on stage to begin their* **concert**.

recital
A **recital** is a performance given by a group of pupils. *The parents enjoyed listening to the music at the piano recital.*

jam session
A **jam session** is an informal meeting of jazz or rock musicians, usually to play for their own enjoyment. *Everyone had brought along their instruments so we decided to start playing a tune we all knew and have a jam session.*

show
A **show** is an entertainment, such as a movie or concert. *Students wrote and directed the show that we are seeing tonight.*

performance
A **performance** is the giving of a play or concert. *The final performance of the play was sold out.*

conclude *verb*

to decide something after thinking about it. *After reading the book carefully, she* **concluded** *that the murderer was not a member of the victim's family.*

deduce
To **deduce** means to work something out by reasoning. *We deduced from the sirens that a nearby building was on fire.*

infer
To **infer** means to form an opinion about something after considering all the facts and information. *They inferred from the spy's report that the enemy would attack early in the morning.*

gather
To **gather** can mean to understand something as a result of things you have heard. *I gather that you had a wonderful time at the picnic.*

reason
To **reason** can mean to decide something by sensible argument. *They reasoned that the river would flood because of the rain and the cattle should be moved to higher ground.*

similar words: **think, solve**

concoct *verb*

to think up something, such as a story or an excuse. *He **concocted** a story to explain why he was late.*

make up
To **make up** means to invent something for a particular reason. *It is no good making up excuses.*

cook up
To **cook up** means to concoct something or to invent it in order to mislead or deceive someone. It is more suited to everyday language. *They have cooked up an explanation between themselves.*

hatch
To **hatch** means to concoct or arrange something, often in secret. *They hatched a clever plan.*

contrive
To **contrive** means to invent or plan something in a clever way. *They contrived a plan to escape.*

similar words: **invent, create**

confine *verb*

to keep or shut someone in a place. *The patient was **confined** to bed during the lengthy illness.*

imprison
To **imprison** means to shut someone up against their will, usually in a prison. *The kidnappers imprisoned their victim in an old farmhouse.*

jail
To **jail** means to put someone in prison. *The judge jailed him for five years.*

lock up
To **lock up** means to shut someone in a place fastened with a lock, such as a prison. *The constable locked up the suspect in a cell until he could be taken before a judge.*

restrain
To **restrain** can mean to take away someone's freedom. *The students should be restrained from doing further damage.*

intern
To **intern** means to keep someone in an enclosed and guarded area, especially during wartime. *Many soldiers were interned by the enemy during the war.*

contrasting words: **free**

conflict   *noun*

a fight, struggle, or disagreement. *We want to avoid a **conflict** between nations so that there will be peace in the world.*

feud	A **feud** is a bitter, long-lasting quarrel, especially one between two families. *We had never met his cousin because of the family feud.*
spat	A short argument over something unimportant. *They have their spats, but they are the best of friends.*
disagreement	A **disagreement** is a failure to agree. *We are having a disagreement over whom to invite to the party.*
clash	A **clash** is an angry conflict. *My friend and I had a clash and we shouted at each other.*

similar words: **argument, fight**

confuse   *verb*

to mix up your mind or your thoughts. *Susan and Diana both tried to show me how to play the game but they only **confused** me.*

muddle	To **muddle** means to make someone confused in mind or unable to think clearly. *The conflicting evidence muddled the jury's thinking.*
fluster	To **fluster** means to make someone nervous and confused. *The boss flustered me when she said I only had ten minutes to finish typing the letter.*
distract	To **distract** means to make someone confused by drawing their attention away from what they are doing. *The TV will distract you while you are doing your homework.*
befuddle	To **befuddle** means to confuse someone, especially by talking cleverly or too quickly. *You befuddle me when you use those big words that I don't understand.*
bamboozle	To **bamboozle** means to confuse or deceive someone. This word is more suited to everyday language. *She bamboozled us by sending us a message written in secret code.*

similar words: **puzzle**
contrasting words: **explain, simplify**

confused *adjective*

feeling unsure or mixed up. *I am so **confused** that I do not know what is the right thing to do.*

puzzled	**Puzzled** means confused or bewildered. *She gave a puzzled frown as she read the strange letter.*
mystified	**Mystified** is so similar to **puzzled** that you can usually use either. *We were mystified when we couldn't find the lunch we brought.*
nonplussed	**Nonplussed** means completely confused and **puzzled**. *I can't think sensibly at the moment because I am nonplussed by his strange behavior.*
undecided	**Undecided** means unsure or not having made up your mind. *I am undecided as to whether I like your new dress.*
ambivalent	**Ambivalent** can mean uncertain or doubtful, because you can't make up your mind. *I have an ambivalent attitude to riding horses and I don't know whether I will continue taking lessons.*

contrasting words: **sure**

confusing *adjective*

hard to understand. *I couldn't follow the **confusing** instructions.*

bewildering	**Bewildering** means so confusing that you don't know what to do. *He couldn't find his way out of the bewildering maze.*
perplexing	**Perplexing** means confusing and troubling, especially by being difficult to understand or answer. *This is a perplexing problem.*
mysterious	**Mysterious** means full of mystery or difficult to explain. *No one can explain the mysterious disappearance of the airplane.*
puzzling	**Puzzling** means difficult to explain or find an answer to. *There did not seem to be a solution to the puzzling problem.*
ambiguous	**Ambiguous** means confusing or **puzzling** because it has more than one meaning. *He gave an ambiguous reply.*

contrasting words: **clear, easy**

continue *verb*

to keep on. *They **continued** to walk in the rain.*

last
: To **last** means to go on or continue. *This lesson will last for half an hour.*

endure
: To **endure** can mean to **last** well. *The appeal of good music endures for years.*

hold on
: To **hold on** means to **last** or continue. *I hope you can hold on until help comes.*

survive
: To **survive** can mean to keep going or remain in existence, especially in the face of some difficulty or change. *The singer's popularity has survived through many music fads.*

persist
: To **persist** can mean to go on and on. *Her toothache persisted even though she had visited the dentist.*

contrasting words: **stop**

continuous *adjective*

going on without stopping. *A **continuous** line of people streamed into the theater.*

constant
: **Constant** means continuing all the time. *His success was a constant source of pleasure to his family.*

steady
: **Steady** can mean continuous and regular. *He made steady progress in learning to play the violin.*

persistent
: **Persistent** means going on and on. *Her persistent efforts paid off when she won the trophy.*

endless
: **Endless** can mean seeming to have no end. *The endless ringing of the burglar alarm brought the police, who arrested the thieves.*

interminable
: **Interminable** means as if without an end. It is very similar to **endless**. *The long heat wave seemed interminable.*

similar words: **permanent**
contrasting words: **erratic**

cool   *verb*

to make someone or something pleasantly cold or less hot. *The gentle breeze* ***cooled*** *us when we sat down after our hot walk.*

fan	To **fan** can mean to cool or refresh someone with, or as if with, a fan. *It was so hot in the assembly hall that I fanned my face with a piece of paper.*
air-condition	To **air-condition** can mean to cool air with a machine that keeps the temperature of a room at a comfortable level. *We'll have to air-condition this office because it's too hot for the computers, as well as the workers.*
chill	To **chill** means to make something cold. *I chilled the drinks quickly with ice cubes.*
freeze	To **freeze** means to turn something to ice. *We froze our orange drinks.*
refrigerate	To **refrigerate** means to make or keep something cold or frozen. *Refrigerate the leftover meat immediately.*

cooperate   *verb*

to work or act together. *The two councils* ***cooperated*** *to build a new library.*

collaborate	To **collaborate** means to work together, especially on a job. *Alice and James collaborated in writing the book.*
team up	To **team up** means to work together for a particular reason. This is more suited to everyday language. *Nathan and Simon teamed up so their sand castle would be the biggest.*
combine	To **combine** means to join or act together. *The two students combined their efforts to finish building the model airplane.*
unite	To **unite** means to join or work together as one. *The whole town united to save the whales.*

contrasting words: **argue, compete**

copy *noun*

something that is made the same as something else. *The secretary took my letter and made two copies.*

duplicate	A **duplicate** is something that is exactly the same as something else. *I have made a duplicate of my essay so that I can give one to the teacher and keep one for myself.*
replica	A **replica** is an exact copy. *He made a small replica of the rocket.*
model	A **model** can be a small copy. *The teacher has a model of the solar system in her room.*
likeness	A **likeness** is something that is similar to something else but not exactly the same. *There is a definite likeness in my family, so that you can tell we are all related.*
effigy	An **effigy** is a crude representation of something, usually of someone disliked. *The crowd hung an effigy of the disgraced judge.*

copy *verb*

to do or make something the same as something else. ***Copy** this chart into your notebook.*

duplicate	To **duplicate** means to make an exact copy of something. *The secretary duplicated the letter.*
reproduce	To **reproduce** means to make a copy or strong likeness of something. *The artist reproduced the famous painting.*
photocopy	To **photocopy** means to make an exact copy of a page of writing or pictures on a machine using a special camera. *He photocopied his birth certificate.*
trace	To **trace** means to copy something by following the lines of the original on transparent paper placed over it. *Anna and Roberto traced the map of Canada.*
match	To **match** can mean to make something similar to or like something else. *Try to make your drawing match mine.*

similar words: **mimic**

correct *verb*

to make something right by removing the mistakes or faults. *I **corrected** my letter carefully before I sent it.*

rectify	To **rectify** means to put something right. *He soon rectified the situation.*
remedy	To **remedy** can mean to correct a wrong or an evil. *You have been treated unjustly, but we will soon remedy that.*
revise	To **revise** means to check or correct something in order to make it better. *I decided to revise my story after reading it through.*
amend	To **amend** means to correct or change something for the better. *You need to amend the rules of this game.*
reform	To **reform** means to improve something by correcting and changing the mistakes or bad parts. It is similar to **amend**. *It was decided to pass a law to reform the system of taxation.*

similar words: **improve, repair**

council *noun*

the governing body of a town, city, or municipality. *The town **council** approved the plan for the new shopping mall.*

parliament	A **parliament** is a group of people elected to make the laws for a country or state. *The Canadian parliament meets in Ottawa.*
senate	A **senate** is one of the decision-making bodies in the government of a country. *She was honored to be elected to the Senate.*
caucus	A **caucus** is the meeting of a group within one political party. *The party held a caucus to decide on its strategy for the election.*
congress	A **congress** can mean the governing legislature of a republic, as well as any meeting of people to discuss ideas of interest to them all. *A congress of health workers was held here last week.*
board	A **board** is a group of people in charge of a business or organization. *The board of the day-care center is holding a meeting next week.*

count

count *verb*

to use numbers to find the sum of a collection of things. *She **counted** the apples to see if there would be enough for everyone.*

add up — To **add up** means to find the sum of a number of things. *Who can add up these three numbers?*

total — To **total** means to find the sum or whole amount of something. *Please total the money to see if any is missing.*

tally — To **tally** means to count up or calculate something. *Will you tally my bill and tell me how much I owe you?*

number — To **number** means to give a number to each of a series of things. *Please number the pages of your story at the top.*

similar words: **calculate**

countless *adjective*

too many to count. *I'm surprised that they haven't broken that window, because their baseball has hit it **countless** times.*

untold — Untold can mean more than can be counted or measured. *It was a nation of untold wealth.*

myriad — Myriad means of a very great but unknown number. *There are myriad stars in the night sky.*

infinite — Infinite can mean **endless** or never seeming to run out. *There are an infinite number of grains of sand on the beach.*

endless — Endless means having or seeming to have no end. *There seemed to be an endless number of chocolates in the box.*

umpteen — Umpteen means an unknown number, especially a very large number that can't be counted. It is more suited to everyday language. *I have told you umpteen times not to put your feet on the table.*

similar words: **numerous**

82

country   *adjective*

coming from or having to do with the land outside the towns and cities. *It's fun visiting our **country** friends on their farm.*

rural

Rural means having to do with the country or with farming. *I prefer a quiet rural road to the crowded city streets.*

agrarian

Agrarian means having to do with farming. *Do you think agrarian work is more healthy than working in an office?*

pastoral

Pastoral can mean having to do with farming, particularly the grazing of animals. *This is rich pastoral land.*

rustic

Rustic means having to do with or living in the country, especially living a simple and peaceful life as opposed to a hectic city existence. *I spend my days in rustic pastimes such as milking cows.*

contrasting words: **civic**

country   *noun*

1. an area of land separated from other areas. *France and Germany are two **countries** in Europe.*

nation

A **nation** is a large group of people living in one country and under one government. *The United States became a nation in 1789.*

republic

A **republic** is a **nation** that has an elected president, not a king or queen. *They elected a new president to be the leader of the republic.*

state

A **state** can be the same as a **nation**. *It is the state's responsibility to ensure that there is justice for all citizens.*

2. the less-developed land outside the towns and cities. *Many people who live in **the country** are farmers.*

countryside

The **countryside** is the rural part of a country, often the scenery of a particular country area. *The countryside was so pretty that we stopped for a picnic.*

the land

The land means the rural areas outside the city. *Many city dwellers yearn to return to the land.*

the outdoors

The outdoors means the world of nature that lies outside the world of human dwellings. *I became a forester because I wanted to work in the outdoors.*

contrasting words: **city**

courage *noun*

the ability to act calmly when threatened by danger. *It took **courage** for the firefighter to enter the burning building.*

bravery   **Bravery** is so similar to courage that you can usually use either. *The mountain climber showed her bravery by going up the cliff first.*

valor   **Valor** is similar to **courage** and **bravery**. It is a rather formal word. *The doctors and nurses were given an award for their valor during the crisis.*

nerve   **Nerve** is the ability to face danger or pressure with a strong mind. *Ramon must have a lot of nerve to be able to dive off of the high board.*

spunk   **Spunk** is the ability to face danger or difficulty in a brave, lively way. It is more suited to everyday language. *Even though it started to rain, they kept their spunk and continued their hike.*

course *noun*

the way along which anything moves. *The map showed the **course** Jacques Cartier followed when he explored the St. Lawrence River.*

path   **Path** can mean a way from one place to another. *The small boat hurried out of the path of the ship.*

route   A **route** is a regular line of travel. *The bus takes the long route home.*

track   A **track** is a rough **path** or trail. *The swimming hole is at the end of the track.*

beeline   A **beeline** is a direct line, like the course bees take when returning to the hive. *The children made a beeline for the food.*

orbit   An **orbit** is the curved **path** or line of flight followed by a planet or satellite around another heavenly body, such as the earth or sun. *The astronomers carefully studied the satellite's orbit around the earth.*

cover *verb*

to lie over or be spread over something. *A fine layer of dust* **covered** *all the furniture.*

blanket	To **blanket** can mean to cover something with a layer or covering. *Crisp, white snow blanketed the ground.*
envelop	To **envelop** can mean to surround something completely. *The heavy fog soon enveloped the whole town.*
wrap	To **wrap** can mean to surround someone or something, often as if with folds. It is similar to **envelop**. *The night wrapped us in its mantle of darkness.*
wreathe	To **wreathe** can mean to surround or cover something in curving or curling masses. *Mist wreathed the mountains and valley.*
shroud	To **shroud** can mean to cover something completely, causing a feeling of mystery. *Darkness shrouded the old gold mine.*

similar words: **enclose**

cower *verb*

to shrink away in fear. *We* **cowered** *among the trees as the snarling lion came into the clearing.*

quail	To **quail** means to shrink with fear or lose courage when in a difficult or dangerous position. *We quailed at the thought of the lion catching sight of us.*
flinch	To **flinch** means to draw back suddenly from something dangerous or unpleasant. *A twig snapped under my foot and we all flinched at the sound.*
waver	To **waver** can mean to act uncertainly, sometimes because of fear. *Our brave guide did not waver as she watched the lion calmly.*
chicken out	To **chicken out** means to back out or go away because you are scared. This is more suited to everyday language. *We chickened out, though, and went back to the truck.*

create *verb*

to make, using your own ideas or imagination. *Danielle **created** a beautiful pattern.*

design
To **design** can mean to invent and then draw up plans for something. *An architect designed our house.*

develop
To **develop** can mean to bring something into being. *The gardener developed a new kind of rose.*

compose
To **compose** means to create literature or music. *Justin composed the tune for this song.*

improvise
To **improvise** means to create or **compose** something on the spot. *Anthony improvised a tune for the song.*

similar words: **invent, concoct, make**

criminal *noun*

someone who is guilty of a crime. *The police were sure she was the **criminal** but they could not prove it.*

offender
An **offender** is someone who has broken the law in some way. This is a rather formal word. *Don't vandalize the railway cars — offenders will be prosecuted.*

felon
A **felon** is someone who has been convicted of a serious offense. *The judge sentenced the felon to life imprisonment.*

outlaw
An **outlaw** is someone who has broken the law and is wanted by the police. *There were pictures of outlaws on posters at the police station.*

gangster
A **gangster** is a member of a gang of criminals. *I saw three of the four gangsters get out of the car and go into the bank.*

hood
A **hood** can be a criminal, often a member of a gang. It is more suited to everyday language. *The hoods attacked the shopkeeper and stole all the money in the cash register.*

similar words: **crook, bandit**

crook   *noun*

a dishonest person. This is more suited to everyday language. *I hope that* **crook** *goes to jail.*

rogue	A **rogue** is a scoundrel or a dishonest person. *There were rogues at the train station who would steal people's luggage.*
cheat	A **cheat** is a dishonest person who tries to get things by deceit or trickery. *He was expelled from school for being a cheat.*
knave	A **knave** is a dishonest and hateful man or boy. It is an old-fashioned word. *The king called him a knave for trying to cheat the trusting old man.*
fraud	A **fraud** is someone who is not what they claim to be. *She said she was an expert dressmaker but she was a fraud.*
shark	A **shark** can be a person who makes money dishonestly from other people, usually through false or unfair deals. *When you want to borrow large sums of money, be careful of loan sharks.*

similar words: **criminal**

crooked   *adjective*

curved or not straight. *The* **crooked** *man had a* **crooked** *stick.*

bent	**Bent** means curved or made into an angled shape. *There was a bent spoke in the wheel of my bike.*
warped	**Warped** means **bent** out of its usual shape. It is most often used about something straight and flat like timber. *The builder could not use the warped plank of wood.*
buckled	**Buckled** means **bent,** or pushed out of shape. *My bike had a buckled wheel after the accident.*
twisted	**Twisted** means pulled into curves and bends. *I used a piece of twisted wire to hold the chain together.*
distorted	**Distorted** means crooked or pulled out of shape. *Her distorted face showed her extreme pain.*

cross *verb*

to go from one side of something to another. *The bridge **crossed** the river just near its mouth.*

traverse
To **traverse** means to pass across or over something. *The hikers traversed the mountain pass as soon as the mist lifted.*

ford
To **ford** means to cross a river where it is shallow enough to walk or ride across. *They had to wait for the flood waters to go down before they could ford the river.*

bridge
To **bridge** means to make a bridge over something so that it can be crossed. *It was easier for the explorers to bridge the deep, narrow gorge than to travel around it.*

span
To **span** means to extend or stretch across something. *The bridge spanned the river at its narrowest point.*

crowd *noun*

a large number of people or things gathered closely together. *Ann pushed her way through the **crowd** of children.*

throng
Throng is so similar to **crowd** that you can usually use either. *A throng of people gathered to watch the parade.*

mob
A **mob** is a large crowd that is sometimes rowdy or violent. *An angry mob gathered outside the Capitol.*

flock
A **flock** is a number of animals of the same kind, especially sheep, goats, or birds, feeding or kept together. It can also be used to mean a crowd of people. *A shepherd looks after a flock of sheep.*

herd
Herd is similar to **flock** but is usually used about cattle. *He drove the herd to a new pasture.*

pack
A **pack** is a group of certain animals living and hunting together. Like **flock** and **herd**, it can also be used to mean a group of people, especially criminals. *A pack of wolves lives in this forest.*

similar words: **group**

cruel   *adjective*

likely or liking to cause pain or unhappiness. *The **cruel** remark made me cry.*

savage   **Savage** can mean cruel or fierce. *The savage dog growled and barked but couldn't leap over the fence.*

brutal   **Brutal** means fiercely or extremely cruel. *It was a brutal blow when the flood destroyed all our crops.*

barbaric   **Barbaric** means extremely **savage** or cruel. *Everyone condemned the army's barbaric treatment of the poor villagers.*

vicious   **Vicious** means very **savage**, cruel, or harmful. *The vicious dog tried to attack the passersby.*

ruthless   **Ruthless** means so cruel that you show no pity or mercy. *The ruthless dictator refused to spend money on food to lesson the effects of the famine.*

---

similar words: **callous, violent**
contrasting words: **lenient**

---

crush   *verb*

to break something into small pieces. *The machine **crushed** the huge rock and we were able to carry the pieces away.*

crumble   To **crumble** means to break something into small pieces, especially something that is soft. *The child crumbled the cake in her hand.*

grind   To **grind** can mean to crush something until fine particles are formed. *We ground the coffee beans and then percolated the coffee.*

mill   To **mill** means to crush something into fine particles using a machine. *You mill wheat to make flour.*

pound   To **pound** can mean to crush something into pieces or powder by beating it with something. *I pounded the herbs in the mortar with the pestle.*

pulverize   To **pulverize** means to crush something until it turns to dust or powder. *Over time, the waves will pulverize the shells into sand.*

cry *verb*

to shed tears. *We all **cried** when our pet dog died.*

weep	To **weep** is so similar to cry that you can usually use either one. *I was so disappointed that I wanted to weep.*
bawl	To **bawl** means to cry loudly. *She bawled when she broke her leg.*
wail	To **wail** means to give a long sad cry. *The crowd wailed when the home team lost the game.*
sob	To **sob** means to cry, making a gulping noise as you breathe. *The little lost girl was sobbing when her father found her.*
whimper	To **whimper** means to cry weakly. *The puppies whimpered when they were taken from their mother.*

contrasting words: **laugh, smile**

cunning *adjective*

able or likely to trick someone. *Here's a **cunning** plan to make them think we've gone away.*

crafty	**Crafty** means cunning or clever in deceiving someone. *The hare was amazed that the crafty tortoise beat him.*
wily	**Wily** is very similar to **crafty**. *The wily old fox escaped the hunters by swimming downstream.*
sly	**Sly** means cunning in a clever or deceitful way. *His sly answer made us think he was innocent.*
devious	**Devious** means tricky, usually not in a completely honest way. *Her devious behavior lost her nearly all her friends.*
artful	**Artful** means clever and cunning in getting what you want. *The artful football fans found a way into the stadium without paying.*

similar words: **dishonest**
contrasting words: **honest**

cut *noun*

an opening in something made with a sharp object. *I have a **cut** on my finger.*

gash   A **gash** is a long deep cut. *The doctor had to stitch the gash in his leg.*

slit   A **slit** is a long straight cut or opening. *The nail has torn a slit in my skirt.*

incision   An **incision** is a deep cut, usually made for a particular reason. *The doctor started the operation by making a deep incision.*

score   A **score** can be a rough cut or deep scratch, especially on wood or metal. *Vandals had made a deep score in the desk.*

notch   A **notch** is a small sharp cut. *There was a notch on the edge of the table.*

---

similar words: **break, groove, opening**

---

cut *verb*

to separate or make something shorter using a sharp instrument. *I **cut** a piece of string.*

snip   To **snip** means to cut something using short quick strokes. *Dad snipped the roses off the bush.*

trim   To **trim** means to shorten something by cutting it. *The barber trimmed his hair.*

clip   To **clip** means to cut off or shorten something using scissors or shears. *She clipped the hedge.*

mow   To **mow** means to cut something off or down with a scythe or machine. *Lisa mowed the lawn.*

shear   To **shear** means to remove hair or fleece from something using large scissors or something similar. *They sheared the sheep.*

---

similar words: **scratch, tear**

---

damage *verb*

to harm, injure, or break a part of something. *He **damaged** the car when he backed into the tree.*

mar
To **mar** means to damage or **ruin** something. *The young child marred the book by scribbling on it.*

sabotage
To **sabotage** means to damage something on purpose or in order to cause problems for the owner. *The spy sabotaged the enemy planes.*

vandalize
To **vandalize** means to damage or destroy something deliberately for no good reason. *Someone vandalized our school last night.*

ruin
To **ruin** means to damage something so badly that you can't use it. *The hailstorm ruined the harvest.*

wreck
To **wreck** is so similar to **ruin** that you can usually use either one. *He wrecked the radio when he dropped it in the water.*

similar words: **destroy, hurt, spoil**
contrasting words: **repair**

dangerous *adjective*

likely to cause harm or injury. *Plastic bags are **dangerous** toys for very young children.*

unsafe
Unsafe is so similar to dangerous that you can usually use either. *The diving board is unsafe because it has a crack in it.*

perilous
Perilous means dangerous because you are exposed to harm or injury. *We breathed a sigh of relief when we finished our perilous climb up the steep slope.*

hazardous
Hazardous means dangerous because there is a possibility of harm or injury. *Most people agree that smoking is hazardous to your health.*

precarious
Precarious means dangerous or not safe. *Robert pulled his brother away from his precarious position at the edge of the cliff.*

risky
Risky means dangerous because there is a chance of injury or loss. *It would be risky to play on the road even though it's not very busy.*

contrasting words: **safe**

dark *adjective*

with little or no light. *I was frightened in the **dark** house.*

dim — **Dim** means without bright light, but not completely dark. *I could just see her shape moving in the dim passageway.*

shadowy — **Shadowy** means slightly dark or having light and shade. *We walked through the shadowy forest.*

murky — **Murky** means unpleasantly and gloomily dark. *We were trapped in the murky cave.*

obscure — **Obscure** can mean dark and out-of-the-way. *He hid in an obscure corner of the room.*

pitch-dark — **Pitch-dark** means completely dark. *The night was pitch-dark and we couldn't see where we were going.*

contrasting words: **bright**

darken *verb*

to make something have very little or no light. *Thick clouds **darkened** the sky.*

shade — To **shade** means to darken something by shutting out light. *Heavy curtains shaded the room.*

dim — To **dim** means to make something less bright. *She dimmed the lights in the sick child's bedroom.*

obscure — To **obscure** means to make something hard to see because of darkness. *A sudden thunderstorm obscured our view of the mountains.*

eclipse — To **eclipse** can mean to block the light of a heavenly body from the earth, thus causing darkness. *Sometimes the moon eclipses the sun and it becomes dark in the middle of the day.*

fog — To **fog** means to make something blurry or hard to see through. *Mist fogged the windshield of our car.*

dart _verb_

to move suddenly and quickly. *I lost sight of him as he **darted** through the crowd.*

scurry	To **scurry** means to move quickly and lightly. *She was too fast for us as she scurried around the corner.*
scamper	To **scamper** means to run or hurry away quickly and lightly. *The rabbit scampered across the road and into its burrow.*
dive	To **dive** can mean to move very quickly into something. *I dived into the train just before the door banged shut.*
scramble	To **scramble** means to climb or move quickly and awkwardly. *Our feet slipped as we scrambled over the rocks to escape the huge wave.*
scoot	To **scoot** means to dart or move along very quickly. It is more suited to everyday language. *I scooted down the stairs and along the path to see what came in the mail.*

similar words: **speed, hurry**
contrasting words: **dawdle, walk, trudge**

dawdle _verb_

to waste time by being slow. *You'll never get there if you **dawdle** so much!*

dally	To **dally** means to waste time or be very slow. *Stop dallying and do your work!*
delay	To **delay** means to move or do something slowly. *If you delay, we'll be late again.*
loiter	To **loiter** means to stay in one place or to move around in a slow aimless way. *I loitered near the park hoping to see someone to play with.*
linger	To **linger** means to stay on in a place because you don't want to leave. *We lingered at the monkeys' cage because they made us laugh.*
tarry	To **tarry** means to wait or be slow in starting to do something or go somewhere. This is an old-fashioned word. *We tarried until it was almost too late to catch the train.*

contrasting words: **hurry, speed, dart**

daydream *verb*

to imagine pleasant things in a dreamy way. *I often **daydream** about being a movie star.*

muse	To **muse** means to think about something so deeply that you become dreamy. *I mused happily on what I would do over the weekend.*
be lost in thought	To **be lost in thought** means to think about something so deeply that you do not pay attention to anything else. *I did not hear what she said because I was lost in thought.*
fantasize	To **fantasize** means to daydream, usually about something that is unrealistic. *My friend likes to fantasize about winning a million dollars.*
let your thoughts wander	To **let your thoughts wander** means to stop concentrating on a particular thing. *I was supposed to be doing homework but I let my thoughts wander.*

similar words: **imagine**
contrasting words: **concentrate on, ponder**

dead *adjective*

no longer alive or useful. *In the autumn, **dead** leaves fall off deciduous trees.*

lifeless	**Lifeless** can mean no longer having life. *They lifted his lifeless body into the ambulance.*
deceased	**Deceased** means dead. It only refers to people. *Both my grandparents are deceased.*
departed	**Departed** is very similar to **deceased**. It is a less common word. *My recently departed uncle left me some money in his will.*
late	**Late** means having recently died. *The late Mr. Jones was well respected in our community.*
fallen	**Fallen** can mean dead. It generally refers to those people who were killed in a war. *On Memorial Day we honor the fallen victims of past wars.*

deal *noun*

financial agreement in which goods, services, or money are exchanged. *I made a* **deal** *with Lavonne to trade her my set of markers for her brushes.*

transaction A **transaction** means any deal in general, especially in business. *I hoped to make money on the transaction.*

arrangement An **arrangement** is any agreement, whether something is exchanged or not. *Marsh and I have an arrangment not to criticize each other any more.*

bargain A **bargain** can mean a deal in which some discussion is involved. *I finally made a bargain to trade some video games with Jason.*

contract A **contract** is a formal agreement, usually in written form. *Kelly signed a contract with her mother to improve her grades in exchange for a later bedtime.*

trade A **trade** is usually an exchange of things. *I got this bat in a trade with Arliss.*

deceive *verb*

to trick someone by not telling the truth. *She **deceived** us by saying she'd found the money when she'd really stolen it.*

dupe To **dupe** means to trick or deceive someone. *He duped them into believing he would pay them for working for him.*

hoodwink To **hoodwink** is very similar to **dupe**. It is usually used in less formal language. *She hoodwinked us with promises she knew she couldn't keep.*

mislead To **mislead** can mean to lead or guide someone wrongly, often on purpose. *You misled us when you said that paint would match our carpet exactly.*

delude To **delude** means to trick or **mislead** someone. *He deluded them into thinking he was an honest person.*

take for a ride To **take for a ride** means to trick or deceive someone. This is more suited to everyday language. *He certainly took you for a ride when he promised to come back with the money he borrowed.*

similar words: **trick, cheat, outwit**

decent *adjective*

acting in a way that is approved by most people. *We thought he was a **decent** man until we saw him cruelly beating his dog.*

proper	**Proper** can mean correct in behavior. *It is not proper for children to sit in a bus while older people stand.*
right	**Right** means fair and good. *It was right for you to refuse to help him cheat in the exam.*
moral	**Moral** means acting according to the rules of what is thought to be right. *She took a moral stand against their shoplifting.*
respectable	**Respectable** means good or worthy of respect, especially in the sense of being socially acceptable. *They are a respectable family, well known for their volunteer work.*
ethical	**Ethical** means in agreement with the rules for **right** and **proper** conduct. *Our school expects high ethical standards from us.*

similar words: **honest**
contrasting words: **indecent, evil**

decrease *verb*

to become less. *The time I take to swim the length of the pool **decreases** the more I practice.*

diminish	To **diminish** is so similar to decrease that you can usually use either. *The number of dancers diminished as the competition became more fierce.*
abate	To **abate** means to become less in strength. *At last the storm abated.*
moderate	To **moderate** means to become less violent or severe. *The winds moderated as the storm moved out to sea.*
wane	To **wane** can mean to grow less gradually, especially in strength of feeling, power, and so on. *Our enthusiasm waned when we realized how long it would take.*

similar words: **shrink**
contrasting words: **increase**

decrepit *adjective*

broken down or made weak by old age. *The **decrepit** house was almost beyond repair. The **decrepit** old man stumbled downstairs.*

infirm
Infirm means weak in body or health. *She's infirm now that she's old, so you'll have to help her.*

timeworn
Timeworn means worn with age or showing signs of disrepair because of long use. *The elderly woman got her timeworn photo album out of the drawer and looked at the faded pictures.*

moth-eaten
Moth-eaten can mean in poor condition or worn out, usually with age. *The old, rather moth-eaten carpets will have to be replaced.*

threadbare
Threadbare can mean worn and thin, usually with age. *My favorite sweater has become threadbare over the years.*

crumbling
Crumbling can mean decaying or disappearing bit by bit. *We looked sadly at the crumbling walls of our old house.*

similar words: **defective**

deed *noun*

something someone does. This is a rather formal word. *Going into the burning house to save the owner was a brave **deed**.*

act
An **act** is something someone does. It can often be used instead of deed. *It was the act of a hero.*

action
An **action** is so similar to **deed** or **act** that you can often choose any of these words. *The newspaper printed a report of her brave action.*

exploit
An **exploit** is a notable and daring deed. *They told fascinating tales of their exploits in the jungle.*

move
A **move** can mean something you do for a particular reason. *Saving his energy for the end of the race was a clever move.*

similar words: **achievement**

defeat *verb*

to overcome someone in a battle or contest. *The army **defeated** the rebels, who didn't have enough ammunition.*

beat To **beat** means to defeat someone, especially in a contest. *The winning team beat us by ten runs.*

conquer To **conquer** means to overcome someone by force. *The enemy was conquered when their fortress was destroyed.*

vanquish To **vanquish** means to defeat someone, especially in battle. It is a more formal word than **defeat** or **conquer**. *The Roman army vanquished the Gauls.*

trounce To **trounce** can mean to defeat someone completely. *We're going to trounce them at volleyball because our team is better.*

defective *adjective*

having a weakness, mistake, or blemish. *The mechanic replaced the **defective** car battery with a new one.*

faulty **Faulty** means having weaknesses or mistakes. *A headlight wasn't working because of faulty wiring.*

unsound **Unsound** means having defects or weaknesses. *The engine was unsound, and had to be repaired.*

substandard **Substandard** means below the normal grade or level, or not as good as it should be. *Mom was angry because the garage's work on the engine was substandard.*

shoddy **Shoddy** means of poor quality or badly made. *She said the mechanic did a shoddy job.*

similar words: **inferior**
contrasting words: **perfect**

defense   *noun*

something that keeps you safe from harm or acts as a protection against attack.
*The moat was an important part of the castle's **defense**.*

protection **Protection** is a form of defense from injury, danger, or annoyance.
We keep a watchdog for protection against burglars.

security **Security** is something that keeps you safe. *Staying together when we
got lost in the woods was our greatest security.*

safeguard A **safeguard** is something that helps protect or defend you. *A
catcher's mask is a safeguard against a head injury.*

shield A **shield** can be anything you use to protect yourself from harm. *She
held her hands to her eyes as a shield against the sun.*

---

contrasting words: **attack**

---

defer   *verb*

to put off something until later. *We'll have to **defer** making a decision about buying
a new computer until we find out how much money we have.*

delay To **delay** means to put off something until later, often because of an
inconvenient interruption. *We can't delay the meeting just because Bob
hasn't arrived.*

postpone To **postpone** means to put off something until a future time. It is
very similar to **defer**. *They postponed the game because of rain.*

adjourn To **adjourn** means to put off something. It is often used about court
cases, sessions of Congress, and other formal proceedings. *The judge
adjourned the trial until the following week.*

suspend To **suspend** can mean to defer something for some time, especially a
punishment or law. *The judge suspended the car thief's sentence for
twelve months.*

shelve To **shelve** can mean to put off considering or thinking about
something for a while. *That's such a tricky problem, I'll have to shelve
it until I find out more about it.*

defiant   *adjective*

boldly going against someone or something in authority. *The **defiant** prisoners would not return to their cells.*

rebellious   **Rebellious** means openly or actively defiant. *The rebellious citizens didn't pay their taxes until the government listened to their complaints.*

antagonistic   **Antagonistic** means disagreeing with and acting against something or someone. *She was antagonistic to any new ideas.*

recalcitrant   **Recalcitrant** means resisting authority or control. *The recalcitrant children complained about their parents' strict rules.*

dissident   **Dissident** means disagreeing or differing, especially with a particular political system. *The dissident groups held a rally to protest against the harsh new laws.*

militant   **Militant** means fighting or ready to fight, especially for a cause. *If the dictator won't resign, the citizens will become militant.*

similar words: **argumentative, disobedient**
contrasting words: **submissive**

deliberate   *adjective*

carefully considered and done on purpose. *Someone had made a **deliberate** attempt to set fire to the house.*

intentional   **Intentional** means done with a purpose or reason. *To fool the other team she made an intentional mistake.*

purposeful   **Purposeful** means having a set reason for doing something. *She set about her work in a purposeful way and soon finished it.*

premeditated   **Premeditated** means planned beforehand. *The judge said it was a premeditated crime and sent the accused to prison for life.*

planned   **Planned** means done according to a plan. *Our planned fishing trip had to be postponed because of bad weather.*

contrasting words: **accidental**

delicious *adjective*

very pleasant to smell or taste. *That was a **delicious** dinner you cooked.*

luscious
Luscious means very pleasant or delicious to taste or smell. *What a luscious peach!*

scrumptious
Scrumptious means very tasty or delicious. It is usually used in less formal language than **luscious**. *We had a scrumptious ice-cream cone while we were shopping.*

appetizing
Appetizing means so delicious that it makes you feel hungry. *The appetizing smell of roast chicken wafted through the house.*

mouth-watering
Mouth-watering means looking or smelling so delicious that you want to eat it right away. *I stared at the mouth-watering cakes and pastries in the shop window.*

yummy
Yummy has the same meaning as **scrumptious**. It is used in less formal language. *We had a yummy snack of fruit and cheese.*

contrasting words: **inedible**

demand *noun*

an urgent or forceful request or need. *Our **demand** for information must be met.*

claim
A **claim** is a demand placed on someone or something that is expected to be met even if it is difficult or unfair. *She had an active social life, even though her job made many claims on her.*

ultimatum
An **ultimatum** is a final statement of terms or conditions that must be accepted. *The ultimatum was that work handed in after Monday would not be graded.*

requisition
A **requisition** can be a formal or official request for something you need. *Our school put in a requisition for a new computer.*

levy
A **levy** is something, often a fee or tax, demanded from you by an official body. *The council imposed an extra levy on people using the parking lot at night.*

similar words: **order**

demand *verb*

to ask for something forcefully, as if it's your right. *He **demanded** an apology.*

order	To **order** can mean to ask for or request something. *I'm going to order a milkshake.*
insist	To **insist** means to demand something very strongly. *I insist that you come with me to see the doctor.*
require	To **require** can mean to demand or **insist** on something. *The boss requires the finished report by this afternoon.*
stipulate	To **stipulate** can mean to demand something as an essential part of an agreement. *The contract stipulated that the work be completed in 60 days.*

similar words: **ask**

dependent *noun*

someone who relies on or needs the support of another person. *Children are the **dependents** of their parents.*

protégé	A **protégé** is someone who is protected or supported by someone else. This comes from a French word. *The musician's protégé was a young pianist who had a lot of potential.*
ward	A **ward** is a young person who has been legally placed under the care or control of a guardian. *He was made a ward of the state because his parents were not able to look after him.*
satellite	A **satellite** can be something that depends on or is dominated by something else. *The new town will be a satellite of the capital city.*
hanger-on	A **hanger-on** is someone who stays around or depends on someone whom they admire. *Rock stars have lots of hangers-on who follow them from one performance to another.*
parasite	A **parasite** can be someone who lives on the money earned by other people without doing anything in return. You use this word about someone whose behavior you don't approve of. *He was such a parasite that he always lived on his parents' money.*

descend *verb*

to go or come down. *The plane has started to **descend**.*

drop
To **drop** can mean to descend very suddenly. *The plane dropped when it entered an air pocket.*

sink
To **sink** can mean to descend gradually to a lower level. *The sun is sinking in the west.*

coast
To **coast** means to go down a hill on a bicycle without pedaling or in a car while it is not in gear. *The hill was so steep that they could coast all the way to the bottom.*

climb down
To **climb down** means to go down, usually using both hands and feet. *The painter climbed down the ladder when the job was finished.*

similar words: **fall**
contrasting words: **climb**

describe *verb*

to give a picture of something or someone using words. *He **described** the accident and how it happened.*

represent
To **represent** can mean to describe or state something in words. *Does his novel really represent the life of an Arizona rancher?*

portray
To **portray** means to describe or explain something in words. *Her story portrayed the excitement she felt when she won the prize.*

depict
To **depict** means to describe or show something in words. *My grandmother tells me stories depicting life when she was a girl.*

illustrate
To **illustrate** can mean to make something clear by giving examples to help people picture or imagine it. *He illustrated his talk on bravery with stories about pioneers.*

express
To **express** means to put thoughts into words. *Try to express your ideas clearly so we all know what you mean.*

similar words: **explain, tell**

destroy   *verb*

to wreck or damage something so completely that it does not exist any more. *The tornado destroyed many houses.*

demolish	To **demolish** means to knock down or destroy something. *The workers demolished the old house.*
wipe out	To **wipe out** means to defeat someone or destroy something completely. *The hailstorm wiped out our garden.*
annihilate	To **annihilate** means to destroy or defeat something completely. *The forest fire had annihilated all of the trees in the valley.*
exterminate	To **exterminate** means to destroy something in order to get rid of it. *We exterminated the cockroaches in the kitchen.*
eradicate	To **eradicate** means to root out or destroy something. *We want to eradicate crime in large cities.*

similar words: **damage**
contrasting words: **make**

deteriorate   *verb*

to become less good in condition or quality. *The house deteriorated while it was not lived in.*

worsen	To **worsen** means to become not even as good as it was before. *The condition of the house worsened after being empty for four years.*
degenerate	To **degenerate** means to become bad or worse than before. *Your health will degenerate if you don't get enough food, sleep, and exercise.*
fall apart	To **fall apart** means to break down or crumble. *Rust caused the old car to fall apart.*
decline	To **decline** can mean to deteriorate or become worse. *His health has declined since he came here.*
waste away	To **waste away** can mean to lose your strength or health, usually from an illness or disease. *Their bodies wasted away during the famine.*

similar words: **rot**
contrasting words: **recover**

die *verb*

to stop living. *My pet dog **died** last week.*

expire To **expire** can mean to die or give out your last breath. It is rather a formal word. *She had been ill for weeks before she expired.*

breathe your last To **breathe your last** means to die. It is similar to **expire,** but less formal. *The king breathed his last at half past two today.*

perish To **perish** means to die in an unnatural way, sometimes from violence or lack of food. *The explorers perished in the desert.*

pass away To **pass away** means to die naturally. People usually use it because they think it is less upsetting than the word die. *I am calling to tell you that your uncle passed away peacefully in his sleep.*

similar words: **become extinct**
contrasting words: **live**

difficult *adjective*

not easy to do or understand. *This is a **difficult** puzzle.*

hard **Hard** can mean difficult to do or explain. *It was a hard exam.*

complex **Complex** means difficult to understand or explain because it is complicated. *She solved the complex puzzle very quickly.*

tough **Tough** can mean very difficult to deal with. *They have a tough job to do.*

arduous **Arduous** means needing a lot of hard work. *She was tired after the arduous canoe trip.*

demanding **Demanding** means needing a lot of time, hard work, and energy. *Nursing is a demanding occupation.*

contrasting words: **easy**

dig   *verb*

to break up, turn over, or remove something, such as earth, using your hands or an implement. *Foxie often **digs** in the vegetable patch so she can bury her bones.*

scoop
To **scoop** means to take something up or out, as with a spoon or your cupped hands. *We scooped sand out to make a moat around our sand castle.*

hollow out
To **hollow out** means to make a hole in something by digging out the inside. *We hollowed out a pineapple and filled it with strawberries and grapes for the party.*

excavate
To **excavate** means to make a hole or tunnel by digging something. *The archeologists excavated the ruined city, hoping to find ancient pottery and coins.*

gouge
To **gouge** means to dig out something roughly or crudely. *Heavy earth-moving machines gouged earth and rocks out of the side of the mountain.*

mine
To **mine** means to dig something, such as earth, to get minerals, precious stones, and so on. *At Dawson, in the Yukon, they mine the earth for gold.*

dirty   *adjective*

covered with dirt or stains. *We had **dirty** hands by the time we had finished cleaning our bikes.*

grubby
Grubby means dirty, messy, or untidy. *Wash your grubby hands before you eat!*

grimy
Grimy means very dirty, especially on the surface. *Underneath the grimy surface the walls were painted bright blue.*

grungy
Grungy means dirty or unattractive. This is more suited to everyday language. *The grungy carpet was dusty and full of holes.*

filthy
Filthy means very dirty or unpleasant. *The beach was filthy where the sewage emptied onto it.*

polluted
Polluted means made dangerously dirty or unfit to use. *The water was too polluted to swim in.*

contrasting words: **clean**

dirty *verb*

to make something unclean, or cover it with marks and stains. *Who **dirtied** the clean floor?*

soil   To **soil** means to make something dirty or stained. *We soiled the new carpets with our muddy feet.*

smear   To **smear** means to rub or spread dirty marks over something. *I didn't mean to smear paint on the walls.*

smudge   To **smudge** means to mark something with dirty streaks. *He smudged his tear-stained face with his grubby hands.*

spot   To **spot** means to mark or stain something. *You have spotted your jacket with ice cream.*

similar words: **spoil**
contrasting words: **clean**

disagree *verb*

to fail to agree about something. *The two reports of the disaster **disagree** as to the number of casualties.*

differ   To **differ** means to disagree or have different ideas or feelings about something. *The brothers differed as to which was the quickest way home.*

dissent   To **dissent** means to disagree or have a different opinion. *Ten members of the club agreed to change the rules and two members dissented.*

dispute   To **dispute** means to argue loudly and for a long time. *They spent the whole day disputing about anything and everything.*

bicker   To **bicker** means to squabble or argue about little things. *The children have been bickering all day.*

wrangle   To **wrangle** means to argue or quarrel noisily. *Don't wrangle with me!*

similar words: **argue**
contrasting words: **agree**

disappear   *verb*

to go out of sight. *He **disappeared** around the corner.*

vanish
To **vanish** means to disappear quickly. *With a wave of the magician's wand the rabbit vanished before our very eyes.*

dematerialize
To **dematerialize** means to disappear without a trace. *In the movie, the hero dematerialized to avoid her enemies.*

fade
To **fade** means to disappear slowly. *Her smile faded as her ice cream fell to the ground.*

dissolve
To **dissolve** means to disappear gradually. *The ghostly shape dissolved into the mist.*

melt
To **melt** means to fade gradually and is very similar to **dissolve**. *He turned the corner and melted into the darkness.*

---

contrasting words: **appear**

---

disappointment   *noun*

failure to have your hopes satisfied. *It was a great **disappointment** to me when it rained on my birthday.*

letdown
A **letdown** is so similar to disappointment you can usually choose either word. *After all our hopes, it was a letdown when we couldn't go to the zoo.*

anticlimax
An **anticlimax** is a disappointing end to something you expected to be very good or exciting. *We were excited about the party and it was an anticlimax when rain caused it to be canceled.*

blow
A **blow** is a sudden shock or disappointment. *It was a blow when the clouds drifted away and the farmers didn't get the rain they needed.*

setback
A **setback** is something that stops or slows down your progress. *It was a setback that was hard to overcome.*

frustration
A **frustration** is something that stops you from getting or achieving what you want. *After many frustrations, they closed down their new business.*

disapprove of   *verb*

to have a bad opinion of something or someone. *I **disapprove of** people who throw litter on the sidewalk.*

frown on To **frown on** means to disapprove or have a bad opinion of something. *My friends frowned on my plan for a picnic in the rain.*

take a dim view of To **take a dim view of** means to have a bad or unfavorable opinion of something. *The neighbors take a dim view of your dog's barking.*

take exception to To **take exception to** means to object to something strongly. *I take exception to what you just called me.*

look down on To **look down on** means to have no respect for someone or to regard them with scorn. *You shouldn't look down on him just because his ideas are different from yours.*

similar words: **fault**
contrasting words: **approve, praise**

disaster   *noun*

any sudden terrible happening that causes great suffering and damage. *The flood was one of the worst **disasters** we've had in years.*

catastrophe A **catastrophe** is a sudden disaster. *The explosion was a catastrophe that we had not expected.*

calamity A **calamity** is a terrible happening. *The newspaper said that building a highway through the national park would be a calamity.*

tragedy A **tragedy** is any very sad or dreadful happening. *It was a tragedy when the family died in the accident.*

debacle A **debacle** is a dreadful disaster. *Their business venture proved to be a debacle in which they lost all their money.*

similar words: **misfortune**

discard   *verb*

to throw something away because you don't need it any more. *We **discarded** all the clothes we'd grown out of.*

shed	To **shed** means to cast off something. *The snake shed its skin by rubbing against a rock.*
jettison	To **jettison** means to throw something off because you don't want or need it. *The pilot jettisoned most of the spare fuel before making the crash landing.*
scrap	To **scrap** means to throw something away because it is useless. *We scrapped any broken toys that couldn't be mended.*
dump	To **dump** can mean to throw something down or get rid of it. *They dumped the garbage in a hole in the ground.*
ditch	To **ditch** means to get rid of something. It is more suited to everyday language. *You should ditch that old bicycle before you hurt yourself.*

contrasting words: **use, keep, store**

discordant   *adjective*

having an unpleasant combination of musical notes. *If the orchestra doesn't tune up properly, the music will be **discordant**.*

dissonant	**Dissonant** means sounding harsh and unpleasant. *We put our hands over our ears to block out the dissonant music.*
cacophonous	**Cacophonous** means loud and lacking any pleasant musical qualities. *A cacophonous clatter and banging came from the workshop.*
atonal	**Atonal** means not in any particular musical key, thus lacking the expected musical qualities. *Not everyone liked the atonal music she wrote.*
flat	**Flat** can mean singing or playing too low or below the correct pitch. *"The violins are flat," shouted the conductor.*
sharp	**Sharp** can mean singing or playing too high or above the correct pitch. *Don't blow your recorder too hard, because the notes will be sharp.*

contrasting words: **musical**

111

discourage *verb*

to try to prevent someone from doing something. *Please **discourage** him from playing with matches.*

dissuade   To **dissuade** means to persuade someone not to do something. *We dissuaded him from leaving home.*

deter   To **deter** means to prevent someone from doing something. *The fact that he doesn't want me to learn to hang-glide won't deter me.*

talk out of   To **talk out of** means to argue with someone in order to stop them from doing something. It is more suited to everyday language. *My parents talked me out of spending all my money on candy.*

advise against   To **advise against** means to tell someone they shouldn't do something. *The sign advised us against taking a truck on the dirt road.*

put a damper on   To **put a damper on** means to discourage someone. It is more suited to everyday language. *The forecast for storms put a damper on our plans to go to the beach.*

contrasting words: **encourage, persuade**

disgust *verb*

to cause you to dislike something totally. *Cruelty **disgusts** me.*

horrify   To **horrify** means to cause someone to feel great disgust and fear. *Hearing about that murder on the news horrified me.*

offend   To **offend** can mean to displease someone or to affect them disagreeably. *Your rudeness offends me.*

sicken   To **sicken** means to make you feel sick. *Violence on TV sickens me.*

nauseate   To **nauseate** means to make you feel you want to vomit. *I was nauseated by the long roller-coaster ride.*

revolt   To **revolt** can mean to make you feel sick and disgusted. *When I saw what the vandals had done it revolted me.*

contrasting words: **please**

dishonest   *adjective*

likely to lie, cheat, or steal. *The **dishonest** employee lost his job.*

deceitful   **Deceitful** means likely to lie or try to trick or mislead people. *His deceitful plans were discovered, and he was asked to resign from the club.*

shifty   **Shifty** means **deceitful** and looking as if you have something to hide. *She was questioned about the crime because of her shifty appearance.*

hypocritical   **Hypocritical** means pretending to be what you are not. *I don't want a hypocritical friend who talks about me behind my back.*

crooked   **Crooked** can mean dishonest or likely to swindle people. It is more suited to everyday language. *The crooked storekeeper was jailed for ten years.*

shady   **Shady** can mean of doubtful honesty or lawfulness. It is more suited to everyday language. *He has been mixed up in some shady deals.*

similar words: **cunning, illegal**
contrasting words: **honest, frank**

dislike   *noun*

a feeling of not liking, or a distaste for, someone or something. *I could not hide my **dislike** of him.*

hatred   **Hatred** means very strong dislike. *They looked at their enemies with hatred.*

aversion   **Aversion** means strong dislike, usually with a feeling of disgust. *I have an aversion to large insects.*

antipathy   **Antipathy** means a long-standing dislike or feeling of disgust. It is very similar to **aversion**. *He has an antipathy to strangers.*

hostility   **Hostility** means unfriendliness or the treating of someone as an enemy. *There was hostility between the two opposing teams.*

animosity   **Animosity** means a feeling of dislike or unfriendliness. It is very similar to **hostility**. *The party was spoiled by the animosity between the two families.*

disobedient *adjective*

refusing to obey. *The **disobedient** girl was asked to explain herself.*

unruly	**Unruly** means disobedient and uncontrollable. *More police had to be called to control the unruly crowd.*
willful	**Willful** means obstinate and determined to have your own way. *The willful boy wouldn't take any notice of the warning.*
delinquent	**Delinquent** means having broken the law. *The delinquent teenagers were helped by a guidance counsellor.*
headstrong	**Headstrong** means hard to control and determined to have your own way. *My headstrong cousin is always telling us what to do.*
insubordinate	**Insubordinate** means not obeying your superiors. *The sailor was sent to the captain for insubordinate behavior.*

similar words: **naughty, defiant**
contrasting words: **obedient, well-behaved, submissive**

disobey *verb*

to refuse to obey someone or something. *They were punished when they **disobeyed** the instructions.*

defy	To **defy** means to boldly refuse to obey someone. *Luke defied his mother when she told him to turn off the television.*
flout	To **flout** means to show no respect for authority by being disobedient. *They flouted the referee's instructions by cheating throughout the game.*
violate	To **violate** means to break a rule or law deliberately. *The United Nations censured the nation that violated the international treaty.*
transgress	To **transgress** means to **flout** or **violate**. It is usually used in connection with religious laws. *They were careful not to transgress any of the holy laws.*
infringe	To **infringe** means to disobey rules or laws. *You'll put yourself in danger if you infringe the rules of the swimming pool.*

contrasting words: **obey**

disorganize *verb*

to throw something into confusion and disorder. *Unexpected visitors **disorganized** our plans and we didn't go to the concert.*

disrupt
To **disrupt** means to interrupt something and throw it into disorder. *The sound of the fire engine going by disrupted the singing lesson and we had to start again.*

disturb
To **disturb** means to unsettle someone or something. *The unexpected news disturbed us and we didn't know what to do next.*

upset
To **upset** can mean to put something into disorder or confusion. *The rain upset our plans for a picnic.*

mess up
To **mess up** can mean to make something confused. *The train strike messed up our holiday plans.*

mix up
To **mix up** means to get something confused. *Douglas and Judith mixed up the time they were to meet and they missed the bus.*

contrasting words: **arrange**

display *noun*

a show or showing of something. *We went to a fireworks **display**.*

exhibition
An **exhibition** is a public showing of something made or done by people. *The handicraft club held an exhibition today.*

demonstration
A **demonstration** can be a public showing of something in order to advertise it. *The microwave cookery demonstration was very helpful.*

parade
A **parade** can be a gathering of people marching or walking for inspection or display. *There was a parade of all the animals and their trainers before the circus began.*

pageant
A **pageant** is a colorful public show, often including a procession of people in costume. *Our town had a pageant to celebrate its centenary.*

preview
A **preview** is a private showing of a film or exhibition before the public is allowed to see it. *The mayor was invited to a preview of the film.*

disprove *verb*

to prove something is not true. *The new experiments **disproved** the old theory.*

refute
: To **refute** means to prove something is false. *The suspect refuted their accusation by showing that he had been away on the day of the crime.*

rebut
: To **rebut** means to show something is false by proof or argument. It is so similar to **refute** that you can usually choose either word. *Karen rebutted their claim by showing them the true information in her encyclopedia.*

invalidate
: To **invalidate** means to show something is not true or sensible. *The first flight to the moon invalidated the theory that it was covered in several yards of dust.*

contradict
: To **contradict** means to be the direct opposite of something. *His happy face contradicted the story we heard that he was always miserable.*

demolish
: To **demolish** can mean to put an end to something, such as a belief or claim. *We demolished their claim to be champions when we beat them so easily.*

contrasting words: **prove**

dissatisfied *adjective*

annoyed because your wishes or needs haven't been fulfilled. *From her **dissatisfied** look I could tell that her holiday had gone badly.*

displeased
: **Displeased** means annoyed or offended. It is very similar to dissatisfied. *I am displeased with your behavior.*

discontented
: **Discontented** means not feeling happy, pleased, or satisfied. *He is discontented with his job.*

disgruntled
: **Disgruntled** means made annoyed and sulky. *He is disgruntled because he has to leave for work so early.*

querulous
: **Querulous** means dissatisfied and complaining. *"Why is this train always late?" he asked in a querulous voice.*

similar words: **angry, annoyed**
contrasting words: **satisfied, glad**

distant *adjective*

far off. *The space probe traveled from Earth to a **distant** planet.*

faraway   **Faraway** is so similar to distant that you can usually use either. *I dream of visiting faraway lands.*

remote   **Remote** means very far off and out-of-the-way. *We visited a remote village in the mountains.*

outlying   **Outlying** means far from the center of things. *The cows had wandered into an outlying field.*

isolated   **Isolated** means separated or apart from other people. *Their isolated cabin was a two-day hike from the nearest town.*

contrasting words: **near**

distinguished *adjective*

having an air or quality that impresses people. *They gathered to honor her career as a **distinguished** politician.*

noble   **Noble** means of a high quality that you admire. *Climbing the tallest mountain in the world was a noble feat.*

refined   **Refined** can mean without any coarseness or roughness. *Our dinner guest had very refined manners.*

genteel   **Genteel** means very polite and careful in your manners, speech, and behavior. *They are so genteel that they won't allow bad manners in their presence.*

classy   **Classy** can mean **refined** or suited to those of high class. It is more suited to everyday language. *We enjoyed going to the classy restaurant even though it was expensive.*

aristocratic   **Aristocratic** can mean proud or distinguished. *Our new black stallion looked aristocratic.*

similar words: **superior, grand**
contrasting words: **ordinary, inferior**

distribute *verb*

to give something out. *Santa Claus **distributed** gifts to the children.*

issue
To **issue** means to give or send out. *Each worker was issued a shovel and work gloves.*

allot
To **allot** means to hand out something. *Their father's will allotted equal shares of the farm to the two brothers.*

dispense
To **dispense** means to deal something out. *The courts dispense justice.*

allocate
To **allocate** means to set something apart for a special purpose. *The children allocated some of their money to buy a chess game.*

ration
To **ration** means to give out the fixed amount of something that is allowed to one person or group. *During the emergency, the authorities rationed food because it was in short supply.*

similar words: **share**

double *adjective*

having two parts. *Only half of the **double** door was open.*

dual
Dual means having to do with two or having two parts. *That book has a dual purpose: to teach you and to entertain you.*

two-piece
Two-piece means having two parts that go together. This is usually used about clothing. *Her two-piece suit had a jacket and skirt.*

twin
Twin can mean having two things that match or look alike. *This plane has twin engines.*

duplicate
Duplicate can mean double or having two parts that are similar or go together. *The twins wanted to look different, and refused to wear duplicate sweaters.*

contrasting words: **single**

doubt *verb*

to be uncertain or unsure of something. *I have reason to **doubt** her excuse for being late.*

distrust
To **distrust** means to doubt or have no confidence in someone or something. *I distrust weather forecasts because they are often wrong.*

disbelieve
To **disbelieve** means to **distrust** or have no faith in something or someone. *I disbelieve anything he tells me.*

question
To **question** can mean to doubt something and want to know more about it before you believe it. *I question the truth of that story.*

query
To **query** means to doubt or ask questions about something. *You should query the manager if you think the price is too high.*

take with a grain of salt
To **take with a grain of salt** means to doubt something someone tells you. *I take the things he says with a grain of salt.*

---

contrasting words: **believe**

---

drab *adjective*

looking dull and uninteresting. *Those **drab** curtains spoil the look of the room.*

somber
Somber can mean dull in color. *His somber clothes gave no sign of his happiness.*

dingy
Dingy means not bright or new-looking. *The abandoned house had a room filled with dingy furniture.*

gloomy
Gloomy can mean dull and dark. *They were locked in the gloomy dungeon.*

mousy
Mousy can mean having a gray-brown or drab color. It is used about the color of hair. *A red hat would brighten up your mousy hair.*

---

similar words: **dull**
contrasting words: **gaudy, colorful, spectacular**

---

dreamy *adjective*

vague or lost in a dream thinking about something else. *He had a **dreamy** look on his face as he thought about his vacation.*

preoccupied **Preoccupied** means completely taken up with your own thoughts. *I was so preoccupied I didn't hear a word you said.*

bemused **Bemused** means lost in thought. *While our teacher read the story my friend had a bemused look on her face.*

half-asleep **Half-asleep** means vague and **preoccupied.** *Because you were half-asleep, you missed the joke.*

inattentive **Inattentive** means not paying attention to what is going on around you. *You were certainly inattentive when I gave out the instructions.*

absent-minded **Absent-minded** means being so vague that you forget things. *What an absent-minded person you are to put on different colored socks!*

contrasting words: **alert, inquisitive**

dreary *adjective*

dull or gloomy. *It was a **dreary** afternoon with no sunshine.*

dismal **Dismal** means causing a feeling of sadness or gloom. *The weather has been dismal for days.*

depressing **Depressing** means causing a feeling of sadness or lack of energy. *It is depressing when it rains all day.*

cheerless **Cheerless** means without brightness or warmth. *They spent the cheerless day trying to get warm.*

bleak **Bleak** means cold and harsh. *It was a bleak winter's day.*

gray **Gray** can mean dark and overcast. *Don't hurry to get up, because it's a gray morning outside.*

similar words: **cloudy**
contrasting words: **fine**

drink   *verb*

to take liquid through your mouth. *I **drink** eight glasses of water a day.*

sip	To **sip** means to drink something in small mouthfuls. *Alison sipped her lemonade to make it last longer.*
imbibe	To **imbibe** means to drink. It is a more formal word. *The ambassador's guests imbibed excellent wine with their dinner.*
quaff	To **quaff** means to drink thirstily. *We quaffed our fruit juice with gusto after winning the tennis match.*
guzzle	To **guzzle** means to drink greedily and noisily. *They were so thirsty that they guzzled the juice straight from the bottle.*
swallow	To **swallow** means to take liquid or food into your stomach through your throat. *Daniel swallowed his nasty medicine quickly and then had a jelly bean.*

drip   *verb*

to let drops fall. *The faucet **drips** all the time.*

dribble	To **dribble** means to flow in small drops. *Soapy water dribbled from the wet cloth.*
trickle	To **trickle** means to flow in a very small or slow stream. *Milk trickled out of the hole in the carton.*
seep	To **seep** means to leak slowly or flow through something gradually. *Water seeped through the hole in the ceiling.*
ooze	To **ooze** means to flow slowly, as if through small openings. It is very similar to **seep**. *Mud oozed through our toes as we walked in the rain.*

similar words: **flow**

drop *verb*

to allow something to fall or go to a lower position. *Careful! Don't **drop** the baby.*

lower To **lower** means to put something in a lower position. *We lowered a rope over the side of the cliff.*

let down To **let down** is so similar to **lower** that you can usually use either. *I had to let down the hem of my pants because I had grown taller.*

dip To **dip** means to lower something briefly before lifting it again. *Dip the ladle into the soup.*

sink To **sink** means to go down to the bottom. *The boat filled with water and sank.*

submerge To **submerge** means to put something under the surface of the water. *The captain submerged the submarine before attacking.*

contrasting words: **lift**

dry *adjective*

not wet or damp. *The lawn was very **dry**, so we watered it.*

arid **Arid** means dry and hot. *We carried plenty of water in our car when we drove across the arid desert.*

parched **Parched** means having become very dry. *The flowers died in the parched garden while we were away on vacation.*

dehydrated **Dehydrated** means having lost all its water or moisture, or having had it removed. *The dehydrated sailors were in desperate need of clean drinking water. Raisins are dehydrated grapes.*

desiccated **Desiccated** means thoroughly dried. *We sprinkled desiccated coconut on the chocolate cake.*

contrasting words: **wet**

dull *adjective*

not bright, shiny, or clear. *The top of this table was very **dull** before I polished it.*

flat Flat can mean not shiny. It is mainly used about paint. *We used flat paint so that the room wouldn't look too bright.*

mat Mat means having a dull surface. *I prefer mat snapshots to glossy ones.*

lackluster Lackluster means without brightness or luster. *The cat's lackluster coat was a sign of its poor health.*

lifeless Lifeless can mean dull and lacking vitality. *If you used brighter colors, your picture wouldn't look so lifeless.*

similar words: **drab**
contrasting words: **shiny**

earth *noun*

the softer part of the dry land, rather than rocks or sand. *The toddlers made mud pies out of **earth** and water.*

clay Clay is a dense earth that holds water and is used in making pottery and bricks. *I need to wet my clay before I make a vase.*

soil Soil is earth, especially the kind in which you can grow plants. *The soil in our garden needs plenty of fertilizer.*

ground Ground is earth or **soil**. *We dug a hole in the ground for the posts.*

dirt Dirt is loose earth or **soil**. You usually think of dirt as being very dry. *I dropped my book in the dirt.*

loam Loam is a loose **soil** made up of clay, sand, and natural fertilizers. *Good crops grow in the loam at the edges of the river.*

easy *adjective*

not difficult or hard to do or understand. *Swimming is **easy** once you have been taught.*

simple	**Simple** means easy to understand, do, or use. *It was a simple explanation.*
uncomplicated	**Uncomplicated** means not hard to use or understand. *She gave me uncomplicated instructions.*
effortless	**Effortless** means done easily or without much effort. *He won the game with an effortless serve.*
foolproof	**Foolproof** means designed not to fail and to be easy to use even if you are inexperienced. *The book has a foolproof recipe for making cookies.*
painless	**Painless** means causing no pain. *I thought it would be hard to get in shape, but the exercises were painless.*

contrasting words: **difficult, complicated, confusing**

eat *verb*

to take food into your mouth and swallow it. ***Eat** your ice cream before you get into the car.*

taste	To **taste** means to eat just a small amount of something to see if you like it. *He tasted the soup to see if it needed more pepper.*
consume	To **consume** means to eat or drink something. It is a more formal word. *The chocolate cookies were so delicious we consumed every one.*
devour	To **devour** means to eat something very hungrily. *I was so hungry I devoured nearly a whole loaf of bread.*
gobble	To **gobble** means to eat something very quickly without chewing it well. *We gobbled our dinner so we could go out to play.*
gulp	To **gulp** means to swallow something quickly, often a large amount at a time. *The large dog gulped his meat down in a minute and then looked for more.*

similar words: **chew, drink**

edge _noun_

a line, side, or boundary where two parts or surfaces meet. *The **edge** of the cardboard box was dented.*

border	A **border** is the edge or side of anything. *I painted a design around the border of my drawing.*
margin	A **margin** is the edge of something. *I wrote my comments in the margin of the page.*
rim	A **rim** is an outer edge, especially of a circular or round object. *The rim of the wheel is bent.*
brim	A **brim** is the top edge of a container, such as a glass or basin. *He filled the glass to the brim.*
brink	A **brink** is the edge of a steep or dangerous place. *They have put up a fence on the brink of the cliff.*

similar words: **outskirts**

educated _adjective_

having had a good education. *We need **educated** people in Congress.*

learned	**Learned** means having a lot of knowledge from study. *Aunt Helen is a learned woman who likes to talk about books.*
erudite	**Erudite** means having knowledge gained from study, especially in history or literature. This is a formal word. *The students enjoyed the lectures of the erudite professor.*
knowledgeable	**Knowledgeable** means having knowledge or understanding, especially about a particular subject. *He is very knowledgeable about the wildflowers of Vermont.*
well-informed	**Well-informed** means having a wide general knowledge or knowledge of a variety of subjects. *My Uncle Daniel helped me with my current affairs project, as he is a very well-informed man.*
cultivated	**Cultivated** means having had your mind and abilities developed and improved. *Cultivated people like to increase their knowledge and to seek out new ideas.*

similar words: **clever, shrewd**
contrasting words: **ignorant**

elastic *adjective*

able to be pulled out or extended and then go back to its original shape again. *The **elastic** sides of the boots stretch to go over my feet and then fit tightly around my ankles.*

stretchy	**Stretchy** means elastic or able to be extended. *This stretchy belt will fit almost anyone.*
springy	**Springy** means elastic or able to regain its shape after being stretched. *We jumped up and down on the springy mattress.*
bouncy	**Bouncy** means able to spring back into shape, or rebound as a ball does. *Look at her thick, bouncy hair.*
rubbery	**Rubbery** means soft and **stretchy**. *The rubbery clay was easy to push and pull into different shapes.*
resilient	**Resilient** means able to bounce back. *Rubber is such a resilient material that many children's toys are made of it.*

similar words: **flexible**

emphasize *verb*

to point out the importance of something. *The manager **emphasized** the necessity for everyone to get to work on time.*

stress	To **stress** is so similar to emphasize that you can usually use either. *The manager stressed the need for punctuality.*
accentuate	To **accentuate** means to make something seem important or noticeable. *He accentuated the main parts of his speech by thumping his fist on the table.*
highlight	To **highlight** means to make something stand out. It is very similar to **accentuate**. *I highlighted the important sentence by underlining it.*
belabor	To **belabor** can mean to develop something in too much detail, usually because you consider it very important. *The camp counselor really belabored the point about how dangerous the trip would be.*
magnify	To **magnify** can mean to make something seem more important than it is. *They always magnify their troubles.*

contrasting words: **minimize**

empty *adjective*

containing nothing. *The children were disappointed when they discovered that the mailbox was **empty**.*

void	**Void** means completely empty or without contents. This is a very formal word. *This statement is void of meaning.*
blank	**Blank** means not written or printed on. *I couldn't think what to write on the blank page.*
finished	**Finished** means empty because everything has been used up. *We ate the chocolates until the box was finished.*
vacant	**Vacant** means not occupied by anyone. *The house has been vacant since the last owner died.*
deserted	**Deserted** means empty of people because they have all gone away. *There was an eerie feeling in the deserted town.*

contrasting words: **full**

enclose *verb*

to shut in or close in on all sides. *A wall **enclosed** the jail.*

box in	To **box in** means to enclose someone or something, as if in a box. *The tall hedges boxed me in and I couldn't get out.*
coop up	To **coop up** means to keep someone or something in a small place. *You shouldn't coop up all the rabbits in the one cage.*
confine	To **confine** means to shut or keep someone or something in. *We'll have to confine our dog in a pen until the vet arrives.*
surround	To **surround** means to go around something completely. *A wooden fence surrounds our house.*
encircle	To **encircle** means to enclose something by making a circle around it. *A deep moat encircled the castle.*

similar words: **cover**

encourage   *verb*

to cheer someone on. *We **encouraged** the team with shouts and flag-waving.*

urge	To **urge** means to push or drive someone or something on. *I urged my brother to try again.*
inspire	To **inspire** means to have an encouraging and uplifting effect on someone. *His bravery inspired the others.*
motivate	To **motivate** means to give someone a strong reason for doing something. *My high class marks motivated me to study hard for the exams.*
set an example for	To **set an example for** means to encourage someone by being a good model for others to follow. *Her physical fitness set an example to everyone in the camp.*

similar words: **persuade**
contrasting words: **discourage**

end   *noun*

the last or final point of something. *I fell asleep before the **end** of the television show.*

finish	**Finish** is so similar to end that you can usually use either. *She ran the race to the finish.*
conclusion	The **conclusion** is the point at which something comes to an end. *At the conclusion of the concert the curtain fell.*
close	**Close** is so similar to **conclusion** that you can usually use either. *We all shook hands at the close of the volleyball game.*
finale	A **finale** is the special last part of a performance that comes just before the end. *The band saved its latest hit for the finale of the concert.*
termination	**Termination** means the bringing of something to an end. *He was sad because of the termination of their friendship.*

contrasting words: **start**

end   *verb*

to come to the finishing point. *The storm **ended** almost as suddenly as it had begun.*

finish To **finish** means to come to an end. *The game finished when it grew too dark to see the ball.*

terminate To **terminate** can mean to end or **finish**. It is usually used in more formal language. *The concert terminated with a solo by the leading tenor.*

stop To **stop** means to **finish** or to come to a halt. *We stopped when the whistle blew.*

cease To **cease** is very similar to **stop**. It may be used in more formal language. *The canary's whistling ceased when I covered its cage.*

expire To **expire** can mean to come to an end. *Please lend me 10 cents, because the time limit on the parking meter has expired.*

similar words: **stop, finish**
contrasting words: **start**

endanger   *verb*

to put someone or something in danger. *They **endangered** their lives going fishing during the fierce storm.*

jeopardize To **jeopardize** means to put something in danger, or to chance its loss or harm. *Don't jeopardize all your good work by being careless now!*

expose To **expose** can mean to leave something open to danger or harm. *The soldiers exposed themselves to the enemy's fire as they made their attack.*

compromise To **compromise** can mean to lay something open to danger, or something similar. *If he had accepted the bribe, he would have compromised his job.*

threaten To **threaten** can mean to be likely to cause damage or harm to something or someone. *The drought threatened our crops.*

put at risk To **put at risk** means to put something in a position or situation where it may be damaged or harmed. *Most doctors agree that smoking puts your health at risk.*

contrasting words: **protect, save**

endure   *verb*

to bear something patiently or without making a fuss, usually for a long time. *The explorers **endured** many hardships before they finally reached civilization.*

put up with
To **put up with** means to endure something that you don't like or that is hard to do. It is more suited to everyday language. *I put up with her teasing for days.*

tolerate
To **tolerate** can mean to endure or **put up with** something. *I tried to tolerate the uncomfortable pillow but in the end I asked for another one.*

stick out
To **stick out** can mean to endure or **tolerate** something, even though you may be tempted not to. *If we can only stick out the bad weather for the next few days, I'm sure our holiday won't be ruined.*

suffer
To **suffer** can mean to endure or **put up with** something that may hurt you very much. *She refused to suffer their insults quietly.*

enemy   *noun*

someone who hates someone else, or wishes to harm them. *He was a good man and had no **enemies**.*

foe
Foe is a rather old-fashioned word for an enemy. *The soldiers went into battle against their foes.*

antagonist
An **antagonist** is an enemy or someone you are striving against, often in an unfriendly way. *The antagonists fought to the bitter end, as they each wanted to win the trophy.*

adversary
An **adversary** is someone you compete against or fight with. *The boxer's adversary weighed much more than he did.*

opponent
An **opponent** is someone who is on the opposite side of you in a contest or argument. *The opponents fought hard to win the last point in the tennis match.*

rival
A **rival** is someone who is aiming at the same thing as another person, or who tries to equal or outdo them. *She is my main rival for the championship.*

contrasting words: **friend**

energetic   *adjective*

strong and active. *Puppies are very **energetic**.*

vigorous	**Vigorous** means strong, energetic, and full of life. *We were hot after our vigorous game of football.*
dynamic	**Dynamic** means energetic and forceful. *The coach of the football team was a dynamic person.*
lively	**Lively** means full of energy and spirit. *The children in the playground are lively.*
animated	**Animated** can mean **lively**. *The birthday party was quite animated, with lots of talking and laughing.*
spirited	**Spirited** means showing lively courage. *The spirited horse wouldn't let anyone ride it.*

similar words: **busy, lively**
contrasting words: **lazy, lethargic, tired, weak**

enlarge   *verb*

to make something bigger. *I am going to **enlarge** this photo and frame it.*

increase	To **increase** can mean to make something bigger, greater, or faster. *We increased our speed as we drove out into the country.*
expand	To **expand** can mean to make something bigger or wider in scope. *She expanded her knowledge by reading.*
augment	To **augment** means to enlarge something by adding to it. *We augmented our dairy farm by building another barn.*
amplify	To **amplify** can mean to enlarge something or make it greater. It is usually used about sound. *Her drums were amplified for the rock concert.*
boost	To **boost** means to raise something or make it bigger or stronger. *Her win in the first heat boosted her confidence.*

similar words: **add**

entertainer *noun*

someone who sings, recites, or amuses people in a public place, usually for payment. *He earns his living as an **entertainer** in clubs.*

performer
A **performer** is someone performs any skill or displays an ability in front of an audience. *You will have to be a good performer to be picked for the musical.*

jester
A **jester** was a clown who entertained a prince or nobleman and his court in medieval times. *"Ask my jester to come and sing to us," shouted the king.*

comedian
A **comedian** is someone who performs in plays, films, or other entertainments that make you laugh. *The comedian was not the star of the play, but we all liked him the best.*

actor
An **actor** is someone who performs in plays, films, on television, or in other entertainments. *The actor signed a contract for a part in a new television series.*

player
A **player** is a rather old-fashioned word for **actor**. It is also used for someone who plays a musical instrument. *The villagers were excited when they heard there was a band of strolling players coming.*

enthusiastic *adjective*

having a lively interest in something. *She is **enthusiastic** about her new job.*

keen
Keen means full of enthusiasm. *She has a keen interest in music and is learning to play the guitar.*

eager
Eager means really wanting to do something. *She is eager to help us build the tree house.*

anxious
Anxious can mean sincerely and earnestly **eager**. *She was anxious to please her father.*

avid
Avid means wanting to do something as often as possible. *He is an avid reader.*

willing
Willing means agreeing happily to do something. *He was a willing helper.*

contrasting words: **apathetic, unwilling**

132

equal   *adjective*

being of the same number, value, or other quality as something else. *Everyone's share is* **equal**.

equivalent	**Equivalent** means of equal or matching value or rank. *An admiral in the navy is the equivalent rank to a general in the army.*
identical	**Identical** means being exactly the same as something else. *The two bikes were identical and I couldn't tell them apart.*
even	**Even** can mean equal. *They have an even number of skills, so they should be paid the same.*
symmetrical	**Symmetrical** means having the parts arranged so that they are balanced or equal in size or shape. *The pattern on the wallpaper is symmetrical.*
uniform	**Uniform** means having the same appearance. *The packages were of uniform size and mass.*

similar words: **similar**
contrasting words: **uneven, unlike**

err   *verb*

to make an error or be incorrect. *I know this answer isn't right, but I can't see where I have* **erred**.

miscalculate	To **miscalculate** means to make a mistake in working out the amount of something. *I thought I bought enough flour for the cake but I miscalculated.*
go wrong	To **go wrong** is so similar to err that you can usually use either. *You have gone wrong in the second line of your multiplication.*
make a slip	To **make a slip** means to make a mistake. *We don't want to make a slip at the last moment.*
trip up	To **trip up** can mean to make a mistake or do badly at something. *I was doing well in the exams, until I tripped up on the last question.*
mistake	To **mistake** means to err, or understand something wrongly. *I have mistaken you for someone else.*

erratic *adjective*

irregular or not steady in behavior or movement. *The coast guard went to investigate the boat because of its **erratic** course.*

unsteady   **Unsteady** means not constant or regular. *It was hard to read by the unsteady light of the campfire.*

intermittent   **Intermittent** means stopping and starting. *There was intermittent rain all day.*

sporadic   **Sporadic** means not very regular or frequent. *We only make sporadic visits to the city, because it is so far away.*

fitful   **Fitful** means stopping and starting in a very irregular way. *The sick man's fitful sleep worried the nurse.*

irregular   **Irregular** means uneven in timing. *Our kitchen clock was irregular until we replaced the old battery.*

---

contrasting words: **continuous, repeated**

---

escapee   *noun*

someone who has broken out of prison. *The newspaper said that the **escapee** might be dangerous.*

fugitive   A **fugitive** is someone who is running away, usually from the police. *The thief had to live as a fugitive so that he wouldn't be caught.*

runaway   A **runaway** is someone who has escaped or run away, often a child who has left home. *The runaway wouldn't tell the police where she lived.*

truant   A **truant** is someone who stays away from school without permission. *She suspected that the boy on the train was a truant.*

refugee   A **refugee** is someone who escapes to another country for safety, especially during war. *The refugees crossed the border and then traveled by sea to their new country.*

---

contrasting words: **prisoner**

---

evil *adjective*

breaking the laws of right or moral behavior. *Snow White's **evil** stepmother tried to poison her.*

wicked

Wicked means evil and causing great harm. *The wicked witch cast a spell on the prince and turned him into a frog.*

sinful

Sinful means **wicked,** and often refers to the breaking of religious laws. *They were told to give up their sinful habits and to live happy and healthy lives.*

malevolent

Malevolent meldans intentionally evil. *The malevolent dragon destroyed the forest with the fire it breathed.*

villainous

Villainous can mean very **wicked** or vile. *The villainous gangsters threatened the bank manager until he gave them the keys to the safe.*

heinous

Heinous means hateful and deserving severe punishment. *Kidnapping is a heinous crime.*

similar words: **indecent, dishonest, illegal**
contrasting words: **decent**

examine *verb*

to inspect or look at someone or something carefully. *The doctor **examined** me to make sure I was not hurt in the accident.*

analyze

To **analyze** means to examine something in detail in order to find out or show its meaning or importance. *The jury analyzed all the facts presented by the lawyers before they came to a decision.*

study

To **study** means to examine or look at something closely. *We studied our bank accounts to see whether we could buy a new washing machine.*

assess

To **assess** means to work out the value of something by examining it in detail. *The mechanic assessed the amount of damage to my car.*

review

To **review** means to examine something, especially in a formal or official way. *The admiral reviewed his fleet to see that all was in order.*

similar words: **investigate, test, inspect**

135

example *noun*

one of several things, or a part of something, that shows what the whole thing is like. *He gave us an **example** of what he wanted us to do.*

sample   A **sample** is a small part or piece of anything that is meant to show what the whole is like. *I have seen a sample of his artwork and will be very happy to sell his paintings in my shop.*

model   A **model** is an example used for copying or comparing. *Her project was used as a model of excellent work.*

specimen   A **specimen** is a part of something, or a single thing, taken as being typical of a larger amount, or a whole group. *The doctor took a specimen of my blood for tests.*

guide   A **guide** can be anything that shows you the way to do something. *The gardening book served as a reliable guide when we planted the vegetables.*

pattern   A **pattern** can be a **model** that shows how something can be made. *When I asked my mother for a new dress, she gave me some material and a paper pattern!*

excellent *adjective*

remarkably good or of the highest quality. *Your schoolwork is **excellent**.*

outstanding   **Outstanding** means so good that it stands out from all others. *She is an outstanding tennis player.*

fantastic   **Fantastic** means extremely good or wonderful. *We saw a fantastic movie last week.*

terrific   **Terrific** means very good or excellent. *The team spirit before the game was terrific.*

sensational   **Sensational** can mean excellent or very pleasing. It is more suited to everyday language. *He always gets onto the team because he's a sensational swimmer.*

exceptional   **Exceptional** means of unusually high quality or ability. *Only exceptional people win the Nobel prize.*

similar words: **good, great, perfect, superior, wonderful, best**
contrasting words: **bad, ordinary**

excess *noun*

an extreme amount. *He had an **excess** of food at the party and was sick afterward.*

surplus A **surplus** is an amount that is more than is needed or used. *We stored the surplus grain in a warehouse, in case we need it next year.*

glut A **glut** is a very big **surplus**. *There was such a glut of beans on the market that they were very cheap.*

oversupply An **oversupply** is too large an amount of something that has been supplied to you. *The weary parents felt their toddler had an oversupply of energy.*

backlog A **backlog** is a piling up of things that need to be done. *I have a backlog of letters to answer.*

superfluity A **superfluity** is a greater amount of something than is needed. *She had a superfluity of paper, so she gave some to her brother.*

contrasting words: **lack**

exchange *verb*

to give one thing in return for another. *I think I'll take this shirt back to the store and **exchange** it for a smaller one.*

swap To **swap** means to exchange. They are so similar you can usually choose either word. *I swapped my apple for my friend's sandwich.*

replace To **replace** something means to renew it or put something else in its place. *I have to replace the cup I broke with a new one.*

substitute To **substitute** means to put something in the place of something else. *The thief substituted a fake for the diamond.*

stand in for To **stand in for** means to act in place of someone. *I will stand in for you while you have lunch.*

transpose To **transpose** means to make two or more things change places. *If you transpose the letters in the word "on" you get "no."*

excited *adjective*

having the strong feelings you get when you are looking forward to something or enjoying something very much. *Jane was **excited** about going to the zoo.*

thrilled	**Thrilled** means very excited. *She was thrilled when she knew you were coming.*
exhilarated	**Exhilarated** means filled with energy and excitement. *They felt exhilarated after the ride on the roller coaster.*
restless	**Restless** means unable to remain quiet and still. *Everyone in the class was restless because it was almost time for the play to begin.*
wrought up	**Wrought up** means overexcited. *Jason got wrought up the night before his birthday.*
frenzied	**Frenzied** means wildly or furiously excited. *The dog began a frenzied barking when he saw his owner.*

contrasting words: **calm, bored**

exciting *adjective*

arousing feelings of eagerness or interest. *This book is so **exciting** I can't put it down.*

exhilarating	**Exhilarating** means filling you with energy and excitement. *I love the exhilarating feeling of zooming across the water in a speedboat.*
stimulating	**Stimulating** means stirring up interest and enthusiasm for something. *That stimulating film on skating made me feel like racing down to the arena.*
rousing	**Rousing** means stirring into action and interest. *She gave a rousing speech at the start of the election campaign.*
thrilling	**Thrilling** means causing a tingling feeling of strong excitement. *I couldn't get to sleep after that thrilling movie.*
breathtaking	**Breathtaking** means causing excitement and admiration mixed with a little fear. *We had a breathtaking view of the mountains from the cable car.*

contrasting words: **boring**

exclude *verb*

to shut or keep something or someone out. *Blinds **exclude** light from rooms.*

preclude	To **preclude** means to rule out or exclude someone. *Animals are precluded from the park unless they are leashed.*
leave out	To **leave out** means to exclude or fail to include someone or something. *Leave out the sugar when you make my coffee.*
drop	To **drop** can mean to exclude someone from a group. *The manager dropped him from the team after he missed several practices.*
skip	To **skip** means to pass over something without reading or noticing it. *He often skips parts when he's reading.*
delete	To **delete** means to take out or wipe out something written. *Delete their names from the list.*

similar words: **ban, isolate**
contrasting words: **include**

expand *verb*

to express something in greater detail so as to make it longer, usually by adding more words. *She **expanded** her short story into a novel.*

develop	To **develop** can mean to expand or enlarge upon the detail of something. *She's trying to develop her ideas about nuclear disarmament before she gives her talk to the class.*
amplify	To **amplify** can mean to expand something by adding more details. *Please amplify your story so that I can understand what happened.*
embellish	To **embellish** means to make a statement or tale more interesting by adding details, mostly imaginary or exaggerated ones. *He embellished his story with a description of the jewels he found in the basement.*
embroider	To **embroider** can mean to improve or make a story more interesting with untruthful additions. *My brother embroidered the tale so much that I could hardly believe what he said.*
pad	To **pad** can mean to fill out a speech or piece of writing with unnecessary words or information. *You padded your essay with too many trivial details.*

contrasting words: **shorten**

139

expect *verb*

to think that something is likely to come or happen. *I **expect** the storm will break in the next half hour.*

anticipate	To **anticipate** can mean to expect something will come to pass. *We anticipate the release of the prisoner tomorrow.*
foresee	To **foresee** means to expect or see something in advance. *We have planned well, and I can foresee success.*
count on	To **count on** means to depend upon or expect something. *The boss is counting on us being on time.*
bargain for	To **bargain for** means to expect or be prepared for something. *We didn't bargain for the crowd at the picnic ground.*
look forward to	To **look forward to** means to expect something with pleasure. *We are looking forward to our holiday.*

expel *verb*

to drive someone out or away with force. *I'm afraid I will have to **expel** you from the school.*

eject	To **eject** means to expel. *If you break the rules, you'll be ejected from the club.*
evict	To **evict** means to turn someone out of a place or remove them. *People were evicted from their homes when the government needed land for the new highway.*
banish	To **banish** means to send someone away as a punishment. *The queen banished the evil magician from her country forever.*
exile	To **exile** means to force someone to leave the country. *The king exiled them for treason.*
throw out	To **throw out** is an informal way of saying **expel**. *The librarian threw out the noisy students.*

similar words: **isolate**

expensive   *adjective*

costing too much money. *Those jeans are **expensive**.*

exorbitant	**Exorbitant** means being far more in amount than you think is reasonable. *Their prices are exorbitant.*
pricey	**Pricey** means costing more money than you think necessary. This is more suited to everyday language. *It is a pricey hotel.*
valuable	**Valuable** means costing a lot of money. *The car they bought was too valuable to park on the street.*
costly	**Costly** means expensive or costing a great deal, usually because it is so precious or fine. *The diamonds were beautiful and costly.*

contrasting words: **cheap**

expert   *noun*

someone who has a lot of skill or knowledge about something. *She is a skating **expert**.*

authority	An **authority** is someone who is a reliable source of information about something. *He is an authority on snakes.*
consultant	A **consultant** is an expert who charges you for advice. *The engineering firm called in a consultant to help plan the new bridge.*
specialist	A **specialist** is someone who has concentrated on a special area of study or work. *The heart specialist explained the operation to her patient.*
ace	An **ace** is an expert who is usually quite famous. *Eddie Rickenbacker, the pilot, was an ace of World War I.*
prodigy	A **prodigy** is someone, usually a child, who has an extraordinary talent for something. *Mozart was a musical prodigy.*

similar words: **star**

explain   *verb*

to make something clear, plain, or easy to understand. *Can you **explain** what you mean?*

clarify	To **clarify** can mean to make something clear or able to be understood. *Can you clarify your answer?*
elucidate	To **elucidate** means to explain something by giving more details about it. *I can't give you an answer until you elucidate what you want.*
spell out	To **spell out** can mean to explain something in a very simple way to make quite sure that nothing has been missed. *Tom is only five, so you had better spell out the rules of the game.*
illustrate	To **illustrate** can mean to explain something by giving examples of it. *He illustrated his theory about leadership with accounts of the lives of some famous explorers.*
interpret	To **interpret** can mean to explain the meaning of something. *I never know what my dreams mean, but my mother can interpret them.*

similar words: **describe, tell**
contrasting words: **confuse, puzzle**

extend   *verb*

to continue or be drawn out over some distance. *The mountain range **extends** right down to the coast.*

reach	To **reach** means to extend over a distance. *The pole reaches into the middle of the cage.*
cross	To **cross** means to go or **reach** from one side or place to another. *They built the bridge to cross over the river.*
spread	To **spread** means to extend or stretch out, especially over an area. *The flood waters spread over the farmland.*
stretch	To **stretch** means to extend for a long distance. *The prairies stretched to the horizon.*
run	To **run** can mean to extend or continue. *A crack runs down the wall.*

extra *adjective*

more than usual or necessary. *There is always **extra** work to do in the garden when we come back from vacation.*

additional	**Additional** is so similar to extra that you can usually use either. *She has additional money because her salary was raised.*
spare	**Spare** can mean extra, or ready as a replacement. *The spare tire was in the trunk of the car.*
superfluous	**Superfluous** means more than is needed. *There were so many helpers that he was superfluous.*
excessive	**Excessive** means more than usual or proper. *The excessive rainfall this week caused the river to flood.*
redundant	**Redundant** means no longer needed because there is already enough. *The factory can't hire new workers as they would be redundant.*

similar words: **sufficient**
contrasting words: **scant, necessary, insufficient**

fail *verb*

to be unsuccessful or fall short in something. *He **failed** in his math test because he could answer only a couple of questions.*

fall through	To **fall through** means to be unsuccessful or to fail. *Their plans fell through because they hadn't prepared well enough.*
collapse	To **collapse** means to fail suddenly. *The plans for the peace talks collapsed when one of the leaders said that she would not attend.*
fizzle out	To **fizzle out** means to fail after a good start. It is more suited to everyday language. *The idea fizzled out even though everyone was enthusiastic to start with.*
miscarry	To **miscarry** means to fail to get the right result or decision. *The terrorist's plan miscarried when the bomb exploded too soon.*
flunk	To **flunk** means to fail in schoolwork. It is more suited to everyday language. *You could flunk the exam if you don't study.*

contrasting words: **succeed, thrive**

failure   *noun*

something or someone that doesn't succeed. *The artist felt that his exhibition was a* ***failure*** *because only a few people came to see it.*

disaster
A **disaster** can mean a total failure. *The school play was a complete disaster because nearly all the actors forgot their lines.*

fiasco
A **fiasco** is an embarrassing or ridiculous failure. *The party was a fiasco because only half the guests turned up.*

flop
A **flop** is something that is a failure. This is more suited to everyday language. *The critics said the play would be a flop because the acting wasn't very good.*

dud
A **dud** is something that proves to be a failure. This is more suited to everyday language. *The car turned out to be a bit of a dud because it kept breaking down.*

loser
A **loser** is someone or something that lacks the ability to succeed. *You can tell that the skinny horse is a real loser.*

---

contrasting words: **achievement**

---

fair   *adjective*

treating everyone equally and not showing favoritism. *He was a very **fair** judge of our projects.*

impartial
Impartial means not taking one side against the other. *The judge in the trial was impartial.*

just
Just means fair or rightly judged. *Most people agreed her decision was just.*

right
Right means fair and good. *He was right not to judge you too harshly.*

objective
Objective means being fair and not allowing your own opinions to influence you. *You need an objective mind to be a judge.*

---

similar words: **neutral**
contrasting words: **unfair**

144

faithful   *adjective*

always staying true to a friend, or a leader, or to what you believe in. *I will be faithful to you until I die.*

loyal **Loyal** means faithful and true. *He stayed loyal to me through all my trouble.*

devoted **Devoted** means loving and **loyal**. *She is my devoted friend.*

trustworthy **Trustworthy** means deserving trust or confidence by showing that you are faithful. *They were our trustworthy allies during the war.*

constant **Constant** means unceasingly faithful. *Their constant love kept their marriage happy for 50 years.*

trusty **Trusty** means faithful and able to be trusted. *My dog has been my trusty friend for 15 years.*

similar words: **reliable, steadfast**
contrasting words: **unfaithful**

fake   *adjective*

made or done in such a way as to trick other people. *We were all fooled by the fake jewels.*

phony **Phony** means not real or genuine. It is more suited to everyday language. *The phony $20 bills were not accepted by the bank.*

false **False** can be so similar to **phony** that you can usually use either. *He wore a false nose to the costume party.*

sham **Sham** means not what it pretends or appears to be. *The army put on a sham battle for the visitors.*

counterfeit **Counterfeit** means made to look exactly like something else in order to deceive people. It is usually used to describe something that is illegal. *Not even the police could identify the counterfeit money at first.*

bogus **Bogus** means **counterfeit** or not real. It is more suited to everyday language. *The man was caught when he tried to use the bogus passport.*

contrasting words: **genuine**

fall *verb*

to come down suddenly from a higher to a lower position because of loss of balance or support. *The cup **fell** to the ground and smashed.*

slip	To **slip** means to lose your footing and fall. *He slipped on the polished floor.*
topple	To **topple** means to fall forward because of lack of balance. *The elderly man felt faint from the heat and toppled over.*
trip	To **trip** means to fall over, or nearly fall, because you struck your foot against something. *I tripped over that toy.*
stumble	To **stumble** means to fall, or nearly fall, when walking or running. It is very similar to **trip**. *She stumbled on the uneven ground.*
pitch forward	To **pitch forward** means to fall forward very suddenly. *The leg of my chair broke and I pitched forward onto the carpet.*

similar words: **descend**

family *noun*

parents and their children. *The whole **family** went on a picnic.*

relatives	**Relatives** are people who belong to your wider, or extended, family, such as uncles, aunts, cousins, and grandparents. *All our relatives came to celebrate our parents' wedding anniversary.*
kin	**Kin** means all your **relatives**. This word is not used as often as **relatives** or **relations**. *Her mother's kin are Greek.*
relations	**Relations** are your **kin** or **relatives**. These words are all so similar you can usually choose any one of them. *Most of Joshua's relations live in Israel.*
flesh and blood	**Flesh and blood** means someone's children or other close **relatives**. This is often used by people who are feeling very emotional about the person they are talking about. *I didn't think my own flesh and blood would do such a thing.*

famous   *adjective*

widely known. *The **famous** runner won his third gold medal.*

renowned	**Renowned** means very widely known and well thought of. *Not a sound was heard as we listened to the adventures of the renowned explorer.*
celebrated	**Celebrated** means so famous that you are publicly recognized and praised. *The celebrated author was surprised and pleased when we gave a dinner in her honor.*
noted	**Noted** means famous or honored for a particular achievement. *Carl Sandburg is a noted American poet.*
notable	**Notable** means important or worthy of being noticed. *He is a notable young writer who has had a lot of success.*
notorious	**Notorious** means famous or well-known for something bad. *He was a notorious basketball player because he was always fouling out.*

similar words: **important**
contrasting words: **insignificant**

fashion   *noun*

a custom or way of doing things. *The **fashion** of entertaining at a barbecue is popular.*

style	A **style** is a fashion. You can usually use either word. *This year, the style is to have short hair.*
vogue	A **vogue** is a fashion at a particular time. *I want to buy shoes that are in vogue to replace the ones I've worn out.*
fad	A **fad** is something that is popular for a short time. *Yoyos are a fad that comes and goes.*
craze	A **craze** is very similar to a **fad**. You can usually choose either word. *Haven't you heard about the latest craze for putting colored gel in your hair?*
trend	A **trend** is a tendency or movement that leads to a fashion. *There is a trend toward buying smaller cars these days.*

fast *adjective*

able to move at a great pace. *She's a very **fast** runner.*

quick	**Quick** means fast or without any delay. *He was so quick he got away before we could catch him.*
rapid	**Rapid** means very fast or **quick**. *Linda's such a rapid worker she did twice as much as Sue.*
speedy	**Speedy** is so similar to **rapid** that you can usually use either word. *Even though her work was speedy, she didn't make one mistake.*
swift	**Swift** means able to move very quickly and smoothly. *With one swift dive the bird grabbed my sandwich in its beak and flew off again.*
express	**Express** means very fast, without stopping or delaying. *She took the express train because she had no time to spare.*

contrasting words: **slow**

fat *adjective*

weighing more than you should. *She said she was quite **fat** after her vacation.*

plump	**Plump** means rather fat and well-rounded. *The new puppies were plump and cuddly.*
chubby	**chubby** means short and fat. *Chubby babies often become tall and slender in their teens.*
overweight	**Overweight** means fat, but it is less likely to be taken as an insult. *His clothes were tight, so he knew he was a bit overweight.*
stout	**Stout** means rather **overweight** and often looking thick and heavy. *He is a stout man with a big, booming voice.*
obese	**Obese** means extremely fat. *Most people who are obese try to lose some weight.*

similar words: **stocky, heavy**
contrasting words: **thin, slight**

fatal *adjective*

causing death. *She suffered **fatal** injuries in the car accident.*

deadly	**Deadly** means likely to cause death. *A rattlesnake's bite can be deadly.*
lethal	**Lethal** is so similar to **deadly** that you can usually use either. *Some household cleaners can be lethal if children swallow them.*
malignant	**Malignant** can mean **deadly** or tending to produce death, as a disease does. *My uncle died from a malignant tumor.*
terminal	**Terminal** can mean causing or happening at the end of your life. *The doctors told him that he had a terminal illness and only had a few months to live.*

fate *noun*

a fixed and inescapable plan for the whole of your life, supposedly designed by some unknown power. *It was due to **fate** that we should meet.*

destiny	**Destiny** is something that had to happen, especially related to the events in someone's life. *It was her destiny to be a great leader.*
providence	**Providence** is the care and protection of God, nature, or some unknown power. *It must have been by providence that the children survived overnight in the woods.*
luck	**Luck** is something, either good or bad, that happens to a person without any apparent reason. *As luck would have it, the bus came just as it started to rain heavily.*
fortune	**Fortune** is so similar to **luck** that you can usually use either. *It was by good fortune that a doctor was close by when I broke my leg.*
chance	**Chance** can be fate or an accidental or unforeseen happening. *If by chance we find the treasure, we will be rich.*

fault *verb*

to find an error or mistake in something. *They couldn't **fault** his wonderful singing.*

criticize — To **criticize** means to find fault with something or someone. *He criticized my table manners in front of my friends.*

condemn — To **condemn** means to express strong disapproval of something or someone. *She condemned the fight in the playground.*

censure — To **censure** means to **condemn** or to find fault with someone or something. This is rather a formal word. *The government censured its opponents for their policy on the budget.*

damn — To **damn** can mean to declare something to be bad, wrong, or illegal. *He damned the activities of the vandals in the neighborhood.*

pick apart — To **pick apart** means to **criticize** something, especially in small details. It is more suited to everyday language. *She picked apart my work and pointed out every little thing that was wrong with it.*

similar words: **scold, disapprove of, accuse**
contrasting words: **approve, praise**

fear *verb*

to feel concern or worry for something. *I always **fear** for your safety while you are rock climbing.*

tremble — To **tremble** can mean to feel so afraid that you can't help shaking. *They trembled when they saw the lightning.*

shudder — To **shudder** can mean to feel so worried and afraid that you suddenly start to shake. *I shuddered at the thought of driving along the icy roads.*

lose your nerve — To **lose your nerve** means to be afraid to do what you set out to do. *The rider lost his nerve when he came to the high fence.*

panic — To **panic** means to feel sudden great terror, sometimes without obvious reason. *He panicked when the fire spread to the fence.*

freak out — To **freak out** means to **panic**. This is only suited to everyday language. *He freaked out when he found he had lost the money.*

similar words: **worry**

fearful   *adjective*

feeling or showing fear. *When I first went to the farm I was **fearful** of the cows.*

timid   **Timid** can mean easily frightened. *The timid kitten hid underneath the furniture.*

cowardly   **Cowardly** means lacking courage in a way that disgraces you. *The cowardly bully only hit people smaller than himself.*

gutless   **Gutless** means having no courage. It is very similar to **cowardly**. *He showed he was gutless when he wouldn't even climb a tree.*

spineless   **Spineless** can mean having no strength of character or courage. *The parachutist wouldn't jump until the others said he was spineless.*

---

similar words: **frightened, nervous**
contrasting words: **brave**

---

feeling   *noun*

a particular physical experience or mental state produced through one of your senses, such as touch or hearing. *There was a **feeling** of warmth in the air as summer approached.*

sensation   A **sensation** is a particular way you feel because of the working of one or more of your senses. *He had the sensation that someone was watching him.*

awareness   An **awareness** is a feeling or knowledge coming to you through your senses. *As she watched the waves beat against the rocks, she felt an awareness of the power of the ocean.*

perception   **Perception** is **awareness** or the gaining of knowledge through your senses. *His perception of a movement in the darkness outside worried him.*

impression   An **impression** can be a vague feeling or indication of something. *She had the impression that nobody was very interested in her story.*

sense   A **sense** can be any physical or mental feeling. *A sense of sadness came over us as we heard the news on the radio.*

female   *noun*

a woman or a girl. This is a formal word that often is used in discussions about medicine and biology. *"**Females** live longer than males," said the professor to her students.*

woman	A **woman** is a mature or adult female. *The two women had their own business selling computers.*
girl	A **girl** is a female who has not reached adulthood. *All of those girls are in grade six.*
young woman	A **young woman** is a female who is almost an adult, or a **girl** who behaves in a mature way. *The mayor called them brave young women for their role in last week's rescue.*
lady	**Lady** is a courteous term for a **woman**. It is used mainly on formal occasions. *Good morning, ladies and gentlemen.*

contrasting words: **male**

fickle   *adjective*

likely to change your mind or behavior. *He's such a **fickle** friend I never know when he is going to be pleasant to me.*

changeable	**Changeable** means likely to change or behave differently from one occasion to another. *He's so changeable that one day he'll smile at you and the next day he'll ignore you.*
flighty	**Flighty** means often changing your mind or feelings. *I'm so flighty today I can't make a decision.*
capricious	**Capricious** means likely to change your mind without any apparent good reason. *He's so capricious I can never be sure of him.*
mercurial	**Mercurial** means rapidly changing in mood. *Jan has such a mercurial nature she can be happy one moment then suddenly become very angry.*
temperamental	**Temperamental** means moody or **changeable** in your behavior. *We had to wait while the temperamental star decided what to wear.*

similar words: **unfaithful**
contrasting words: **reliable**

fidget *verb*

to move about restlessly and not be able to keep still. *I **fidgeted** nervously as I waited for my turn.*

squirm	To **squirm** means to move around uncomfortably or uneasily. *The performer squirmed with embarrassment when the audience caught the mistake.*
wriggle	To **wriggle** means to move or twist about because you are feeling uneasy. *We wriggled in our chairs until we heard our names called.*
writhe	To **writhe** means to twist and **squirm** because you are embarrassed or uneasy. *His loud comments that everyone could hear made me writhe.*
toss and turn	To **toss and turn** means to move about restlessly, not able to feel comfortable. *My frightening dreams made me toss and turn all night.*

fight *noun*

a violent struggle or contest. *Adrian's arm was bruised in the **fight**.*

brawl	A **brawl** is a noisy struggle or fight. *The argument developed into a brawl.*
fray	A **fray** is a noisy fight or quarrel. *When we joined the fray the whole playground was in an uproar.*
battle	A **battle** is a large-scale or serious fight. *A battle was fought between the two armies.*
combat	A **combat** is a fight or struggle. *Soldiers are trained for combat.*
skirmish	A **skirmish** is a small **battle**. *The armies met but it was only a skirmish.*

similar words: **conflict**

fight *verb*

to take part in a violent contest. *They **fought** over who owned the ball.*

struggle   To **struggle** means to fight with an enemy, usually without weapons. *He struggled with the thief.*

grapple   To **grapple** means to **struggle** or fight while gripping someone firmly. *The angry men grappled with each other.*

tussle   To **tussle** means to fight roughly. *The children tussled on the grass.*

scuffle   To **scuffle** means to **struggle** or fight in a confused way. *A few people in the crowd began to scuffle when the referee sent a player off.*

come to blows   To **come to blows** means to start fighting with someone. *They came to blows over whose turn it was to use the computer.*

find *verb*

to come upon something by chance or after a search. *He **found** his glasses under a chair.*

discover   To **discover** means to find, especially for the first time. *I discovered a new way home.*

locate   To **locate** means to find the place where something is. *At last I located the fault in the engine.*

unearth   To **unearth** can mean to find or uncover something by chance or after a search. *Mom unearthed a lot of old clothes that she thought she had thrown out.*

detect   To **detect** means to notice or find, especially after looking carefully. *She detected storm clouds on the horizon.*

trace   To **trace** can mean to find by looking in an orderly way. *I had to look through the index of the book to trace the passage I wanted.*

fine *adjective*

with the sun shining, or without rain. *I'm enjoying the **fine** weather that we are having at the moment.*

sunny   **Sunny** means having plenty of sunshine. *It was a lovely sunny day before the clouds came over.*

balmy   **Balmy** means fine or pleasant. *In the balmy spring weather they were often outdoors.*

mild   **Mild** can mean not cold, severe, or extreme. *Why don't we go for a walk tonight since the temperature is so mild?*

fair   **Fair** can mean bright and free from clouds as the sky can be. *The forecast was for fair weather all weekend.*

temperate   **Temperate** can mean having a moderate temperature or climate. *We've had a temperate October with very little frost.*

contrasting words: **wintry, cloudy, dreary**

finish *verb*

to bring something to a satisfactory final point. *I am trying to think of an interesting way to **finish** my story.*

end   To **end** is so similar to finish that you can usually use either. *The referee ended the game when two players were injured.*

close   To **close** can mean to finish something or shut it down completely or only for a short time. *She closed the meeting by thanking everyone who came.*

conclude   To **conclude** can mean to finish something or bring it to an end. *We will conclude the lesson by reading the poem.*

complete   To **complete** can mean to bring something to an end after having done everything necessary. *We completed our plans for the surprise party just in time.*

terminate   To **terminate** means to bring something to an end, often something that could have gone on further. *The severe injury to his leg terminated the dancer's career.*

contrasting words: **begin, initiate**

flat *adjective*

having a fairly regular surface that is at right angles to something that is upright. *The long, **flat** road stretched out in front of us.*

level	**Level** means having no part higher than any other part. *We found a level area of ground where we could pitch our tents.*
smooth	**Smooth** means having no bumps or lumps. *The road had only recently been built and was smooth compared with the rough track we had just left.*
even	**Even** can mean flat, **smooth**, or **level**. *A basketball court should have an even surface.*
horizontal	**Horizontal** means parallel or in line with the horizon. *When you are laying paving bricks, use a horizontal piece of string as a guide.*

flatter *verb*

to try to please someone by complimenting or praising them even if you don't mean it. *He **flattered** me so I would invite him to the party.*

sweet-talk	To **sweet-talk** means to persuade someone to do what you want by saying very nice things. It is more suited to everyday language. *If we sweet-talk them enough they might take us to the circus.*
cajole	To **cajole** means to persuade someone through flattery to do something. *I cajoled him into running the errand by telling him how fast he is.*
soft-soap	To **soft-soap** means to use very smooth, pleasant, or insincere words to persuade someone to do what you want. It is more suited to everyday language. *The salesperson soft-soaped the customers.*
butter up	To **butter up** means to flatter someone in an open and obvious way. It is only used in everyday language. *Let's butter up Mom so she'll give us money for ice cream.*

similar words: **praise**

flee *verb*

to run away, especially from danger. *They **fled** from the burning house.*

escape	To **escape** means to get away, especially from somewhere unpleasant or dangerous. *He escaped from prison.*
abscond	To **abscond** means to run away secretly. *The treasurer absconded with the funds.*
elope	To **elope** means to run away secretly to be married. *They didn't want a big wedding so they eloped.*
take to your heels	To **take to your heels** means to run away quickly. It is more suited to everyday language. *They took to their heels when the rain started.*
take off	To **take off** can mean to run away, especially so as to avoid being caught. It is more suited to everyday language. *I've got to take off before they find out I'm here.*

similar words: **leave**

flexible *adjective*

easily bent into a different shape. *I need some **flexible** wire to tie around this gate.*

pliable	**Pliable** means easily bent. It is similar to flexible. *Bamboo is a kind of pliable grass used for weaving baskets.*
supple	**Supple** means able to bend easily without breaking or being harmed. *An athlete needs a strong, supple body.*
malleable	**Malleable** means easily worked or moulded into a different shape. *Clay is a malleable material used by potters.*
floppy	**Floppy** means bending in a droopy way, often out of its usual shape. *My beach hat has a big, floppy brim.*

similar words: **elastic**
contrasting words: **hard**

flood *verb*

to supply someone with a great amount of anything. *Our neighbors **flooded** us with gifts when our house was burned down.*

swamp
To **swamp** can be so similar to flood you can usually choose either word. *Everyone swamped us with kindness and offers of help.*

overwhelm
To **overwhelm** can mean to come upon you so that you feel crushed. *Our feeling of helplessness almost overwhelmed us.*

inundate
To **inundate** can mean to load or heap someone with a very large amount of something. *Orders for the new dictionary inundated the publisher.*

smother
To **smother** can mean to surround someone with too much of something. *They smothered us with toys, books, and all kinds of presents.*

engulf
To **engulf** means to surround or swallow up someone with something. *Sorrow engulfed them after their tragedy.*

flourish *verb*

to grow strongly. *The apple tree we planted began to **flourish** after we gave it some fertilizer.*

bloom
To **bloom** can mean to flourish and produce flowers. *Our rose bush blooms in summer.*

flower
To **flower** means to grow flowers. It is usually used about plants, often those whose flowers form and develop into fruit or vegetables. *Our tomato plant flowered early this year.*

blossom
To **blossom** can mean to produce flowers. It is usually used about trees. *Many trees blossom in the spring.*

sprout
To **sprout** means to send up shoots as a seed does. *I planted some carrot seeds last week and they sprouted.*

germinate
To **germinate** means to begin to grow and send up shoots. *The seeds germinated and now we can see the little green shoots above the ground.*

similar words: **thrive**

flow   *verb*

to move along in, or as if in, a current. *The river **flows** out to the sea.*

stream   To **stream** means to flow steadily or continuously. *Tears streamed from his eyes.*

surge   To **surge** means to rush forward or upward in, or as if in, waves. *The heavy rain caused the river to rise and surge over its banks.*

spurt   To **spurt** means to flow suddenly. *Dirty water spurted out of the faucet when we turned it on.*

wash   To **wash** means to flow against or over something. *The waves washed against the sides of the boat.*

gush   To **gush** means to flow suddenly in large amounts. *The sea gushed through the hole the rock had made in the side of the ship.*

similar words: **drip**

fluctuate   *verb*

to change all the time. *He **fluctuated** between yes and no until I decided for him.*

waver   To **waver** means to be unsure or show doubt. *Even after he said yes he began to waver.*

vacillate   To **vacillate** means to be unsure or to put off making a decision. *He vacillated right up to the moment we got on the train.*

oscillate   To **oscillate** means to change your mind back and forth between two different opinions or ideas. *I oscillated between buying the toy and saving my money.*

blow hot and cold   To **blow hot and cold** means to keep on changing your mind. *She blew hot and cold on the idea of going winter camping.*

change your tune   To **change your tune** means to change your attitude or way of looking at something. *We changed our tune about joining in when we saw how much fun everyone was having.*

fluent *adjective*

able to speak easily. *My cousin is a **fluent** speaker of Italian.*

articulate   **Articulate** means able to say what you mean clearly. *Mary was chosen to explain the situation because she is very articulate.*

eloquent   **Eloquent** means able to speak in a flowing, expressive manner. *She was so eloquent that I was nearly crying by the time she finished.*

silver-tongued   **Silver-tongued** means able to speak so expressively that you can persuade people easily. *That auctioneer is successful because he is silver-tongued.*

smooth   **Smooth** can mean having a pleasant speaking manner, especially when insincere. *His smooth talk was flattering, but I wasn't fooled.*

slick   **Slick** can mean having a pleasant and clever way of talking, although insincere. It is similar to **smooth**. *He is a slick salesperson.*

contrasting words: **inarticulate**

fly *verb*

to move through the air with the help of wings, wind, or some other force. *Amyra watched the hawk **fly** high above the trees.*

flap   To **flap** can mean to fly by moving the wings up and down. *The colony of bats suddenly took off and flapped across the darkening sky.*

flutter   To **flutter** can mean to fly by moving the wings quickly up and down. *Brightly colored butterflies fluttered among the flowers.*

flit   To **flit** means to move lightly and quickly. *Dragonflies flitted through the long grass.*

soar   To **soar** means to fly upward. *The airplane soared through the clouds into the blue sky above.*

hover   To **hover** means to stay in one spot in the air as if hanging. *Bees hovered just above the flowers, collecting nectar.*

follow *verb*

to come or go after someone or something. *You go ahead and I'll **follow** you.*

pursue   To **pursue** means to follow in order to catch someone or something. *The police pursued the youths who had stolen a car.*

chase   To **chase** means to follow quickly in order to catch or overtake someone or something. *The cat chased the mouse.*

shadow   To **shadow** can mean to follow someone secretly. *The police officer shadowed the suspect to find out where he was going.*

tag along   To **tag along** can mean to follow someone closely, especially without being invited. *The dog tagged along with her wherever she went.*

track   To **track** can mean to follow, or hunt by following, the footprints or tracks of someone or something. *The photographer tracked the tiger through the jungle.*

similar words: **seek**

food *noun*

anything that can be eaten to keep your body alive and help it grow. *My favorite **food** is fruit.*

cuisine   **Cuisine** is food or a certain style of preparing food. This comes from a French word. *That restaurant serves Japanese cuisine.*

fare   **Fare** is the food provided by someone. *At home we have simple fare, like hearty stew.*

nourishment   **Nourishment** is food, especially the goodness of food. *The pony needs lots of nourishment to help it grow.*

provisions   **Provisions** are supplies of food. *They took provisions for ten days on their camping trip.*

victuals   **Victuals** are food or **provisions**. It is an old-fashioned word. *The stagecoach robbers asked for the travelers' money and victuals.*

similar words: **meal**

force *noun*

the ability to have a strong effect or influence on something, especially a physical one. *The **force** of the wind caused a lot of damage.*

power   **Power** can be so similar to force that you can usually use either. *Her easy leap over the fence showed the power of her legs.*

strength   **Strength** means the quality of being strong or having great **power** or effect. *The strength of the earthquake caused huge buildings to crumble.*

might   **Might** means force or **power**. *We felt the might of the tornado as it tore great trees out of the ground.*

muscle   **Muscle** can mean **strength** or force. It is usually used about people. *You need to put some muscle into chopping up that wood.*

vigor   **Vigor** means **strength** and energy, usually of a kind that helps you do something easily or happily. *We attacked the difficult job with vigor.*

force *verb*

to make someone do something, often by using threats or violence. *The thief **forced** them to hand over the money.*

compel   To **compel** means to make someone do something, usually because you are more powerful. *They can compel us to go to school.*

coerce   To **coerce** means to force someone to do something, usually with arguments or threats. *The armed thief coerced the shopkeeper to open the cash register.*

drive   To **drive** can mean to use a lot of effort to make yourself or someone else do something. *He always drives himself hard to get his work finished on time.*

bully   To **bully** means to hurt, frighten, or order around someone who is smaller and weaker than you. *She bullied us into agreeing with her.*

bulldoze   To **bulldoze** can mean to force someone to do something without caring whether the person wants to or not. It is more suited to everyday language. *You can't bulldoze us into going if we don't want to.*

similar words: **threaten**

forecast   *noun*

an opinion about or warning of what is going to happen in the future. *The forecast for tomorrow is rainy weather.*

prediction	A **prediction** is similar to a forecast and can often be used in the same way. *She made a prediction that the school team would win this year.*
prophecy	A **prophecy** is similar to a **prediction** or a **forecast**. *My prophecy is that you will win the election!*
prognosis	A **prognosis** is a doctor's opinion of how an illness will affect a patient. *Dr. Mack's prognosis was that my sister would recover.*
omen	An **omen** is a sign of something that might happen in the future. *She thought that breaking the mirror was an omen of bad luck.*
tip	A **tip** is a piece of useful information about something that might happen. *He gave us a tip that you might come.*

foreign   *adjective*

from a country other than your own. *We learned a foreign language to help us when we traveled.*

immigrant	**Immigrant** means moving to another country to live after leaving your own. *The immigrant family left France to live in Canada.*
alien	**Alien** means living in a country without being a citizen of it. *The alien residents decided to become citizens.*
ethnic	**Ethnic** means having to do with the customs, history, or language of a particular group of people. *We saw colorful costumes from all over the world during the display of ethnic dancing.*
imported	**Imported** means brought in from another country. *A lot of people buy imported cars from Japan.*
exotic	**Exotic** means foreign or not belonging naturally to your own country. *Many exotic animals can be seen at the zoo.*

forgive *verb*

to give up bad feelings against someone or any wish to punish them. *I will forgive you if you say you are sorry.*

excuse — To **excuse** can mean to overlook a wrongdoing or fault. *I'll excuse your bad behavior this time, but don't do it again.*

let off — To **let off** can mean to **excuse** and not punish someone. *I'll let you off this time, but never call him rude names again.*

pardon — To **pardon** can mean to forgive and not punish someone. This can be a legal word. *The judge pardoned the accused man and let him go free.*

spare — To **spare** means to forgive and not harm someone you have power over. *The king spared his treacherous cousin.*

clear — To **clear** can mean to free someone from blame. *The jury's verdict cleared her of guilt.*

contrasting words: **accuse**

formal *adjective*

following the proper and usual procedure. *They decided to have a **formal** wedding.*

established — **Established** means done in the customary or usual way. *This is the established method of applying for a passport.*

official — **Official** means properly approved or arranged. *We made an official request for a pedestrian crossing outside our school.*

ceremonial — **Ceremonial** means following the proper procedure used on an important occasion. *They wore their best clothes to the ceremonial opening of the new museum.*

ritual — **Ritual** means following the set procedure used on special or religious occasions. *Many peoples perform ritual dances to celebrate the harvest season.*

similar words: **legal**
contrasting words: **informal**

fragile *adjective*

very easily broken or damaged. *I held the **fragile** china cup very carefully and admired its fineness.*

delicate	**Delicate** means easily damaged or weakened. *I dusted everything on the shelf except the delicate glass animals.*
frail	**Frail** can mean easily destroyed or broken. *The frail lace curtain tore as we pulled it.*
brittle	**Brittle** means likely to break very easily. *We packed the brittle seashells in cotton wool to keep them safe.*
breakable	**Breakable** means easily fractured or broken into pieces. *I put away the pans while Dad dried all the breakable plates and glasses.*

frank *adjective*

open or free of pretending. *We had a **frank** discussion about our differences of opinion.*

direct	**Direct** can mean going straight to the point. *His direct question about the financial affairs of the committee embarrassed the treasurer.*
straightforward	**Straightforward** is so similar to **direct** that you can usually use either. *The straightforward directions you gave made it easy to find your house.*
candid	**Candid** means honest and sincere. *He gave a candid answer to the judge's question.*
forthright	**Forthright** means speaking your mind openly. *He is a very forthright person and sometimes hurts people's feelings without meaning to.*
genuine	**Genuine** can mean showing real, not pretended, feelings. *She was genuine in her praise of my painting.*

similar words: **honest**
contrasting words: **dishonest**

free   *adjective*

not confined, restricted, or limited. *In a democracy people are **free** to express their opinions.*

uninhibited	**Uninhibited** means behaving just as you like without worrying about what people think. *He was quite uninhibited about doing somersaults across the classroom floor.*
unconventional	**Unconventional** means not doing things according to the usual or accepted ways. *People were curious about his unconventional way of dressing.*
spontaneous	**Spontaneous** means doing things in a natural and sometimes unexpected way. *Her spontaneous smile pleased me because I didn't think she liked me.*
open	**Open** can mean doing things in a way that shows you are not hiding anything. *He was quite open about trying to take my place on the team.*
wild	**Wild** can mean not restrained or controlled. *Our parents had to stop the wild party.*

free   *verb*

to set at liberty or enable persons or animals to move or act as they wish. *I want to **free** my caged canary but it may not survive in the wild.*

release	To **release** means to set someone or something free, especially from being locked up. *The government decided to release the convicted man when new evidence was brought forward.*
liberate	To **liberate** means to set someone or something free, especially from some kind of oppression. *The army liberated the enemy-occupied town.*
emancipate	To **emancipate** means to set someone free from any kind of restraint. *Abraham Lincoln wanted to emancipate the slaves in the southern United States.*
rescue	To **rescue** means to free someone or something from a dangerous situation, being locked up, or evil. *We told the police our plan to rescue our kidnapped friend.*
deliver	To **deliver** can mean to save someone or set them free. *The rescuers delivered me from certain death as my raft neared the waterfall.*

contrasting words: **subdue, confine, capture**

friend   *noun*

someone you like and who likes you. *My **friend** and I spend our spare time together.*

playmate	A **playmate** is someone you play with. *The girl next door has been my playmate since we were little.*
pal	A **pal** is a good friend. This is more suited to everyday language. *Good pals do things for each other.*
companion	A **companion** is someone you go out with or travel with. *I like to go to movies with a companion.*
teammate	A **teammate** is someone who is on the same team as you. *My teammates and I were excited about winning the field hockey game.*
acquaintance	An **acquaintance** is someone you don't know very well. *He is only an acquaintance I talk to on the bus.*

similar words: **associate**
contrasting words: **enemy**

friendly   *adjective*

showing friendship or acting like a friend. *Everyone at the party was **friendly**.*

warm	**Warm** can mean kind and affectionate. *They gave us a warm welcome.*
neighborly	**Neighborly** means kind and friendly. *The Goh family gave us some neighborly help when we moved next door.*
outgoing	**Outgoing** means able to mix with people easily. *Outgoing people usually make friends quickly.*
sociable	**Sociable** means wanting to be with other people. *Sociable people are easy to talk to.*
genial	**Genial** means having a warm and friendly manner. *His genial behavior made us all feel relaxed.*

similar words: **agreeable, kind**
contrasting words: **unfriendly**

frighten   *verb*

to fill someone with fear. *The barking dog **frightened** the baby.*

scare   To **scare** means to fill someone with sudden fear. *The loud clap of thunder scared us all.*

alarm   To **alarm** means to frighten and make someone feel in danger. *The smell of smoke in the house alarmed me.*

petrify   To **petrify** can mean to make someone stiff with fear and unable to move. *The snarling dog petrified me.*

terrify   To **terrify** means to frighten someone very, very much. *The sound of someone trying to open the back door terrified me.*

terrorize   To **terrorize** can mean to cause someone to feel very great fear. *The gang terrorized the local shopkeepers and then demanded money from them.*

similar words: **shock, threaten**
contrasting words: **pacify**

frightened   *adjective*

showing or feeling fear. *The **frightened** children huddled together during the storm.*

scared   **Scared** means feeling sudden fear. *The scared boys ran away from the angry man.*

afraid   **Afraid** means frightened or feeling great fear. It is never used before the noun it is describing. *They were afraid of being punished.*

panicky   **Panicky** means feeling so frightened that you can't think clearly or act sensibly. *The Scout leader calmed the panicky boys who had seen the snake.*

alarmed   **Alarmed** means frightened suddenly. *They were alarmed when they realized they were late for class.*

petrified   **Petrified** can mean feeling so frightened that you can hardly move or do anything sensible. *The petrified children wished they hadn't gone into the haunted house.*

similar words: **nervous, fearful**
contrasting words: **calm, brave**

frightening *adjective*

causing you to feel afraid. *The car accident was a **frightening** experience.*

scary	**Scary** means causing fear or fright. It is more suited to everyday language. *Walking along the road at night is scary.*
creepy	**Creepy** means frightening or unpleasant. *We got a creepy feeling when we found the skull in the garden.*
hairy	**Hairy** can mean very frightening. It is more suited to everyday language. *It was a hairy drive down the mountain when the brakes failed.*
grim	**Grim** can mean having such a fierce or angry appearance that it makes you feel afraid. *When we saw his grim face, we knew we could expect no mercy.*
forbidding	**Forbidding** means dangerous and frightening. *The forbidding appearance of the cliff made us decide not to climb to the top.*

similar words: **horrible**

frisk *verb*

to leap around playfully, as a lamb or kitten does. *They **frisked** around joyfully in the warm, spring sunshine.*

dance	To **dance** can mean to move about quickly and lightly, usually because you are excited or happy. *We danced for joy when we heard the good news.*
caper	To **caper** means to jump or **dance** around. *They were so excited that they capered around the room.*
gambol	To **gambol** means to jump around in play. *Jean and Robert gamboled along the water's edge.*
skip	To **skip** means to jump lightly from one foot to the other. *He skipped up the path and through the open door.*
prance	To **prance** means to leap around gracefully. *The crowd cheered as the horses pranced into the ring.*

similar words: **jump**
contrasting words: **walk, limp, trudge**

frown *verb*

to wrinkle your forehead to show you are annoyed. *They stopped talking when she* *frowned at them and shook her head.*

glare To **glare** means to give a long fierce look to show that you are angry. *He glared at them when they rudely laughed at him.*

glower To **glower** means to look or stare in a bad-tempered way. *Paul just sat and glowered when he didn't get his own way.*

scowl To **scowl** means to have an angry look on your face. *I scowled when she said I couldn't go.*

pout To **pout** means to push out your lips in a sulky way. *He pouted until we gave in and let him play with us.*

contrasting words: **smile**

full *adjective*

filled up. *The milk carton was **full**.*

crowded **Crowded** means filled with people or objects. *We couldn't see our friends on the crowded footpath.*

packed **Packed** means so full that no more people or things can fit in. *The pianist played to a packed hall.*

bursting **Bursting** means very full, as if ready to break open. *The bag of apples was filled to the bursting point.*

laden **Laden** means having a full load or holding a lot. *We climbed the heavily laden apple tree to pick the fruit while it was ripe.*

crammed **Crammed** means stuffed tight. *Nothing else would fit into my crammed suitcase.*

contrasting words: **empty**

funny *adjective*

causing you to laugh. *We all enjoyed his **funny** stories.*

amusing	**Amusing** means causing laughter or smiles. *We watched the clown's dogs perform many amusing tricks.*
comical	**Comical** means funny, often because it is odd or unusual. *The clown's dogs were comical walking on their hind legs and wearing clothes.*
humorous	**Humorous** means funny or full of humor. *His humorous comment about being able to run as fast as a snail made us laugh.*
hilarious	**Hilarious** means very, very funny. *We had a hilarious time playing charades.*
droll	**Droll** means amusingly odd. *His droll sense of humor made us realize how funny the situation was.*

further *verb*

to help, improve, or develop something. *Regular training will **further** your chances of becoming a top swimmer.*

advance	To **advance** means to develop something and make it better. *Nuclear weapons do not advance the cause of world peace.*
promote	To **promote** means to further something so that it has a better rank or position. *They promoted the new drink by putting ads on television.*
facilitate	To **facilitate** means to help or further something by making things easier. *The open window facilitated the burglar's entry into the house.*
ease	To **ease** means to help something by taking away any problems or difficulties. *Talks between the United States and the Soviet Union eased the tension between the two nations.*

similar words: **help**
contrasting words: **hinder, block**

future *adjective*

having to do with, or happening in, the time that has not yet come. *Our future plans are to rent a boat for the holidays.*

prospective   **Prospective** means happening in the future, especially something pleasant. *We are looking forward to our prospective holiday.*

next   **Next** can mean immediately following in time. *At last we could say that our vacation would begin the next day.*

imminent   **Imminent** means likely to happen at any moment. *We said good-bye and boarded the plane when we knew its departure was imminent.*

impending   **Impending** means near at hand or **imminent**. *Our departure was delayed by the impending arrival of another plane.*

contrasting words: **past**

gasp *verb*

to struggle for breath with your mouth open. *The people who were trapped in the smoke-filled room were gasping for air.*

pant   To **pant** means to breathe hard and quickly because of effort or emotion. *All the runners were panting after the relay.*

wheeze   To **wheeze** means to breath with difficulty, making a whistling sound. *My brother has to stay home from school when he wheezes with asthma.*

puff   To **puff** means to breathe quickly, especially after vigorous exercise. *You shouldn't be puffing after such a short run.*

blow   To **blow** can mean to produce a strong current of air with your mouth. *Take a long, deep breath, then blow out slowly.*

heave   To **heave** can mean to breathe heavily and noisily, with a great effort. *The exhausted swimmer heaved and gasped for air after the long race.*

gather   *verb*

to bring together. *I **gathered** my belongings and put them in a bag.*

collect
To **collect** means to gather things together, usually in order to keep examples of them for a particular reason. *She collects stamps.*

accumulate
To **accumulate** means to bring something together or heap it up in a large quantity. *He has accumulated a great deal of money.*

amass
To **amass** means to gather things together for yourself. *By the end of her life the successful businesswoman had amassed a large fortune.*

pile up
To **pile up** means to bring things together into a pile. *We piled the junk up outside the house ready for the garbage collection.*

rake in
To **rake in** means to gather or **collect** a lot of something. It is more suited to everyday language. *They raked in donations during the telethon for the new hospital.*

similar words: **store**
contrasting words: **scatter**

gaudy   *adjective*

very bright or ornate in order to attract attention. *My **gaudy** towel is very easy to find on the crowded beach.*

showy
Showy means attracting attention in a very obvious way. *The peacock's brightly colored tail is very showy.*

flashy
Flashy means bright and **showy**. *We went for a ride in the flashy red sports car.*

loud
Loud can mean very brightly colored, usually in an unpleasant way. *I thought his new tie was too loud.*

tawdry
Tawdry means cheap and gaudy. *She said the glass beads I bought at the fair were too tawdry to wear.*

tacky
Tacky means **showy** or gaudy in a way that you think is in bad taste. It is more suited to everyday language. *I thought the pink and yellow plastic roses were tacky.*

similar words: **colorful, spectacular**
contrasting words: **drab, simple**

generous *adjective*

unselfish or ready to give money or gifts. *A **generous** woman has given a lot of new books to our library.*

liberal	**Liberal** is very similar to generous. *We were glad to receive her liberal gift.*
lavish	**Lavish** means very generous in giving. *He is lavish with his money.*
hospitable	**Hospitable** means being very welcoming and generous to strangers or your guests. *Our hospitable neighbors invited us to dinner the day we moved to our new house.*
charitable	**Charitable** means giving money or help to people who need it. *Our school collects money for charitable organizations.*
magnanimous	**Magnanimous** means unselfish and generous in a noble way. *She is too magnanimous to hold a grudge.*

similar words: **kind**
contrasting words: **mean, selfish**

genuine *adjective*

true or real. *She has a **genuine** antique grandfather clock.*

authentic	**Authentic** means genuine or known to be what it claims to be. *We saw an authentic Egyptian mummy at the museum.*
legitimate	**Legitimate** can mean true or reasonable. *He had a legitimate excuse for being late.*
factual	**Factual** means based on facts. *This book gives a factual account of life in China.*
proven	**Proven** means shown to be true or right. *It is a proven fact that worn car tires cause accidents.*

similar words: **actual, true**
contrasting words: **fake**

get *verb*

to obtain. *I **got** high marks on my math exam.*

gain   To **gain** means to get or obtain, usually something you desire. *You will gain more confidence if you practice making the speech.*

acquire   To **acquire** can mean to get as your own, usually through your own action or effort. It is a more formal word. *She acquired a wonderful tan during the summer.*

win   To **win** can mean to get something by making a special effort. *She won fame as a result of her courageous behavior during the marathon.*

receive   To **receive** can mean to get something or have it given to you. *He received some good books for his birthday.*

procure   To **procure** means to get or obtain, especially using a lot of care or effort. *The detective procured all the evidence he needed to arrest the thief.*

similar words: **grab, buy**
contrasting words: **give**

ghost *noun*

the spirit of someone who has died, imagined as visiting living people. *I screamed because I thought the white shape in the corner was a **ghost**.*

specter   **Specter** is so similar to ghost that you can usually use either. *Shakespeare's play* Hamlet *is about a man who is visited by the specter of his father.*

phantom   A **phantom** is a ghost or a ghostly appearance. *She wrote a story about the phantom that haunted the old house.*

spook   A **spook** is a ghost. It is more suited to everyday language. *The attic is supposed to be full of spooks.*

apparition   An **apparition** is something, such as a ghost, that appears in an out-of-the-ordinary way. *He fainted because he said he saw an apparition of a very old man in the mirror.*

wraith   A **wraith** is the ghostlike appearance of a living person, supposed to be seen just before that person's death. *Some people thought they saw the wraith of the dying king in the palace grounds.*

gift *noun*

something that is given to you. *A skateboard was my favorite birthday* **gift**.

present — **Present** is so similar to gift that you can usually use either. *I always give birthday presents to my brothers and sisters.*

legacy — A **legacy** is a gift of money or property made after someone's death through their will. *He left her a legacy of $5000 as well as his house.*

donation — A **donation** is a gift, usually of money. *We made a donation to the fund for freedom from hunger.*

contribution — A **contribution** is a **donation** or a gift of money. *Our family made a contribution to the appeal for aid to the drought victims.*

allowance — An **allowance** is a certain amount of money given to someone regularly, usually by parents to their children. *I saved my allowance for a new baseball glove.*

give *verb*

to hand something over freely. *They will* **give** *Karen a present before she moves.*

donate — To **donate** means to give something as a gift. *We donated some money to the Red Cross.*

present — To **present** means to give, especially in a formal way. *The mayor presented the prizes.*

award — To **award** means to give somebody something for merit or achievement. *The school awards prizes for pupils who do very well in a subject.*

confer — To **confer** means to give something to somebody as a gift, favor, or honor. *The fire chief conferred a medal for bravery on the boy.*

grant — To **grant** means to give somebody something that has been requested. *The farmer granted them permission to hike through his fields.*

contrasting words: **take, get**

give in   *verb*

to admit that you are defeated. *Do you **give in** now that you know you can't win?*

yield   To **yield** means to give in because you are powerless to go on. *The country yielded to the invader.*

surrender   To **surrender** means to give yourself up into someone else's power. *They surrendered when they ran out of bullets.*

capitulate   To **capitulate** means to give in without making any terms or conditions. *They capitulated after only a short battle.*

submit   To **submit** means to give in in obedience. *He finally submitted to the orders.*

succumb   To **succumb** means to give in to a stronger force. *In the end she succumbed to temptation and bought a milkshake.*

---

contrasting words: **resist**

---

glad   *adjective*

happy about something. *I am **glad** that you have arrived safely.*

pleased   **Pleased** means happy or satisfied with something. *We are pleased that you are working hard.*

delighted   **Delighted** means very glad. *We are delighted that the holidays are starting soon.*

thrilled   **Thrilled** means so glad that you feel excited. *Her face had a thrilled expression when she heard they were going to the circus.*

tickled pink   **Tickled pink** means greatly **pleased** or amused. It is more suited to everyday language. *She was tickled pink by his compliments.*

---

similar words: **happy, joyful, satisfied**
contrasting words: **sad, miserable, glum, angry, annoyed**

---

glue *noun*

a substance used to stick things together. *Buy a special hobby **glue** to stick the pieces of your model plane together.*

paste

Paste is a mixture of flour and water used for sticking paper onto another surface. *Make up some paste so you can put these pictures in your scrapbook.*

adhesive

An **adhesive** is any substance used for sticking things together. *What's the best adhesive for mending this broken chair leg?*

cement

Cement is a soft substance that hardens or sets to join or bind things together very strongly. *I'll need some special cement to stick these broken tiles back together.*

mortar

Mortar is the special mixture used for joining bricks together. *If you don't use enough mortar the bricks won't stick firmly and the wall will fall down.*

glum *adjective*

unhappy or depressed. *After trying so hard he was really **glum** when he failed.*

moody

Moody means angry or unhappy. *She was moody when her parents were away on vacation.*

sullen

Sullen means angry, silent, and ill-mannered. *He is sullen because he was accused of cheating.*

surly

Surly means unfriendly and bad-tempered. *Nobody was friendly to him because of his surly manner.*

morose

Morose means bad-tempered or unfriendly because you are unhappy. *It was hard for him not to be morose when everything was going wrong.*

gloomy

Gloomy can mean feeling unhappy or depressed. *I'm gloomy today because our picnic was rained out.*

similar words: **sad, miserable**
contrasting words: **happy, joyful, glad**

go   *verb*

to move away from or toward something or someplace. *Alex **goes** to the dentist twice a year.*

depart	**Depart** means to go away or leave. *The train departs from Grand Central Station at 1:00 p.m.*
leave	**Leave** is so similar to **depart** that you can usually use either. *When did you leave the party?*
advance	**Advance** means to move forward, often in a steady, orderly way. *Due to difficult conditions, the troops advanced slowly.*
proceed	**Proceed** means to go ahead with or continue. *After looking both ways, Chris proceeded through the intersection.*

good   *adjective*

of a high standard or worthy of praise. *This is a **good** piece of work.*

satisfactory	**Satisfactory** means good enough to meet your requirements. *He gave a satisfactory answer.*
fine	**Fine** can mean very good or of a high quality. *He's a fine musician.*
commendable	**Commendable** means worthy of praise. *They held a party for Donna to thank her for her commendable work.*
all right	**All right** means **satisfactory**. *She did an all right job for us in very demanding circumstances.*
neat	**Neat** means **fine** or pleasing. It is more suited to everyday language. *That was a neat party last night!*

similar words: **great, excellent, nice, best**
contrasting words: **bad, nasty**

gossip   *noun*

silly or unkind chatter about another person's business. *I don't listen to **gossip** because it is often harmful or untrue.*

talk
: **Talk** can be so similar to gossip that you can usually use either word. *Have you heard the talk about Tessa's argument with Bruce?*

rumor
: A **rumor** is a story that is widely spread, without any proof as to the facts. *Are the rumors true about your leaving school next year?*

hearsay
: **Hearsay** is so similar to **rumor** that you can usually use either word. *It's just hearsay that they are going to sell their farm.*

whisper
: A **whisper** can mean a **rumor** or private information. *I heard a whisper that you are planning a surprise party.*

---

similar words: **information**

---

grab   *verb*

to take something suddenly. *Don't **grab** the ball before it's your turn.*

seize
: To **seize** means to take hold of something suddenly or by force. *She seized her brother to keep him from running across the busy street.*

snatch
: To **snatch** means to take hold of something suddenly or rudely. *The thief snatched my purse as I walked down the crowded street.*

snap up
: To **snap up** means to grab something quickly. *The shoppers snapped up the bargains at the department store sales.*

nab
: To **nab** means to catch or **seize** someone suddenly. It is more suited to everyday language. *My father nabbed me as I was trying to sneak off to play.*

nail
: To **nail** can mean to catch or **seize** someone, usually a criminal. It is more suited to everyday language. *"We've nailed you!" said the police as they burst into the criminals' hide-out.*

---

similar words: **take, capture**

---

grade   *noun*

a particular position on a scale of standing, status, quality, or value. *She earned the highest **grade** on the science test.*

step   A **step** can be a particular position or degree on a scale. *We must all understand the first step before we can learn anything new.*

stage   A **stage** is a single **step** on a scale or in a particular process. *Now we are ready to go on to the next stage.*

level   A **level** is one person's position on a scale compared with other people's positions. *She was promoted to a higher level of the company because of her good work.*

rank   A **rank** can be an official position or grade. *He reached the rank of colonel before the war ended.*

class   **Class** can be someone's place in society, judged by their work, possessions, or family. *In the Depression, factories closed down and many members of the working class were unemployed.*

grand   *adjective*

fine, splendid, or important. *The royal wedding made a **grand** spectacle.*

lofty   **Lofty** can mean very noble or high in character. *I wish everyone had her lofty ideals.*

dignified   **Dignified** means showing nobleness of mind or character. *Her dignified conduct when she lost the race inspired us.*

magnificent   **Magnificent** means very fine or impressive. *There is a magnificent view of the mountains from this park.*

majestic   **Majestic** can mean great or impressive in appearance. *The majestic view left them speechless.*

stately   **Stately** means looking formal, grand, or **majestic**. *The stately tree was tall and beautiful and very old.*

similar words: **important, distinguished**
contrasting words: **humble**

grateful   *adjective*

feeling or showing gratitude or thanks. *Mom said she was **grateful** that I cooked dinner when she was sick.*

thankful
Thankful means feeling or showing thanks to someone who has been kind. It is very similar to grateful. *I was thankful when Tessa offered to drive me home when it was raining.*

appreciative
Appreciative means showing or feeling appreciation or gratitude. *Colin was most appreciative of Ian's offer to help him paint the house.*

obliged
Obliged means feeling under an obligation because of a kindness that has been shown. *I am obliged to you for lending me your car while mine is being repaired.*

indebted
Indebted means feeling that you owe a great debt of gratitude for help, a favor, or the like. *I am indebted to you for looking after the baby when I had to go to work.*

beholden
Beholden means bound to feel grateful or **indebted**. It is a very old-fashioned word. *Pam never accepts help because she hates to be beholden to anybody.*

contrasting words: **ungrateful**

gray   *adjective*

of a color between black and white. *We looked at the **gray** sky and knew there would be a storm.*

charcoal
Charcoal means of a very dark gray that is almost black. *After the forest fire the tree trunks had turned a charcoal color.*

slate
Slate means of a dull, dark bluish-gray. *The paint we chose was a slate color to match the tiles on the roof.*

silver
Silver means of a shiny whitish-gray color. *The snail left a silver trail on the grass.*

steel
Steel means of a dark bluish-gray color with a metallic look. *Our new car is a shiny steel color.*

great *adjective*

very good or fine. When **great** is used this way it is more suited to everyday language. *We had a **great** time at the party.*

splendid	**Splendid** means extremely good. *The orchestra gave a splendid performance.*
superb	**Superb** is so similar to **splendid** that you can usually use either. *The meal was superb.*
super	**Super** means extremely good or pleasing. It is more suited to everyday language. *We had a super holiday at the beach.*
first-rate	**First-rate** means very good or outstanding. It is more suited to everyday language. *She got a high mark for her first-rate work.*

similar words: **good, excellent, best, superior**
contrasting words: **bad, nasty**

greedy *adjective*

wanting an unreasonable amount of something, especially food or money. *Those **greedy** children ate all my chocolates.*

avaricious	**Avaricious** means greedy for money. *The avaricious boss underpaid his workers.*
grasping	**Grasping** means wanting much more than you are entitled to. *The grasping landlord said he was going to raise the rent.*
rapacious	**Rapacious** means taking things from other people in a greedy and violent way. *The rapacious outlaw robbed the villagers and burned their houses.*
insatiable	**Insatiable** means never being satisfied with what you have. *The politician had an insatiable desire for power.*
voracious	**Voracious** means eager or greedy for something, especially food. *I have a voracious appetite when I come home from school.*

contrasting words: **satisfied**

green *adjective*

of the color of growing leaves and grass. *Sheep and cattle grazed along the lush,* ***green*** *banks of the river.*

emerald	**Emerald** means having a clear, bright green color. *The dewy emerald fields glistened in the sun.*
lime	**Lime** means having a greenish-yellow color. *We mixed some yellow and green together to make a lime paint for the kitchen.*
hazel	**Hazel** means having a greenish-brown color. *He stared at me through his large, hazel eyes.*
olive	**Olive** means having a dull brownish-green color. *We recognized the army trucks by their olive color.*
turquoise	**Turquoise** means having a bright greenish-blue color. *The peacock displayed the beautiful turquoise feathers in his tail.*

grieve *verb*

to feel very sad because you have suffered some sorrow. *I* ***grieved*** *for our broken friendship.*

mourn	To **mourn** can mean to grieve or express sorrow because someone you love has died. *He mourned for a long time after his wife died.*
lament	To **lament** means to feel or express deep sorrow or grief. *She lamented over the disappearance of her new kitten.*
pine away	To **pine away** means to become sick from grief and longing. *She has been pining away since her pet dog died.*
brood	To **brood** can mean to worry or think moodily about something. *He brooded for a long time after they said such hurtful things to him.*
mope	To **mope** means to be sunk in an unhappy mood. *He has moped ever since he was dropped from the team.*

contrasting words: **rejoice**

groove   *noun*

a long narrow cut or hollow, especially one made by a tool. *There is a groove in my desk for my pencils.*

rut	A **rut** is a groove made in the ground. *The whirling wheels of the car made deep ruts in the mud.*
furrow	A **furrow** is a groove, especially one made in the earth by a plough. *The farmer planted wheat in the furrows.*
ditch	A **ditch** is a long narrow hollow dug in the earth. *I fell off my bicycle into the muddy ditch by the side of the road.*
channel	A **channel** can be a **ditch** dug for water to flow through. *Farmers pump water from irrigation channels to water their crops.*
trench	A **trench** is a deep **ditch,** especially one dug by soldiers to protect themselves from the enemy. *The soldiers in the trenches fired at the approaching enemy.*

group   *noun*

a number of people connected in some way and sometimes gathered together. *He has a large group of friends.*

bunch	A **bunch** can be a group of people. It is more suited to everyday language. *She is one of our bunch.*
gang	A **gang** is a group of people acting together. *They were robbed by a gang of outlaws.*
band	A **band** is a group of people organized to act together. It is similar to **gang**. *Robin Hood had a band of merry men.*
troop	A **troop** is an organized group of people. It is similar to both **gang** and **band**. *Franca and a troop of her friends went camping.*
huddle	A **huddle** can be a small group of people crowded together to discuss something in private. *The huddle of friends whispered together in a corner.*

similar words: **crowd, club**

grumpy *adjective*

bad-tempered. *I'm always **grumpy** when I wake up in the mornings.*

cross	**Cross** means annoyed or slightly angry about something. *I'm cross if someone else is in the bathroom when I want to use it.*
irritable	**Irritable** means easily annoyed. *I'm irritable until I've eaten my breakfast.*
snappy	**Snappy** can mean speaking angrily or sharply. *The shopkeeper was snappy with the customer who was always complaining.*
crotchety	**Crotchety** means bad-tempered or **irritable**. *My crotchety neighbor wouldn't let me go in to get my ball when it went over the fence.*
petulant	**Petulant** means showing impatient annoyance, especially over something unimportant. *The petulant student threw the pen on the floor when it wouldn't write.*

similar words: **annoyed, touchy, angry**
contrasting words: **happy**

halt *noun*

a stop, especially a temporary one. *The union leaders called a **halt** to the work.*

stoppage	A **stoppage** is a situation or time during which everything has stopped. *Cargo could not be unloaded from the ships because of the stoppage at the wharf.*
stalemate	A **stalemate** is a situation where no progress can be made. *The management and the unions have reached a stalemate in the dispute.*
deadlock	A **deadlock** is the point in an argument when neither side will give way. *Brian and Jenny have reached a deadlock over who is going to use the car tonight.*
standstill	A **standstill** is a **stoppage**, especially of work or movement. *Work came to a standstill in the factory when the power went off.*

similar words: **end**
contrasting words: **start**

happen   *verb*

to take place. *The accident **happened** just as we were leaving home.*

occur

To **occur** is so similar to happen that you can usually use either word. *The incident occurred yesterday.*

arise

To **arise** means to happen or to come into being. *The problem arose when they couldn't find the map showing them how to get there.*

transpire

To **transpire** can mean to happen or take place. *It transpired that the goat had eaten the map.*

come about

To **come about** means to **occur** or to happen in the due course of time. *It came about that after a hundred years a prince kissed Sleeping Beauty and she awoke from her long sleep.*

fall

To **fall** can mean to happen or take place. *My birthday falls on a Monday this year.*

happiness   *noun*

pleasure, contentment, or gladness. *The children's **happiness** was complete when they were given a puppy.*

merriment

Merriment is happiness mixed with laughter. *The house was filled with sounds of merriment.*

mirth

Mirth is amusement and laughter, such as is caused by something silly. *The audience rocked with mirth at the clowns' tricks.*

high spirits

High spirits is a very happy mood. *We went to the party in high spirits.*

joy

Joy is a strong feeling of pleasure or happiness. *The good news filled us with joy.*

glee

Glee is a feeling of **joy**. *We set out for the beach with glee.*

contrasting words: **misery**

happy   *adjective*

delighted, pleased, or glad about something. *I was very **happy** when he invited me to the concert.*

cheerful   **Cheerful** means happy and full of high spirits. *She is a cheerful person to be with.*

merry   **Merry** means happy and laughing. *We were a merry group as we hiked along.*

jolly   **Jolly** means good-humored and full of fun. *The bus driver was jolly and made us laugh a lot.*

blithe   **Blithe** means happy or **cheerful**. *He was blithe and carefree as he walked along in the sunshine.*

gleeful   **Gleeful** means very happy or full of joy. *They were gleeful at the thought of the long summer holidays.*

similar words: **joyful, glad**
contrasting words: **sad, miserable, glum, solemn**

hard   *adjective*

solid and not able to be pushed out of shape. *Rocks and wood are **hard**.*

stiff   **Stiff** means hard or not easily bent. *The stiff collar of my new shirt was uncomfortable.*

firm   **Firm** means solid, hard, or **stiff**. *I like to sleep on a firm mattress.*

rigid   **Rigid** means not able to be bent or moved. *The tent pole was rigid and withstood the strong winds of the storm.*

tough   **Tough** means not easily broken or cut. *The vines growing in the forest were so tough that we couldn't hack our way through them.*

contrasting words: **soft, flexible, elastic**

harden *verb*

to make or become solid or firm to the touch. *The icing on the cake had to* ***harden*** *before we could cut it.*

set	To **set** means to become hard or solid. *The gelatin had set in time for dinner.*
stiffen	To **stiffen** means to become so hard and firm that it is not easily bent. *It's so cold that my mittens have stiffened with ice.*
solidify	To **solidify** means to become firm or solid right through. *The molten metal solidified as it cooled.*
petrify	To **petrify** can mean to become changed into stone or something like stone. *It took millions of years for the dinosaur's skeleton to petrify.*
freeze	To **freeze** can mean to become hard by being exposed to very low temperatures. *I hope the lake freezes well enough to skate on.*

contrasting words: **soften**

hardy *adjective*

able to stand up to rough treatment or conditions. *Only a* ***hardy*** *cyclist would be able to ride up that hill.*

durable	**Durable** means lasting for a long time. *Winter boots should be made of durable material.*
sturdy	**Sturdy** means strong and able to stand up to rough use. *Use this sturdy spade.*
tough	**Tough** can mean not easily broken or damaged by bad conditions. *They tied up the boat with a tough rope.*
heavy-duty	**Heavy-duty** means strong and designed for heavy use. *A heavy-duty battery will last you much longer than an ordinary one.*
rugged	**Rugged** can mean hardy and strong in your body. *We admired the rugged mountain climber.*

similar words: **strong**
contrasting words: **weak**

hate   *verb*

to regard something or someone with strong dislike. *I **hate** washing the dishes.*

detest   To **detest** means to dislike something or someone intensely. *I detest people who break their promises.*

loathe   To **loathe** means to feel strong opposition, hatred, or distaste for something or someone. *I loathe having to tidy my room.*

despise   To **despise** means to look down on someone or something, especially with hate or scorn. *They despised him for not daring to admit his mistakes.*

abhor   To **abhor** means to think of something or someone with disgust and hatred. *I abhor cruelty to animals.*

abominate   To **abominate** means to regard something or someone with great hate or disgust. It is very similar to **abhor**. *I abominate irresponsible manufacturers who pollute our environment.*

contrasting words: **love, worship**

healthy   *adjective*

free from disease or sickness. ***Healthy** children have lots of energy.*

well   **Well** means in good health. *Now that I've had some time off, I'm well again.*

fine   **Fine** is so similar to **well** that you can usually use either. *He was in the hospital last week but is fine now.*

sound   **Sound** means healthy or in good condition. *Even though Grandpa is 96 his heart is sound.*

fit   **Fit** can mean strong and healthy. *She is very fit after the weekend training camp.*

robust   **Robust** means strong, healthy, and hardy. *They chose only the most robust mountaineers to climb Mt. Everest.*

contrasting words: **sick**

heap *noun*

a group of things lying one on top of another. *My favorite socks were somewhere in the **heap** of laundry.*

pile	A **pile** can be a group of things lying one on top of another in a fairly orderly way. *He carried the pile of dirty dishes into the kitchen.*
stack	A **stack** is an orderly **pile** of things. *She took a large log off the stack of firewood.*
mound	A **mound** is a heap of earth or stones. *Vinnie planted the potatoes in a mound of soil.*
levee	A **levee** is a **mound** of earth built beside a river to keep it from overflowing. *They built a levee to protect their homes from the flood.*
rampart	A **rampart** is a wide **mound** of earth built around a fort to protect it. *We were safe because the attacking soldiers couldn't climb over the ramparts.*

heavy *adjective*

hard to lift or carry. *The piano was so **heavy** that three people had to move it for us.*

massive	**Massive** means large and extremely heavy. *They blasted the massive boulder with dynamite and took away the pieces in trucks.*
hefty	**Hefty** means heavy. It is more suited to everyday language. *Those books are a hefty load for you to carry.*
solid	**Solid** can mean heavy or not flimsy, slight, or light. *She's a solid child and I can't carry her now.*
leaden	**Leaden** means heavy like the metal lead. *After weightlifting, her arms felt so leaden she could hardly lift them.*
ponderous	**Ponderous** means large and heavy. *He's a ponderous dog and can't move quickly.*

similar words: **stocky**
contrasting words: **light**

help   *noun*

support, or something that makes what you have to do easier. *Keep hanging on because **help** is on its way.*

assistance	**Assistance** is support or help. *Sometimes I ask for my older sister's assistance when I do my homework.*
aid	**Aid** is so similar to help and **assistance** that you can usually use any one of these. *The government sends aid to the developing countries of the world.*
relief	**Relief** can be freedom or release from pain, unhappiness, or worry. *During the crisis, volunteers provided some relief for the overworked nurses.*
charity	**Charity** can be help or **aid** given to people who need it. *Our mayor thanked the government for the charity our town was given after the flood.*
backing	**Backing** means support of any kind, such as money made available to help a project. *Is the sportswear company going to give you their backing?*

help   *verb*

to do something with someone so that it is done more easily. *Will you **help** me with my homework, please?*

assist	To **assist** means to help someone do something, often in a time of trouble. *She assisted me when I lost my job.*
aid	To **aid** means to help or to make something easier for someone. *Studying will aid you in your exams.*
oblige	To **oblige** means to help by doing someone a favor. *Please oblige me by giving me a lift home.*
support	To **support** means to give help, strength, or courage to someone. *He supported her with kindness and advice when she failed the exam.*
nurse	To **nurse** can mean to help something or someone by careful tending. *She nursed the seedlings until they were big enough to plant in the garden.*

similar words: **befriend, further**
contrasting words: **hinder**

helper   *noun*

someone who does something with you so that it is done more easily. *I need three* **helpers** *to set out the paints.*

assistant   An **assistant** is someone who helps another person, especially one in a more important position or job. *The scientist hired an assistant to do some of the experiments.*

aide   An **aide** is a personal helper or **assistant**, especially to an important official such as an army officer or a politician. *The general's aide handed out the new orders.*

supporter   A **supporter** is someone who pledges aid to another person. *During her victory speech, the politician thanked her loyal supporters.*

deputy   A **deputy** is a person chosen to assist or act for another person. *We elected a deputy to take over for the president of our club when she was away.*

attendant   An **attendant** is someone who helps or looks after someone else. *The attendant at the door will show you to your seats.*

similar words: **associate, friend, clerk**

helpful   *adjective*

willing to help or support someone. *Thanks for being so* **helpful** *and clearing the table.*

useful   **Useful** means of use or service to someone or something. *Tidying your bedroom would be a useful thing to do.*

cooperative   **Cooperative** means showing a desire to be helpful. *He was cooperative and did the chores the first time he was asked.*

obliging   **Obliging** means willing to do someone a favor or be of service. *The salesperson was most obliging and showed us lots of shoes to choose from.*

accommodating   **Accommodating** means helpful and easy to deal with. *The bank teller was most accommodating when I opened my account.*

supportive   **Supportive** means giving help, strength, and encouragement to someone else. *My friends were very supportive when I was unhappy.*

hermit   *noun*

someone who lives alone and keeps away from other people. *The **hermit** came out of the forest once a month for his supplies.*

recluse A **recluse** is someone who lives alone and doesn't mix with other people. *The artist became a recluse so that no one could interrupt her work.*

loner A **loner** is someone who doesn't like being with other people. *He was such a loner that no one remembered to invite him to their parties.*

introvert An **introvert** is someone who is mainly interested in their own thoughts and feelings. *She did not make many friends because she was an introvert.*

monk A **monk** is a member of a religious group of men living apart from the rest of the world. *The monks lived in the monastery and spent their days praying and working in the grounds.*

hide   *verb*

to keep something from being seen or discovered. *Pirates used to **hide** their treasure by burying it.*

conceal To **conceal** means to hide something or keep it out of sight. *She concealed the present at the top of her cupboard.*

cover To **cover** can mean to put something on or over a thing in order to hide it. *She covered her mouth with her hand when she yawned.*

disguise To **disguise** means to try to hide your true identity, or the way something really is by changing your appearance, or making it seem different. *I disguised myself by wearing a wig. She tried to disguise her anger by smiling sweetly.*

mask To **mask** means to hide or **disguise** something. *We laughed and joked to mask our disappointment at not being chosen for the team.*

camouflage To **camouflage** can mean to do something that you hope will hide or **disguise** the way things really are. *He had left his radio on to camouflage his absence from the room.*

contrasting words: **show, reveal**

high-pitched *adjective*

played, sung, or spoken at a high pitch of sound. *It annoys me when my brother's digital watch makes a **high-pitched** beep every hour.*

shrill	**Shrill** means loud and high-pitched. *We could hear the shrill yapping of the playful puppy.*
high	**High** can mean sharp in sound. *I can't sing the very high notes in that song.*
treble	**Treble** means of the highest pitch or range when referring to a voice part, singer, or instrument. *I'll play the treble recorder and you can play the alto one.*
soprano	**Soprano** means of the range of notes that can be sung by a woman or boy with a high voice. *She sang in the soprano section of the choir.*
falsetto	**Falsetto** means very high-pitched. *The man used a falsetto voice when he pretended to make the puppet speak.*

hinder *verb*

to slow down something or make it difficult. *My sore leg **hindered** my efforts to run.*

hamper	To **hamper** means to hold back or hinder something or someone. *The loose wheel hampered his progress in the bike race.*
frustrate	To **frustrate** means to hinder or stop someone or something by putting difficulties in the way. *We wanted to arrive early but the traffic jam frustrated us.*
retard	To **retard** means to hinder something or someone, slowing it down. *The muddy road retarded our progress.*
impede	To **impede** means to slow down or block the way of something or someone. *The road construction impeded the traffic.*
inhibit	To **inhibit** means to hold back or control something or someone. *Black plastic spread over your garden should inhibit the growth of weeds.*

similar words: **prevent, block, interrupt**
contrasting words: **further, help**

hint *verb*

to make an indirect suggestion. *She **hinted** she'd like to come to my party.*

suggest To **suggest** can mean to hint, or give the idea of something indirectly. *I think his appearance suggests a serious illness.*

insinuate To **insinuate** means to **suggest** something unpleasant without saying so outright. *I was angry when he insinuated I had cheated.*

imply To **imply** means to **suggest** something without actually stating it. *My parents implied that my present was hidden in their closet, but I couldn't be sure.*

allude to To **allude to** means to refer casually to something. *He alluded to the book he had just read.*

hit *verb*

to give a hard blow to someone or something. *He **hit** the nail with a hammer.*

strike To **strike** means to hit or give a blow to something or someone. *I'm going to strike that log with my ax and split it in two.*

knock To **knock** can mean to bump or **strike** something. *She knocked his hat off his head.*

bat To **bat** means to hit something with, or as if with, a bat. *She batted the ball over the fence.*

clip To **clip** can mean to give someone a short sharp hit. *He clipped his attacker on the jaw.*

tap To **tap** means to hit something or someone lightly. *We tapped the wall to find the secret closet.*

similar words: **beat**

hold   *verb*

to have or keep something in your hands or arms. *I **held** the books while she put them on the shelf.*

grip
To **grip** means to hold something very firmly or strongly. *They gripped the rope tightly as they climbed down the cliff.*

grasp
To **grasp** means to seize something or hold it firmly in your hands. *I grasped the railing to stop myself from falling.*

clutch
To **clutch** means to hold or **grip** something tightly in your hands. *She clutched her hat so it wouldn't blow away.*

clasp
To **clasp** means to take a firm hold of something. *He clasped his teddy bear tightly and wouldn't let me hold it.*

cling to
To **cling to** means to hold tightly to something. *The frightened little boy clung to his father's hand.*

similar words: **hug, grab**

hole   *noun*

an opening in or through something. *Do you think this **hole** in the cliff is an entrance to a cave?*

gap
A **gap** is a break or opening in something. *Here's a small gap in the fence that we can crawl through.*

slit
A **slit** can be a straight narrow opening. *He peeked through a slit in the fence.*

perforation
A **perforation** is a hole punched or pierced through something. *I made some perforations in the top of the box so the silkworms could breathe.*

chink
A **chink** can be a narrow opening in something. *I could just slip my fingers through the chink in the wall.*

aperture
An **aperture** can be any hole or opening. It is often used about the opening in a camera that limits the amount of light entering the lens. *We squeezed through the narrow aperture in the rocks.*

similar words: **break, cut**

holy *adjective*

set apart for a religious purpose, or having religious significance. *We visited the ruins of the **holy** temples.*

sacred	**Sacred** means holy or worthy of religious respect. *The Koran is the sacred book of the Muslims.*
hallowed	**Hallowed** means regarded or honored as holy. *In some religions you must take off your shoes before you walk upon hallowed ground.*
blessed	**Blessed** means set apart as holy. *In many cultures, the birth of a child is considered to be a blessed event.*
saintly	**Saintly** means like or suited to a saint. *The woman was honored for her saintly acts of compassion.*

similar words: **religious**

home *noun*

the place where someone lives, usually with their family. *I'd like you to come to my **home** and have dinner with us.*

abode	An **abode** is someone's home. It is a rather old-fashioned word. *"Come to my abode and rest," said the kind man to the weary traveler.*
residence	A **residence** is the place where someone lives. It is a more formal word than **home**. *The White House is the official residence of the President of the United States.*
dwelling	A **dwelling** is a place for someone to live in. It is a formal word like **residence**. *Several small stone dwellings were all that remained of the ancient village.*
household	A **household** is a home, including the people who live there and the things they do. *Our household is a busy place because we have a big family.*

honest *adjective*

fair, not lying, cheating, or stealing. *If you are always **honest**, people will know they can trust you.*

truthful **Truthful** means showing you can be relied on to tell the truth. *I don't doubt his story, as he is always truthful.*

honorable **Honorable** means acting with high principles and honesty. *I believe what you say because you are an honorable person.*

upright **Upright** means honest and just. *That police officer is an upright person whom we all respect.*

sincere **Sincere** means expressing true and honest feelings. *Her sincere compliment pleased me.*

scrupulous **Scrupulous** means being very strict about doing what is right. *He was scrupulous in his dealings with his customers.*

similar words: **frank, decent**
contrasting words: **dishonest, cunning**

horrible *adjective*

causing a strong feeling of fear and disgust. *We couldn't bear to look at the **horrible** accident.*

dreadful **Dreadful** means causing great fear or terror. *They spent a dreadful night when the hurricane struck the town.*

horrendous **Horrendous** means horrible and **dreadful.** *He never recovered from the horrendous sight of his house burning down.*

terrible **Terrible** means causing great fear. *In my nightmare a terrible giant was chasing me.*

frightful **Frightful** means alarming and unpleasant. *They had a frightful time trying to cross the flooded river.*

similar words: **nasty, frightening**
contrasting words: **nice**

hot *adjective*

having a high temperature or giving out heat. *Don't touch the stove, because it's very **hot**.*

blazing	**Blazing** means very hot or burning fiercely. *The blazing fire soon warmed the whole room.*
sweltering	**Sweltering** can mean causing you to feel very hot and damp with perspiration. *We were glad of the air conditioning on that sweltering day.*
fiery	**Fiery** can mean like fire. *A blast of fiery heat hit me as I opened the door.*
tepid	**Tepid** means lukewarm or slightly warm. *I can't drink that tea because it's tepid now.*
warm	**Warm** means having some heat that can be felt. *Are you warm enough or shall I put the heater on?*

similar words: **humid**
contrasting words: **cold, wintry**

hug *verb*

to put your arms tightly around someone in order to show your affection for them. *I **hugged** my father when I went home.*

cuddle	To **cuddle** means to hug someone gently. *My father cuddles me if I am hurt or unhappy.*
embrace	To **embrace** means to hug or hold someone in your arms. This is a more formal word. *The two sisters embraced each other after their long separation.*
cradle	To **cradle** means to hold and rock someone or something gently, especially a baby. *The mother cradled her sick baby in her arms.*
press	To **press** can mean to hug someone tightly or hold someone close to you. *He pressed her to him and begged her never to leave.*

similar words: **hold**

huge *adjective*

very, very large or immense. *We couldn't even see the top of the **huge** mountain.*

gigantic **Gigantic** means extremely large or huge. *The gigantic man towered over everyone else.*

colossal **Colossal** means huge or of extremely great size. *There was a colossal pile of dishes to wash after my party.*

enormous **Enormous** means much larger than usual. *The enormous tree was very old.*

tremendous **Tremendous** means very large or **enormous**. It is more suited to everyday language. *We saw a tremendous moose crashing through the bush.*

vast **Vast** means huge or of very great area, bulk, or size. *Vast mountains cover much of the West.*

similar words: **big, heavy**
contrasting words: **small**

humble *adjective*

being aware of your weaknesses and having a low opinion of your own importance or abilities. *She was too **humble** to try out for a part in the class play.*

modest **Modest** means having a moderate opinion of yourself and your abilities. *We were surprised at the modest behavior of such a famous performer.*

meek **Meek** means being obedient and patient in a humble way, even though you are treated badly. *The boy was so meek that he didn't complain about being bullied.*

self-effacing **Self-effacing** means keeping yourself in the background because you feel humble. *My self-effacing partners are too modest about the good work they did.*

lowly **Lowly** means being humbly obedient and not having a high opinion of your abilities. *There is no reason for you to behave in a lowly manner.*

contrasting words: **proud, pompous, conceited, grand**

humid *adjective*

moist and damp, especially when it's also warm. *We perspired a lot in the **humid** weather.*

muggy	**Muggy** means unpleasantly warm and humid. *The air became very muggy as we approached the marsh.*
sultry	**Sultry** means unpleasantly hot and humid. *The air was sultry before the thunderstorm.*
close	**Close** can mean lacking fresh air. *The room was close and someone fainted.*
oppressive	**Oppressive** can mean causing discomfort because the heat or humidity is so great. *The heat was so oppressive we couldn't do any work outside.*

similar words: **hot**

hurry *verb*

to act quickly to save time. ***Hurry** or you'll miss the bus.*

dash	To **dash** means to move very quickly and suddenly. *I dashed into the elevator just before the doors closed.*
rush	To **rush** means to move very quickly or to do something in a great hurry. *Sally rushed to finish her dinner so she could go out to play.*
hasten	To **hasten** means to move or act quickly. *He hastened to catch the glass before it fell.*
shake a leg	To **shake a leg** means to hurry as fast as your legs will carry you. This is more suited to everyday language. *If you don't shake a leg, the train will leave without you.*
get a move on	To **get a move on** means to hurry up. This is more suited to everyday language. *Get a move on or you won't finish in time!*

similar words: **speed, dart**
contrasting words: **dawdle, walk**

hurt *verb*

to cause pain or damage to someone or something. *She **hurt** her hand in the accident.*

harm
To **harm** means to hurt or damage someone or something. It is mostly used when there has been a danger of some hurt or damage but it hasn't happened. *The hijacker did not harm his hostages.*

injure
To **injure** means to hurt a living thing, especially a person or animal. *He injured his knee when he fell off his bike.*

wound
To **wound** means to hurt someone, using a weapon of some kind. *She fired at the escaping prisoner but only wounded him.*

maim
To **maim** means to cause an injury to someone, especially to an arm or leg. *The accident maimed him for life.*

mutilate
To **mutilate** means to injure or disfigure someone or something very badly. *The doctor operated on the worker's hand, which had been mutilated by a machine.*

similar words: **damage**

ignorant *adjective*

knowing little or nothing. *He was quite **ignorant** before I started teaching him.*

uneducated
Uneducated means not having been taught or instructed. *He's completely uneducated and can't read or write.*

illiterate
Illiterate means unable to read or write. *Our school offers night classes for illiterate adults.*

uninformed
Uninformed can mean **uneducated** about a particular subject. *This simple explanation of nuclear power is especially for the uninformed people in the audience.*

contrasting words: **educated**

illegal   *adjective*

not allowed by law. *Smoking in theaters is **illegal**.*

illicit

Illicit means unlawful or not having permission to operate. *The police raided the illicit gambling house.*

criminal

Criminal means having to do with crime. *His criminal activities soon became known to the police.*

felonious

Felonious means having to do with a serious crime, such as murder or burglary. *He was jailed for his felonious assault on the security guard.*

fraudulent

Fraudulent means having to do with deliberate trickery or cheating. *The manager discovered his bookkeeper's fraudulent attempt to fake the accounts.*

contraband

Contraband means having to do with goods that have been imported or exported illegally. *The smuggler was fined for trying to bring contraband radios into the United States.*

---

similar words: **dishonest, evil**
contrasting words: **legal**

---

imaginary   *adjective*

existing only in your mind. *When everyone else is busy I play with my **imaginary** friend.*

made-up

Made-up means invented or worked out in your mind. *It was only a made-up story about a unicorn.*

fanciful

Fanciful means unreal or imaginary. *I read a fanciful story about a flying carpet.*

fictitious

Fictitious means not real or genuine, coming instead from your own imagination. *We didn't believe their fictitious story about meeting a goblin at the bottom of the garden.*

fantastic

Fantastic can mean imaginary or without basis or reason. *Don't let such fantastic fears worry you!*

mythical

Mythical can mean imaginary or invented. *The dragon is a mythical creature.*

---

contrasting words: **actual**

---

imagine *verb*

to form a picture of something in your mind. ***Imagine*** *you are exploring a new continent.*

dream   To **dream** can mean to imagine something that is usually pleasant or enjoyable. *I dreamed about becoming a famous actor.*

pretend   To **pretend** means to imagine something to be true, usually as a game. *The children pretended they were on a desert island.*

make believe   To **make believe** is so similar to **pretend** that you can usually use either. *Let's make believe we are pirates.*

feign   To **feign** means to **pretend** or to appear to have something, usually in order to deceive someone. *She feigned illness so that she could stay home.*

similar words: **think, daydream**

important *adjective*

having great influence or power. *We planned a special welcome for the **important** visitor.*

great   **Great** can mean notable or important. *We went to a concert of the great composer's works. The great occasion was celebrated with fireworks and parades.*

eminent   **Eminent** means well-known or high in rank. *The eminent scientist talked to us about her experiments.*

prominent   **Prominent** means very important or standing out ahead of others. *Because she was a prominent member of the council, everyone listened to her.*

pre-eminent   **Pre-eminent** means most important or much better than others. *He is the pre-eminent scientist in his field.*

prestigious   **Prestigious** means having a high reputation or standing. *The famous singer earned his prestigious position by practicing for hours every day.*

similar words: **grand, famous**
contrasting words: **insignificant**

impossible   *adjective*

not able to be done or used. *It is **impossible** for my son to carry me.*

inconceivable	**Inconceivable** means not being able to be imagined or believed. *It was inconceivable to me how she managed to survive the accident.*
unattainable	**Unattainable** means not able to be achieved even with great effort. *I have an unattainable ambition to be able to fly like Superman.*
unthinkable	**Unthinkable** can mean not able to be done or imagined. *A hundred years ago it was unthinkable that people would ever walk on the moon.*
hopeless	**Hopeless** means not likely to be carried out. *Escape from the maximum security prison was hopeless.*

contrasting words: **possible, likely**

improve   *verb*

to make something of higher quality or bring it into a better condition. *I want to **improve** my handwriting.*

better	To **better** means to improve something or to increase its good qualities. *You'll have to better your playing if you want to be a professional musician.*
enrich	To **enrich** means to improve the quality of something. *Farmers enrich the soil with fertilizer.*
upgrade	To **upgrade** can mean to improve the standard of something. *They upgraded the plumbing in their home by putting in new pipes.*
enhance	To **enhance** means to increase or improve something. *A coat of paint should enhance the value of the house.*
perfect	To **perfect** can mean to improve something or bring it nearer to perfection. *The inventor perfected the machine before selling it.*

similar words: **correct, repair**

inarticulate   *adjective*

not able to use clear speech that everyone can understand. *His rage made him inarticulate and we didn't know what he was trying to say.*

hesitant	**Hesitant** can mean pausing while or before speaking, usually because you are unsure of yourself or of what you are saying. *We could tell from their hesitant answer that they didn't understand the question.*
faltering	**Faltering** can mean **hesitant** or often stopping and starting again when speaking. *His faltering speech showed us how nervous he was.*
tongue-tied	**Tongue-tied** means not able to speak, usually because you are too shy or nervous. *Don't be surprised if you are tongue-tied for a minute the first time you give a speech in public.*
disjointed	**Disjointed** means not fitting together properly. *His story was so disjointed we couldn't figure out who had really hidden the chocolate cookies.*
quavering	**Quavering** means shaking or trembling as your voice does sometimes. *It was hard to understand the frail man's quavering voice.*

contrasting words: **fluent**

include   *verb*

to consist of or contain as a part. *Education **includes** what we learn both at home and at school.*

comprise	To **comprise** means to include or be composed of something. *This school comprises a kindergarten and the primary grades.*
involve	To **involve** means to include as a necessary part of something. *The job of an art gallery guide involves a knowledge of art history.*
incorporate	To **incorporate** means to include something and make it part of something else. *We incorporated several ideas into the design of the house.*
embrace	To **embrace** can mean to include or contain something. *The committee's decision embraced all the points raised in the meeting.*
cover	To **cover** can mean to provide for something or take it in. *This book covers the whole French course.*

contrasting words: **exclude**

incompetent *adjective*

lacking the skill or ability you should have. *The **incompetent** plumber couldn't fix the leaking faucet.*

unskillful **Unskillful** means showing or having very little skill. *He made an unskillful attempt to fix it.*

amateurish **Amateurish** means having very little skill or knowledge of a job. *Dad did an amateurish job of painting the house.*

fumbling **Fumbling** means handling something clumsily. *His fumbling fingers tore open the parcel.*

inept **Inept** means awkward or lacking in skill. *She made an inept attempt to sew on the button.*

similar words: **inexperienced, clumsy**
contrasting words: **competent, skillful**

incomplete *adjective*

not being whole or having some parts missing. *This jigsaw puzzle is **incomplete**.*

partial **Partial** can mean not total or complete. *Here are partial instructions, and I'll give you the rest tomorrow.*

fragmentary **Fragmentary** means broken or not whole. *The news was fragmentary because the radio picked up so much static.*

unfinished **Unfinished** means incomplete or not brought to an end. *I have some unfinished business I have to take care of before tonight.*

piecemeal **Piecemeal** means done piece by piece. *She is very disorganized and has a piecemeal approach to her work.*

deficient **Deficient** means incomplete or lacking something. *The crops died because the water supply was deficient.*

similar words: **insufficient**
contrasting words: **whole, thorough**

incorrect *adjective*

wrong or having mistakes. *Your answer is **incorrect**.*

inaccurate   **Inaccurate** means not right or exact. *This copy is inaccurate.*

untrue   **Untrue** means not true or right. *He knew his statement was untrue.*

false   **False** means incorrect or not true. *He made a false accusation about me to cause me trouble.*

erroneous   **Erroneous** means incorrect or containing a mistake. *Your theory about the crime is erroneous.*

off base   **Off base** means wrong or incorrect. This is more suited to everyday language. *That answer is so far off base it's not even close.*

---

contrasting words: **true**

---

increase *verb*

to become more or bigger. *The population of the world **increases** every year.*

expand   To **expand** can mean to increase in size, especially by spreading out. *The more he blew into the balloon, the more it expanded.*

grow   To **grow** means to become bigger. *The town began to grow when gold was discovered nearby.*

multiply   To **multiply** can mean to increase in amount or number. *Every time you put some money in the bank, your savings multiply.*

mount   To **mount** can mean to increase in amount. It is similar to **multiply**. *Our costs are mounting every day.*

accumulate   To **accumulate** can mean to increase by growing into a heap. *Don't let too much junk accumulate on your desk.*

---

contrasting words: **decrease**

---

indecent   *adjective*

not proper or in good taste. *We were shocked by his **indecent** language.*

immoral	**Immoral** means wicked or wrong. *I think that cheating is immoral.*
corrupt	**Corrupt** means dishonest or able to be bribed. *The corrupt judge had been in the pay of criminals for years before he was found out.*
depraved	**Depraved** means evil or morally bad. *He was as depraved as the cruel, wicked thieves he mixed with.*
degenerate	**Degenerate** means becoming bad or worse than before. *People are becoming more and more greedy in this degenerate decade.*
perverted	**Perverted** means turned from what is right or proper in your behavior or beliefs. *His perverted sense of humor gets him into a lot of trouble.*

similar words: **evil, dishonest**
contrasting words: **decent**

independent   *adjective*

not needing or relying on the help of others. *As children get older they are more **independent** and want to move away from home.*

self-sufficient	**Self-sufficient** means able to supply your own needs. *They led a self-sufficient life because they grew all their own food.*
separate	**Separate** means not connected to anything or anyone else. *Although they lived in the same apartment building, they led completely separate lives.*
unattached	**Unattached** can mean not connected with any particular person or group. *The new student enjoyed sports, but was unattached, for a while, to any school teams.*
autonomous	**Autonomous** means self-governing or able to govern or rule on your own. *The Philippines has been an autonomous nation since 1946.*
freelance	**Freelance** means not working for a wage but selling work to more than one employer, especially as a writer does. *The freelance journalist sold his stories to several magazines and newspapers.*

indicator   *noun*

something that points to or shows something. *The **indicator** on the gas gauge showed that the car was nearly out of fuel.*

sign
A **sign** can be anything that shows something exists or is likely to happen. *Dark clouds are a sign of rain.*

marker
A **marker** is something used to mark or indicate something. *We used a pile of stones as a marker to show the others which way we had gone.*

pointer
A **pointer** is anything that draws your attention to something of interest. *The pointer of the barometer showed that rain was coming.*

guide
A **guide** is something or someone who shows you the way. *The reflectors on the posts by the side of the road are a guide to drivers at night.*

clue
A **clue** is something that guides or directs you to the solution of a puzzle or mystery. *The fingerprints on the window were the best clue to the identity of the burglar.*

inedible   *adjective*

not able or fit to be eaten. *Those biscuits are so hard they're **inedible**.*

unpalatable
Unpalatable means tasting so unpleasant it is difficult to eat. *The dinner was so unpalatable even the dog wouldn't eat it.*

stale
Stale means so old it is no longer pleasant to eat. *Give the stale bread to the squirrels and we will eat the fresh loaf.*

rotten
Rotten can mean unfit for eating because it is old and decaying. *The rotten apples were soft and brown.*

rancid
Rancid means having a stale sour smell or taste. *Don't use that butter, because it is rancid and will make the sandwiches taste awful.*

contrasting words: **delicious**

inexperienced   *adjective*

lacking the knowledge or skill you gain from doing, seeing, or living through something yourself. *An **inexperienced** driver has to be particularly careful in wet weather.*

raw **Raw** can mean inexperienced or not trained. *Daily drills and training turned the raw recruits into fine soldiers.*

amateur **Amateur** can mean not skilled, or having only slight knowledge of a job. *He is an amateur bricklayer and his wall is very uneven.*

untrained **Untrained** means having had no training for a particular activity. *She is an untrained singer but has a lovely voice.*

callow **Callow** means young and inexperienced. *He was a callow youth but has grown into a self-confident young man.*

green **Green** can mean **untrained** or inexperienced. It is usually used after a verb. *You could see he was green by the way he tried to start a fire with wet wood.*

similar words: **incompetent, naive**
contrasting words: **experienced, competent**

inferior   *adjective*

of low quality or value. *I'm afraid that I think your work is **inferior**.*

poor **Poor** can be so similar to **inferior** that you can usually use either. *That is a very poor novel.*

shoddy **Shoddy** means badly made. *This cupboard is so shoddy the doors won't close properly.*

crummy **Crummy** means of low quality. It is more suited to everyday language. *I want a new bike because my old one is crummy.*

worthless **Worthless** means of such low quality as to have no value. *This worthless toy broke two days after I bought it.*

dud **Dud** means useless or **worthless**. This is more suited to everyday language. *The enemy dropped a dud bomb so no damage was done.*

similar words: **defective, mediocre**
contrasting words: **superior, distinguished**

influence *noun*

some force that affects or produces a change in someone or something else. *He is a good **influence** on his brother.*

power   **Power** can mean strength or force, especially in controlling others. *The new government will have the power to change many things.*

hold   **Hold** can mean a controlling force or influence. *The politician had a hold on her leader because she knew about his dishonesty.*

clout   **Clout** can mean influence or effectiveness. *You need some clout to get a good job like that.*

sway   **Sway** can mean control or rule. *The dictator has held sway for many years.*

charisma   **Charisma** is the power to attract and influence people. *A successful leader should have charisma.*

influence *verb*

to have an effect on someone or something. *Try to make up your own mind without letting your friends **influence** you too much.*

manipulate   To **manipulate** can mean to influence someone cleverly or unfairly. *He always gets his own way because he manipulates people.*

prejudice   To **prejudice** means to influence someone without sensible reason. *They were prejudiced against her because she came from another town.*

bias   To **bias** means to influence someone, usually unfairly. *He tried to bias my opinion about the film by telling me what he didn't like about it.*

condition   To **condition** means to influence or affect someone by training in a particular way. *What we are taught by our parents and teachers conditions the way we live.*

brainwash   To **brainwash** means to have an extreme influence over someone's way of thinking or beliefs. *The guards tried to brainwash the prisoner so that he would speak out against the leader of his country.*

similar words: **persuade**

inform   *verb*

to give news or knowledge to someone. *I **informed** him of your success.*

instruct   To **instruct** can mean to inform or give information to someone. *The man instructed me to go straight ahead and then turn left.*

notify   To **notify** means to inform someone of something, especially in an official way. *The committee notified them that the meeting time had changed.*

advise   To **advise** can mean to give someone information about something important. *We advised the bank that we were moving to the country.*

keep posted   To **keep posted** means to inform someone about a particular situation. *Please keep me posted so I'll know what to do.*

announce   To **announce** means to tell something to someone or make it known in public. *The date of the track meet was announced during the assembly.*

similar words: **tell, reveal, publish**

informal   *adjective*

without ceremony or formality. *The President had an **informal** talk with the visiting athletes.*

unofficial   **Unofficial** can mean not done formally or without official approval. *According to an unofficial report 10,000 people were killed in the earthquake.*

casual   **Casual** can mean informal or not having to do with special occasions. *We wore casual clothes to the picnic.*

relaxed   **Relaxed** can mean informal and at ease. *Once the ceremony was over, the wedding guests were more relaxed.*

easygoing   **Easygoing** means not being strict about the way things are done. *Our relatives are easygoing people who don't mind if we arrive late for dinner.*

contrasting words: **formal**

information *noun*

knowledge given or received about some fact or happening. *It is always a good idea to get some **information** about a country if you plan to visit it.*

news
News can be information considered suitable for reporting or not known before. *Have you heard any news about the presidential election?*

data
Data are facts or information, especially a group of facts from which a conclusion will be drawn. *If you give me the data, I'll figure out what's wrong.*

intelligence
Intelligence can be information or knowledge of an event or happening given to or received from someone. *The agents listened to the latest intelligence from the FBI.*

propaganda
Propaganda is information that is used to try to convince you of a certain point of view. *The magazine was full of political propaganda.*

similar words: **gossip**

inhabit *verb*

to live or dwell in a place, as people or animals do. *Polar bears **inhabit** the arctic regions of Alaska.*

populate
To **populate** can mean to inhabit or live in a place, as a group of people do. *The rocky land around our town is sparsely populated.*

occupy
To **occupy** can mean to **settle** or take possession of a place. *The settlers occupied land on both sides of the river.*

settle
To **settle** means to go to live in a new, undeveloped place. *The pioneers took many risks so that they could settle the new land.*

colonize
To **colonize** means to start a settlement in a new land ruled by the parent country. *France and England colonized much of North America.*

similar words: **reside**

initiate *verb*

to begin something or to set it going. *I'm going to **initiate** a discussion about the movie I saw last night.*

establish
To **establish** means to set something up. *There were so many children they had to establish a new school.*

found
To **found** means to set something up or **establish** it. *Dawson was founded when gold was discovered at Bonanza Creek.*

institute
To **institute** means to set something up or set it going. *Our sports club instituted a new course in judo.*

launch
To **launch** means to set something going. *We launched the fishing boat at dawn.*

pioneer
To **pioneer** means to begin something or to be one of the first to do it. *Banting and Best pioneered the research of diabetes.*

---

similar words: **begin, invent**
contrasting words: **finish, cancel, stop**

---

inquiry *noun*

a search or probe into a matter. *The police **inquiry** into the robbery took several weeks.*

investigation
An **investigation** is a close look at something. *The investigation into the cause of the fire showed that there had been an electrical fault.*

examination
An **examination** means the act of careful looking and testing. *The dentist's examination of her teeth revealed a broken filling.*

analysis
An **analysis** means the separation of something into its basic parts to discover something about it. *Current affairs programs give an analysis of the most important issues in the news.*

survey
A **survey** is the act of asking the views of people in order to write a report about what people think or do. *They did a survey to see what people thought about the new soft drink.*

poll
A **poll** means a counting of people, votes, or opinions. *The TV station did a telephone poll on the government's plans to change the tax system.*

inquisitive   *adjective*

wanting to find out all about something. *Our new cat was very **inquisitive** and looked all around our house.*

questioning   **Questioning** can mean being so inquisitive about the world around you that you can't help asking questions. *He has such a questioning mind that he spends a lot of time looking things up in the library.*

inquiring   **Inquiring** means seeking information or knowledge. *The child had an inquiring mind and was eager to learn.*

curious   **Curious** can mean wanting to learn, especially about things that are strange or new. *We were curious about the new person in our class.*

nosey   **Nosey** means interested in things that aren't your business. *Our next-door neighbor was nosey and always wanted to know what we were doing.*

snoopy   **Snoopy** means prying into things in a mean or sly way. *My snoopy sister was always trying to discover where I hid my diary.*

similar words: **alert**

insert   *verb*

to put or set in something. ***Insert** the key in the lock.*

enclose   To **enclose** can mean to put something in. *I enclose a photograph with this letter.*

slip   To **slip** can mean to put or pass something into anything else with a smooth, sliding movement. *I slipped the money into my pocket.*

introduce   To **introduce** can mean to bring or put something new into a place, surroundings, and so on. *The biologist introduced a new species of fish into the aquarium.*

ease   To **ease** can mean to move something or someone slowly and carefully into anything. *I eased the logs into the fireplace so sparks wouldn't fly.*

insinuate   To **insinuate** can mean to get yourself gradually and slyly into a certain position. *Brian insinuated himself into the boss's favor.*

similar words: **add**
contrasting words: **remove**

inside *noun*

the inner part or side of something. *The **inside** of their house is always gloomy.*

interior The **interior** is the internal or inside part of something. *The interior of the shop was decorated with striped wallpaper.*

contents The **contents** are whatever is inside or contained in something. This is a plural noun. *We were keen to discover the contents of the old box we found in the storeroom.*

innards **Innards** can be the essential or inner parts of something. This is a plural noun. It is more suited to everyday language. *She looked at the innards of the broken engine to find the problem.*

belly A **belly** can be the inside of anything. *The sailor crawled right into the belly of the ship to look for the leak.*

---

similar words: **center**
contrasting words: **outside**

insignificant *adjective*

not having much power or not worth consideration. *He is an **insignificant** member of the club and won't take on any responsibilities.*

unimportant **Unimportant** means not powerful or worthy of notice. *The color of your boots is unimportant so long as your feet are warm.*

dispensable **Dispensable** means able to be done without. *Our new house is much smaller and we had to decide which furniture was dispensable.*

expendable **Expendable** means able to be sacrificed or used up for a purpose. *Those old bottles are expendable, so don't worry if a couple of them break.*

peripheral **Peripheral** means not essential or important. *The work of the social committee was peripheral to the club's main purpose of raising money for the hospital.*

small-time **Small-time** means of little importance. This is more suited to everyday language. *The police kept a watch on the small-time criminal and hoped he would lead them to the mastermind of the bank robberies.*

---

similar words: **minor, subordinate**
contrasting words: **significant, main, important**

inspect   *verb*

to look carefully at something. *The general **inspected** his troops.*

look over To **look over** means to view or examine something carefully. *We looked over several houses before we decided which one we would buy.*

search To **search** means to look at or through something very carefully, hoping to find something. *The detective searched the ground for footprints.*

survey To **survey** means to take a general view of something. *We surveyed the beautiful valley from the top of a hill.*

scan To **scan** means to look at something closely. *The doctor scanned the blood sample for any evidence of disease.*

reconnoiter To **reconnoiter** means to look carefully at a place in order to gain useful information. *The scouts reconnoitered the village before the soldiers marched in.*

similar words: **examine, see**

insufficient   *adjective*

not enough or not having as much as is wanted or needed. *There is **insufficient** paint to give the room a second coat.*

inadequate **Inadequate** means not enough to fill a need. *The crops were small because of inadequate rain.*

lacking **Lacking** means showing the lack or absence of some important part. *This soup is lacking in flavor.*

deficient **Deficient** means incomplete or **lacking**. *Eat plenty of fresh fruit and vegetables or you will be deficient in vitamins.*

short **Short** can mean not having or being enough. *Please lend me $2, because I'm short of money. Don't use the photocopier, because we're short on paper at the moment.*

similar words: **scant, incomplete**
contrasting words: **enough, abundant, extra**

insult   *verb*

to act or speak rudely to someone. *I was hurt when she **insulted** me in front of everyone.*

slight To **slight** means to treat someone rudely. *You slighted me by not replying to my invitation.*

snub To **snub** means to insult someone by ignoring them. *He snubbed me when I met him in the street.*

humiliate To **humiliate** means to make someone feel ashamed or foolish. *His rude remarks humiliated me.*

belittle To **belittle** means to make someone feel unimportant. *The supervisor belittled their efforts, even though they had done their best.*

affront To **affront** means to hurt someone's feelings or pride. *He affronted her visitors by making rude comments about their appearance.*

---

similar words: **tease**
contrasting words: **worship**

---

intend   *verb*

to have as an idea you are going to carry out. *I **intend** to make a model airplane this weekend.*

mean To **mean** is to intend or have a particular purpose. *Rita means to learn to skate during the holidays.*

plan To **plan** is to form a purpose or scheme. *We plan to build a tree house next week.*

vow To **vow** is to declare your intention solemnly. *He vowed to be very careful if he ever went hiking by himself.*

have in mind To **have in mind** is to be thinking about or to intend. *What do you have in mind for us to do today?*

choose To **choose** can mean to decide or prefer to do something. *Justine chose to go to the movie instead of the zoo.*

intense *adjective*

very great or strong. *I couldn't walk when I sprained my ankle because of the* ***intense*** *pain.*

severe **Severe** can mean harsh or extreme. *The severe cold of a winter wind can lead to frostbite.*

profound **Profound** means very deep, not superficial. *We thought for a long time about the wise woman's profound words.*

vivid **Vivid** means strong and clear. *She is a good writer because she has a vivid imagination.*

passionate **Passionate** means showing a strong feeling or emotion. *She had a passionate belief in her plan to encourage politicians to stop the new development.*

violent **Violent** can mean forceful or intense in a rough way. *The violent wind made us worried.*

---

contrasting words: **moderate**

---

interrupt *verb*

to stop someone or something, or break into the middle of what they are doing. *She* ***interrupted*** *me many times with her questions.*

disturb To **disturb** means to interrupt in a way that hinders or interferes with what someone is doing. *Your constant chatting is disturbing me and I am taking longer to finish.*

punctuate To **punctuate** can mean to interrupt quite often. *They punctuated his speech with cheers.*

cut off To **cut off** means to break in in the middle of something. *I cut his speech off before he finished.*

disconnect To **disconnect** means to break a connection or link between two things. *We were disconnected in the middle of our telephone conversation.*

---

similar words: **hinder**

---

intrude *verb*

to enter or force yourself in where you are not wanted or invited. *We were having fun playing together until he **intruded**.*

interfere	To **interfere** means to take part in someone else's affairs without being asked. *She always interferes by trying to tell us what to do.*
meddle	To **meddle** means to **interfere** with something that doesn't concern you. *He finished his own work early and then started to meddle in ours.*
butt in	To **butt in** means to interrupt or **interfere**. This is more suited to everyday language. *We were having a private talk when John butted in.*
barge in	To **barge in** means to intrude in a forceful and obvious way. This is more suited to everyday language. *I'm going to barge in on their meeting and tell them what I think.*
interject	To **interject** means to make a remark that interrupts a conversation or speech. *I interjected loudly because I didn't agree with what he said.*

invent *verb*

to think up something new. *Do you know who **invented** the automobile?*

originate	To **originate** means to invent or start something. *The game of basketball was originated by a Canadian.*
devise	To **devise** means to think out, plan, or invent something. *I have devised a way for us all to earn some extra money for our trip.*
conceive	To **con aceive** means to think of or form something. *We have conceived a new plan.*
innovate	To **innovate** means to bring in something new. *He innovated a lot of rules wlkhen he first came to our school.*
coin	To **coin** means to make or invent something. *She coined a word that no one had heard before.*

similar words: **create, concoct**

investigate *verb*

to look into or examine something closely. *The police are **investigating** the murder at the moment.*

probe	To **probe** means to examine or search something thoroughly. *The police have to probe the whole area in order to solve the murder.*
scrutinize	To **scrutinize** means to examine something closely and carefully. *The art dealer scrutinized the painting to see whether it was genuine.*
explore	To **explore** means to examine or go over something very carefully. *They explored the whole cave to see if there was another way out.*
research	To **research** means to study something closely or scientifically in order to understand or learn more about a subject. *The students researched the topic thoroughly for their geography assignment.*
delve into	To **delve into** means to search or look into something thoroughly or in great depth. *He delved into all the encyclopedias he could find for information for his project.*

similar words: **examine, test**

invisible *adjective*

unable to be seen. *We could all hear the airplane even though it was **invisible** in the sky.*

unseen	**Unseen** means invisible or not seen. *The unseen animals could be heard crashing through the woods.*
hidden	**Hidden** means kept from sight. *The entrance to the rabbit's burrow was hidden in the long grass.*
concealed	**Concealed** means placed out of sight. *Dad had a concealed safe installed in his study after we were robbed.*
inconspicuous	**Inconspicuous** means not standing out or not noticeable. *The Prime Minister's bodyguard was inconspicuous in the crowd.*
imperceptible	**Imperceptible** means not easily seen or noticed. *The slope in the ground was so imperceptible that I did not notice I was climbing a small hill.*

contrasting words: **visible**

irrational   *adjective*

absurd or not based on sound judgment. *Jan had an **irrational** fear of water.*

illogical	**Illogical** means not based on sensible or correct thinking. *Wearing an overcoat on a hot day is illogical.*
unreasonable	**Unreasonable** means not based on good sense. *It's unreasonable to insist on going skiing when there's no snow.*
groundless	**Groundless** means without any reason or basis. *I know you are frightened, but your fears are groundless.*
inconsistent	**Inconsistent** means having no order or agreement between the parts of something. *Your inconsistent behavior is very confusing; we never know if you'll be angry or not.*
arbitrary	**Arbitrary** means based on your own feelings and ideas rather than on rules or reasons. *The teacher made an arbitrary decision as to who was going to be the first on the stage.*

similar words: **silly, fickle**
contrasting words: **sensible, sane**

irritate   *verb*

to annoy someone or make them angry. *The audience's chatter **irritated** the speaker.*

vex	To **vex** means to annoy or worry someone. *I'm vexed by all this rainy weather.*
pique	To **pique** means to annoy and upset someone. *Mary's refusal to help Craig piqued him.*
provoke	To **provoke** means to make someone or something angry or annoyed. *He provoked me by telling me I was useless.*
goad	To **goad** can mean to tease someone until you make him or her angry. *They goaded me until I lost my temper.*
bug	To **bug** means to annoy or irritate someone. It is more suited to everyday language. *His silly questions bugged me.*

similar words: **annoy**
contrasting words: **please**

isolate   *verb*

to set or place someone or something apart from everything else so that they are alone. *The guards **isolated** the most dangerous prisoners.*

ostracize   To **ostracize** means to keep someone away from others or send them away from everyone else, especially as a punishment. *The other children ostracized the boy who ratted on his friends.*

quarantine   To **quarantine** means to isolate people or animals for a certain period of time to make sure they don't spread a disease to others. *The officials quarantined the animals that had been in contact with the sick cow.*

segregate   To **segregate** means to set someone or something apart from other people or things. *We should segregate all the damaged supplies so that no one uses them by mistake.*

shut away   To **shut away** means to hide or confine someone or something. *The evil magician shut away the enchanted prince so that no one would find him.*

similar words: **expel, exclude**

jealous   *adjective*

wanting very much to have what other people have. *Peter is **jealous** of his brother's good looks.*

envious   **Envious** means feeling or showing discontent and ill will at seeing what someone else has. It is very similar to **jealous**. *I am envious of your good luck in winning the prize.*

covetous   **Covetous** means wanting what someone else has very much. *David was so covetous of her new book that he took it without asking.*

possessive **Possessive** means wanting to control or possess someone or something all by yourself. *My little brother is very possessive of his remote-control car.*

green   **Green** can mean extremely jealous. It is more suited to everyday language. *I was green with envy I saw his new bike.*

job *noun*

employment for which you are paid. *I have a **job** selling newspapers after school.*

work	Your **work** can be the job by which you earn money. *His work is teaching.*
occupation	Your **occupation** is your usual job or employment. *What is your mother's occupation?*
business	A **business** is the job or trade you have in order to earn a living. *We have a business building swimming pools.*
career	A **career** is the job or profession you hope to have for the rest of your life. *She wants to make acting her career.*
vocation	A **vocation** is a particular job or profession that you believe to be very important. *I want to make nursing my vocation.*

similar words: **profession, position**

join *verb*

to put two or more things together. *I have **joined** the broken pieces with glue.*

connect	To **connect** means to join or unite something. *Carl connected the ends of the toy railway track.*
link	To **link** is so similar to join and **connect** that you can usually use any of them. *You can link these rings together to make a chain.*
couple	To **couple** means to join one thing to another. *The workers had to couple the cars together before the train could leave.*
unite	To **unite** means to join two or more people or things together as one. *The three of us are united in our efforts to organize a school dance.*
knit	To **knit** means to join people or things closely and firmly together. *The coach knitted the players into an unbeatable team.*

similar words: **combine**
contrasting words: **separate**

joke *noun*

something that is said or done to make people laugh. *She told us a **joke** about a man who took a refrigerator to the South Pole.*

jest	A **jest** is a joke that is sometimes a mocking one. *He made a jest about his clumsiness to hide his embarrassment.*
laugh	A **laugh** is something that makes you laugh. It can be used to mean the opposite of what is being said. *Walking through the Hall of Mirrors was a laugh. "That's a laugh," he said when I asked if he had any money.*
gag	A **gag** is a joke or funny trick. *The comedian's gag kept the audience laughing.*
crack	A **crack** can be a joke, often an unkind one. It is more suited to everyday language. *He made a crack about my red hair.*

similar words: **wisecrack**

journey *noun*

a course you take when traveling from one place to another, especially by land. *Our **journey** took us across the prairies and into the foothills of the Rockies.*

trip	A **trip** is a journey, usually taken for pleasure. *We'll plan a trip to the city on the holiday weekend.*
tour	A **tour** is an organized journey through a place or from one place to another. *We went on a bus tour to the main historical sites.*
expedition	An **expedition** is a journey made for a special reason. *Many explorers made expeditions to discover the Northwest Passage.*
excursion	An **excursion** is a short journey or **trip**, usually taken for a special reason. *Our class is going on an excursion to the zoo.*
jaunt	A **jaunt** is a short **trip** made for fun. *Let's go on a jaunt to the beach.*

joyful *adjective*

full of great happiness and delight. *The family had a **joyful** reunion when their grandparents came from Poland.*

jubilant	**Jubilant** means joyful because you have been successful. *We were jubilant when we got permission to make an outdoor skating rink.*
elated	**Elated** means in very high spirits. *The children were elated when they started their vacation.*
ecstatic	**Ecstatic** means having a sudden feeling of great joy. *They were ecstatic when they met each other at the airport.*
rapturous	**Rapturous** means filled with great joy and happiness. *We spent a rapturous hour watching the sun set over the lake.*
blissful	**Blissful** means extraordinarily happy. *They had a blissful time together after so many years apart.*

similar words: **happy, glad**
contrasting words: **glum, miserable, sad**

judge *verb*

to form an opinion about something. *I didn't **judge** the width of the car properly so I scratched the car door on the wall of the garage.*

adjudicate	To **adjudicate** means to make a judgment about something. This is a rather formal word. *The older students adjudicated the speeches in our debate.*
evaluate	To **evaluate** means to test and find the value or quality of something. *Our essay topic was to evaluate the statement: "Smoking is bad for you."*
appraise	To **appraise** means to judge the value of something. *The judges appraised the paintings in the competition.*
value	To **value** means to form an opinion about how much something is worth. *The jeweler valued Mom's ring at $1000.*
size up	To **size up** something means to form an idea about it. *The police officer walked around the smashed cars and sized up the situation.*

similar words: **measure**

jump *verb*

to move yourself suddenly from the ground or some other support, using your leg muscles. *She was so happy she **jumped** up and down.*

leap	To **leap** means to jump lightly and quickly. *I leaped over the puddle in the middle of the track.*
spring	To **spring** means to **leap** or move upward with sudden energy. *She sprang out of her seat when the bell went. The dog sprang into the air.*
bound	To **bound** means to move with jumps or big steps. *He bounded right over the fence and ran up the path.*
hop	To **hop** means to move by springing, often using only one leg. *He hopped over to the tree when he sprained his ankle.*
vault	To **vault** means to jump, often with your hands on something to support you. *She vaulted onto her horse. When she couldn't open the gate she vaulted over it.*

similar words: **frisk**

justify *verb*

to show an act, or something similar, to be right or reasonable. *The police officer had to **justify** the shots he fired at the suspect as he ran away.*

warrant	To **warrant** can mean to show there is a good reason or need for something. *The urgency of the situation warranted her hasty action.*
explain	To **explain** can mean to account for something or make the reason for it clear. *Please explain your absence.*
excuse	To **excuse** can mean to justify or serve as a reason for a fault or wrongdoing. *Your tiredness does not excuse your rudeness.*
vindicate	To **vindicate** means to show someone or something to be innocent or right. This is rather a formal word. *The evidence of the witnesses vindicated the man who had always claimed he was innocent.*

similar words: **prove**

keep *verb*

to make something continue in the same way or state. *We must **keep** our room as clean as we can.*

maintain	To **maintain** means to keep something up or keep it in good condition. *You maintain a bike by oiling it and keeping the tires filled.*
preserve	To **preserve** means to keep something from going bad. *We picked so much fruit from our tree that we had to preserve some of it.*
retain	To **retain** means to keep or keep on using something. *The plumbers retained our house key until they finished the job.*
sustain	To **sustain** means to keep something up. *It's hard to sustain a conversation with him because he gives such short answers to my questions.*
prolong	To **prolong** means to make something last longer. *We should prolong our vacation because we're having such a good time.*

similar words: **store**
contrasting words: **change, discard**

kill *verb*

to cause the death of something or someone. *We **killed** the rats with poison.*

murder	To **murder** means to kill someone deliberately. *The detective overheard the plan to murder the security guard.*
assassinate	To **assassinate** means to **murder** a well-known person, such as a politician. *The man who assassinated the President was arrested with the gun in his hand.*
execute	To **execute** can mean to put someone to death in a way allowed by the law. *I heard in the foreign news that a political criminal was executed by a firing squad.*
slay	To **slay** means to kill someone or something using violence. It is an old-fashioned word. *The princess grabbed the sword to slay the dragon.*

kind *adjective*

warm-hearted, friendly, and wishing good things for other people. *It was **kind** of him to show the new boy around the school.*

nice Nice can mean kind or pleasant. *They were nice people to play with.*

thoughtful **Thoughtful** means thinking of other people and considering their needs. *It was thoughtful of you to give me some flowers when I was feeling sad.*

considerate **Considerate** means kind or thinking of other people's needs and feelings. *Although he could hardly keep his eyes open, the considerate boy read his sister her favorite story.*

unselfish **Unselfish** means thinking about other people and not just yourself. *It was very unselfish of you to share your last piece of cake.*

well-meaning **Well-meaning** means having good intentions in the way you act or treat people. *She is very well-meaning but when she attempted to help she managed to flood the kitchen.*

similar words: **friendly**
contrasting words: **selfish, mean**

label *noun*

a piece of paper put on something to show what it is, who owns it, or where it is going. *I put a **label** showing my name and address on my suitcase.*

tag A **tag** is a piece of cardboard or strong paper attached to something as a label. *I took the price tag off the shirt before I gave it to Dad.*

tab A **tab** is a small label. *A tab with the manufacturer's name was sewn on the inside of the collar of the shirt.*

ticket A **ticket** is a label or **tag** showing how much something costs. *The clothes in the sale all have red tickets.*

sticker A **sticker** is an adhesive or gummed label, usually with an advertisement or other information printed on it. *The bag of fruit had a sticker with the price on it.*

label *verb*

to describe something with a label. *We always **label** our suitcases when we travel on trains or planes.*

mark
To **mark** means to put a sign or label on something to give some information about it. *I marked my roller skates so I could tell they were mine.*

brand
To **brand** means to **mark** something with the name of the owner or maker. *The rancher brands the new calves every year.*

tag
To **tag** can mean to put a tag or label on something giving information about it. *The shopkeeper tagged every item of new stock when it came into the store.*

identify
To **identify** means to establish or prove as being a particular thing or person. *As soon as he comes on the air, the disc jockey plays this song to identify his program.*

lack *noun*

absence of something you want or need. *The explorers became ill due to the **lack** of good food.*

shortage
A **shortage** is a lack in the supply of something. *There was a serious shortage of water during the long drought.*

insufficiency
An **insufficiency** can be an amount that is less than you need for something. *The club had an insufficiency of funds to pay for the new sports equipment.*

deficiency
A **deficiency** can be an inadequate amount of something. *We made up for our deficiency in numbers by working extra hard to finish on time.*

dearth
A **dearth** is a lack or very small supply of something. *The dearth of medical supplies made the situation even more serious.*

deficit
A **deficit** is an amount lacked, especially money. *Dad promised that if I saved up half the money he would make up the deficit.*

contrasting words: **excess**

lake _noun_

a large area of water surrounded by land. *We canoed in a circle around the shoreline of the small **lake**.*

lagoon	A **lagoon** is a pond of shallow water that is often separated from the sea by low banks of sand. *The children played safely in the lagoon only a hundred meters from the crashing surf.*
basin	A **basin** is an area of water in a hollow surrounded by higher land. *The river basin lies between the two mountain ranges.*
pond	A **pond** is a body of still water smaller than a lake. *The pond was filled with lily pads and weeds.*
dam	A **dam** is a barrier built to hold back water. *The farmers use water from the dam to irrigate their crops.*
reservoir	A **reservoir** is a place where water is stored. *Pipes carry water from the dam to the town reservoir.*

similar words: **bay, swamp**

land _verb_

to come to rest by the shore or on the ground. *The ship will **land** late this afternoon. The jet **landed** so smoothly that the passengers hardly felt the jolt.*

touch down	To **touch down** is similar to land but is only used about aircraft. *The plane will touch down at Richmond and then Baltimore.*
alight	To **alight** means to get down out of a vehicle after a journey. *The passengers alighted from the bus.*
dismount	To **dismount** means to get off a horse or a bike after a ride. *He pulled up outside the gate and dismounted hurriedly.*
disembark	To **disembark** means to get off a ship or out of a plane after a journey. *Passengers should check their luggage before they disembark.*

similar words: **come**

language *noun*

the arrangement of words we use when we speak or write. *English is the most widely spoken language in the world.*

dialect   A **dialect** is a variety of a language spoken in a particular area or by a particular group of people. *U.S. dialects differ on the meanings of* bucket *and* pail.

tongue   **Tongue** can be another word for a language or a **dialect**. *The stranger spoke in a foreign tongue.*

jargon   **Jargon** is the language made up of special words and phrases used only by people in a particular job or occupation. *Most people find it hard to understand the legal jargon of documents.*

slang   **Slang** is everyday language that is not suitable for formal speech or writing. *Try not to use slang in your essays.*

laugh *verb*

to make sounds that show amusement, happiness, or scorn. *The children laughed as the waves wet their feet.*

chuckle   To **chuckle** is to laugh softly with amusement. *I chuckled as I read Justine's funny letter.*

chortle   To **chortle** means to laugh loudly. *We chortled with glee when they invited us to the circus.*

cackle   To **cackle** means to laugh with the harsh noisy sound a hen makes after laying an egg. *The witch cackled as she stirred her magic brew.*

guffaw   To **guffaw** means to laugh loudly and noisily. *The workers guffawed when they saw their companion stuck in the mud.*

break up   To **break up** can mean to explode into or collapse with laughter. This is more suited to everyday language. *We broke up laughing when she came in wearing the funny mask.*

similar words: **smile**
contrasting words: **cry**

lawyer   *noun*

someone whose work is to give advice about the law and to argue on behalf of people in law courts. ***Lawyers*** *have to know all about new laws so that they can advise their clients.*

attorney
An **attorney** is someone, usually a lawyer, who represents or advises you in legal matters. It usually can be used wherever **lawyer** is used. *We need to consult our attorney before we sign this.*

counsel
A **counsel** is a lawyer who represents a client in a court case. *My counsel convinced the judge that I had been wrongly charged, and the case was dropped.*

advocate
An **advocate** is someone who speaks on behalf of other people or of causes. *The lawyer devoted himself to being an advocate for conservationists who are arrested.*

state attorney
The **state attorney** is the lawyer whose job it is to represent the state that employs him or her, either as a prosecutor or defense attorney. *The state attorneys of Mississippi and Louisiana met to negotiate an agreement on interstate pollution.*

district attorney
A **district attorney** is a lawyer who prosecutes criminal cases in a certain judicial district. *The district attorney questioned the man accused of assaulting his neighbor.*

paralegal
A **paralegal** is someone who performs some legal services but who is not qualified as a lawyer. *We went to a paralegal instead of a lawyer when we incorporated our family business.*

layer   *noun*

a single thickness. *The wedding cake had three **layers**.*

stratum
A **stratum** is a horizontal layer of any material. *We could see a stratum of granite running across the cliff face.*

seam
A **seam** can be a thin layer of a different kind of rock or mineral in the ground. *The new seam of coal discovered yesterday will keep the miners working for another year.*

vein
A **vein** can be a layer of metal or ore in the middle of rock. *The miners were excited when they found the rich vein of gold.*

deposit
A **deposit** can be a layer that collects on a surface. *As the flooding river went down, it left a deposit of rich soil on the farmer's land.*

laze *verb*

to be lazy or spend your time doing very little. *It was so hot that I just **lazed** around all weekend.*

idle To **idle** can mean to spend your time doing nothing. *Instead of doing her homework she just idled at the table.*

loaf To **loaf** means to do nothing. It is similar to **laze** and to **idle**. *You can loaf all through your vacation.*

lounge To **lounge** can mean to spend your time relaxing. It is similar to **loll**. *He lounged around the pool instead of working.*

not pull your weight To **not pull your weight** means to avoid doing your fair share of something. *You won't be popular with us if you don't pull your weight.*

loll To **loll** means to lean or lie around in a lazy way. *He said he just wanted to loll on the bed all day.*

similar words: **rest**
contrasting words: **work**

lazy *adjective*

not liking work or effort. *The **lazy** boy wouldn't help his mother cut the lawn.*

idle **Idle** means not doing or wanting to do anything. *We were idle until the blizzard stopped.*

indolent **Indolent** means lazy or tending to avoid work. *He is so indolent that he spends the weekends lying in front of the television.*

slack **Slack** can mean lazy, careless, and neglectful. *She is slack about doing her homework.*

slothful **Slothful** means extremely lazy. It is often used in an insulting way. *Thanks to your slothful ways, our project won't be finished in time.*

similar words: **lethargic**
contrasting words: **busy, energetic**

learn *verb*

to come to have knowledge about or skill in something. *She wants to **learn** to speak Spanish before she visits Peru.*

memorize — To **memorize** means to put something into your memory or learn it by heart. *The singer memorized the words to several songs.*

absorb — To **absorb** can mean to take something into your mind. *The student absorbed all the facts.*

assimilate — To **assimilate** means to learn or **absorb** something so completely that it becomes part of you. *I assimilated all the information I could find about horses until I could give the talk without using any notes.*

take in — To **take in** can mean to understand and remember something. *Did you take in what she was telling you?*

digest — To **digest** can mean to think something over and take it into your mind. *Make sure you have time to digest all the information before the exam.*

---

contrasting words: **teach**

---

leave *verb*

to go away from somewhere. *We will **leave** when our taxi comes.*

depart — To **depart** means to leave. It is a more formal word. *The train departs at 10 a.m.*

withdraw — To **withdraw** means to take yourself away from a place, especially a room. *She withdrew to her study.*

retreat — To **retreat** means to go back. *The soldiers retreated to a safer position.*

retire — To **retire** can mean to go away from other people or leave what you are doing for a particular reason. *Sometimes I retire to my cottage to get away from the city crowds.*

emigrate — To **emigrate** means to leave your own country to go to live in another one. *Many people have emigrated from Europe to the United States.*

---

similar words: **flee**
contrasting words: **come, advance**

---

legal *adjective*

allowed or decided by law. *She took **legal** action to stop people walking across her property to the beach.*

lawful	**Lawful** means allowed by law. *He got a speeding ticket because it isn't lawful to drive fast through town.*
legitimate	**Legitimate** means in accordance with the law or established rules. *Being sick is a legitimate reason for staying home.*
permissible	**Permissible** means allowed. *Talking loudly is not permissible behavior in this library.*
authorized	**Authorized** means having been given the legal power to do something. *The babysitter was authorized to send the children to bed.*
proper	**Proper** means right or approved. *If you see someone breaking into a house, the proper thing to do is to call the police.*

similar words: **formal**
contrasting words: **illegal, dishonest**

lengthy *adjective*

long or using many words. *He gave us a **lengthy** explanation.*

rambling	**Rambling** can mean lengthy and not keeping to one train of thought. *Their rambling account of what happened puzzled us.*
wordy	**Wordy** means using more words than are needed. *We didn't listen to the wordy explanation.*
tedious	**Tedious** means too long and boring. *We didn't listen to the politician's tedious speech.*
verbose	**Verbose** is a more formal word for **wordy**. *That five-minute speech was a verbose way of saying thank you.*
long-winded	**Long-winded** means talking for too long. *He is so long-winded that he talks for half an hour if you ask him the simplest question.*

contrasting words: **brief**

lenient   *adjective*

not harsh or severe in treatment. *The judge was **lenient** because it was Alice's first offense.*

merciful

Merciful means showing kindness by not punishing someone, or not being cruel. *She was merciful, even though she knew he had broken the vase through carelessness.*

compassionate

Compassionate means showing pity and kindness to someone. *The compassionate children fed the stray kitten.*

humane

Humane means showing feelings of pity or tenderness in the way that kind and decent human beings should. *The warden of the jail was well-known for his humane treatment of prisoners.*

mild

Mild means not severe or harsh. *His mild manner made me feel less worried about the scolding.*

gentle

Gentle can mean not rough or violent. *Her gentle rebuke showed how kind and understanding she is.*

---

contrasting words: **strict**

---

lesson   *noun*

an amount or unit of teaching given at one time. *Ed has a one-hour drum **lesson** this afternoon.*

lecture

A **lecture** is a long speech made in front of an audience or class and meant to teach or inform. *We had a very interesting lecture on road safety today.*

seminar

A **seminar** is a meeting of students to discuss a particular subject. *I enjoyed the discussion in our history seminar and I asked lots of questions.*

claitss

A **class** can be the information taught to a student or students at one time. It is similar to **lesson**. *We had a class on Inuit folktales.*

course

A **co hurse** is a series of lessons. *I'm taking an art course once a week for the next ten weeks.*

lethargic   *adjective*

being in a state of sleepy laziness. *I feel so **lethargic** today that I don't want to do anything energetic.*

listless	**Listless** means having no energy or interest in anything. *It was such a hot day that we were all very listless.*
sluggish	**Sluggish** means moving slowly with no energy. *The car was very sluggish going up the hill.*
languid	**Languid** means weak, tired, or slow-moving. *Don't be surprised if your cold makes you languid.*
inert	**Inert** means slow or not active. *The inert python digested its meal in the shelter of a fallen tree.*

similar words: **apathetic, lazy, tired**
contrasting words: **energetic, lively, busy**

lift   *verb*

to move or bring something upward or to a higher position. *Please **lift** this heavy box for me.*

raise	To **raise** is so similar to **lift** that you can usually use either. *He was so tired that he couldn't raise his head from the pillow.*
elevate	To **elevate** can mean to lift or **raise** something. This meaning is usually used in more formal language. *The sculpture was elevated so that everyone could see it.*
hoist	To **hoist** means to lift something up, often with an effort. *The lumberjacks hoisted the log onto tr heir shoulders.*
lever	To **lever** means to lift and move something by putting a bar under it and pushing down on the other end of the bar. *The worker levered the boulder out of the way.*
jack up	To **jack up** means to lift something very heavy with a special tool called a jack. *We had to jack up the car so that we could change the tire.*

contrasting words: **drop**

240

light *adjective*

of little or less than usual weight. *I'm glad to be wearing **light** clothing in this heat.*

feathery   **Feathery** means light and airy like feathers. *The ballet dress was soft and feathery.*

thin   **Thin** means having opposite surfaces close together or having small thickness. *The birthday present was covered in thin wrapping paper that you could almost see through.*

fine   **Fine** can mean very **thin** or slender. *I don't think this thread will be strong enough because it's too fine.*

flimsy   **Flimsy** means not strongly made. *This flimsy fence will probably blow down in the wind.*

contrasting words: **heavy**

like *verb*

to find someone or something pleasant. *I **like** everyone in my class.*

enjoy   To **enjoy** means to take pleasure in something. *I enjoy barbecues.*

relish   To **relish** means to **enjoy** something to the full. *My grandmother relishes a hot cup of tea.*

appreciate   To **appreciate** means to value or be aware of the good things about something or someone. *He appreciates my cooking.*

welcome   To **welcome** can mean to receive or regard something or someone with pleasure. *I welcome the cooler weather after all this heat.*

similar words: **love**
contrasting words: **hate**

likely *adjective*

reasonably or apparently going to happen. *It is **likely** that it will rain tomorrow.*

probable	**Probable** is so similar to **likely** that you can usually use either. *Do you think it is probable that she will arrive by this afternoon?*
expected	**Expected** can mean likely to happen or come about. *The expected result in the election is for the tax increase to pass.*
liable	**Liable** can mean likely. It is so similar that you can usually use either. *Problems are liable to come up.*
apt	**Apt** means likely or inclined to do something. *He is apt to lose his temper at any moment.*

similar words: **possible, believable**
contrasting words: **unbelievable, impossible**

limit *verb*

to keep something within a certain amount or space. *I **limit** myself to one soft drink a week.*

restrict	To **restrict** is so similar to **limit** you can usually choose either word. *We had to restrict the time we spent watching TV so that we could finish our homework.*
control	To **control** can mean to keep something in check. *We had to control our spending so that our pocket money would last all week.*
curb	To **curb** means to **control** or hold back something. *I tried to curb my anger when my bike got a flat tire.*
inhibit	To **inhibit** means to hold back or hinder something. *No one supported Melanie's idea and this inhibited her enthusiasm.*
stifle	To **stifle** can mean to keep back or stop. *She stifled her giggles in class.*

limp *verb*

to walk unevenly and with difficulty because one leg or foot is injured or lame. *My foot ached as I **limped** along on my sprained ankle.*

hobble   To **hobble** means to walk unevenly and with difficulty. *I hobbled around after stubbing my toe.*

shuffle   To **shuffle** means to walk slowly, dragging your feet along the ground. *Bruce was so tired after the long walk that he shuffled straight off to bed.*

stagger   To **stagger** means to walk or move along very unsteadily, looking as though you might fall over. *He staggered during the last few meters of the marathon to cross the finish line in third place.*

totter   To **totter** means to sway or to walk unsteadily. *The boxer tottered around the ring and then fell to the mat.*

toddle   To **toddle** means to walk with short unsteady steps. *The baby toddled along on his chubby little legs.*

---

similar words: **walk, march, trudge**
contrasting words: **frisk**

---

line *noun*

something arranged like a thin mark or stroke made on a surface. *A **line** of trees grew on either side of the street.*

row   A **row** is a line of people or things. *We saw the movie from the back row of the theater.*

string   A **string** is a **row** or line of things. *There is a string of islands off the coast of Japan.*

file   A **file** is a line of people or things one behind the other. *The teacher told us to walk in single file.*

rank   A **rank** is a **row** or line, especially of soldiers. *The soldiers stood in their ranks waiting to be inspected.*

---

liquid *adjective*

flowing like water. *Oil is sometimes referred to as **liquid** gold because it is so valuable.*

fluid
: **Fluid** means liquid or able to flow. *Lava is the fluid rock that comes out of a volcano.*

runny
: **Runny** means pouring out liquid, or flowing. *The little boy had a runny nose because he had a cold. The runny apple pie spread all over the plate.*

sloppy
: **Sloppy** means wet and slushy. *The sloppy baby food ran down the infant's chin.*

molten
: **Molten** means made liquid by heat. *The fire had to be very, very hot to make the molten metal.*

list *verb*

to make a set of the names of things written down one under the other, so that you'll remember them. ***List** all the books you need from the library and I'll try to get them for you.*

index
: To **index** means to make an alphabetical list of names, places, or subjects in a book, showing their page numbers. *If you write a thesaurus, it is a good idea to index all the words you have included and put it at the back.*

tabulate
: To **tabulate** means to make a plan or chart listing things that are related to one another. *We tabulated the results of our experiment to show how we reached our conclusions.*

itemize
: To **itemize** means to give details about each part of an overall group. *We itemize our accounts so that our customers know exactly what they are paying for.*

enumerate
: To **enumerate** means to name things one by one or make them clear in a list. *Let's enumerate the arguments for and against buying it before you decide.*

similar words: **arrange, record**

live   *verb*

to be alive. *I will never forgive you as long as I **live**.*

be   To **be** can mean to live or have reality. *I'm afraid he is no more.*

exist   To **exist** can mean to have life or be real. *Do ghosts exist?*

breathe   To **breathe** can mean to **exist** or have life. *Everything that breathed was destroyed in the flood.*

survive   To **survive** means to stay alive or in existence, especially after someone's death or the end of something. *Three people were killed in the accident and one survived.*

remain   To **remain** can mean to stay alive. *Of my grandmother's ten brothers and sisters, now only two remain.*

---

contrasting words: **die**

---

lively   *adjective*

full of energy or spirit. *We had a **lively** party, with lots of dancing and laughter.*

frisky   **Frisky** means jumping around in a lively way. *The horses were very frisky after their long rest in the corral.*

vivacious   **Vivacious** means lively and energetic. *We have a vivacious teacher who makes our classes interesting and fun.*

playful   **Playful** means full of fun. *The playful puppy loved to run after the ball.*

frolicsome **Frolicsome** means enjoying happy or energetic play. *The playground was full of frolicsome children.*

jaunty   **Jaunty** means lively and confident. *He walked into the room with a jaunty step.*

---

similar words: **energetic**
contrasting words: **lethargic**

---

lonely   *adjective*

without friendly company. *He was **lonely** when his best friend was away.*

alone	**Alone** means by yourself. *She was alone in the house.*
lone	**Lone** means unaccompanied or not with anyone. *They could see a lone traveler coming toward them.*
solitary	**Solitary** means quite **alone** or without any companions. *I went on a solitary walk when I wanted time to think.*
reclusive	**Reclusive** means wanting to live by yourself and not see other people. *He is reclusive by nature but his family tries to visit him often.*

loot   *noun*

anything that has been obtained by stealing. *The burglars became frightened and ran away without any **loot**.*

booty	**Booty** is something stolen, especially by violence or in war. *The pirates shared their booty of gold.*
plunder	**Plunder** is something stolen by open force, as in a war. It is similar to **booty**. *The soldiers came home with a lot of plunder.*
spoils	**Spoils** are all sorts of loot taken by violence. It is similar to **booty** and **plunder**. *The outlaws held up three coaches but the spoils were not worth much.*
pickings	**Pickings** can be things obtained easily or in a way that is not strictly honest. *There were plenty of pickings for the cleaners when the crowd had left the sports ground.*

loud   *adjective*

producing a lot of sound so that you can hear it easily. *The **loud** noise startled me.*

blaring   **Blaring** means producing a loud harsh sound. *It was hard to relax at the beach because there were so many blaring radios.*

deafening   **Deafening** means so loud that it could make someone deaf. *The jackhammers were deafening so the workers had to wear ear plugs.*

raucous   **Raucous** means harsh-sounding. *We heard raucous laughter coming from the party.*

shrill   **Shrill** means loud and piercing. *The canary's shrill whistle woke us up every morning.*

resonant   **Resonant** means deep and booming. *He has a resonant baritone voice that can be heard all through the auditorium.*

contrasting words: **quiet**

love   *verb*

to feel strong affection for another person. *I **love** my parents and my brothers and sisters.*

adore   To **adore** means to feel very strong love for something or someone. *The children adored their puppy.*

dote on   To **dote on** means to love someone or something so much that you appear to be silly. *She dotes on horses and talks about them all the time.*

cherish   To **cherish** can mean to feel love for someone or hold them dear. *He cherishes his grandfather and enjoys making him presents.*

care for   To **care for** means to have a fondness for someone or something. *I don't care for spinach.*

similar words: **like, worship**
contrasting words: **hate**

loving *adjective*

feeling or showing love. *Her **loving** parents always tried to do the best for her.*

affectionate   **Affectionate** means having and showing feelings of love toward someone. *The affectionate puppy kept licking my hand.*

fond   **Fond** means having warm feelings toward someone. *I have fond memories of the people we met during our holidays.*

tender   **Tender** can mean loving in a romantic way. *The film ended with the two lovers in a tender embrace.*

devoted   **Devoted** means showing a very strong attachment to something or someone. *He is devoted to his pets and spends hours caring for them.*

lucky *adjective*

having good luck or good fortune. *We were **lucky** to find a parking spot so close to the arena.*

fortunate   **Fortunate** means being lucky or having good fortune. *You were fortunate to find the money you lost.*

happy   **Happy** can mean **fortunate** or lucky for everyone concerned. *It was a happy coincidence to meet you at the movies.*

promising   **Promising** means likely to turn out well. *The weather looks promising, so perhaps we could have a picnic.*

auspicious   **Auspicious** means favorable or showing signs of success. *All the signs were auspicious, so our parents decided to set up their own business.*

contrasting words: **unlucky**

mad   *adjective*

mentally ill or unbalanced. *The dog went **mad** and behaved dangerously because it had rabies.*

crazy	**Crazy** is so similar to **mad** that you can usually use either. *The book is about a crazy man who really thinks he can fly.*
insane	**Insane** means mentally ill. It is similar to **mad** and **crazy** but is often used in a more serious way. *The explorer almost went insane from loneliness and starvation.*
maniacal	**Maniacal** means violently or dangerously mad. *I was scared because his face had a maniacal look.*
disturbed	**Disturbed** can mean emotionally or mentally unstable. *The doctor told the disturbed patient to relax and rest for a few weeks.*
nutty	**Nutty** can mean **crazy** or odd. It is only suited to everyday language. *Barking like a dog sure is a nutty way of showing that you are upset.*

similar words: **silly**
contrasting words: **sane**

main   *adjective*

most important or biggest. *My **main** reason for training so hard is to get onto the swimming team for the Olympics.*

major	**Major** means greater in importance or size. *His major interest in life is playing the guitar.*
chief	**Chief** means most important or main. *My chief problem is with spelling.*
key	**Key** means main or important. *The goalie is a key member of the hockey team.*
fundamental	**Fundamental** means most important or basic. *You have to learn the fundamental rules of the road before you can get a license to drive a car.*
primary	**Primary** means first in order of importance. *My primary concern is finding enough food to feed all of the guests.*

similar words: **significant, best**
contrasting words: **minor**

make   *verb*

to bring something into being. *Paul and I are **making** a batch of cookies.*

produce
To **produce** means to bring something forth or into existence. *My favorite author produces a new book every year.*

manufacture
To **manufacture** means to make or **produce** something by hand or machine, especially in large numbers. *Dad works for a company that manufactures furniture.*

form
To **form** means to make or **produce** something. *The children piled up sand to form a sand castle.*

prepare
To **prepare** means to make something ready. *I am practicing every day to prepare myself for the performance.*

whip up
To **whip up** means to make something quickly. *Mom and Dad had to whip up a meal when their friends made a surprise visit.*

---

similar words: **create, build, produce**
contrasting words: **destroy**

---

male   *noun*

a man or a boy. *Our experiment was designed to find out why some **males** go bald.*

man
A **man** is a mature or adult male. *My father is known to be a friendly man.*

boy
A **boy** is a male who has not reached adulthood. *The boys played outside on their skateboards.*

young man
A **young man** is a male who is almost an adult, or a **boy** who behaves in a mature way. *The principal said she was proud of all the young men and women who were entering high school.*

gentleman
Gentleman is a courteous term for a man. It is used mainly on formal occasions. *Ladies and gentlemen, thank you for attending this meeting.*

---

contrasting words: **female**

maltreat *verb*

to treat someone roughly or cruelly. *The dog bit him when he **maltreated** it.*

abuse
To **abuse** means to treat someone in a way that causes emotional or physical hurt. *Don't abuse me again in front of my friends.*

victimize
To **victimize** means to punish or harm someone unfairly. *We felt victimized when the whole class had to stay after school because two students caused trouble.*

torment
To **torment** means to cause someone a lot of pain or suffering. *Please don't torment me anymore with your teasing.*

hound
To **hound** means to worry or pursue someone unkindly and continually. *The detective hounded the suspect night and day.*

torture
To **torture** means to cause severe pain, sometimes to make someone tell you something. *The explorers were tortured by the cruel heat of the desert sun.*

similar words: **subdue**

manage *verb*

to be in charge of something or someone. *She was asked to **manage** the store while the owner was away.*

run
To **run** can mean to conduct or administer something, such as a business or an experiment. *My parents run a small printing business.*

direct
To **direct** can mean to guide something or someone by giving instructions. *Our class teacher will direct the school play this year.*

govern
To **govern** can mean to guide and have a controlling influence over something or someone. *Public opinion governed the committee's decision to stop the project.*

control
To **control** means to be in charge of or **direct** someone or something. *The teacher had to control a large group of children on the field trip to the zoo.*

supervise
To **supervise** means to manage, keep an eye on, or be responsible for someone or something. *The principal supervised my class the day the French teacher was absent.*

similar words: **rule**

manager   *noun*

someone who runs a business or supervises other people at work. *My **manager** gave me an outline of my activities for the month.*

director

A **director** can be one of a group of people who control the affairs of a company or a government department. *The board of directors meets once a month to review the progress of the project.*

superintendent

A **superintendent** is someone who is in charge of work being done, a business, or a building. *The superintendent is in charge of all the repairs carried out in our apartment.*

administrator

An **administrator** is someone who directs or manages something according to set rules or ways. *She was a good administrator and her employees were happy to follow her directions.*

commissioner

A **commissioner** can be someone in charge of a government department. *They rewarded her for her years of good work by making her a commissioner.*

official

An **official** is someone who has the authority to do a particular job, usually in connection with government. *The municipal official said he would tell the garbage collectors not to be so noisy.*

similar words: **boss**

manner   *noun*

a way of behaving or of doing things. *The doctor has a good bedside **manner**.*

attitude

An **attitude** can be the way you hold your body or behave. *The students have a positive attitude about school.*

bearing

Your **bearing** is the way you behave or stand. *She had the grace and the strong bearing of an athlete.*

carriage

Your **carriage** is the way you hold your head and body when you walk or stand. *He has the tall, straight carriage of a soldier.*

stance

Your **stance** is the position of your body when you are standing. *Her confident stance showed that she was used to winning.*

posture

Your **posture** is the particular position of your body at any time. *He photographed them in a kneeling posture.*

similar words: **appearance**

march   *verb*

to walk like a soldier, with swinging arms and even steps. *We **marched** in time to the drumbeat.*

parade   To **parade** means to march, often in a procession or for display. *Our band paraded into the auditorium for the assembly.*

stride   To **stride** means to walk with long bold steps. *She strode quickly along the street without looking to the left or right.*

strut   To **strut** means to walk in a proud or pompous way, with your back straight and your head held high. *The actor strutted across the stage to accept the award.*

swagger   To **swagger** means to walk in a pompous way, hoping to draw attention to yourself. *He was so proud of his new clothes that he swaggered along when he wore them.*

---

similar words: **walk, limp, trudge**

---

meal   *noun*

food eaten at more or less fixed times each day. *Breakfast is my favorite **meal**.*

snack   A **snack** is a small quick meal. *I have a snack every afternoon after school.*

feast   A **feast** is a large meal set out for many guests. *They held a feast after the wedding.*

spread   A **spread** can be a large meal for many people. It is similar to **feast** but is more suited to everyday language. *They put on a wonderful spread to welcome their friends from overseas.*

repast   A **repast** is a meal. It is a slightly old-fashioned or formal word. *Let us sit down to our evening repast.*

---

similar words: **food**

---

mean *adjective*

bad-tempered and cruel. *A **mean** neighbor yelled at us for cutting across the lawn.*

unkind   **Unkind** means not very friendly or warm-hearted. *Don't be unkind and leave me alone when I'm afraid.*

shabby   **Shabby** can mean unfair or mean. *That's a shabby way to treat a good friend.*

contemptible   **Contemptible** means disgraceful and mean. *Tripping the other runner was a contemptible thing to do.*

despicable   **Despicable** means disgraceful and deserving contempt and scorn. *It was despicable of you to lie to your friends.*

similar words: **resentful**
contrasting words: **kind**

meaning *noun*

something that is intended to be said or shown. *The teacher explained the **meaning** of the poem.*

gist   **Gist** is the most important part of something. *I understood the gist of her message, so I can explain it to you.*

drift   **Drift** can be the general meaning of something. *Did you get the drift of that argument?*

significance   **Significance** can be so similar to **meaning** that you can usually use either. *The guide explained the significance of the sculpture.*

sense   **Sense** can be the particular meaning of a word, statement, or a passage in a book. *In what sense is the poet using that word?*

essence   **Essence** is the basic nature or character of someone or something. *The artist has caught the essence of the President in that portrait.*

measure   *verb*

to decide the size or quantity of something by using a special instrument, such as a ruler or scales. *We **measured** the length of rope we would need.*

gauge	**Gauge** means to measure the size, capacity, amount, or force of certain things. *Airports have instruments to gauge the rate at which the wind is blowing.*
estimate	To **estimate** means to measure or work out roughly the quantity, size, or amount of something. *We estimated how much food we would need for our camping trip.*
survey	To **survey** can mean to find out the form and boundaries of land by measuring it. *He surveyed the new area and marked the corners of the lot.*
rate	To **rate** means to measure by comparing one thing with another. *The swimming coach records times so that our progress can be rated.*
sound	To **sound** can mean to measure how far below the surface of the water something is. *The trawler sounded the channel to locate the school of fish.*

similar words: **judge, calculate**

mediocre   *adjective*

neither good nor bad. *It was a **mediocre** film but we watched it to the end.*

indifferent	**Indifferent** can mean neither good nor bad in quality or character. *I am a very indifferent chess player.*
second-rate	**Second-rate** can mean mediocre, or not very good. *He's a second-rate actor and is often out of work.*
middling	**Middling** can mean mediocre or **second-rate**. It is more suited to everyday language. *Most new players are only middling at tennis.*
banal	**Banal** means unoriginal or dull because it has been used too much. *The plot of the TV soap opera was so banal we could guess everything that was going to happen.*
mundane	**Mundane** means ordinary, dull, or boring. *We rejected his mundane suggestion when Sarah made a better one.*

similar words: **ordinary, inferior**
contrasting words: **superior**

meet *verb*

to come face to face with someone. *I **meet** my friend on the way to school each morning.*

encounter To **encounter** means to meet someone, especially unexpectedly. *I encountered an old friend in town yesterday.*

come across To **come across** means to meet someone by chance. *Whom do you think I came across yesterday?*

run into To **run into** can be so similar to **come across** that you can usually use either. *She ran into her uncle at the carnival.*

bump into To **bump into** means to meet someone by chance. *I bumped into him at the supermarket.*

join up with To **join up with** means to meet someone by arrangement. *I will join up with you at your place after dinner.*

meeting *noun*

an arrangement to come together for a purpose. *Next week's **meeting** of the chess club will be on Wednesday.*

appointment An **appointment** can be an arrangment made between people to meet to do something. *Daniel has an appointment to have his hair cut this afternoon.*

date A **date** is an **appointment**, usually made with a friend to do something enjoyable. *Clare and Tessa have a date to go to the movies.*

rendezvous A **rendezvous** is a meeting arranged beforehand. *Delroy has agreed to be at our rendezvous at 7:00 tonight.*

assignation An **assignation** is a secret or forbidden meeting. *The ship's captain sent word to the smugglers to come to an assignation at midnight.*

tryst A **tryst** is a **rendezvous**, especially between lovers. *Romeo and Juliet arranged a secret tryst in the garden.*

mess   *noun*

a dirty or untidy state. *The garage was a **mess** after I took apart my bike.*

jumble   A **jumble** is a confused mess. *I left my room in a jumble this morning because I slept in.*

clutter   A **clutter** is an untidy group or pile of things. *There was a clutter of paper on the floor after we had opened our presents.*

shambles   **Shambles** means any place or thing that is in confusion or disorder. *The classroom was a shambles after the vandals had broken into it.*

litter   **Litter** is garbage scattered about. *The park ranger was angry about the litter the picnickers had left.*

message   *noun*

information sent to one person from another. *Evan took a **message** about the picnic from Dorothy to Charles.*

letter   A **letter** is a written or printed message addressed and sent to someone. *We received a long letter from Susan when she went to Paris.*

note   A **note** is a short letter. *My mother sent a note to my teacher when I stayed home sick.*

memo   A **memo** is a brief **note**. It is the short form of the word "memorandum." *The principal sent a memo to the teachers, asking them to attend a meeting.*

dispatch   A **dispatch** is an official message sent by a messenger. *Captain Collins sent a dispatch to the general asking for reinforcements.*

communiqué   A **communiqué** is an official news report. *After the meeting the premiers issued a communiqué to the public.*

similar words: **report**

messenger   *noun*

someone who carries a message. *Large companies often employ* **messengers** *to take letters to their customers or to branch offices.*

courier
A **courier** is someone who carries messages, letters, or parcels for other people. *The courier took the important document across the city to be signed.*

mail carrier
A **mail carrier** is someone who takes letters and packages from post offices to the people to whom they are addressed. *The mail carriers are always extra busy in December.*

envoy
An **envoy** is someone who is sent to represent another person or a country. *The general sent an envoy to the besieged town demanding that its troops surrender.*

correspondent
A **correpondent** can be a person employed to contribute news regularly from a particular place. *The news correspondent had information about the earthquake.*

method   *noun*

a way of going about something, especially in an orderly way. *If you follow this* **method** *when you do the problem, you will find it easy.*

approach
An **approach** is a particular way of going about something. *A new approach to reading has been accepted at our school.*

procedure
A **procedure** is a way of doing something. *She followed the usual procedure for applying for a job and was offered an interview.*

technique
A **technique** is a particular way of doing or performing something. *His serving technique is influenced by his tennis instructor.*

means
Means can be a method or way used to reach an end or a goal. *Cars, buses, and trains are the common means of transportation in cities.*

mimic   *verb*

to copy someone's voice or movements. *Some birds can **mimic** human voices.*

imitate

To **imitate** means to copy or to use someone as a model. *She often imitates her mother talking on the phone.*

ape

To **ape** means to copy or mimic someone, sometimes without thinking about or realizing what you are doing. *He is only four but he apes his big brother.*

mock

To **mock** means to **imitate** someone in an exaggerated way in order to make fun of this person. *The comedian mocked the singing styles of several musicians.*

caricature

To **caricature** can mean to mimic someone by exaggerating or making fun of the person's unusual features. *The actor caricatured the Secretary of State.*

impersonate

To **impersonate** means to pretend to be someone else. *The thief impersonated a police officer to persuade the guard to open the door.*

minimize   *verb*

to make something seem as small or unimportant as possible. *We must not **minimize** the risks we are taking.*

lessen

To **lessen** can mean to make less. *The cold pack lessened the swelling.*

trivialize

To **trivialize** means to make something important seem unimportant. *That book trivializes the subject of war.*

play down

To **play down** means to treat something as unimportant in order to keep attention away from it. *She played down the amount of help she had given.*

make light of

To **make light of** means to treat something as unimportant or amusing. *She made light of her injuries.*

laugh off

To **laugh off** means to treat something lightly, even though you may not really feel that way. *He laughed off the pain he was feeling.*

---

contrasting words: **emphasize**

---

minor *adjective*

lesser in importance or size. *His plan had only a few **minor** faults.*

secondary   **Secondary** means next after the first in order of importance. *Moving the damaged cars was secondary to attending to the injured people.*

trivial   **Trivial** means of very little importance. *Trivial everyday chores seem to take up more time than they are worth.*

trifling   **Trifling** is so similar to **trivial** you can usually use either word. *I interrupted her work but she said it was a trifling matter that could wait.*

petty   **Petty** means of little importance. *We ignored petty complaints about the paint we used on the tree house.*

slight   **Slight** can mean minor or small. *There is a slight change in our plans to go away next week.*

similar words: **insignificant, subordinate**
contrasting words: **main, significant**

miracle *noun*

an occurrence that is surprising because it is thought to be very unlikely or impossible. *It is a **miracle** that you weren't hurt when you fell out of the tree.*

wonder   A **wonder** is a surprising or odd event. *It's a wonder that Trish telephoned me just when I was thinking about her.*

marvel   A **marvel** is so similar to a **wonder** that you can usually use either. *The acrobats performed one marvel after another.*

sensation   A **sensation** can be an event that makes someone surprised or excited. It is more suited to everyday language. *The roller coaster ride was a real sensation!*

curiosity   A **curiosity** can be an odd event. *The strange disappearance of my slippers is a curiosity.*

miserable   *adjective*

very unhappy. *We were **miserable** because we couldn't take a day off.*

depressed	**Depressed** means feeling dejected or miserable. *She was depressed when she realized she had forgotten about the party.*
despondent	**Despondent** means feeling downhearted or in low spirits. *He was despondent when he realized that he had no chance of winning the race.*
forlorn	**Forlorn** means miserable because you are left all alone. *The sick boy was forlorn when his friends went camping without him.*
heartbroken	**Heartbroken** means completely overcome with sadness or grief. *She was heartbroken when her best friend died.*
blue	**Blue** means sad or **depressed**. It is more suited to everyday language. *He was blue when everyone went to the movie except him.*

similar words: **sad, glum**
contrasting words: **happy, joyful, glad**

misery   *noun*

great unhappiness. *He caused **misery** to his parents when he was arrested for shoplifting.*

sorrow	**Sorrow** means grief or sadness. *Families feel great sorrow when relatives move far away.*
anguish	**Anguish** is very great **sorrow** or worry. *The parents of the lost child suffered terrible anguish.*
depression	**Depression** is the state of your mind when you feel worried, miserable, and hopeless. *He suffered from depression when he was told his broken leg would take several weeks to heal.*
melancholy	**Melancholy** is a feeling of sadness or **depression**. *Her melancholy was so deep none of us could cheer her up.*
gloom	**Gloom** can be a feeling of unhappiness or **depression**. *Gloom fell on us all when we heard about our classmate's accident.*

contrasting words: **happiness**

misfortune   *noun*

bad luck. *Losing your lunch money was a **misfortune**.*

accident	An **accident** is an unwanted or unlucky happening. *Our car accident stopped us from going on our trip.*
mishap	A **mishap** is an unfortunate accident. *I had a mishap on my way to school − I fell over and hurt my knee.*
hardship	**Hardship** means bad luck or suffering in the way you live. *Many families endured great hardship during the Depression.*
blow	A **blow** is a sudden shock or misfortune. *It was a blow to discover our flight would be delayed for several hours.*
evil	An **evil** is something that can cause suffering or misfortune or disaster. *The pollution of our environment is an evil we can prevent.*

similar words: **disaster**

misrepresent   *verb*

to describe or show something in an incorrect or false way. *Our real complaints were **misrepresented** in the bad newspaper article.*

twist	To **twist** can mean to change the meaning of something on purpose. *You twisted what I said to make it sound as though I agreed with you.*
distort	To **distort** can mean to misrepresent or **twist** something. *The reporter distorted the facts, so it was difficult to know the truth.*
slant	To **slant** can mean to present or tell something in a way that makes one particular thing seem more important. *They slanted the report to make their own ideas seem more sensible.*
exaggerate	To **exaggerate** means to say more than is true about something to make it sound better. *He exaggerated the story until it sounded as though he alone had saved the whole town.*
falsify	To **falsify** means to represent something in a false or incorrect way. *The accountant falsified the records to cover up her stealing.*

mistake   *noun*

something someone has done wrongly without realizing it. *I made three **mistakes** in my spelling.*

error	An **error** is so similar to mistake you can usually use either word. *I saw my error and corrected it.*
slip	A **slip** is so similar to mistake and **error** that you can usually choose any of them. *I made a slip in adding up the bill.*
blunder	A **blunder** is a silly mistake. *What a blunder to tell you the wrong day!*
misunderstanding	A **misunderstanding** is a mistake of meaning, or a misinterpretation. *A misunderstanding occurred because he did not receive the whole message.*
faux pas	A **faux pas** is an embarrassing **slip** in speech or behavior. It is a French word. *It was a faux pas to invite them both to the same party, since they dislike each other.*

mix   *verb*

to combine or blend things together. *I **mixed** the eggs, sugar, milk, and flour together and made some pancakes.*

mash	To **mash** means to mix something by pounding or crushing. *I mashed the potatoes until they were soft and creamy.*
emulsify	To **emulsify** means to mix things together so that they form a liquid that looks like milk and is often rather oily. *I shook the jar of salad dressing to emulsify the oil and vinegar.*
stir	To **stir** means to mix something by moving a spoon or something similar around in it. *When you make a sauce you have to stir it all the time it is cooking.*
fold	To **fold** can mean to mix something in gently by turning one part over another with a spoon or something similar. *The cook folded the flour into the mixture to make a sponge cake.*

similar words: **combine**

mixture *noun*

any combination of different kinds, parts, qualities, and so on. *We need a* **mixture** *of foods in our diet to keep healthy.*

assortment	An **assortment** is a **collection** of things of various kinds. *We have a wide assortment of travel books in our library.*
collection	A **collection** is a group of things gathered together from different places. *A collection of stamps from around the world was on display in the library.*
jumble	A **jumble** is a confused or disorderly group of things. *Her clothes were in a jumble on the floor.*
hodgepodge	A **hodgepodge** is an unordered mixture. It is so similar to **jumble** you can often use either word. *Her bookshelves were a hodgepodge of books, magazines, and photo albums.*
medley	A **medley** is a mixture of different kinds of things, especially a piece of music combining passages from other musical compositions. *The band played a medley of jazz music.*

moderate *adjective*

keeping within proper bounds, or not extreme. *We put a* **moderate** *price on the goods at our school sale and sold everything.*

reasonable	**Reasonable** means fair or moderate. *We made a reasonable profit at the garage sale.*
modest	**Modest** can mean of medium value, quality, or amount. *They bought a modest home in the country.*
restrained	**Restrained** means controlled or kept in check. *There was polite but restrained applause for the amateur singer.*
middle-of-the-road	**Middle-of-the-road** means moderate or not going to extremes in thought or behavior. *The politician's opinions about pollution are middle-of-the-road.*
temperate	**Temperate** means moderate or controlled. *She has a temperate and easygoing personality.*

contrasting words: **intense**

modern *adjective*

belonging to or used in the present time. *Modern airplanes are much bigger and faster than the early ones.*

contemporary	**Contemporary** can mean modern or existing now. *The house was decorated in a contemporary style.*
current	**Current** means belonging to the present time. *We read about many of the current problems of the world in the newspaper.*
up-to-date	**Up-to-date** can mean modern or to do with the newest ideas and styles. *He used only the most up-to-date books to teach us science.*
recent	**Recent** can mean made or done not long ago. *The teacher hasn't had time to grade our most recent project.*
late	**Late** can mean new or **recent**. *My mom likes late model cars because they run better.*

similar words: **new**
contrasting words: **old-fashioned, old**

momentary *adjective*

lasting for a very short space of time. *There was a **momentary** flash of light before we heard the explosion.*

brief	**Brief** can mean short in time. *We are having a brief rest before finishing our work.*
fleeting	**Fleeting** means passing swiftly away. *We had a fleeting view of the race cars as they went round the bend.*
passing	**Passing** can mean **brief** or going by quickly. *They hope my passion for very loud music is only a passing phase.*
ephemeral	**Ephemeral** means not lasting for very long. *The beauty of a rose is ephemeral, as it fades and dies within a day or two.*
transitory	**Transitory** means continuing only for a brief time. *Rainstorms in this area are transitory; they come and go quickly.*

similar words: **temporary**
contrasting words: **permanent**

move *verb*

to change from one place or position to another. *David was so comfortable in his hammock he didn't want to **move**.*

shift
To **shift** means to move from one place or position to another. This is a more informal word than move. *Shift your weight from your left foot to your right as you do the exercise.*

stir
To **stir** can mean to move gently or in a slight way. *The leaves of the tree stirred in the gentle breeze.*

budge
To **budge** means to move away. This is usually used with the word *not* or *can't*. *We tried to push the truck out of the ditch, but it would not budge.*

give way
To **give way** can mean to move or yield. *We all tried to push the heavy rock and it finally gave way.*

moving *adjective*

changing from place to place. *The **moving** shadows on my bedroom wall frightened me.*

mobile
Mobile means able to move or be moved. *After two weeks in bed with a broken leg, Timothy is mobile again.*

maneuvrable
Maneuvrable means easy to move around. *The small car was very maneuvrable in busy traffic.*

dynamic
Dynamic means having to do with the power that causes movement. *A battery is the dynamic force in some children's toys.*

kinetic
Kinetic means having to do with movement. *A mobile is an example of kinetic art.*

contrasting words: **steady, still**

mumble   *verb*

to speak softly and not clearly. *If you **mumble** no one will know what you are saying.*

mutter   To **mutter** means to speak or grumble in a low voice that is hard to understand. *He muttered angrily to himself.*

lisp   To **lisp** means to speak in such a way that you pronounce "s" and "z" like the "th" sound of *thin. I have been lisping less since I have been going to a speech therapist.*

stammer   To **stammer** means to speak with breaks and pauses that you can't control or with repetitions of some words or sounds. *He was so surprised and pleased he could only stammer out his thanks.*

murmur   To **mumur** means to make a low, indistinct sound. *The patient was murmuring while regaining consciousness.*

sputter   To **sputter** means to talk quickly and in a confused way, making it difficult to pronounce the words. *He sputtered with rage when he heard the news.*

---

contrasting words: **pronounce**

---

musical   *adjective*

pleasing to your ears like music. *The **musical** tones of the robins drifted through the meadow.*

tuneful   **Tuneful** means full of or producing pleasant and agreeable sounds. *We enjoyed the tuneful singing of the children.*

melodious   **Melodious** means having an attractive sound like a melody or tune. *We were wakened by the melodious ringing of nearby church bells.*

lyrical   **Lyrical** means having the form and musical quality of a song. *He recited the lyrical poem in his light singsong voice.*

mellow   **Mellow** can mean having a very deep and rich sound. *The last mellow notes of the organ echoed around the concert hall.*

sweet   **Sweet** can mean light and pleasant to your ears. *She fell asleep to the sweet sounds of the lullaby.*

---

contrasting words: **discordant**

---

musician   *noun*

someone who plays or composes music. *She wants to be a **musician** in an orchestra when she leaves school.*

virtuoso   A **virtuoso** is a highly skilled musician. *He is a virtuoso on the violin.*

instrumentalist   An **instrumentalist** is someone who plays a musical instrument. *There were six instrumentalists at the chamber concert.*

soloist   A **soloist** is someone who performs a piece of music for one singer or player, with or without an accompaniment. *The soloist at the concert was a violinist.*

accompanist   An **accompanist** is someone who provides a musical backing for a melody. *I played the piano as the accompanist for my sister, who played a violin solo.*

naive   *adjective*

ignorant, or understanding little about the affairs of the world. *His **naive** comment showed us that he had no idea how serious the situation was.*

simple   **Simple** can mean lacking knowledge, ignorant, or unaware. *He was a simple soul who wanted nothing more than to tend his garden and his animals.*

unworldly   **Unworldly** means having little or no knowledge of the ways of the world. *The scientist was an unworldly woman whose main concern was her research.*

unsophisticated   **Unsophisticated** means not changed by or experienced in the interests and pleasures of the world. *She has lived in many cities, but she still dresses in a casual, unsophisticated way.*

gullible   **Gullible** means easily deceived or cheated. *People always played practical jokes on him because he was so gullible.*

innocent   **Innocent** can mean having the simplicity of a person who isn't experienced in the ways of the world. *He had an innocent air that was free of worry.*

name   *noun*

what something or someone is called. *Have you thought of a **name** for your new kitten?*

title A **title** is a name given to someone to show occupation or rank in society. *She earned the title "Doctor" by studying hard for her medical degree.*

pseudonym A **pseudonym** is a made-up name used instead of a writer's real name. *He decided to use a pseudonym so nobody would know he had written the book.*

pen name A **pen name** is the same as a **pseudonym**. *Some authors use pen names so they can remain anonymous.*

alias An **alias** is a false name someone uses to try to hide who he or she really is. *The criminal gave an alias to get a new passport and flee the country.*

nickname A **nickname** is a name people call you, usually in a friendly way, instead of your real name. *Her nickname is "Spike" because she's a great volleyball player.*

name   *verb*

to give a name to someone or something. *They **named** the baby Emma.*

call To **call** can be so similar to **name** that you can usually use either word. *They called the kitten Whiskers.*

title To **title** means to **call** or name something. *What have you titled your new book?*

dub To **dub** can mean to make up a name or title to use instead of someone's real name. *We dubbed him "The Rat."*

tag To **tag** can mean to use a special word or phrase to describe someone. *They tagged him a genius.*

term To **term** means to name someone or something, or to give it a label. *According to this fitness chart, you would be termed "very healthy."*

narrow *adjective*
not wide. *The path through the garden was very **narrow**.*

tight
    Tight can mean fitting closely, especially too closely. *We all got into the bus but it was a tight squeeze.*

close
    Close can mean narrow or **tight**. *During the train trip we'll be living in close quarters.*

small
    Small can mean narrow or not great in extent. *The rabbit squeezed through a small hole in the fence.*

confined
    Confined means restricted to a very small space. *The lion lived in a very confined area at the zoo.*

cramped
    Cramped can mean narrow or not having enough space. *The room was cramped with three desks in it.*

contrasting words: **wide, spacious, thick**

narrow-minded *adjective*
lacking in understanding of other people's ideas. *He's so **narrow-minded** he doesn't understand the opinions of others.*

intolerant
    Intolerant means not allowing other people to have or express opinions different from your own. *She is very intolerant of people who like to go to movies instead of playing sports on the weekend.*

bigoted
    Bigoted means holding an unreasonable opinion and being **intolerant** of the opinions of others. *The bigoted man said rude and foolish things.*

biased
    Biased can mean having a strong opinion that stops you from seeing the other side of an argument. *The soccer player was too biased in favor of his sport to see any good in baseball.*

prejudiced
    Prejudiced means influenced without a sensible or balanced reason. *The dog-show judge was prejudiced in favor of the poodle because he has one himself.*

conservative
    Conservative means opposed to new ideas and sudden changes of any kind. *She is so conservative in her dress that she never wears jeans.*

contrasting words: **broad-minded, neutral**

nasty *adjective*

unpleasant or discourteous. *Don was **nasty** to me after our argument.*

malicious   **Malicious** means wanting to cause harm for no reason. *Ruining the wedding cake was the act of a malicious person.*

spiteful   **Spiteful** means likely to hinder or to cause harm in little ways. *I wouldn't trust her when she's in that spiteful mood.*

disagreeable   **Disagreeable** means wanting to be unpleasant. *People learned to recognize the clerk's disagreeable moods and wait to talk to him.*

similar words: **resentful, mean, rude**
contrasting words: **kind, polite, nice, agreeable**

naughty *adjective*

behaving in an annoying or irritating way. *The **naughtiest** person in the class had to stay after school.*

badly behaved   **Badly behaved** means not behaving properly. *I was badly behaved because I didn't like my babysitter.*

mischievous   **Mischievous** means behaving in a way that is naughty without meaning serious harm. *The mischievous toddler threw his daddy's shoes in the bath.*

incorrigible   **Incorrigible** means showing that you intend to do what you like even though it's wrong. *The incorrigible child had every intention of pouring water all over the kitchen floor.*

uncooperative   **Uncooperative** means not helpful or unwilling to work together. *The work will take longer if you are uncooperative.*

perverse   **Perverse** means deliberately going against what is expected or wanted. *She is in a perverse mood and won't go to bed.*

similar words: **disobedient**
contrasting words: **well-behaved, obedient**

nautical   *adjective*

having to do with ships, sailors, or sailing. *If you want to learn to sail, you will have to learn the proper **nautical** terms.*

seafaring
: **Seafaring** means traveling on the sea. *It has been a seafaring nation for generations.*

seagoing
: **Seagoing** means designed for or able to sail on the open sea. *They have bought a seagoing launch and are going to sail around the world.*

maritime
: **Maritime** means having to do with ships or the sea. *International maritime law states that any ship must go to the aid of another ship in trouble.*

seaworthy
: **Seaworthy** means in a fit condition to sail at sea. *The inspector said the boat was seaworthy and they could start as soon as they wished.*

naval
: **Naval** can mean having to do with ships, these days only warships. *They fought a naval battle not far from the islands.*

near   *adjective*

being at a short distance from something. *As he lives **near** the school, it only takes him two minutes to get home.*

close
: **Close** can have almost the same meaning as **near**. *My house is close, so we'll go there now.*

next
: **Next** means nearest in place or position. *I'll just be in the next room.*

adjacent
: **Adjacent** means lying near or alongside something. *The school bought the adjacent block of land to give us a bigger playground.*

neighboring
: **Neighboring** means living or placed near something or someone. *We went to play in the neighboring park.*

warm
: **Warm** sometimes means being quite near to something you're looking for, usually in a game. This is usually used in everyday language. *Keep looking, you're very warm now.*

contrasting words: **distant**

necessary *adjective*

unable to be done without. *Water is **necessary** for life.*

essential	**Essential** means absolutely necessary. *Flour is an essential ingredient in bread.*
vital	**Vital** can be so similar to **essential** that you can usually use either. *Careful preparations are vital if this project is to be a success.*
crucial	**Crucial** means of the greatest importance. *Checking the air tanks before you go scuba diving is crucial.*
imperative	**Imperative** means necessary or not to be avoided. *It was imperative that our boat reach the shore before the storm came.*
obligatory	**Obligatory** means necessary, required, or considered as binding. *Typing will be an obligatory part of this job.*

contrasting words: **extra**

neglect *verb*

to pay no attention to something, usually by ignoring it. *He **neglected** his appearance when he was on vacation.*

overlook	To **overlook** means to miss or ignore something. *The burglars overlooked the ring because it was in a cheap box.*
leave out	To **leave out** means to forget about or ignore someone or something. *He did badly on the test because he left out one question.*
omit	To **omit** means to **leave out** or fail to do something. *He omitted phoning before he came over and had to wait for us to get home.*
disregard	To **disregard** means to fail to pay any attention or thought to something or someone. *She disregarded my wishes.*
forget	To **forget** can mean to fail to remember someone or something, sometimes on purpose. *Forget about going to his place and come with me instead.*

contrasting words: **remember**

negotiate *verb*

to deal with someone in order to prepare some kind of agreement, such as between countries or in business. *The two countries **negotiated** to write a peace treaty to end the fighting.*

decide To **decide** can mean to settle something in doubt. *Let's ask the teacher to decide for us.*

arbitrate To **arbitrate** means to judge or settle a disagreement between other people. *Will you arbitrate for us, because we can't agree?*

mediate To **mediate** means to come between people who are arguing to try to help them to agree. *The consumer affairs official mediated between the store and the customer until they reached an agreement over the damaged goods.*

intervene To **intervene** means to step in, in order to solve a problem. *When the unions still couldn't agree, the government finally intervened.*

intercede To **intercede** means to speak or act on behalf of someone in trouble. *She interceded for the student in his argument with the principal.*

nervous *adjective*

worried or frightened, especially about something that might happen in the future. *I am **nervous** about going to my new school.*

anxious **Anxious** means very worried or uneasy. *We were anxious when the hikers didn't get back on time.*

apprehensive **Apprehensive** means afraid of what might happen. *We were apprehensive about meeting our new teacher.*

edgy **Edgy** means nervous and irritable. *It makes most people edgy to be caught in a traffic jam.*

jumpy **Jumpy** means so nervous that you are likely to make sudden uncontrolled movements. *I'm jumpy if I'm alone in the house at night.*

jittery **Jittery** means nervous or **jumpy**. *We were jittery before the race started.*

similar words: **frightened, upset, fearful**
contrasting words: **calm, patient**

neutral   *adjective*

not taking one side or the other. *Sweden was a **neutral** country in the war.*

even-handed   **Even-handed** means not favoring or preferring one side to the other. *The referee was known for his even-handed treatment of players.*

disinterested   **Disinterested** means not directly involved in something. *They called for a disinterested outsider to settle the dispute.*

noncommittal   **Noncommittal** means not giving your decision or opinion so you can't be held to it. *His noncommittal answer could have meant anything.*

detached   **Detached** means remaining apart or not being concerned with or involved in something. *She maintained a detached attitude throughout the whole dispute.*

similar words: **fair**
contrasting words: **unfair, narrow-minded**

new   *adjective*

recently arrived, obtained, or come into being. *This is the first show in the **new** TV series.*

novel   **Novel** means new or different, usually in an unusual way. *He had a novel excuse each day for not doing his homework.*

original   **Original** can mean newly thought up or invented, and not like anything else. *The car shaped like a rocket won a prize for the most original design.*

innovative   **Innovative** means completely new in a clever or creative way. *We admired the innovative projects they displayed in the classroom during Education Week.*

fresh   **Fresh** can mean new or different. *That is a very fresh approach to our problem.*

avant-garde   **Avant-garde** means modern and usually produced as an experiment, especially drawing, painting, architecture, or something similar. *Not everyone admired the avant-garde sculpture.*

similar words: **modern**
contrasting words: **old-fashioned, old**

nice *adjective*

pleasing or delightful. *She was wearing a **nice** dress.*

pleasant **Pleasant** means agreeable or pleasing. *We all had a pleasant day at the zoo.*

enjoyable **Enjoyable** means pleasing or to your liking. *The party was enjoyable because everyone chatted happily together.*

lovely **Lovely** can mean very **pleasant** or good. *The weather was lovely while we were away.*

acceptable **Acceptable** means pleasing to the person receiving it. *The meal was quite acceptable even though it was not really hot enough.*

welcome **Welcome** can mean pleasing and wanted. *Her letter was especially welcome as I hadn't heard from her for a long time.*

similar words: **agreeable, good**
contrasting words: **unpleasant, pathetic, annoying, horrible**

noise *noun*

any kind of sound, especially a sound that is too loud or that you don't like. *Stop making that **noise**, I can't hear the TV!*

din A **din** is a loud noise that goes on and on. *The children made a terrible din as they set the table.*

hubbub A **hubbub** is a loud confused noise, like that made by many voices. *There was a hubbub in the room as everyone talked at once.*

racket A **racket** can be a loud confused noise. *The carpenter building our deck made a racket as he moved the wood and hammered in the nails.*

uproar An **uproar** is a noisy disturbance. *The audience was in an uproar when the rock concert was canceled at the last minute.*

pandemonium **Pandemonium** means wild and noisy confusion. *There was pandemonium when the people in the shopping center heard about the gas leak.*

similar words: **commotion**
contrasting words: **whisper**

nonsense   *noun*

words that are silly or without meaning. *The explanation sounded like* **nonsense** *to me.*

drivel

Drivel can be so similar to nonsense that you can usually use either. *That's the kind of drivel you would expect from an uninformed person.*

rubbish

Rubbish can be so similar to **drivel** and nonsense that you can usually use any of them. *You won't convince me if you keep talking rubbish.*

mumbo jumbo

Mumbo jumbo is meaningless words, especially when thought to have a magical effect. *The magician said some mumbo jumbo as he did his trick.*

piffle

Piffle means nonsense or idle talk. It is more suited to everyday language. *We were unconvinced by the argument because we thought it was utter piffle.*

gibberish

Gibberish is meaningless words. *She listened to her brother speak gibberish in his sleep.*

number   *noun*

a word or symbol you use to indicate an amount or the position of something. *Everyone in the game was given a* **number** *so they would know when it was their turn.*

figure

A **figure** is a symbol that stands for a number. *Write the figure 3 next to the circle with three crosses in it.*

numeral

A **numeral** is a word, figure, or group of figures that stands for a number. *The Roman numeral for 100 is C.*

digit

A **digit** is any of the **numerals** from 0 to 9. *There are only ten digits.*

integer

An **integer** is any whole number. *We made a list of all the integers up to a hundred that could be divided evenly by three.*

fraction

A **fraction** is a part of a whole number or **integer**. *I know that $\frac{3}{4}$ is a fraction.*

numerous   *adjective*

very many. *The pennies in the jar were too **numerous** to count.*

multiple **Multiple** means having or involving many parts. *The man who fell over the cliff had multiple injuries.*

multitudinous **Multitudinous** means forming a great number or crowd. This is an old-fashioned word. *The multitudinous waves swamped the buccaneer's boat.*

innumerable **Innumerable** means more than can be counted. *As soon as we started our picnic, innumerable flies descended on us.*

legion **Legion** means great in number. *She is such a lovely person that her friends are legion.*

similar words: **countless, abundant**
contrasting words: **scarce, single**

obedient   *adjective*

following someone else's wishes or orders. *The **obedient** puppy is being trained as a guide dog.*

docile **Docile** means quiet and easy to manage. *The children learned to ride on the docile horse.*

tractable **Tractable** means easily managed. *Animals with tractable natures make ideal pets.*

law-abiding **Law-abiding** means obeying the laws. *The law-abiding citizens helped the police in their search.*

compliant **Compliant** means agreeing with someone else readily or willingly. *He was so compliant that he seemed to have no mind of his own.*

dutiful **Dutiful** means doing what you should do. *The dutiful mechanic worked for hours repairing the car.*

similar words: **well-behaved, submissive**
contrasting words: **disobedient, naughty**

obey *verb*

to carry out the commands of someone. *The children **obeyed** their parents.*

heed
To **heed** means to pay attention to someone or something. *We decided to heed the "No Swimming" notice at the lake.*

observe
To **observe** can mean to obey or **follow** rules or laws. *You should observe the traffic rules when riding a bicycle on the road.*

follow
To **follow** can mean to accept someone or something as a guide. *I'll follow your instructions.*

comply with
To **comply with** means to act in accordance with rules, laws, or requests. *The audience complied with the request to remain in their seats.*

contrasting words: **disobey**

obsession *noun*

a strong idea or feeling that controls someone's behavior. *She has an **obsession** about horses and goes riding every weekend.*

hang-up
A **hang-up** is something that worries you and that you can't get off your mind. This is more suited to everyday language. *He had a hang-up about wearing hats.*

complex
A **complex** is so similar to **hang-up** that you can usually use either. This is more suited to everyday language. *He had a complex about speaking in public.*

phobia
A **phobia** is an overpowering fear. *Some people have phobias about crowds.*

fetish
A **fetish** is an obsession that is usually expressed by ritualistic behavior. *He had a fetish about cleanliness and washed his hands three or four times an hour.*

obstacle *noun*

something that is in your way or that holds you up. *We could see that the* **obstacle** *holding up the traffic was a fallen tree.*

hindrance   A **hindrance** is something that slows you down or hinders your progress. *Lack of money has been a real hindrance to our school's plans to buy more computers.*

hitch   A **hitch** is something that obstructs or makes things difficult. *The total fire ban was a hitch in our camping plans.*

handicap   A **handicap** is any disadvantage that makes success harder. *Wearing uncomfortable shoes turned out to be a handicap for him in the cross-country race.*

drawback   A **drawback** is a disadvantage or an inconvenience. *The plan is great except for one drawback — we haven't got enough money.*

barrier   A **barrier** is anything that bars or blocks the way. *Not being able to speak the same language can often be a barrier between people.*

obvious *adjective*

easily seen. *It was* **obvious** *from his red eyes that he had been crying.*

clear   **Clear** can mean obvious or without any doubt. *It was very clear to us that we would miss the bus if we didn't run.*

evident   **Evident** can mean obvious or easily understood. *It's evident from your red face that you are embarrassed.*

plain   **Plain** can mean clearly seen. It can be very similar to **clear** and **evident**. *The tangle in your knitting is a plain case of what happens if you start before you know what you are doing.*

apparent   **Apparent** can mean able to be seen. *My failure to follow the recipe was apparent because the cake was as flat as a pancake.*

distinct   **Distinct** can mean obvious and unmistakable. *Don't worry, you will see a distinct difference between the twins.*

similar words: **visible, clear**

offer   *noun*

something that is presented to someone to consider or accept. *We made him an* **offer** *of help but he refused.*

proposal
A **proposal** is a plan or scheme offered to someone for approval. *We presented our proposal for the new swimming pool to the committee.*

proposition
A **proposition** is a plan or subject suggested as something to be acted upon or discussed. *Our neighbors suggested that we should have a picnic, but I had a better proposition.*

bid
A **bid** is an offer of money for something, especially one made at an auction. *She made a bid of $200 for the table.*

submission
A **submission** is a plan or piece of work presented to others for consideration. *Jenny's submission for the essay contest arrived a day late.*

---

similar words: **suggestion**

---

offspring   *noun*

the baby animal or child of a particular parent. *A lion's* **offspring** *is called a cub.*

young
Young can be offspring, usually of animals. *The female kangaroo carries its young in a pouch.*

issue
Issue can be offspring, usually of people. This is a rather formal word. *The king's first male issue was the heir to the throne.*

descendant
A **descendant** is an offspring or a person who has descended from a particular ancestor. *I'm a descendant of the family who cleared this land over a hundred years ago.*

progeny
Progeny means the offspring or **descendants** of people or animals. *Before long I didn't have any more room for my pet rabbits' progeny.*

---

contrasting words: **ancestor**

---

old *adjective*

of or from an earlier time. *In the **old** days there were hardly any cars on the roads.*

ancient	**Ancient** means of, happening, or living a very long time ago. *We read stories about the gladiators in ancient Rome.*
antique	**Antique** means dating from earlier times. *They found some antique statues in the pyramid.*
prehistoric	**Prehistoric** means belonging to the time before history was written or records were kept. *We saw the fossils of a prehistoric dinosaur in the museum.*
vintage	**Vintage** can mean from a time in the past. *We saw some vintage airplanes at the air show.*

similar words: **old-fashioned**
contrasting words: **modern, new**

old-fashioned *adjective*

belonging to a time in or style of the past. *We dressed up in **old-fashioned** clothes and pretended we were pioneers.*

out-of-date	**Out-of-date** means not in fashion or no longer used. *You need a modern computer to replace that out-of-date one.*
obsolete	**Obsolete** means no longer used because something newer and more fashionable has replaced it. *My computer is so obsolete that it only belongs in a museum.*
antiquated	**Antiquated** means old-fashioned or **out-of-date**. *That antiquated textbook has some interesting diagrams in it that show how people thought the human body worked in those days.*
archaic	**Archaic** means very old-fashioned or belonging to the very distant past. *"Thee" and "thou" are archaic words that are not used very often today.*
dated	**Dated** means **out-of-date**. *In the play, the actor wore dated clothes that were popular ten years ago.*

similar words: **old**
contrasting words: **chic, new, modern**

opaque *adjective*

not able to be seen through. *I couldn't see who was there because the glass in the door was **opaque**.*

dense	**Dense** can mean too thick to see through. *The airport was closed due to the dense fog.*
thick	**Thick** can often be used instead of **dense**. *The smoke was so thick we couldn't see where we were going.*
turbid	**Turbid** means not clear or **dense**. This is a rather formal word. *I could only see white through the window as the plane flew through the turbid clouds.*
cloudy	**Cloudy** can mean not clear. *We added ammonia and now the water is cloudy.*
muddy	**Muddy** can mean not clear or **turbid**. *The water was too muddy for us to see the bottom of the creek.*

contrasting words: **transparent**

opinion *noun*

what you think or decide. *What is your **opinion** about the upcoming election?*

attitude	An **attitude** can be the way you behave toward or feel about something. *I tried to keep a positive attitude toward all my classmates.*
outlook	An **outlook** is an **attitude** or point of view. *Diana has a friendly nature and an optimistic outlook on life.*
viewpoint	A **viewpoint** is a way of considering or thinking about something or someone. *He asked me my viewpoint about having three terms or four in the school year.*
stand	A **stand** can be a definite opinion that you declare openly. *The governor took a strong stand about fighting acid rain.*
conviction	A **conviction** can be an opinion or belief that you hold strongly. *It is my conviction that we would all be safer if nuclear weapons had never been invented.*

opposite *adjective*

completely different in every way. *His behavior was **opposite** to what I had expected.*

converse	**Converse** means turned about or opposite in direction, action, or meaning. *The letters of "Madam, I'm Adam" read the same in converse order.*
antithetical	**Antithetical** means in direct or complete opposition or contrast. *Which of these two antithetical statements will you believe?*
contradictory	**Contradictory** means in exact or direct opposition. It is very similar to **antithetical**. *The results of your experiments are contradictory.*
contrary	**Contrary** means opposed to or different from something else, but it may not be exactly opposite. *My opinion is contrary to yours.*
conflicting	**Conflicting** means clashing, disagreeing, or in opposition. *We were surprised at our conflicting ideas about religion.*

contrasting words: **similar**

optimistic *adjective*

expecting that things will turn out well. *Her **optimistic** outlook helped us all believe we would be rescued.*

positive	**Positive** can mean tending to see what is good or gives hope. *His positive approach helped him to find a solution to the problem.*
confident	**Confident** means having a strong belief, or feeling quite certain about something, usually something that is good or desirable. *I am confident that they will find us soon.*
hopeful	**Hopeful** means looking forward to or expecting something, especially something good. *We were hopeful of finding the hikers before nightfall.*
buoyant	**Buoyant** means light-hearted and cheerful. *They expressed the buoyant feelings they had by laughing and joking as they set out.*
happy-go-lucky	**Happy-go-lucky** means trusting cheerfully to luck. *They're so happy-go-lucky that their preparations were not adequate and they lost their way.*

contrasting words: **pessimistic**

orange *adjective*

having a reddish-gold or yellow color. *We planted some seeds and weeks later dug up huge **orange** carrots.*

amber	**Amber** means having a yellowish-brown color. *Dad slowed the car, ready to stop, when he saw the amber light.*
terracotta	**Terracotta** means having a brownish-red color. *We have terracotta pots for all of our plants.*
ginger	**Ginger** means having a reddish-brown color. *I named my cat Ginger after her ginger fur.*
peach	**Peach** means having a light pinkish-orange color. *Their cheeks were a healthy, peach color after their swim.*
gilt	**Gilt** means having a golden-orange color. *I bought a frame with a gilt edge to put my favorite photograph in.*

order *noun*

an instruction that you must obey. *The general gave the **order** to march.*

command	A **command** is so similar to an **order** that you can usually use either word. *At last the command to stop was heard.*
decree	A **decree** is an official order, usually made by a government or someone in a position of power. *The new government decree stated that no one could go out at night during the state of emergency.*
instructions	**Instructions** are orders. This is a plural noun. *My instructions are to ask everyone for a ticket.*
summons	A **summons** is an order to appear in a certain place, often a law court. *I received a summons to appear as a witness at his trial.*
warrant	A **warrant** is a paper given by a justice of the peace to the police allowing them to arrest someone or search a building. *We have a warrant for your arrest.*

similar words: **demand**

285

ordinary   *adjective*

usual or normal. *It was just another **ordinary** working day.*

average Average can mean usual or ordinary. *An average Monday consists of school, basketball practice, dinner, homework, and TV.*

standard Standard can mean normal or ordinary. *Any sports store will have a tire for your bike, because it's a standard size.*

fair Fair can mean of an ordinary or moderately good standard. *His marks in the exam were fair.*

nondescript Nondescript means very ordinary-looking without any easily recognizable qualities. *It's hard to describe the house because it's quite nondescript.*

so-so So-so means ordinary, or not very good or very bad. *We had a so-so holiday at the beach, with sunny but cool weather.*

similar words: **mediocre**
contrasting words: **excellent, unusual**

organization   *noun*

a group of people that runs or manages something. *We need to set up a fund-raising **organization**.*

company A company can be a group of people brought together to run a business. *This book is produced by a publishing company.*

firm A firm is a business organization. It is very similar to company. *She went to work for a firm located downtown.*

corporation A corporation is a business company, especially one established by law. *The government set up a broadcasting corporation.*

syndicate A syndicate is a group of business people or business organizations, especially one formed to carry out a particular project. *The engineering firms formed a syndicate to build the big new hotel.*

outfit An outfit can be a business organization or group of people working together. *He belongs to an outfit that paints houses.*

286

outside   *noun*

the outer part or side of something. *We covered the **outside** of the box with colored paper.*

exterior	**Exterior** means the outer part of something. *The exterior of the building was in bad shape and needed painting.*
surface	**Surface** can mean the top or outer side of something. *The workers were repairing the surface of the road because it was full of potholes.*
face	**Face** can mean the main side or front of something. *The face of the cliff was too steep to climb.*
facade	A **facade** is the front of something as seen from the outside, especially of a building. *The historic building had a very attractive facade although the inside was quite plain.*

similar words: **side**
contrasting words: **inside**

outskirts   *noun*

the outer areas. This is a plural noun. *There are small farms on the **outskirts** of the city.*

periphery	The **periphery** is the outside edge of an area or thing. *The chairs were arranged around the periphery of the room.*
perimeter	The **perimeter** is the outside edge of a shape or area. *The spectators sat around the perimeter of the oval.*
boundary	The **boundary** is the outside edge that separates one area from another. *The farmhand rode around the boundary of the farm checking that there were no broken fences.*
limit	The **limit** is the outermost point of an area. *The king sent messengers out to the limits of his kingdom to find someone who could slay the dragon.*
frontier	A **frontier** is the outer area or end of known territory. *The early settlers explored the frontier.*

similar words: **edge**
contrasting words: **center**

outwit *verb*

to trick or fool someone by being more intelligent or clever. *I have a brilliant plan that will **outwit** the other team and let us win.*

circumvent To **circumvent** means to defeat or outwit someone through skillful planning. *The citizen's group, after much preparation, circumvented the government's proposal to raise taxes.*

get the better of To **get the better of** means to defeat or be superior to someone. *My love of food got the better of me and I had two desserts.*

foil To **foil** means to stop someone from doing something or accomplishing a plan. *The hero foiled the villain's attempt to rob the bank.*

pull a fast one To **pull a fast one** means to outwit someone in order to achieve an unfair result. *He pulled a fast one on me and now he's got my baseball glove.*

similar words: **deceive, trick**

overturn *verb*

to turn something over on its side, back, or face. *I **overturned** the wheelbarrow to tip the grass onto the compost.*

invert To **invert** means to turn something upside down, inside out, or inward. *The magician inverted the glass of water without spilling any.*

upset To **upset** can mean to knock or turn something over. *When the cat jumped on my lap, it upset my cup of tea.*

flip To **flip** can mean to turn something over. *He flipped the rock over to see what was underneath.*

bowl over To **bowl over** can mean to knock someone or something over forcefully. *The big wave bowled me over.*

tip over To **tip over** means to topple something over. *The cat tipped its milk dish over as it ran out the door.*

contrasting words: **steady**

288

own *verb*

to have something that belongs to you. *My parents **own** the house we live in.*

possess To **possess** means to own or have something. *The art gallery possesses several valuable paintings.*

hold To **hold** means to have in your possession. *She holds a large number of shares in several businesses.*

have all to yourself To **have all to yourself** means to have something completely for your own use. *You will have the house all to yourself this weekend because we are going away.*

monopolize To **monopolize** means to get or have complete control of something. *The new children found it hard to join in because the others had monopolized all the toys.*

occupy To **occupy** can mean to own or live in a building or house. *The new owners moved in to occupy our house as soon as we sold it.*

pacify *verb*

to make something or someone quiet or peaceful. *She quickly **pacified** the frightened horse.*

mollify To **mollify** means to make someone calmer or less angry. *The shop owner mollified the angry customer by replacing the faulty iron.*

appease To **appease** means to make someone peaceful, quiet, or happy. *The factory manager appeased the angry workers by promising them a pay raise.*

calm To **calm** means to make someone or something less excited or emotional. *The teacher calmed the hysterical children and told them the vicious dog had been caught.*

quiet To **quiet** can mean to make someone or something more calm or peaceful. *The speaker came back on stage to quiet the jeering crowd.*

defuse To **defuse** can mean to **calm** a tense situation. *When the argument started to get nasty, Leah defused the situation by cracking a joke.*

similar words: **comfort**
contrasting words: **anger, frighten**

pain   *noun*

a feeling of hurt or soreness in a particular part of your body. *My brother had a lot of **pain** in his leg after he broke it.*

ache	An **ache** is a dull continuous pain. *I had an ache in my ankle for two days after I twisted it.*
twinge	A **twinge** is a pain that lasts only a moment. *My grandmother gets twinges of rheumatism in her hands.*
stitch	A **stitch** can be a sudden sharp pain, especially between your ribs. *I had a stitch after my aerobics class.*
cramp	A **cramp** is a sudden tightening of a muscle in your body. *My mother suggested that I pull my foot forward when I had a cramp in my leg.*
spasm	A **spasm** is an uncontrolled movement of your muscles. *I had a spasm in my leg after the cross-country run.*

pardon   *noun*

a formal declaration of forgiveness for a crime. *The government gave the prisoner a **pardon** because he was too old and sick to be in jail.*

release	A **release** can be the act of setting someone free from imprisonment, arrest, or other confinement. *The newspaper report about the prisoner's release said that the police didn't have enough evidence to charge him.*
stay	A **stay** is a delay in carrying out an order of a court of law. *There was a stay of the trial decision while the appeal was heard.*
amnesty	An **amnesty** is a pardon given to everyone, especially for crimes against the government. *An amnesty was granted to all of the illegal immigrants in the country.*
acquittal	An **acquittal** is a declaration of innocence. *The man's acquittal by the jury was announced on the news.*

part   *noun*

a piece or fragment of something. *Daniel cut **part** of the shelf off to make it fit.*

portion   A **portion** is a part or share of something. *I left my lunch at home, so Jasper gave me a portion of his.*

section   A **section** is a part or division of something. *I play the trumpet in the brass section of our school orchestra.*

segment   A **segment** is a piece or a **section**. *Alexandra divided her orange into segments and gave each of her friends one.*

proportion   A **proportion** is a part of something compared to the whole of it. *Enrico did a larger proportion of the work than anyone else.*

fraction   A **fraction** can be a small amount or piece. *Dominic did his composition in a fraction of the time the rest of the class took.*

---

similar words: **share, piece**

---

pass   *verb*

to go by or move past something. *We **passed** the station on our way to the shops.*

overtake   To **overtake** means to catch up with and pass someone or something. *The police overtook the speeding driver and made her stop.*

outstrip   To **outstrip** can mean to pass and leave behind someone or something when running or traveling quickly. *I outstripped my nearest rival in the 100-meter sprint.*

beat   To **beat** can mean to defeat or do better than someone. *She beat him in the race.*

lose   To **lose** can mean to leave someone or something far behind in a race or a chase. *The winner of the marathon lost the other runners toward the end of the race and won by nearly half a kilometer.*

lap   To **lap** can mean to get ahead of other competitors by a complete round of a racing track or length of a swimming pool in a race. *The winning car lapped the others early in the race and never gave up its lead.*

past *adjective*

gone by in time. *My **past** hobby was hiking but now I prefer mountain climbing.*

former   **Former** means coming before someone or something else in time, or from an earlier or past time. *The former principal of our school came back to visit us.*

bygone   **Bygone** means past or gone by. *We read stories about bygone days when people traveled on horseback.*

sometime   **Sometime** means having been formerly or in the past. *She is a sometime champion and now coaches younger athletes.*

late   **Late** can mean having recently died. *The young prince took over the throne of his father, the late king.*

previous   **Previous** means earlier or **former**. *Please go back and reread the previous chapter.*

---

contrasting words: **future**

---

pathetic *adjective*

causing feelings of pity or sadness. *The picture of the starving children on TV was a **pathetic** sight.*

pitiful   **Pitiful** means causing or deserving pity. *The mouse made a pitiful attempt to escape as the cat pounced on it.*

wretched   **Wretched** means **pitiful** and causing misery. *The homeless people were living in wretched conditions after the earthquake.*

miserable   **Miserable** can mean causing unhappiness or distress. *I wish I could get rid of this miserable cold.*

dismal   **Dismal** means feeling or causing deep sadness. *Our plan to raise a lot of money was a dismal failure.*

woeful   **Woeful** means **miserable** and deserving pity. *He has been so woeful since his best friend moved.*

---

similar words: **bad**
contrasting words: **nice**

---

patient *adjective*

waiting quietly and calmly. *The **patient** customer waited for his turn.*

tolerant	**Tolerant** means putting up with or allowing things that you may not like or feel happy about. *She was very tolerant of the noise we made playing with our new toys.*
long-suffering	**Long-suffering** means continually putting up with something that annoys or hurts you. *My long-suffering friend puts up with my moodiness.*
persevering	**Persevering** means continuing to do something even though it is very difficult. *His persevering work brought him success on the exams.*
persistent	**Persistent** means keeping on doing something until you have finished, no matter how hard it is. *We were persistent and at last completed the job.*
stoical	**Stoical** means behaving in a patient and calm way that shows you have courage. *We were impressed by your stoical behavior while you were waiting to be rescued.*

contrasting words: **nervous**

pay *noun*

the money you are paid for the work you do. *Most people try to save some of their **pay**.*

salary	A **salary** is the money you earn, especially for office work. *The bank manager earns a bigger salary at his new branch.*
wage	A **wage** is the money you are paid for working, especially in a factory or as a laborer. *The mechanic earned a good wage.*
commission	**Commission** is the extra money paid to someone who sells things for an employer. *The car salesperson earned 10% commission on each car she sold.*
fee	A **fee** is the money charged for a service or privilege. *There was a $200 fee for joining the golf club.*
income	**Income** is all the money you get from your work or investments. *You have to pay tax on your income.*

similar words: **profit**

pay *verb*

to give money, or something similar, in return for goods or services. *I **paid** $20 for the new tire for my bike.*

spend
: To **spend** means to pay out money, wealth, or something similar. *I spent a lot of my savings at the show.*

expend
: To **expend** can mean to pay out or **spend** money, usually large amounts. *We expended nearly all our capital on the new farm machinery.*

outlay
: To **outlay** means to **spend** or pay out money in order to obtain something worthwhile. *They outlaid a lump sum to make sure the team was well trained for the competition.*

invest
: To **invest** means to pay out a large sum of money for something, hoping that you will make more money from the deal. *She invested her inheritance in real estate and before long became a millionaire.*

similar words: **buy, repay**

peaceful *adjective*

calm and free from strife or trouble. *We enjoyed living in the **peaceful** country town where people were so friendly.*

serene
: **Serene** means peaceful or showing no signs of stress or strife. *She has a serene personality that naturally relaxes people.*

tranquil
: **Tranquil** means peaceful, calm, or free from disturbance. *We found a tranquil spot on the bank of a river to have a rest.*

quiet
: **Quiet** can mean calm and peaceful. *We enjoyed a quiet evening at home after a hard day at school.*

gentle
: **Gentle** can mean not rough or violent. *The gentle little boy loved to cuddle his baby brother.*

harmonious
: **Harmonious** means showing agreement in feeling or action. *The harmonious atmosphere in the club returned when the president told the troublemakers to go.*

similar words: **calm**
contrasting words: **violent**

perfect *adjective*

with nothing missing and no faults. *It was a **perfect** day to go on a picnic.*

faultless   **Faultless** means without any mistakes or blemishes. *They gave a faultless performance at the concert.*

impeccable   **Impeccable** means completely free from any faults. It is very similar to **faultless**. *His manners were impeccable during his visit.*

immaculate   **Immaculate** means free from any fault, blemishes, or errors. *Their work was immaculate.*

ideal   **Ideal** means a perfect example of something. *She will make an ideal captain for the team.*

complete   **Complete** can mean perfect in every way. *Our happiness was complete as we rode beside the river.*

similar words: **excellent, precise**
contrasting words: **defective**

permanent *adjective*

lasting forever or for a very long time. *There is **permanent** snow on the top of the highest mountains.*

everlasting   **Everlasting** means lasting or continuing for a long time or forever. *I'm sick of your everlasting complaints.*

eternal   **Eternal** means lasting forever or not having any end. *Some people believe that the universe will have an eternal existence.*

immortal   **Immortal** means lasting or living forever. *In Greek mythology, the gods and goddesses were powerful and immortal beings.*

perpetual   **Perpetual** means without a fixed end or lasting forever. *I don't think we'll ever have rain to break this perpetual drought.*

perennial   **Perennial** means continually coming back or lasting for a long time. *The perennial flowers in our garden bloom each spring.*

contrasting words: **temporary, momentary**

permission   *noun*

agreement to let someone do something. *I have **permission** to go.*

leave	**Leave** is so similar to **permission** that you can usually use either. *I need my parents' leave before I can go.*
approval	**Approval** can mean permission or **consent**. *We had to get the approval of the coach before we chose our team jackets.*
clearance	A **clearance** can be official permission to go ahead with something. *They needed clearance from the town council to add an extra story to their house.*
consent	**Consent** means permission or agreement to do something. *The doctor asked for her patient's consent before operating.*
dispensation	**Dispensation** can be special permission given to break a rule for a particular occasion. *He was given a dispensation to pay his debt in a year's time instead of immediately.*

persist   *verb*

to continue or keep on with something, even when people oppose you. *He **persisted** with his questions even though his teacher wanted him to stop.*

persevere	To **persevere** means to continue with something you have started, even though it may be difficult. You can often use it instead of persist. *Although I am tired, I will persevere with my work.*
last the distance	To **last the distance** means to keep on with a difficult task or some physical activity until you have finished. *He knew he couldn't win the race but he was determined to last the distance.*
hang in	To **hang in** can mean to **persevere** or to keep on trying, even though you may want to give up. This is more suited to everyday language. *We'll just hang in until this job is finished.*
stick to your guns	To **stick to your guns** means to keep your position in an argument when people oppose you. *My friends tried to talk me out of going to the concert but I stuck to my guns.*

persistence *noun*

the fact or action of continuing to do something in spite of opposition from someone. *Because of his **persistence** in asking for a bike, his parents finally gave in.*

perseverance	**Perseverance** is the determination to continue to do something in spite of difficulty. *We admired his perseverance in doing the painful exercises after his accident.*
tenacity	**Tenacity** means the stubborn determination to continue to do something. *The ant's tenacity in dragging the huge crumb to its nest amazed us.*
stamina	**Stamina** is physical strength or power, especially to fight off sickness or tiredness. *The cross-country race will test your stamina.*
endurance	**Endurance** is the ability to bear or hold out against some difficulty or problem. *The early settlers in the American colonies showed their endurance by not giving in to the hardship they had to face.*
grit	**Grit** can mean courage or strength of character. *He showed a lot of grit in overcoming the difficulties of life in a wheelchair.*

persistent *adjective*

continuing in spite of opposition. *We watched with interest the spider's **persistent** attempts to put its web across the path we use every day.*

tenacious	**Tenacious** means stubbornly persistent. *The detective's tenacious questioning of the witness finally got her the evidence she needed.*
determined	**Determined** means firm in purpose. *We are determined to win the championship again this year.*
dogged	**Dogged** means unflinching, or resolved not to give in. *Anthony's parents rewarded his dogged attempts to learn to swim.*
single-minded	**Single-minded** means showing you have decided or resolved to succeed in a particular thing. *Amanda is single-minded about saving her allowance to buy a bicycle.*
unflagging	**Unflagging** means not weakening or giving up. *They were unflagging in their efforts to raise money for the charity.*

similar words: **stubborn**

persuade *verb*

to cause someone to do or believe something by advising, arguing with, or influencing. *We **persuaded** her to come with us.*

convince
To **convince** means to make someone believe or feel sure about something. *His test results convinced him that he had to work harder at school.*

talk into
To **talk into** means to persuade someone to do something by talking. *We finally talked them into taking a vacation this year.*

induce
To **induce** can mean to cause someone to decide something. *I will induce him to join the drama club.*

coax
To **coax** means to persuade someone gently and patiently. *She coaxed the sick child to eat.*

lobby
To **lobby** means to try to get political support for a particular issue or cause. *The environmental group lobbied various politicians on the issue of acid rain.*

similar words: **influence, encourage**
contrasting words: **discourage**

pessimistic *adjective*

expecting that things will turn out badly. *He was **pessimistic** about our chances of being rescued.*

discouraging
Discouraging means making things appear in the worst possible way. *The discouraging talk began to make us lose hope.*

disheartening
Disheartening means **discouraging,** or causing a loss of good spirits. *I heard the disheartening news that my friend is moving to another town.*

gloomy
Gloomy means causing great unhappiness or depression. *Our gloomy situation looked even worse as it grew dark.*

depressing
Depressing means causing gloom or misery. *We finally told him to keep his depressing comments to himself.*

contrasting words: **optimistic**

piece *noun*

a bit or part of something. *I cut off a **piece** of my new dress material to show Pat.*

scrap
A **scrap** is a small piece. *Hamish made a toy car out of a scrap of wood.*

fragment
A **fragment** is a part that has been broken off. *He cut his foot on a fragment of the broken bottle lying in the grass.*

morsel
A **morsel** is a very small piece or amount. *She was too tired to eat more than a morsel of food before she fell asleep.*

particle
A **particle** is a very small bit. *A particle of dust got in her eye and made it very sore.*

sliver
A **sliver** is a small thin piece. *We used a sliver of wood as a wedge to stop the window from rattling.*

similar words: **trace, part**

pity *noun*

a feeling of sorrow for the suffering of others. *We looked at the poor trapped animal with **pity**.*

sympathy
Sympathy is a feeling of sorrow you share with someone else who is sad or in trouble. *We felt great sympathy for our neighbors when their house burned down.*

compassion
Compassion means pity together with a feeling that you want to help. *The Red Cross asked us to show compassion for the victims of the earthquake by sending money.*

tenderness
Tenderness is a gentle loving feeling of pity. *The father cared for his sick baby with tenderness.*

mercy
Mercy is the pity or kindness you show when you don't punish someone for doing something wrong. *The lawyer asked the jury to show mercy on the young man because it was his first offense.*

similar words: **comfort**

place   *noun*

a particular area or part of space. *We're going to a new **place** for our vacation.*

position	A **position** is a particular place. *I chose a position near the window.*
spot	A **spot** can be a less formal word for a **place**. *Pick a good spot for the barbecue.*
location	A **location** can be a particular place or area. *The post office has been moved to a new location nearer the shopping mall.*
site	A **site** is a particular place where something has happened or is going to happen, or the place where something is or will be built. *Many people gathered at the site of the rocket launch. We want a house on a site overlooking the lake.*
niche	A **niche** is a hollow spot in a wall. *The statue fit perfectly in a niche near the door..*

place   *verb*

to put something in a particular position. *When he finished drinking, he **placed** his cup back on its saucer.*

set	To **set** can be so similar to **place** that you can usually use either word. *He set the vase on the table.*
rest	To **rest** can mean to lie or lean one thing against another. *She rested the ladder against the wall.*
deposit	To **deposit** can mean to put something down. *She deposited her bag on the bed.*
stick	To **stick** can mean to place something. It is more suited to everyday language. *She's going to stick all her old toys in the attic.*
park	To **park** means to place something in a particular position. It is more suited to everyday language. *He parked himself right in the middle of the doorway.*

similar words: **position**

plan *verb*

to make careful preparations for something. *We **planned** the picnic so that we wouldn't forget anything.*

arrange   To **arrange** can mean to prepare or plan something. *We arranged a party for the last day of school.*

organize   To **organize** can mean to **arrange** something or make plans for it. *We organized a holiday at the beach.*

engineer   To **engineer** means to plan or **arrange** something in a clever way. *Everyone was surprised when she engineered a friendly meeting between the two rivals.*

mastermind   To **mastermind** means to plan and direct something in a skillful, clever way. *Not a thing went wrong when she masterminded the concert.*

schedule   To **schedule** means to plan the times when certain events should or will happen. *Our music teacher scheduled a band practice for Monday at four in the afternoon.*

---

similar words: **plot**

---

please *verb*

to make someone happy. *The gift **pleased** them very much.*

delight   To **delight** means to give someone great pleasure. *Being invited to the party delighted me.*

charm   To **charm** can mean to please very much. *Her personality charmed me.*

attract   To **attract** means to draw or win someone by your appearance, behavior, and so on. *His smile attracts me.*

appeal to   To **appeal to** means to have the ability to attract or interest someone. *This perfume appeals to me.*

satisfy   To **satisfy** means to please or make someone happy. *My test results satisfied my parents.*

---

contrasting words: **disgust, irritate, annoy**

---

plot *noun*

a secret plan or idea, usually to harm someone. *The captain discovered that there was a **plot** for a mutiny.*

conspiracy   A **conspiracy** is similar to a plot. It always involves more than one person. *The FBI arrested the people involved in the conspiracy against the government.*

scheme   A **scheme** can be a secret plan. *They worked out a scheme to kidnap the millionaire's son.*

intrigue   An **intrigue** can be a secret plan made by dishonest or sly people. *Political intrigue caused the downfall of the government.*

ruse   A **ruse** is a dishonest trick or plan. *His mother saw through his ruse to avoid mowing the lawn.*

stratagem   A **stratagem** is a plan or trick for deceiving an enemy. *The Greeks' stratagem for conquering the city of Troy was to hide inside a wooden horse.*

similar words: **trick**

plot *verb*

to plan secretly, especially something harmful or evil. *They **plotted** to overthrow the government.*

scheme   To **scheme** can mean to plot or make up a secret plan. *We schemed all night planning his surprise party.*

conspire   To **conspire** means to plan secretly with another person or group of people. *The terrorists conspired to hijack a plane.*

collude   To **collude** means to **conspire** to cheat people. *The ship's captain colluded with the smugglers to escape the customs officers.*

intrigue   To **intrigue** means to plot in a crafty way. This is a rather old-fashioned way to use this word. *He knew they were intriguing against him behind the locked door.*

connive   To **connive** can mean to work together secretly. *The spy connived with the government scientist to steal the secret plans for the new rocket.*

similar words: **plan**

poisonous *adjective*

containing poison that may kill you or make you very sick if you swallow it or it pierces your skin. *Drinking the **poisonous** concoction was the cause of his death.*

venomous	**Venomous** means producing a poisonous substance that can kill you or make you very sick. It is used about some snakes and spiders. *The rattlesnake is a venomous reptile.*
toxic	**Toxic** can mean poisonous, or acting as a poison. *The toxic waste from the mill was killing the fish in the river.*
noxious	**Noxious** means harmful to your health. *Many people were taken to the hospital when the noxious gas escaped from the factory.*
carcinogenic	**Carcinogenic** means able to cause cancer in your body. *Any known carcinogenic chemicals and food additives are banned by law.*

polish *verb*

to make something smooth and bright by rubbing. *He **polished** his shoes until they glistened.*

shine	To **shine** can mean to polish or make something sparkle or glisten. *Dad decided to shine all the silver cutlery in the drawer.*
buff	To **buff** means to polish metal or give a smooth bright glow to other surfaces. *He buffed the brass knocker on our door.*
burnish	To **burnish** means to make something glistening and bright by rubbing. It is similar to **buff**. *He burnished the copper kettle, too.*
furbish	To **furbish** can mean to polish or **burnish** armor or weapons. It is a rather old-fashioned word. *The knight furbished his sword and put it carefully into its sheath.*
wax	To **wax** means to polish something by rubbing it with wax. *We asked the garage to wax our car.*

similar words: **smooth**
contrasting words: **roughen**

polite *adjective*

having good manners. *What a **polite** girl you are to offer me your seat on the bus.*

courteous
Courteous is so similar to polite you can usually use either word. *He asked in such a courteous way that we all agreed to do what he said.*

gracious
Gracious means very kind and **courteous**. *Alison was a gracious host and thanked everyone for coming to her party.*

gallant
Gallant means very polite and helpful. *It was a gallant act to carry my heavy suitcase for me.*

chivalrous
Chivalrous means very polite and attentive. It is usually only used about men's behavior toward women. *Have you read the story of the chivalrous knights of King Arthur and the Round Table?*

similar words: **well-behaved**
contrasting words: **rude, bold, vulgar, abrupt**

pompous *adjective*

showing too much sense of your own importance. *The **pompous** teenager gave commands to the other people in the group.*

pretentious
Pretentious means having an exaggerated outward show of importance, wealth, and so on. *The pretentious woman always talked about the important people she knew and the expensive clothes she bought.*

uppity
Uppity means behaving in a bold or forward way, or acting as if you are superior. It is more suited to everyday language. *The people who lived in the big house next door were rather uppity.*

affected
Affected can mean behaving in an artificial way to impress people. *That actor is very affected, especially in the way he speaks.*

snooty
Snooty means **snobbish**, proud, or arrogant. It is more suited to everyday language. *Don't get snooty just because you are captain of the team.*

snobbish
Snobbish means looking down on people who are not as wealthy, important, or clever as you. *He has been snobbish ever since he won the award.*

similar words: **proud**
contrasting words: **humble**

ponder *verb*

to consider or think deeply or carefully about something. *We **pondered** the question of whether we would let him join our band.*

contemplate To **contemplate** means to consider something thoughtfully. *He contemplated the letter for several minutes.*

weigh To **weigh** can mean to consider carefully by thinking about all aspects of something. *Give me some time to weigh your suggestion in my mind.*

meditate on To **meditate on** means to think long and deeply about something. *If you meditate on a problem you can often find a solution to it.*

reflect on To **reflect on** means to think carefully about something. *I reflected on the moral of the story.*

pore over To **pore over** means to read or study something very carefully. *The students pored over their books.*

similar words: **concentrate**

poor *adjective*

having little money, property, or means of producing wealth. *The **poor** nation borrowed money from other countries.*

needy **Needy** means very poor or not having enough money or belongings. *There are many organizations that help needy people by giving them food, clothes, and furniture.*

impoverished **Impoverished** means having been made very poor. *The farmers were impoverished after the many years of drought.*

disadvantaged **Disadvantaged** can mean not having a reasonable standard of living because you don't have enough money or the means of making it. *During the Depression, disadvantaged people crossed the country looking for work.*

hard up **Hard up** means very poor or urgently in need of money. It is more suited to everyday language. *I was so hard up I had to borrow some money for lunch today.*

similar words: **broke**
contrasting words: **wealthy**

position   *noun*

a job or duty for which you are employed. *He began his career in the bank with a* ***position*** *as a teller.*

post	A **post** is a job or duty. *She has a teaching post.*
situation	A **situation** is a position in which you are employed. *I've been looking for a new situation ever since I lost my last job.*
station	A **station** can be a place or position of duty. *She took up her new station as supervisor.*
office	An **office** is a position of trust or power, usually in the government or a business. *She has the office of press secretary to the mayor.*
appointment	An **appointment** is a job or special position someone is given. *We were pleased at his appointment as general manager of the company.*

similar words: **job, profession**

position   *verb*

to put in a particular place. *He **positioned** his chair right in front of the television.*

locate	To **locate** means to put something in a particular position or area. *The council located the new parking lot near the railway station.*
site	To **site** means to place something in a certain position. It is very similar to **locate**. *They sited the new hospital on the other side of town.*
station	To **station** means to place someone or something in a position for a particular reason. *The police stationed guards at every exit.*
install	To **install** means to put something into place so it can be used. *Dad installed the new stove just in time to cook us lunch.*
establish	To **establish** means to set up. *They established the new school exactly where the old one had been.*

similar words: **place**

possible   *adjective*

able to be done or be used. *It is **possible** to drive there in one day.*

feasible   **Feasible** means likely to work. *I think your plan is feasible.*

viable   **Viable** means possible or able to succeed in operation. *I don't think it is viable for us all to go in your car.*

workable   **Workable** means able to be put into operation. *I have thought of a workable plan.*

practicable   **Practicable** means able to be done or put into practice because it is sensible or uses what you have. *It will be more practicable for us to go there by bus.*

similar words: **likely, useful**
contrasting words: **impossible, useless**

poverty   *noun*

the condition of having little money, few possessions, or means of producing wealth. *The farmer lived in **poverty** for a year after the crops failed.*

want   **Want** is the condition of not having the necessities of life. It is very similar to poverty. *There are people living in want in all our big cities.*

need   **Need** can mean a situation or time when you do not have the things necessary to live. *They were in great need when they lost all their belongings in the fire.*

distress   **Distress** can mean the state of suffering or hardship caused by poverty. *Try to imagine a whole African nation in distress.*

destitution   **Destitution** means the state of having no money or the means of getting any. *Their relatives sent them gifts of food and clothing to relieve their destitution.*

deprivation   **Deprivation** can mean the state of being without the things you need because you have no money. *When she was unemployed, she suffered deprivation with dignity.*

contrasting words: **wealth**

powerful   *adjective*

having great force, authority, or influence. *The President is one of the most* **powerful** *people in the world.*

mighty	**Mighty** means having or showing power, force, or ability. It is rather an old-fashioned word. *Some of the ancient kings were mighty rulers.*
forceful	**Forceful** means strong, powerful, and able to influence people. *The politician was a forceful speaker.*
potent	**Potent** can mean strong or having great power. *There are potent arguments against building the new airport so close to the city.*
dominant	**Dominant** means most important or powerful. *The dominant group at the meeting was the one that supported the mayor.*
strong	**Strong** can mean having great power of effect. *She is such a strong principal that all the children respect her.*

contrasting words: **powerless**

---

powerless   *adjective*

not having the power or ability to do things. *With my hands and feet tied up I was* **powerless** *to escape.*

impotent	**Impotent** is very similar to powerless. *The townspeople wanted to prevent the flooding, but they were impotent against the force of the storm.*
incapacitated	**Incapacitated** means having been made powerless or unable to do something. *The ambulance carried the incapacitated victims of the traffic accident to the hospital.*
feeble	**Feeble** means lacking in force, strength, or effectiveness. *The tired survivors could only make feeble attempts to yell for help.*
pathetic	**Pathetic** can mean showing a great lack of ability. *I made such a pathetic attempt at writing my essay that I decided to try again.*
weak	**Weak** can mean lacking in power or strength. *The boy was too weak to use the heavy sledgehammer.*

similar words: **useless**
contrasting words: **powerful**

practical   *adjective*

sensible and facing things as they really are. *It is not **practical** to try to build the tree house so high.*

realistic   **Realistic** means facing life as it really is. *She had realistic ideas concerning our fight against pollution.*

down-to-earth   **Down-to-earth** means practical and sensible. *He's always down-to-earth in the way he solves his problems.*

matter-of-fact   **Matter-of-fact** means so sensible that it is rather uninteresting. *He gave a matter-of-fact speech rather than an imaginative one.*

pragmatic   **Pragmatic** means thinking about the results or usefulness of your actions. *The pragmatic politician planned a successful election campaign.*

---

similar words: **sensible**

---

practice   *noun*

a performance or action that is repeated regularly to improve skill. *With **practice**, you will get better at playing field hockey.*

drill   A **drill** can be an exercise or a strict way of training that is repeated regularly. *We must have a fire drill once a month.*

training   **Training** can be a session to develop fitness or a time to practice certain physical skills. *We go to football training twice a week.*

run-through   A **run-through** is a quick trial or practice, usually before the official performance. *We had a run-through of what we were going to say before we went in to see the mayor.*

warm-up   A **warm-up** is a short period of preparation for a sporting event, or a musical or theatrical performance. *The orchestra had a warm-up before the performance.*

rehearsal   A **rehearsal** is a private practice of something before giving a public performance. *We had several rehearsals before the opening night of our school play.*

---

praise *verb*

to say that you admire or approve of someone or something. *Although we didn't win the game, the coach **praised** our efforts.*

compliment
To **compliment** means to praise or say that you admire someone or something. *She complimented me on my new sweater.*

commend
To **commend** means to say that you admire and approve of someone or something. *I commend you for your hard work this year.*

speak well of
To **speak well of** means to say very good or complimentary things about someone or something. *I heard your teacher speak well of your friend.*

congratulate
To **congratulate** means to express your happiness at someone's accomplishments or good fortune. *I will congratulate Golda on her victory in the election.*

glorify
To **glorify** means to praise someone or something very highly. *The statue was built to glorify the nation's leader.*

---

similar words: **acclaim, approve**
contrasting words: **disapprove of, fault, slander**

---

precise *adjective*

absolutely right in every detail. *Do you know the **precise** time?*

exact
Exact can mean completely right. It is very similar to **precise**. *Please tell me the exact date.*

accurate
Accurate can mean careful and **exact**. *Is that an accurate copy of the original?*

specific
Specific means clear and **accurate**. *Her directions were very specific, so we didn't get lost.*

definite
Definite means precise and clearly stated. *I found the definite instructions you gave me very helpful.*

---

similar words: **perfect**
contrasting words: **vague**

---

predict _verb_

to tell what is going to happen in the future. *The journalists tried to **predict** which party would win the election.*

divine	To **divine** means to use magic to guess what will happen in the future. *The fortuneteller looked into her crystal ball to divine my future.*
foresee	To **foresee** means to see what is going to happen before it does. *I foresaw trouble when the kitten got into the knitting basket.*
forecast	To **forecast** is so similar to predict that you can often use either word. **Forecast** is mostly used to tell about the weather. *The weather bureau has forecast rain for next weekend.*
prophesy	To **prophesy** means to tell what you believe is going to happen. *He prophesied a huge flood after the hurricane.*
foretell	To **foretell** means to predict. *I will read your palm to foretell the future.*

similar words: **warn**

prefer _verb_

to regard one thing or person as better than another. *I **prefer** caramel topping to chocolate on my ice cream.*

favor	To **favor** can mean to prefer someone or something unfairly. *I favor dogs rather than cats.*
single out	To **single out** means to pick or choose someone or something ahead of others. *They singled her out for a special award because of her kindness.*
opt for	To **opt for** means to choose one thing instead of another or other things. *I opt for the train because it's faster.*
elect	To **elect** can mean to pick out or choose something. *I elected to try out for the gymnastics team.*

similar words: **choose**

press   *verb*

to act upon something with mass or force. *We **pressed** the button at the pedestrian crossing and waited for the "walk" sign.*

compress To **compress** means to press things together, or force something into less space. *The workers compressed the wool into bales ready for transportation.*

jam To **jam** can mean to push or force something into a space tightly. *I jammed the books into the small bookcase.*

squeeze To **squeeze** can mean to press hard so as to remove something. *Let's squeeze some oranges so that we can have a drink of fresh orange juice.*

squash To **squash** means to flatten or crush something or someone. *The wheel squashed my hat.*

trample To **trample** means to crush or tread heavily on something or someone. *The neighbor's dog trampled the flowers in our garden.*

pretty   *adjective*

pleasant or pleasing to look at, especially in a dainty or graceful way. *The **pretty** girl was admired by everyone. I bought a **pretty** vase.*

fair **Fair** can mean very pretty or beautiful. This is a rather old-fashioned way of using the word. *The prince fell in love with the fair maiden.*

good-looking **Good-looking** means pleasant to look at. *Everyone in my family is good-looking.*

handsome **Handsome** means having a fine or pleasant appearance. *Her brother is very handsome.*

attractive **Attractive** means quite pleasing to look at. *It's an attractive color scheme.*

similar words: **beautiful**
contrasting words: **ugly**

prevent *verb*

to keep or hinder something or someone from doing something. *We'll build a high fence to **prevent** the animals from getting out.*

stop	To **stop** can mean to prevent, restrain, or hinder someone or something from doing something. *I'm going to stop you from going to the dance.*
prohibit	To **prohibit** can mean to prevent or hinder. *I'm afraid your bad leg prohibits your jumping the hurdles.*
oppose	To **oppose** can mean to hinder or stand in the way of something. *We are opposing the building of the highway so close to our house.*
suppress	To **suppress** can mean to keep something hidden or from being known or published. *They will try to suppress the news of his death.*
forbid	To **forbid** can mean to prevent or make it impossible for someone to do something. *The train strike forbids his return home.*

similar words: **hinder, block, ban**
contrasting words: **allow**

price *noun*

the amount of money for which something is bought or sold. *I'll buy it if the **price** is right.*

cost	The **cost** is the price to be paid for something. *What's the cost of the bike with the red handlebars?*
charge	The **charge** is the price or **cost** of something. *There's a charge of $2 for the long-distance phone call.*
expense	The **expense** is the amount of money to be paid for something. *We couldn't go by plane because the expense was too great.*
rate	The **rate** is a specially worked out **charge** or payment for something. *The lawyer's rate was over $100 per hour.*
outlay	An **outlay** can be the amount of money spent in getting something. *We rented two videos for the party for a very small outlay.*

prison   *noun*

a place where criminals are kept locked up. *The bank robber was sent to* **prison** *for ten years.*

jail
A **jail** is so similar to a prison you can usually use either word. *He spent ten years in jail.*

penitentiary
A **penitentiary** is a prison for people who have committed serious crimes. *The penitentiary had high walls and was heavily guarded.*

compound
A **compound** can be a closed-off area with buildings where people can be kept. *The soldiers guarded the captured pilots in a compound for prisoners of war.*

lockup
A **lockup** is a small prison, often attached to a police station, where offenders are kept until they appear in court. *The detective took the drunken driver to the lockup.*

prisoner   *noun*

someone who is kept somewhere against their will. *The* **prisoners** *were locked in their cells after dinner.*

captive
A **captive** is someone who has been taken prisoner. *The terrorists kept the captives locked up for almost a year.*

convict
A **convict** is someone who has been found guilty of a crime and is serving a prison sentence. *Police are searching for the escaped convict.*

inmate
An **inmate** is someone who has to stay in an institution, such as a prison. *She counseled the inmates to prepare them for life outside of prison.*

internee
An **internee** is someone who is held as a prisoner in a guarded area during wartime. *The German internees in England tried to escape from their compound and return to Germany.*

similar words: **criminal**
contrasting words: **escapee**

prize *noun*

a reward for winning something, such as a race or competition. *The winner's prize was a free trip to the zoo.*

trophy	A **trophy** is a prize won in a contest, usually a silver cup or something similar. *My trophy for winning the race was a cup with my name on it.*
award	An **award** is a prize won for good work or achievement. *She was given an award for her brave action.*
medal	A **medal** is a metal disk or cross given as a prize or an **award** for bravery. *The soldier received a medal for bravery under fire.*
pennant	A **pennant** is a triangular flag, often given as a prize in a sporting event. *Our football team has won three pennants.*

produce *verb*

to bring something or someone into being. *This soil produces good crops.*

bear	To **bear** can mean to produce by natural growth or to give birth to a child. *This tree bears oranges. The queen bore a son who would one day be the king.*
yield	To **yield** can mean to produce or **bear** something. It is not used to refer to animals or people. *The crops will yield a good harvest this year.*
breed	To **breed** can mean to raise young, or produce young by encouraging the parents to mate. *He breeds prize bulls.*
grow	To **grow** means to develop or cause to come into being. *We grew these plants from seeds.*

similar words: **make**
contrasting words: **destroy**

profession *noun*

an occupation in which special knowledge is needed. *She is a doctor by profession.*

craft
A **craft** is an occupation for which you need special skill with your hands. *His craft is watchmaking.*

trade
A **trade** is a particular kind of work using your hands, for which you need special training. *He decided that carpentry was the best trade to learn.*

apprenticeship
A **apprenticeship** is a time in which someone learns a trade or art by working for someone with experience. *My apprenticeship with the glass sculptor lasts two years.*

calling
A **calling** is someone's usual occupation or **trade**. *She always felt her calling was to be a doctor.*

---

similar words: **job, position**

---

profit *noun*

money made by selling something for more than it cost to produce or buy. *The barbecue factory made a big **profit** this year.*

proceeds
Proceeds means the money you get when you sell something. *The proceeds of the sales were higher than the costs of running the factory.*

return
A **return** can be the extra money you receive as a profit from an investment and so on. *The owners were pleased with the return on the money and work they had put into the factory.*

dividend
A **dividend** is your share in the profit made by a business. *They paid a good dividend to the investors in the business.*

bonus
A **bonus** is extra money paid to a worker as a reward for good work. *Each worker received a bonus because sales had been high.*

royalty
A **royalty** is money paid to writers, composers, or inventors as a share of the profits made from their work. *The inventor of the gas barbecue received a royalty each year.*

---

similar words: **pay**

---

promise   *noun*

a statement telling someone that you will be sure to do or stop doing something. *I made a **promise** to be good.*

pledge   A **pledge** is a promise made very seriously. *She made a pledge that she would not be late again.*

vow   A **vow** is a solemn promise. It is very similar to a **pledge**. *The secret agent took a vow not to reveal any secret information.*

oath   An **oath** is a promise you make that what you say will be true. *When you give evidence in court, you take an oath that you will tell the truth.*

word   Your **word** is a serious promise you make to someone that what you say can be trusted. It is an abbreviation of the expression "word of honor." *I give you my word that I won't do it again.*

pact   A **pact** is a solemn promise or agreement. *We made a pact that we would always be friends.*

pronounce   *verb*

to make the sound of a word or letter. *I **pronounced** the word slowly so he could learn how to say it.*

enunciate   To **enunciate** means to pronounce words or sounds in a particular manner, usually clearly. *He enunciates his words very well although he is only three.*

articulate   To **articulate** means to speak words or sounds clearly. *He articulated every word so that everyone could hear.*

sound   To **sound** can mean to speak, pronounce, or express words or sounds clearly. *He sounded each letter as he went.*

voice   To **voice** means to express a thought or feeling with your voice. *She voiced her opinion.*

utter   To **utter** means to speak or pronounce. *The judge uttered the decision so that everyone could hear.*

contrasting words: **mumble**

property *noun*

something that is owned by a person or group of people. *Everything with my name on it is my **property**.*

possessions **Possessions** are the things someone owns. *We hired a van to move all our possessions to our new house.*

belongings **Belongings** are things that you own. It is very similar to **possessions**. *I had to decide where to put my belongings in my new bedroom.*

paraphernalia **Paraphernalia** means things you own, especially things you don't really need. *We didn't realize how much paraphernalia we had collected until we had to pack and move it all.*

assets **Assets** are things you own, especially things that are valuable. *Our house and car are our most important assets.*

gear **Gear** can be equipment used for a particular purpose. *We packed our camping gear in two knapsacks.*

protect *verb*

to keep something or someone from injury, danger, or annoyance. *The construction workers wore helmets to **protect** their heads.*

guard To **guard** means to protect or keep safe from harm. *Our dog guards our house and barks if strangers come.*

defend To **defend** means to protect or keep safe, especially from attack. *The soldiers defended the town from the enemy.*

shield To **shield** can mean to protect someone or something with anything that acts as a shield. *I shielded my small brother with my body.*

screen To **screen** can mean to protect or shelter someone or something with anything that acts as a screen. *The gigantic beach umbrella screened him from the sun.*

secure To **secure** means to make something safe from harm or danger. *A burglar alarm will secure the house against intruders.*

contrasting words: **endanger**

protrude *verb*

to stick out or stretch out more than is usual. *I need braces on my teeth because the bottom row **protrudes**.*

jut To **jut** means to stick out sharply. *Watch out for the shelf that juts from the wall.*

project To **project** means to stand out or stick out beyond the surface. *Frogs' eyes project noticeably.*

bulge To **bulge** means to stick out as a rounded mass or hump. *The squirrel's cheeks were bulging with nuts.*

swell To **swell** means to **bulge** out. *After I sprained my ankle, I put ice on it so that it wouldn't swell so much.*

billow To **billow** means to **bulge** out because of being filled with air. *The clothes on the line flapped and billowed in the strong breeze.*

proud *adjective*

thinking well of yourself. *I am **proud** that I won the wheelchair race.*

self-confident **Self-confident** means believing strongly in your own ability to do something. *She is a self-confident reporter because she has years of experience.*

self-reliant **Self-reliant** means counting on your own abilities to accomplish something. *We need a self-reliant person who can work without supervision.*

smug **Smug** means showing or feeling that you are very pleased with yourself. *I gave a smug smile when I won first prize.*

arrogant **Arrogant** means showing that you think you are very important. *Pete was arrogant until Carla beat him in the debate.*

similar words: **pompous, conceited**
contrasting words: **humble**

prove   *verb*

to show something to be true or genuine. *The jeweler's appraisal of my gold necklace* **proves** *its worth.*

confirm
To **confirm** means to strengthen or make more certain someone's belief in something. *Nicola's news confirmed my suspicions about how ill he really was.*

corroborate
To **corroborate** means to make something more certain by giving additional, similar information about it. *The information I gave the police officer corroborated Geoffrey's report of what had happened.*

substantiate
To **substantiate** means to prove something by producing evidence. *You will have to substantiate your accusation that she stole your book.*

verify
To **verify** means to prove something is true or correct. *You can verify the spelling of a word by looking it up in a dictionary.*

bear out
To **bear out** means to prove someone or something is right. *The facts you have given him bear me out.*

---

contrasting words: **disprove**

---

public   *adjective*

used by or having to do with the people of a community or the people as a whole. *Many people use* **public** *transportation to go to the city so that they don't have to worry about finding a parking place.*

general
General means concerning all or most people. *The general feeling at the meeting was that the school dance should be postponed.*

popular
Popular means widely liked by a particular group or people in general. *Lots of people listen to this radio station because it plays popular music.*

collective
Collective means having to do with a group of people taken as a whole. *The job will be done more quickly if we make a collective effort.*

communal
Communal means shared by several people. *The apartments have lockers and a communal laundry room in the basement.*

common
Common means shared by two or more people. *The two friends shared a common interest in stamp collecting.*

publication   *noun*

something that has been printed for sale to the public. *This library contains mainly Mexican* **publications**.

newspaper   A **newspaper** is a publication that is produced daily or weekly and contains news reports and advertisements. *We read the newspaper every day so that we know what's happening in our town and the rest of the world.*

magazine   A **magazine** is a paper or a booklet containing stories, articles, and advertisements, usually issued once a week or once a month. *We enjoy reading the weekly sports magazine.*

journal   A **journal** is a **magazine** that is issued regularly by a professional or learned group to inform or educate the readers. *The doctor always reads the monthly medical journals.*

pamphlet   A **pamphlet** is a very small paper-covered book or a single sheet of paper with advertisements printed on it. *We found a pamphlet on the department store sale in our mailbox.*

---

similar words: **book**

---

publish   *verb*

to make something known to the public. *The newspaper* **published** *the story about the hijack.*

report   To **report** means to describe or give an account of something. *At the meeting, he reported that his latest overseas trip had been successful.*

declare   To **declare** means to announce something or make something known officially. *The government declared war.*

proclaim   To **proclaim** means to announce something publicly. *The governor proclaimed a new state holiday.*

advertise   To **advertise** means to draw attention to something or someone, especially in order to sell a product or services. *We advertised our car in the newspaper because we wanted to sell it.*

broadcast   To **broadcast** means to spread information, especially by radio or television. *The radio station broadcast the latest news on the disaster.*

---

similar words: **inform, reveal**

---

pull

pull *verb*

to move something by tugging it toward you. *I **pulled** my fishing line into the boat but the bait was gone.*

haul — To **haul** means to pull something hard. *We hauled the anchor into the boat.*

drag — To **drag** means to pull something slowly or heavily along. *We dragged the sofa across the floor.*

draw — To **draw** means to pull, move, or take something in a particular direction. *I quickly drew my hand away from the hot stove.*

tow — To **tow** means to **drag** or pull something behind you using a rope or chain. *The tractor towed our car out of the flooded river.*

lug — To **lug** means to pull or carry something along with a great deal of effort. *We lugged our heavy suitcases from the taxi into the railway station.*

contrasting words: **push**

punish *verb*

to make someone suffer in some way because of a wrong. *He **punished** the bullies by making them stay in at lunchtime.*

discipline — To **discipline** means to punish in a way that will teach someone not to do the same thing again. *He disciplined us for being careless by making us pay for the new window.*

chastise — To **chastise** means to punish or scold someone. *Their mother chastised them for being late for dinner.*

penalize — To **penalize** means to punish a person by taking something away or by not letting the person do some activity. *She penalized them for being late by not letting them have any dessert.*

correct — To **correct** can mean to scold someone, especially a child, or tell someone about something done wrong so it won't happen again. *She corrected him when he snatched the ball without asking for it.*

similar words: **scold**

purple *adjective*
colored dark reddish-blue. *The plums are **purple**.*

magenta **Magenta** means colored reddish-purple. *The blood in your veins is a magenta color.*

mauve **Mauve** means colored light purple. *If you mix purple and white paint you get a mauve color.*

lilac **Lilac** means colored pale reddish-purple. *The flowers on a lavender bush are a lilac color.*

indigo **Indigo** means colored a deep violet blue. *One of the bands of the rainbow is an indigo color.*

cerise **Cerise** means having a clear red or bright pinkish-red color. *Some cherries are cerise.*

push *verb*
to move something by pressing or leaning against it. *Julian likes to **push** the stroller with his baby brother in it.*

shove To **shove** means to push something roughly. *Someone shoved me from behind and I fell over.*

thrust To **thrust** means to force or push something hard. *She thrust the knife into the watermelon to cut it.*

drive To **drive** means to make someone or something go forward. *The sheepdog drove the sheep into the pen.*

ram To **ram** can mean to push or **drive** something with great force. *Tom rammed the earth down around the fence posts.*

propel To **propel** means to push or **drive** something forward energetically. *The rowers propelled their boat across the finish line.*

contrasting words: **pull**

puzzle *verb*

to make someone uncertain or unable to understand. *The signpost **puzzled** me because the name of the street was spelled differently on the map.*

perplex	To **perplex** means to make someone confused and uncertain. It is very similar to puzzle. *That exam question perplexed me because we haven't had any lessons about how bees find their way home.*
baffle	To **baffle** means to puzzle or confuse someone. *The disappearance of the suspect baffled the police.*
bewilder	To **bewilder** means to confuse someone hopelessly. *He was bewildered by the question and couldn't think of a reply.*
mystify	To **mystify** means to confuse someone completely with something that seems strange or unusual. *The mark on the wall mystified her until she realized there was a secret sliding door there.*
confound	To **confound** means to puzzle and surprise someone. *She confounded the experts by solving the mystery.*

similar words: **confuse**
contrasting words: **explain**

question *verb*

to ask someone for information about something. *The doctor **questioned** the patient about her symptoms.*

inquire	To **inquire** can mean to question or to ask about. *She inquired about the cost of the table.*
interrogate	To **interrogate** means to question someone closely in order to find out something. *The police interrogated the suspect for several days.*
interview	To **interview** means to meet with someone formally in order to ask them particular questions, often related to getting a job or as part of a radio or television program. *The hospital superintendent interviewed all the doctors who applied for the job.*
quiz	To **quiz** means to ask someone many questions. *My mother quizzed me on all the work I had studied for my test.*

contrasting words: **answer**

quiet *adjective*

free from or making little noise or sound, especially an annoying sound. *This is a **quiet** street because there is no through traffic.*

soft	**Soft** can mean making little sound. *We could hardly hear his soft voice.*
faint	**Faint** can mean lacking loudness or strength. *We could hear the faint sound of singing in the distance.*
low	**Low** can mean not loud. *The owl gave a low hoot.*
indistinct	**Indistinct** can mean not sounding clear. *On the long-distance phone call, my mother's voice was indistinct and I had trouble understanding her.*
muffled	**Muffled** means deadened or made less in sound, usually because of being covered by or wrapped in something. *When we were playing hide-and-seek, I heard a muffled laugh coming from behind the clothes in the closet.*

contrasting words: **loud**

quit *verb*

to give up or leave something. *He **quit** his job.*

evacuate	To **evacuate** means to leave a place in order to escape danger. *We evacuated the building when the fire started.*
vacate	To **vacate** means to leave a house or building, usually because someone else wants it. *We had to vacate our hotel room before lunch.*
abandon	To **abandon** means to leave a place and intend to stay away. *We had to abandon the sinking ship.*
desert	To **desert** means to leave a place where you are on duty and not come back. *The sentry deserted his post.*
forsake	To **forsake** means to give up someone or something. *She decided to forsake her career to study art.*

rain *verb*

to come down from the sky in drops of water. *We won't have to water the garden because it **rained** all night.*

sprinkle	To **sprinkle** can mean to rain lightly. *Let's keep walking, because it's only sprinkling.*
drizzle	To **drizzle** means to rain gently and steadily in fine drops. *I wish the sun would come out, because it has been drizzling for days.*
pour	To **pour** means to rain heavily. *It started to pour and we were soaked coming home from school.*
storm	To **storm** means to rain with accompanying violent winds. *It stormed for three hours last night and many power lines were blown down.*
flood	To **flood** means to rain heavily enough to create a water overflow. *The rain storm flooded all the streets and yards in our neighborhood.*

ramble *verb*

to talk or write without keeping to the subject. *He **rambled** on and on about things that I didn't understand.*

wander	To **wander** can mean to move or turn idly toward another thing. *Her mind wandered off the subject and she started to talk about her youth.*
stray	To **stray** can mean to turn aside from the subject you were talking or writing about. *I strayed from the topic of my essay and wrote about horses instead.*
digress	To **digress** means to **wander** away from the main subject when writing or speaking. *I started to lecture on the effects of smoking but I'm afraid I have digresssed.*
diverge	To **diverge** can mean to **wander** off or turn aside from a plan, discussion, and so on. *We have diverged from the points on the agenda and I'd like to return to them.*

rash   *adjective*

acting too quickly and without thought of possible danger or trouble. *Diving into the shallow creek was a **rash** act.*

reckless — **Reckless** means not caring about danger, often in a foolish way. *Riding a bike without lights at night is a reckless thing to do.*

foolhardy — **Foolhardy** means foolishly adventurous or not thinking about danger. It is quite similar to **reckless**. *You were foolhardy to explore the cave by yourself.*

impetuous — **Impetuous** means acting quickly and thoughtlessly, but not necessarily in a dangerous way. *The impetuous boy rushed off without hearing the end of what his mother was saying.*

hasty — **Hasty** means acting in a hurry and without thinking. *He was sorry later for his hasty decision.*

harebrained — **Harebrained** means **reckless** or not sensible. *It was his harebrained idea to go skiing at midnight.*

contrasting words: **wary**

rave   *verb*

to talk wildly making little sense, especially when you are very ill. *The delirious patient was **raving**, so the nurse gave him a sedative to put him to sleep.*

babble — To **babble** means to speak words quickly and unclearly. *The shy boy babbled in reply to her question.*

jabber — To **jabber** means to speak words quickly, unclearly, or foolishly. *The teacher looked annoyed as the student jabbered on and on about why the homework wasn't finished.*

prattle — To **prattle** means to speak or write vaguely and for a long time. *His speech was boring because he just prattled on and on.*

talk nonsense — To **talk nonsense** means to say something that has no meaning. *Don't talk nonsense.*

similar words: **talk**

reaction *noun*

something done as a result of an action by someone else. *Our **reactions** to the play were very favorable.*

response   A **response** is a reaction caused by something that provokes it. *The sunflower turns in response to light.*

reply   A **reply** can be so similar to **response** that you can usually use either. *When I stroke my cat her reply is to purr.*

answer   An **answer** can be an action done in **response** to another. *His answer to my teasing was to step on my toe.*

feedback   **Feedback** can be information passed back about something that has been done or said. *I've had a lot of feedback about my new book.*

acknowledgment   An **acknowledgment** can be a thing done or given to show that you are grateful or think highly of something. *My friends bought me some flowers in acknowledgment of the help I had given them.*

read *verb*

to look at and understand writing or printing. *My father **reads** a story to my little sister every night.*

browse through   To **browse through** means to glance through a book in a casual and leisurely way. *I browsed through a magazine while I was waiting to see the dentist.*

leaf through   To **leaf through** means to turn the pages of a book, or something similar, quickly. *I leafed through the book to make sure it was the one I needed to borrow from the library.*

skim   To **skim** can mean to glance over something without taking everything in. *I skimmed the headlines of the newspaper while I was having my breakfast this morning.*

study   To **study** can mean to look at something closely. *The lawyer studied all the documents for the case.*

wade through   To **wade through** can mean to make your way through something with difficulty or with a lot of effort. *We waded through all our receipts and papers so that we could fill out our tax return.*

ready   *adjective*

in the right condition for immediate action or use. *I'm always **ready** to leave for school at 8 o'clock.*

prepared	**Prepared** means made ready for something. *When you go camping you should be prepared for any emergency.*
equipped	**Equipped** means provided with whatever is needed to do something. *The plumber was equipped for a very dirty and difficult job.*
available	**Available** means easily attainable or ready. *The books will be available for you to pick up at two o'clock.*
fit	**Fit** means in a condition suitable for use. *Our old car is not fit for long trips.*

realize   *verb*

to find out or come to understand clearly. *At last I **realized** the truth.*

discover	To **discover** can mean to find out something you didn't know before. *They soon discovered the truth about the smashed windows.*
learn	To **learn** can mean to find out or come to know something. *She was surprised when she learned what a good swimmer he was.*
ascertain	To **ascertain** means to find out or make sure of something. *I am trying to ascertain the facts.*
glean	To **glean** can mean to gather something slowly and with difficulty, one bit at a time. *It took them many weeks to glean all the information they needed.*
catch on	To **catch on** can mean to understand something, often something you should have understood earlier. It is more suited to everyday language. *It didn't take her long to catch on to the problem, and soon the motor was fixed.*

similar words: **sense, understand**

rebel *verb*

to fight against the government or resist those who rule or have power. *The people* *rebelled* *against the president and exiled him.*

disobey	To **disobey** means to refuse to do as you are told. *We should not disobey the school rules.*
mutiny	To **mutiny** means to rebel against someone in authority. It is usually used about sailors or soldiers. *The crew mutinied because of their captain's unfair treatment.*
rise up	To **rise up** is so similar to **rebel** that you can usually choose either. *The people rose up against the cruel king.*
revolt	To **revolt** means to rebel against those who have power over you. *The prisoners revolted against their jailers.*
run riot	To **run riot** means to behave without control and ignore those in authority. *The audience ran riot at the concert and smashed the seats.*

similar words: **resist**
contrasting words: **give in**

rebellion *noun*

a refusal to obey someone who is in charge or who has power over you. *There was a* *rebellion* *against the dictator's harsh new laws.*

revolt	A **revolt** is so similar to rebellion that you can usually choose either word. *Several guards were injured in the revolt at the prison.*
revolution	A **revolution** is the complete overthrow of a government or a complete change in the form of government. *After the revolution in 1917, Russia no longer had a Czar.*
uprising	An **uprising** is a violent rebellion against the government or other authority by a large number of people. *The citizens were displeased with the military dictator, and an uprising occurred in which part of the city was damaged.*
coup	A **coup** is a sudden successful move, especially against a government. *The generals have been in power since the army coup.*
mutiny	A **mutiny** is a rebellion against authority, especially by sailors or soldiers against their officers. *The captain was killed in the mutiny.*

record   *verb*

to write down information so that it can be kept. *I'll **record** all the events of my trip in this journal.*

note
To **note** means to write something down, usually so you can remember it. *I noted the time of my dentist's appointment on the calendar.*

register
To **register** means to write down, or have written down in a list of names, acts, or events that are to be kept as a record. *Dad registered our new car at the government office where licenses are issued.*

enter
To **enter** can mean to write something on a list. *Luke entered his name on the list of volunteers.*

log
To **log** can mean to write down important details of a voyage or flight, such as the weather, speed, and so on. This is usually done by the captain of the ship or plane. *The captain logged the weather information as soon as he received it.*

similar words: **list**

---

recover   *verb*

to get well again after being sick. *He has now **recovered** from his accident.*

recuperate
To **recuperate** is so similar to recover that you can usually use either word. *She is recuperating from measles.*

bounce back
To **bounce back** can mean to recover or regain your health. This is rather an informal word. *He bounced back well after the doctor treated him with antibiotics.*

convalesce
To **convalesce** means to grow stronger after an illness. *He is convalescing at home after his operation.*

rally
To **rally** can mean to begin to recover or gain fresh strength, often after an illness. *We were relieved when she rallied after her cast came off.*

brighten
To **brighten** can mean to become more lively or cheerful, especially if you haven't been feeling well. *She gradually brightened as her fever went down.*

contrasting words: **deteriorate**

red

red *adjective*
colored like a ripe tomato. *The **red** peppers looked lovely in the green lettuce salad.*

crimson **Crimson** means colored a deep, purplish-red. *The school colors were gold and crimson.*

scarlet **Scarlet** means colored a bright red. *The guards at Buckingham Palace wear scarlet coats.*

ruby **Ruby** means rich red-colored, like the precious stone called a ruby. *The stop light shone ruby red through the mist.*

maroon **Maroon** means having a dark brownish-red color. *She held the chestnut up to the light to admire its rich maroon color.*

pink **Pink** means having a pale red color.

similar words: **rosy**

refresh *verb*
to fill someone with new energy and strength. *You'll be ready to work again after you **refresh** yourself with a short nap.*

revive To **revive** can mean to bring someone or something back into a lively state. *A drink of cool water will revive me after that long walk.*

renew To **renew** can mean to restore someone or something to the way it was before. *The rain renewed the grass and it turned green again.*

invigorate To **invigorate** means to fill someone with life and energy. *Her morning swim invigorated her and made her feel wide awake.*

stimulate To **stimulate** can mean to interest someone and make him or her want to do something. *The advertisement stimulated him to buy the new book.*

refuge *noun*

a place giving shelter or protection from danger or trouble. *The cave was a perfect* **refuge** *during the storm.*

shelter
A **shelter** is a place that provides protection or safety when there is danger or trouble. *Many people built lead-lined shelters in case there was a nuclear war.*

haven
A **haven** can be a place of safety and protection. *The fishing boats used the sheltered bay as a haven whenever the sea became too rough.*

asylum
An **asylum** can be any refuge offering safety or care. *My grandmother's quiet house is my asylum in time of trouble.*

retreat
A **retreat** is a sheltered remote place where people go to find peace and quiet. *We go to our retreat by the lake nearly every weekend.*

sanctuary
A **sanctuary** can be a place protected by law where plants and animals cannot be harmed. *The wildlife sanctuary was a perfect place to see animals living in their natural state.*

refuse *verb*

to say you will not accept something offered to you. *He* **refused** *my help and said he could manage by himself.*

decline
To **decline** means to refuse to accept something in a polite way. *He declined my invitation to the party.*

reject
To **reject** means to refuse to accept or use something, usually because it isn't satisfactory. *They rejected my story because they said they couldn't read my writing.*

renounce
To **renounce** means to refuse to accept something that you are entitled to. *The man renounced his legal right to the money.*

turn down
To **turn down** can mean to refuse or **reject** something. This is more suited to everyday language. *Mom turned down their offer to buy our house because it was too low.*

rebuff
To **rebuff** means to refuse to accept something in a definite and strong way. *She rebuffed all his attempts to be friendly.*

similar words: **prevent, ban**
contrasting words: **allow**

rejoice *verb*

to be glad or delighted. *The whole family **rejoiced** when the baby was born.*

celebrate   To **celebrate** means to have a party for a special reason. *When the exams are over we are going to celebrate.*

revel   To **revel** means to have a wild party. *Our neighbors reveled all night and kept us awake.*

exult   To **exult** means to rejoice greatly. *We exulted in our good luck at being rescued.*

go crazy   To **go crazy** can mean to **revel**, or behave in a very wild manner. It is more suited to everyday language. *Everyone will go crazy if our team wins.*

whoop it up   To **whoop it up** means to have a party or celebration. It is only suited to everyday language. *He really whooped it up on his birthday.*

contrasting words: **grieve**

related *adjective*

of a similar kind or having something in common. *Geography and geology are **related** subjects of study.*

connected   **Connected** can mean thought of as related. *The detective gathered a connected set of clues that solved the crime.*

associated   **Associated** means related to or **connected** with something in your mind or thoughts. *Holidays and their associated pleasures are memories you have all your life.*

allied   **Allied** means joined together in reality or in your thoughts. *Running and its allied sport, hurdling, interest me a lot.*

relevant   **Relevant** means related to what is being discussed. *Her remark about people landing on the moon was very relevant to the topic of space travel.*

similar words: **similar**
contrasting words: **unrelated**

reliable *adjective*

trusted or able to be relied on. *He is such a **reliable** friend I know he will keep his promise.*

responsible
Responsible means reliable, or able to accept and be trusted with special responsibilities or duties. *We need a responsible person to be in charge of the sports equipment.*

dependable
Dependable is so similar to reliable that you can usually use either word. *We let Alison do the shopping because we knew she was dependable.*

conscientious
Conscientious means reliable because you are very careful and particular in what you do. *We gave the most important jobs to Scott because he was such a conscientious worker.*

dutiful
Dutiful means always doing what you think is right. *We elected her again because she had been a very dutiful club president.*

---

similar words: **faithful, steadfast**
contrasting words: **fickle**

---

religion *noun*

any particular system of worship that usually involves confidence and trust in a supernatural power that created the world. *When we studied different **religions** in school, we learned that each **religion** has a number of values and morals that followers are taught to believe.*

faith
Faith can mean a particular religion with its collection of principles and teachings. *He was brought up in the Jewish faith.*

belief
Belief can be very similar to **faith**. *Their family is of the Hindu belief.*

denomination
Denomination means a large, organized religious group, especially in the Christian church. *She belongs to the Baptist denomination.*

theology
Theology means the collection of beliefs held by a particular religion. *In the theology of the ancient Greeks, there were many gods and goddesses.*

religious   *adjective*

believing in a particular religion. *The **religious** man went to church every week.*

pious	**Pious** means showing religious devotion and respect. *They are so pious they will not do any work on the Sabbath.*
devout	**Devout** means sincerely believing in and praising your God. *The devout Muslim prayed to Allah every day.*
reverent	**Reverent** means showing deep respect for the goodness and greatness of God. *The little girl's reverent behavior in church was appreciated by the congregation.*
faithful	**Faithful** can mean full of belief in a religion. *In the temple, the faithful Buddhists meditated.*

similar words: **holy**

remains   *noun*

what is left. This is a plural noun. *The police inspected the **remains** of the building after the fire.*

remnants	**Remnants** are parts or amounts that are left. This is a plural noun. *I made a patchwork cushion from remnants of material.*
odds and ends	**Odds and ends** are scraps or **remnants**. This is a plural noun. *We made toys out of odds and ends from our parents' workshops.*
residue	**Residue** is something that is left. This is a singular noun. *Most of the grass cuttings went into the catcher of the lawnmower and I raked up the residue.*
leftovers	**Leftovers** are things that remain or were not used, especially from a meal. This is a plural noun. *We gave the leftovers to the dog.*
leavings	**Leavings** are remains or useless **leftovers**. This is a plural noun. *We scraped the leavings into the garbage can.*

remember   *verb*

to bring something back to, or to keep it in your mind. *I **remember** the way to do that puzzle.*

recollect
To **recollect** is very similar to remember and you can often choose either word. *I recollect the fun we had at the beach last summer.*

recall
To **recall** means to remember or **recollect** something. These three words are so similar you can usually use any of them. *He does well in tests because he can recall facts very easily.*

place
To **place** can mean to remember someone or something by connecting them in your mind with certain places, events, or other things. *I could only place her when I heard her sing the same song she sang at our last concert.*

recognize
To **recognize** means to know someone or something again when you see or hear them at a later time. *I recognized him even though I met him over a year ago.*

remove   *verb*

to take something off or away. *Please **remove** your shoes before coming inside the house.*

withdraw
To **withdraw** means to take something out. *I withdrew some money from the bank.*

extract
To **extract** means to pull or take something out. *The dentist extracted my tooth.*

excise
To **excise** means to cut something out. *The doctor excised the wart from my finger.*

dislodge
To **dislodge** means to remove something from its existing position. *When the workers were pruning the tree, they dislodged a bird's nest.*

erase
To **erase** means to remove something by rubbing. *We erased the writing from the blackboard.*

contrasting words: **insert, add**

repair   *verb*

to bring something back into a good condition. *I have to **repair** my old bike.*

mend　　　To **mend** means to put something into working order. It often refers to repairing an item of clothing. *Dad is going to help me mend my shirt.*

fix　　　To **fix** means to repair or **mend** something. These three verbs are so similar you can usually choose any one of them. *I will have to fix the broken headlight.*

restore　　　To **restore** means to bring something back to its original condition. *The Historical Society wants to restore the first house built in our town.*

renovate　　　To **renovate** means to repair something so that it is like new. *We are going to renovate our house.*

patch up　　　To **patch up** means to repair something, especially in a hasty or makeshift way. *When the car broke down, we patched it up until we could find a garage.*

---

similar words: **improve, correct**
contrasting words: **damage**

---

repay   *verb*

to pay back or return something. *I want to **repay** the money you lent me.*

reimburse　　　To **reimburse** means to pay back to someone money they have spent on behalf of someone else. *I bought new tennis balls and the treasurer reimbursed me.*

recompense　　　To **recompense** means to make a repayment, especially for time or trouble spent in doing something. *I recompensed the dressmaker for the extra time spent looking for matching buttons.*

compensate　　　To **compensate** means to make something up to someone. *We will compensate you for the cost of repairing your car.*

refund　　　To **refund** means to give or pay back money you have already spent. *The theater refunded the cost of our tickets when the show was canceled.*

reward　　　To **reward** means to give something to someone in return for work or help. *The neighbors rewarded me for feeding their dog while they were on vacation.*

---

similar words: **pay**

338

repeated *adjective*

done again and again. *They were exhausted after making **repeated** attempts to pull the boat up onto the beach.*

regular	**Regular** means following a rule or pattern, especially having to do with fixed times. *Regular eating and sleeping habits help keep you healthy.*
periodic	**Periodic** means happening or appearing at regular intervals. *It is a good idea to pay periodic visits to your dentist.*
recurrent	**Recurrent** means happening or appearing again and again. *She has recurrent attacks of hay fever in July and August.*
rhythmical	**Rhythmical** means happening in a regular pattern of timing. *The rhythmical beat of the music set our feet tapping.*
frequent	**Frequent** means happening often. *We make frequent visits to the beach during summer.*

contrasting words: **erratic**

repel *verb*

to drive away or force back someone or something. *Our bug spray **repelled** the black flies.*

repulse	To **repulse** is so similar to repel that you can usually use either. *The soldiers repulsed the enemy's attack.*
scare off	To **scare off** means to drive away by frightening someone or something. *We made loud noises to scare off the lion.*
dispel	To **dispel** means to drive or send something away in all directions. *His explanation of what the noise really was dispelled all my fears.*
rebuff	To **rebuff** means to drive someone away who is offering you something, or trying to be pleasant. *I went to put my arms around him but he rebuffed me.*
spurn	To **spurn** means to refuse to have anything to do with someone or something because you are scornful. *At the ball the prince spurned Cinderella's wicked sisters.*

contrasting words: **attract**

report   *noun*

an account of the important facts, especially of a meeting, an event, or someone's progress at work or school. *Could you write me a **report** on how your committee will be set up?*

document	A **document** is a paper giving information or evidence. *Keep an important document like your birth certificate in a safe place.*
statement	A **statement** is something spoken or written that presents facts or details about something or someone. *The officer told us that we'd have to make a statement at the police station after the accident.*
dossier	A **dossier** is a bundle of documents containing information about a person or subject. *The police kept a dossier on the bank robber.*
brief	A **brief** is an outline of information or instructions on a subject, especially for use by a lawyer conducting a legal case. *The lawyer prepared a brief on the case for his supervisor.*
bulletin	A **bulletin** is a short written or spoken report or account, especially of news or events. *Did you see the latest TV bulletin on the floods?*

similar words: **summary, message**

resentful   *adjective*

having a feeling of jealousy, hurt, or anger about someone or something. *They were **resentful** of his rapid success.*

bitter	**Bitter** can mean filled with sour feelings. *She is bitter toward her friend because he would not help her.*
spiteful	**Spiteful** means full of a bad-tempered wish to annoy or hurt someone else. *The spiteful child hit the little girl for no reason.*
malicious	**Malicious** means having the desire to harm or hurt someone. *She was just being malicious when she broke his pencil.*
vindictive	**Vindictive** means paying someone back for something done to you. *He could be a vindictive person when things didn't go his way.*
vengeful	**Vengeful** means wanting to take revenge. *The vengeful boy pushed me over when I accidentally bumped into him.*

similar words: **angry, mean**

reside   *verb*

to have your home in a particular place. It is a fairly formal word. *We **reside** in Arizona now.*

live
       To **live** means the same as reside. It is a much less formal word. *He lives in a friendly country town.*

dwell
       To **dwell** means to **live** in a particular place or condition. It sounds rather old-fashioned and isn't used as much as **live**. *They dwell in peace and harmony.*

board
       To **board** means to pay for the use of a room and for meals. *He has to board at school because his parents live in the country.*

stay
       To **stay** means to **live** somewhere for a time. *This summer I will stay with my uncle in Fredericksburg.*

squat
       To **squat** can mean to **live** without permission on land or in a property you don't own. *The vagabonds squatted in the derelict houses until they were evicted.*

---

similar words: **inhabit**

---

resist   *verb*

to stand up to or fight against someone. *The army **resisted** the invaders until they retreated.*

defy
       To **defy** can mean to resist someone or something boldly. *I defied the bully to take my bike away from me.*

oppose
       To **oppose** means to disagree with and resist someone or something. *Our town was opposed to the plan to build the shopping mall so close to the park.*

withstand
       To **withstand** means not to give way to something or someone. *She tried hard to withstand their pleas but eventually gave in.*

obstruct
       To **obstruct** means to **oppose** someone by making things difficult. *The captured spy obstructed the enemy's efforts to get information by refusing to talk.*

counter
       To **counter** means to act against someone or something. *The manager countered the workers' demands by closing the factory.*

---

contrasting words: **give in**

---

respect   *noun*

feelings of admiration. *I have the greatest **respect** for people who do volunteer work.*

regard	**Regard** can be respect for, or a favorable opinion of, someone or something. *I have a very high regard for her knowledge of these matters.*
esteem	**Esteem** is the good opinion you have of someone. *His courage earned him the esteem of the whole team.*
honor	**Honor** can mean respect or **esteem**. *The scientist was treated with honor when she visited her old school.*
veneration	**Veneration** means a feeling of deep respect and love. *We were filled with veneration for our grandfather, who had saved the little boy from drowning.*
devotion	**Devotion** can be loyalty or great affection. *She was an excellent manager and won the devotion of her staff.*

contrasting words: **scorn**

rest   *noun*

a time of ease or recovery. *I think I'll have a **rest** after I finish my homework.*

break	A **break** is a short rest. *They took a break from work.*
recess	A **recess** is a period of rest from work. *The judge said we would take an hour recess before continuing with the trial.*
pause	A **pause** can be a brief period of inactivity or rest. *They took a pause from climbing to catch their breath.*
leisure	**Leisure** is time that is free from work. *We were given a day of leisure to do whatever we wanted.*

contrasting words: **work**

rest *verb*

to take time off from working. *Little children often **rest** in the afternoon.*

relax	To **relax** means to rest and feel at ease. *You can sit down and relax for an hour.*
wind down	To **wind down** means to rest after working very hard. *Watching TV helps me wind down after a busy day.*
put your feet up	To **put your feet up** means to lie down and have a rest. It is more suited to everyday language. *What a busy day! Let's put our feet up and listen to some music.*
take it easy	To **take it easy** means to have a restful time. It is more suited to everyday language. *You should take it easy after running such a long cross-country race.*

similar words: **laze**
contrasting words: **work**

restaurant *noun*

a place where you can buy and eat a meal. *That **restaurant** serves both American and Chinese food.*

café	A **café** is a restaurant that serves coffee, tea, and small meals. *We had lunch in a café.*
bistro	A **bistro** is a small restaurant or wine bar. *Let's meet in the French bistro on the corner.*
cafeteria	A **cafeteria** is an inexpensive self-service restaurant. *Is there a cafeteria in this store?*
snack bar	A **snack bar** is a counter where beverages and small meals are served. *There is a snack bar in this store where we can get a sandwich.*
diner	A **diner** is a small inexpensive restaurant, usually on the roadside for travelers. *We parked and went into the diner for a quick meal.*

result   *noun*

something that springs or proceeds from an action or event. *The success of the play was the **result** of our group's terrific effort.*

outcome	An **outcome** is something that results from what has happened previously. *My book was so exciting, I couldn't wait to discover the outcome.*
effect	An **effect** is a result, or something that is produced by some cause. *Wrinkles are an effect of aging.*
consequence	A **consequence** is the inevitable or expected result of something. *This mess is the consequence of your foolishness.*
conclusion	**Conclusion** can mean a final result. *The signing of an agreement was the conclusion of the peace talks.*
sequel	A **sequel** can be anything that follows or results from something. *The author wrote a sequel to her popular novel.*

retaliate   *verb*

to strike back. *If you tease him he will **retaliate**.*

reciprocate	To **reciprocate** means to act in a similar way in return. *If you are spiteful to me, I will reciprocate.*
get even	To **get even** means to retaliate or strike back. *I hid his books and now I'm afraid he'll try to get even.*
take revenge	To **take revenge** means to cause hurt or damage because of something someone has done to you. *When they spoiled our game, we took revenge by hiding their bikes.*
settle a score	To **settle a score** means to avenge a wrong done to you. *She settled a score with Jayne by not going to her party.*

reticent *adjective*

not inclined to talk a lot or openly. *She is a **reticent** person and doesn't talk about her problems.*

reserved **Reserved** means inclined to keep your feelings or thoughts to yourself. It is similar to reticent. *He seems unfriendly but he is really only reserved.*

quiet **Quiet** can mean shy and not inclined to talk. *The new boy in the class is rather quiet.*

taciturn **Taciturn** means not inclined to communicate by talking. *He is rather taciturn when he is in a bad mood.*

laconic **Laconic** means using few words when talking. *She is often laconic in her replies.*

secretive **Secretive** means liking to keep things to yourself. *A lot of people mistrust her because she is secretive.*

similar words: **shy**
contrasting words: **talkative**

reveal *verb*

to uncover something or make it known. *He **revealed** the secret of the door to the hidden room.*

disclose To **disclose** can mean to tell something or allow it to be known. *He disclosed the history of the castle.*

show To **show** can mean to explain something or make it clear. *He showed the special technique to me so I could open the secret door too.*

expose To **expose** can mean to reveal something that has been hidden from most people. *The story he told me exposed many family secrets.*

unfold To **unfold** can mean to reveal or explain something little by little. *As he unfolded the whole saga I began to understand his pride in his family's history.*

similar words: **admit, publish, inform, blab**
contrasting words: **hide**

345

reverse   *verb*

to turn back or go backward. *We came to a dead end and had to **reverse** direction.*

back
To **back** can mean to move backward. *Dad backed into the garage.*

recede
To **recede** means to move back and become more distant. *As we drove away, the hills receded into the distance.*

ebb
To **ebb** means to flow back or away. *We waited until the tide ebbed before we walked around the rocks.*

rebound
To **rebound** means to bounce or spring back. *The ball rebounded off the wall.*

---

contrasting words: **advance**

---

rhythm   *noun*

the pattern of regularly repeated groups of strong and weak pulses, stresses, or accents in music, poetry, or speech. *They clapped to the **rhythm** of the music.*

beat
Beat can be the units of time in a piece of music, or the rate at which accents or stresses follow one another, giving a feeling of pattern or regularity. *Pop music usually has a strong, regular beat.*

time
Time can be the speed of movement of a piece of music. *This music is marked to be played in waltz time.*

tempo
Tempo is the speed at which you perform a piece of music, and is usually indicated for you. It is very similar to **time**. *This song has a fast, lively tempo.*

swing
Swing can be a steady marked rhythm or movement in music or speech. *Everything the band played had a swing to it.*

ridiculous   *adjective*

so silly or funny that people feel like laughing, often with contempt. *Why are you wearing that **ridiculous** hat?*

absurd	**Absurd** can mean ridiculous or foolish. *He wore absurd rabbit ears to the costume party.*
nonsensical	**Nonsensical** means foolish or making no sense. *We found ourselves in a nonsensical situation that no one could explain.*
ludicrous	**Ludicrous** means so ridiculous that no one could take it seriously. *Your suggestion that we walk from Richmond to Atlanta is ludicrous.*
preposterous	**Preposterous** means annoyingly ridiculous. *Don't come to me with any more of your preposterous suggestions.*
farcical	**Farcical** means so ridiculous that it doesn't seem like a real situation. *It was farcical the way we kept on not recognizing each other.*

similar words: **silly**
contrasting words: **sane**

ring   *verb*

to make or give out a clear musical sound. *The bells are **ringing**.*

peal	To **peal** means to ring loudly and for a long time. *The bells pealed in celebration of the prince's wedding.*
chime	To **chime** can mean to make the sound of a bell that has been struck. *This clock chimes on every hour.*
knell	To **knell** means to ring slowly and with a sad sound. *The church bells knelled for her funeral.*
toll	To **toll** means to ring with single, slow, sad sounds, usually at a funeral. It is similar to **knell**. *Do you know for whom the bell is tolling?*

room *noun*

a part of a building separated by walls from other parts. *Our house has eight* **rooms.**

chamber	A **chamber** is a private room, usually a bedroom. It is an old-fashioned word. *The sick man received visitors in his chamber.*
den	A **den** can be a quiet, cosy, private room. *My father likes to read in the den.*
compartment	A **compartment** is a room or separate section in a railway car, ship, or aircraft. *We shared our compartment with two other passengers.*
cubicle	A **cubicle** is a very small, partly enclosed room. *We left our clothes in the changing cubicle.*
cell	A **cell** can be a small room in a prison, a convent, or monastery. *The prisoners were locked in their cells each night.*

rosy *adjective*

pink and healthy-looking. *She had lovely* **rosy** *cheeks and a clear skin.*

flushed	**Flushed** means having skin that has gone red. *His face was flushed from running in the heat.*
ruddy	**Ruddy** means having a healthy red color. *They came home from their camping trip with ruddy faces and strong muscles.*
florid	**Florid** means red-colored. *His florid cheeks showed that he had a fever.*
bloodshot	**Bloodshot** means having eyes with red streaks from enlarged blood vessels. *Her eyes were bloodshot from staying up late for too many nights.*
inflamed	**Inflamed** means made red by emotion or an infection. *His inflamed eyes showed he had been crying.*

similar words: **red**

rot   *verb*

to go bad. *The garbage is **rotting**.*

decay
To **decay** can be so similar to rot that you can usually use either. *The apples fell from the tree and decayed on the ground.*

decompose
To **decompose** means to break up as it rots. *The leaves decomposed on the forest floor.*

putrefy
To **putrefy** can mean to rot with a very unpleasant smell. *If we don't get the refrigerator working, the meat will putrefy.*

fester
To **fester** means to go bad and form pus. This is mostly used about a wound or a sore. *Put some ointment on that cut before it festers.*

---

similar words: **deteriorate**

---

rough   *adjective*

feeling uneven or not smooth. *I touched the **rough** skin of the pineapple.*

bumpy
Bumpy means having a lumpy or uneven surface. *That toad has bumpy skin.*

gnarled
Gnarled can mean rough and worn by old age or the weather. *He stroked his beard with his gnarled, old hand.*

coarse
Coarse means thick or not having a fine smooth feel. *This dog has coarse hair.*

shaggy
Shaggy can mean rough and matted. *The pony's coat was so shaggy that I couldn't brush it easily.*

bristly
Bristly means rough because of having short stiff hairs. *I don't like kissing Dad's bristly face before he's had a shave.*

---

contrasting words: **smooth**

---

roughen   *verb*

to make something feel worn or not smooth. *Hard work has **roughened** his hands.*

coarsen

To **coarsen** can mean to make something feel rough or no longer fine. *Too much sun has coarsened her skin.*

chap

To **chap** means to make your skin cracked, red, and rough. *The cold wind chapped her hands.*

chafe

To **chafe** means to wear down or make something sore by rubbing it roughly. *The saddle chafed the horse's back.*

rasp

To **rasp** means to scrape something with a rough tool. *The carpenter rasped the piece of wood with a file.*

ruffle

To **ruffle** means to spoil the smoothness of something. *Birds ruffle their feathers when they are cleaning themselves.*

contrasting words: **smooth**

rubbish   *noun*

useless leftover material or matter. *We took our **rubbish** to the dump.*

garbage

Garbage is so similar to rubbish you can often use either word. *Our household garbage is collected every week and taken away in trucks.*

refuse

Refuse is **garbage** or waste material. *Rain washed refuse off the sidewalks into the gutters.*

debris

Debris is the rubbish left when something is broken or destroyed. *The rescuers had to clear away piles of debris to get to the victims of the earthquake.*

junk

Junk means old or unwanted things. *We are going to clean out all the junk from our garage tomorrow.*

trash

Trash is rubbish or anything that you think is worthless or useless. *We put our pile of trash outside to be collected, but we saw some people take things they could use from it.*

rude   *adjective*

bad-mannered or not behaving politely. *The **rude** woman did not thank the boy who opened the door for her.*

impolite

Impolite is so similar to rude that you can usually choose either word. *It's impolite to talk when someone else is speaking.*

cheeky

Cheeky means not showing respect. *The annoyed employee made a cheeky reply to his boss's question.*

impudent

Impudent means rude and disrespectful. *The teacher was cross with the student's impudent answer.*

insolent

Insolent means boldly and openly rude and disrespectful. *We were surprised by their insolent behavior toward their parents.*

insulting

Insulting means showing rudeness by saying hurtful things. *I ignored his insulting remark about my shabby clothes.*

---

similar words: **bold, vulgar, abrupt**
contrasting words: **polite**

---

rule   *noun*

an instruction telling you what to do. *I'll read out the **rules** of the game.*

law

A **law** is a rule made by a government or ruler for all the people to follow. *There is a law that says you must wear your seat belt in a car.*

regulation

A **regulation** is a rule made by an authority such as a school or a municipality. *Local regulations forbid you to walk on the grass in the park.*

convention

A **convention** is a rule, often not written down, that everyone understands and follows. *It is a convention to say "hello" when you answer the telephone.*

precept

A **precept** is a general rule or saying about behavior. *"Look before you leap" is a wise precept.*

formula

A **formula** is a rule or recipe that you should follow. *Helping others is a formula that brings happiness.*

rule *verb*

to have or exercise power over something or someone. *The queen **ruled** over her subjects wisely.*

reign
To **reign** means to rule or use authority as a king or queen does. *Queen Victoria reigned over her people for many years.*

preside
To **preside** means to have control over something. *The chairperson's job is to preside over the meeting.*

officiate
To **officiate** means to perform the duties that accompany a particular position. *My father was the umpire who officiated at our baseball game last week.*

dominate
To **dominate** can mean to rule or control because you have the most power. *Some people dominate conversations and don't let others talk.*

command
To **command** can mean to give orders or be in charge. *The sergeant commanded, and the soldiers obeyed immediately.*

---

similar words: **manage**

---

sacrifice *verb*

to give up something for a particular reason. *I **sacrificed** my leisure time on Saturday to help my friend fix her bike.*

relinquish
To **relinquish** means to give up or let go of something. It is a rather formal word. *The thief was asked to relinquish the stolen goods.*

forego
To **forego** means to sacrifice or **do without** something. *She decided to forego her vacation to stay with her sick grandfather.*

do without
To **do without** means to get along without something you would like to have. *He has to do without a new sweater because he can afford only a jacket.*

resign
To **resign** means to **relinquish** something, especially a job or position. *He resigned his job when he moved to another state.*

safe

sad *adjective*

sorrowful or miserable. *I was **sad** when my best friend left our school.*

unhappy **Unhappy** means not cheerful or happy. *He was unhappy when he couldn't go to the picnic.*

homesick **Homesick** means **unhappy** because you are not living at home. *I was homesick for my first two days at summer camp.*

low **Low** can mean **unhappy** or sad. *He was in low spirits when he didn't pass the test.*

hurt **Hurt** can mean sad because someone has been unkind to you. *I was hurt when she didn't invite me to her house to play.*

upset **Upset** means feeling sad or **hurt**. *She was upset when she wasn't picked for the team.*

---

similar words: **miserable, glum**
contrasting words: **happy, joyful, glad**

---

safe *adjective*

free from danger or risk. *We knew we were **safe** when the wind and waves died down.*

protected **Protected** means guarded or shielded from danger or harm. *I was protected as I huddled in the tiny cave away from the storm.*

sheltered **Sheltered** means **protected** from bad weather, danger, and so on. *We planted the seedlings in a sheltered corner of the garden.*

secure **Secure** means safe or free from danger. *We were secure knowing we had a map and compass in case we lost our way.*

immune **Immune** means free or **protected** from danger, harm, or disease. *We knew the desert so well we were immune to most of its dangers.*

---

contrasting words: **vulnerable, dangerous**

---

sag   *verb*

to hang loosely. *His trousers **sagged** over his hips.*

droop	To **droop** means to bend or hang down. *Her head drooped with tiredness.*
collapse	To **collapse** can mea fn to fall down suddenly, often from weakness. *The sick man collapsed onto the bed.*
loll	To **loll** can mean to hang loosely, or sink down. *The dog's tongue lolled from its mouth as it panted.*
slump	To **slump** means to drop heavily and loosely. *He slumped into the chair.*
slouch	To **slouch** means to sit or walk not holding yourself up straight. *He slouched along the street.*

sail   *verb*

to travel in a ship or boat. *During our vacation we **sailed** around Cape Hatteras.*

cruise	To **cruise** means to sail from place to place, especially for pleasure. *We cruised among the islands looking at the lovely scenery.*
glide	To **glide** can mean to move slowly and easily through the water. *The sailboat glided across the calm lake.*
skim	To **skim** can mean to move lightly across the surface of the water. *The canoe skimmed across the still lake.*
coast	To **coast** can mean to sail from port to port along a coast. *The ship coasted from Vancouver to Prince Rupert.*
float	To **float** means to move gently on top of the water. *We floated on our raft for a couple of hours after our launch sank.*

sailor   *noun*

a member of a ship or boat's crew. *Every **sailor** had a special job to do to make sure the ship traveled safely across the sea.*

seafarer	A **seafarer** is someone who travels on the sea, especially someone who does it for a living. *The Vikings of long ago were brave and warlike seafarers.*
mariner	A **mariner** is someone who makes a living as a sailor. *Because he loved boats and traveling to new places, he decided to be a mariner.*
mate	A **mate** can be a ship's officer below a captain. *She signed on as first mate for the sailing trip to the West Indies.*
marine	A **marine** is someone who belongs to a naval troop that serves both on ships and on land. *The marines left their ship and fought the enemy on the nearby island.*

sane   *adjective*

sensible or based on common sense. *When we realized that we were lost, we knew the only **sane** thing to do was to find shelter for the night.*

sound	**Sound** can mean sure or reliable. *He always gives me sound advice when I'm in trouble.*
well-balanced	**Well-balanced** can mean sane or sensible. *This is a well-balanced approach to the problem.*
coherent	**Coherent** means consistent or thought of in the same way throughout. *Her essay had a coherent argument.*
logical	**Logical** can mean based on sensible or correct reasoning. *The logical course of action, now that it's pouring, is to go inside.*

similar words: **sensible**
contrasting words: **irrational, mad**

satisfied   *adjective*

pleased and happy because your wishes or needs are fulfilled. *She looked at her test results with a **satisfied** smile.*

content   **Content** means satisfied with what you have. *We are very content with our new house.*

complacent   **Complacent** means satisfied or quietly pleased, especially with yourself. *The committee members are too complacent to realize they have to work harder.*

comfortable   **Comfortable** can mean having enough to be satisfied. *They live a comfortable life.*

satiated   **Satiated** means satisfied to a very great extent. *We were satiated with pleasure after our day at the circus.*

similar words: **glad**
contrasting words: **dissatisfied, greedy**

save   *verb*

to keep, free, or deliver someone or something from danger or harm. *Their life jackets **saved** them from drowning.*

rescue   To **rescue** means to save someone or something from danger. *Anita climbed up the tree and rescued the terrified kitten.*

preserve   To **preserve** can mean to keep something or someone safe. *Our guide preserved us from any dangers along the trail.*

safeguard   To **safeguard** means to protect something or someone or to keep it from harm. *We all took turns watching the bird's nest to safeguard it from wild animals.*

salvage   To **salvage** means to save or recover something, especially from a shipwreck or fire, or something similar. *We salvaged most of the cargo before the ship sank.*

similar words: **protect**
contrasting words: **endanger**

saying *noun*

something that is often said. *My mother has a funny **saying** for every situation.*

adage
An **adage** is a wise saying. *"Haste makes waste" is a common adage.*

proverb
A **proverb** is a short, popular, usually wise saying that has been used by people for a long time. *"A stitch in time saves nine" is an old proverb.*

epigram
An **epigram** is a short witty saying that goes straight to the point of a matter. *"Speech is silver, but silence is golden" is a well-known epigram.*

maxim
A **maxim** is a saying containing a general truth or rule. *"Look before you leap" is a wise maxim.*

motto
A **motto** is a short saying, often taken as summing up the aims or beliefs of a particular organization or group. *The motto of the Scouts is "Be prepared."*

scant *adjective*

barely enough of something. *There was only enough water for a **scant** mouthful each.*

sparse
Sparse can mean of small amount, especially when what exists is thinly spread out or scattered. *Shade trees were sparse after the long drought.*

skimpy
Skimpy can mean having less thickness, size, or amount than you would like. *My skimpy coat could not keep me warm in the icy wind.*

meager
Meager means of a small amount or of poor quality. *We gulped down a meager breakfast of bread and butter before we raced for the bus.*

paltry
Paltry means having such a small amount of something that it is not of much use or value. *That was a paltry sum of money to pay for such a beautiful painting.*

measly
Measly means having an annoyingly small amount of something. It is more suited to everyday language. *There was only a measly two cents left in my purse.*

similar words: **insufficient**
contrasting words: **extra, abundant, sufficient**

scarce   *adjective*

not often seen or found. *Many forms of wildlife are becoming* **scarce** *as their natural habitat is destroyed.*

rare
: **Rare** means unusual or uncommon. *Vaccination has made polio a rare disease today.*

infrequent
: **Infrequent** means not happening very often. *Our grandparents' visits to us have been very infrequent since they sold their car.*

sporadic
: **Sporadic** means irregular and not very frequent. *You could tell he was not a hockey fan by his sporadic attendance at the games.*

occasional
: **Occasional** means happening or appearing sometimes. *I've only received an occasional letter from Sally since she went to England.*

similar words: **unusual**
contrasting words: **numerous, countless**

scatter   *verb*

to throw something loosely about. *I* **scattered** *crumbs for the birds to eat.*

strew
: To **strew** means to scatter or throw things everywhere. *The wind strewed the leaves all over the lawn.*

distribute
: To **distribute** can mean to put or scatter something around. *She distributed the fertilizer over the lawn.*

disperse
: To **disperse** can mean to scatter something around. *The wind dispersed my pile of leaves and blew them into the air.*

spread
: To **spread** can mean to scatter something or send it around. *Cover your mouth when you cough or you will spread your germs to everyone else.*

dissipate
: To **dissipate** means to scatter something or use it wastefully. *He dissipated his money by gambling.*

contrasting words: **gather, store**

scholar   *noun*

a learned person. *A rabbi is a **scholar** and teacher of the Jewish religion.*

intellectual   An **intellectual** is someone who shows great mental ability. *Peter Mark Roget was an intellectual who devised the first English thesaurus.*

philosopher   A **philosopher** is someone who searches for truth and wisdom. *The philosopher has written many books containing her thoughts on the meaning of life.*

sage   A **sage** is a very wise person. *People come from far and near to consult the sage about their problems.*

genius   A **genius** is an unusually talented or clever person. *Everyone regards Leonardo da Vinci as a genius.*

mastermind   A **mastermind** can be a very clever or knowledgeable person. *She scored so well in the general knowledge quiz she must be a mastermind.*

---

similar words: **student**

---

scold   *verb*

to find fault with someone. *She **scolded** me for being careless.*

rebuke   To **rebuke** means to scold someone or show them you disapprove of their behavior. *He rebuked us for splashing in the bath.*

reprimand   To **reprimand** means to scold or **rebuke** someone, especially in a formal way. *The bus driver reprimanded them for standing on the seats.*

reprove   To **reprove** means to find fault with or blame someone. *The teacher reproved the student for speaking out of turn.*

admonish   To **admonish** means to warn or caution someone not to do something. *We admonished the boys not to be noisy.*

---

similar words: **fault**
contrasting words: **praise, acclaim**

---

scorn *noun*

a complete and obvious lack of respect. *She showed her **scorn** for his remark by turning her back on him.*

contempt   **Contempt** is the feeling you have for someone or something that is mean and disgraceful. *I have nothing but contempt for anyone who is cruel to animals.*

disrespect   **Disrespect** is rudeness and lack of respect. *The demonstrators showed their disrespect for the new law by heckling the Premier.*

disdain   **Disdain** is a feeling of dislike for something or someone you think is unworthy. *She gave the rude young man a look of disdain.*

ridicule   **Ridicule** is words or actions meant to cause scornful laughter at a person or thing. *The ridicule of his shyness made him blush with embarrassment.*

derision   **Derision** is the act of laughing or making fun of someone or something. *They had nothing but hoots of derision for the bad TV show.*

contrasting words: **respect**

scratch *verb*

to mark or cut something roughly. *The knife **scratched** the polished table.*

nick   To **nick** means to cut something slightly. *She nicked her hand with the scissors.*

lance   To **lance** means to cut something open with a sharp instrument. *The doctor lanced my boil.*

score   To **score** means to make a deep scratch, especially in wood or metal. *The screwdriver slipped and scored the wood.*

graze   To **graze** means to scratch the skin of part of your body. *He grazed his hand against the wall.*

similar words: **cut, tear**

scruffy   *adjective*

dirty, shabby, and uncared for. *The scruffy little boy looked as though his clothes had never been washed or ironed.*

unkempt	**Unkempt** means in an uncared for or untidy condition. *He did not get the job because of his unkempt appearance.*
disheveled	**Disheveled** means untidy and disordered. *Her disheveled appearance was surprising, as she was usually very neat.*
bedraggled	**Bedraggled** means wet, dirty, and hanging limply. *Their clothes were bedraggled when they came out of the storm.*
shabby	**Shabby** means worn or threadbare. *Your old slippers are starting to look shabby.*
sloppy	**Sloppy** means loose and untidy. *On weekends he enjoyed wearing jeans and sloppy sweatshirts.*

similar words: **untidy**
contrasting words: **tidy**

secret   *adjective*

done or made without others knowing. *The police uncovered the secret plan to steal the diamonds.*

confidential	**Confidential** means secret or not public. *Don't let anyone else read this confidential letter.*
classified	**Classified** can mean known or used by only a few people, and not made public, especially top-secret military or government information. *Lock the classified files away where no one else can read them.*
private	**Private** can mean secret or not public. *I won't let anyone read my private diary.*
hush-hush	**Hush-hush** means extremely secret. It is more suited to everyday language. *Their meeting was so hush-hush they wouldn't even tell us what it was about.*

similar words: **secretive**

secretive *adjective*

liking to keep things secret or to yourself. *She is very **secretive** about her research work.*

stealthy	**Stealthy** means done or made in a hidden or sly, secretive way in the hope that it won't be discovered. *We knew something was wrong when we heard a faint, stealthy movement in the next room.*
furtive	**Furtive** means done or acting in a **stealthy** or secretive way. *She gave us a quick, furtive look and then disappeared through the hole in the fence.*
surreptitious	**Surreptitious** means made, done, or behaving in a secret or **stealthy** way. *He didn't notice the surreptitious glance we gave him as we walked past.*
underhanded	**Underhanded** means secret and sly, usually in regard to things that are not very honest or honorable. *They met in the middle of the night to carry out their underhanded dealings in stolen goods.*
cagey	**Cagey** means secretive or careful not to reveal much. *He was very cagey when I asked him where he went yesterday afternoon.*

similar words: **secret**
contrasting words: **frank**

see *verb*

to take things in with your eyes. *I **see** the cows coming across the field.*

observe	To **observe** means to see or look at something. *Douglas observed the hooded men entering the bank.*
view	To **view** means to look at or see something. *We went to the art gallery to view the collection of Ansel Adams photographs.*
notice	To **notice** means to see or take note of something. *I noticed she was wearing a new dress.*
watch	To **watch** means to look at something attentively. *The pupils watched a film on gold mining.*
witness	To **witness** means to be present at and see something. *We witnessed the accident.*

similar words: **inspect**

seek *verb*

to try to find or get something. *Dick Whittington set out for London to **seek** his fortune.*

hunt for To **hunt for** means to look for something. *I hunted for my pencil everywhere but I couldn't find it.*

search for To **search for** means to look for something thoroughly. *I searched for a four-leafed clover all summer but I didn't find one.*

pursue To **pursue** can mean to try hard to find or get something. *In the Wizard of Oz, Dorothy helped the tin man pursue his goal of getting a heart.*

quest after To **quest after** means to look for or seek. It is the sort of old-fashioned word that you might find in poetry. *Jason and the Argonauts quested after the Golden Fleece.*

strive for To **strive for** means to struggle to find or get something. *Paul is striving for top grades.*

similar words: **follow**
contrasting words: **avoid**

selfish *adjective*

thinking only of your own interests. *The **selfish** girl never shared her toys with the other children.*

self-centered **Self-centered** means being interested only in yourself. *She didn't know that she had hurt my feelings because she was too self-centered.*

inconsiderate **Inconsiderate** means not caring about other people's rights or feelings. *It was inconsiderate to slam the door when the baby was asleep.*

spoiled **Spoiled** means selfish because you are used to getting your own way. *Don't pout like a spoiled child just because you can't see a movie tonight.*

possessive **Possessive** means wanting to have or control something all by yourself. *Don't be so possessive! Let the others play with the kitten too.*

similar words: **ungrateful**
contrasting words: **kind, generous**

sell *verb*

to give up something in exchange for money. *I **sold** my skates for $20.*

auction	To **auction** means to sell something by holding a public sale where items are sold to the person who offers the highest amount of money. *We auctioned our old car.*
wholesale	To **wholesale** means to sell large quantities of goods to store owners rather than directly to the public. *Tim's father manufactures and wholesales furniture.*
peddle	To **peddle** means to take things around from place to place in order to sell them. *A man was peddling brooms from house to house.*
hawk	To **hawk** means to offer things for sale in the street or by calling at people's homes. It is similar to **peddle** and more suited to everyday language. *The student needed money, so he tried to hawk his paintings.*
retail	To **retail** means to sell directly to the consumer. *She retails her pottery through small craft shops.*

contrasting words: **buy**

seller *noun*

someone who sells something or gives up goods in exchange for money. *The **seller** of the second-hand piano I bought was moving to a small apartment.*

vendor	A **vendor** is someone who sells things, especially small articles. *Everyone crowded around the ice cream vendor on the beach.*
retailer	A **retailer** is someone, such as a shopkeeper, who sells things directly to the public. *My uncle is a furniture retailer.*
merchant	A **merchant** is someone who buys and sells goods to make a profit, usually not dealing directly with the public. *The timber merchant was busy all the time.*
dealer	A **dealer** is someone who buys and sells things. *That dealer only sells second-hand cars.*
broker	A **broker** is someone who buys or sells things for someone else. *They asked the broker to invest their money for them.*

contrasting words: **buyer**

send   *verb*

to cause something to go somewhere. *I'll **send** a postcard as soon as I get there.*

dispatch	To **dispatch** means to send something off. *I dispatched an urgent message asking Dad to come home at once.*
forward	To **forward** means to send something on. *Will you forward my mail to me while I'm away?*
pass on	To **pass on** means to send something or give it to someone. *Would you like me to pass on your message when she gets home?*
relay	To **relay** means to pass or send something on. *They relayed the storm warning to the ship by radio.*
transmit	To **transmit** means to send something over or along to a person or place. *The captain of the ship transmitted a distress call over the marine radio.*

similar words: **carry**

sense   *verb*

to notice or feel something with your senses. *You could **sense** the excitement at the start of the race.*

experience	To **experience** means to meet with, or have something happen to you that you can sense. *She experienced a lot of friendliness from other people during her visit.*
feel	To **feel** can mean to sense or **experience** something. *She doesn't like winter because she feels the cold. He felt sad when he heard the news.*
perceive	To **perceive** means to come to know or realize something through one of your senses, such as sight, hearing, and so on. *He perceived a faint smell of roast chicken wafting out of the house.*
recognize	To **recognize** can mean to realize or understand something clearly. *I recognized my mistake almost immediately, but it was too late to do anything about it.*

similar words: **realize, understand**

sensible *adjective*

able to act with good judgment. *The **sensible** boy made sure the cars had stopped before he stepped into the crosswalk.*

wise
Wise can mean showing good judgment. *He made a wise decision to take no notice of that stupid dare.*

level-headed
Level-headed means being calm and sensible, with good judgment. *The level-headed girl quickly got the class out of the room when the fire started.*

sage
Sage means sensible or **wise**, especially as a result of learning or experience. *The sage woman advised the young couple to forgive each other after their quarrel.*

prudent
Prudent means showing you are careful and sensible in a practical way. *Prudent people always lock their houses when they go out.*

reasonable
Reasonable means showing good sense or sound judgment. *Reasonable people don't leave their keys in their cars.*

similar words: **shrewd, sane, practical**
contrasting words: **silly**

separate *verb*

to put things apart. *Rebecca **separated** her pencils from her crayons.*

divide
To **divide** means to split up or separate into parts. *A river divides the two parts of the city.*

disconnect
To **disconnect** means to separate two things that are usually connected to each other. *Dennis disconnected the antenna of the television.*

detach
To **detach** means to separate or unfasten one thing from another. *Please detach the top piece of paper and keep it.*

break off
To **break off** means to separate one thing from another using force. *The storm broke off a large branch of the tree.*

free
To **free** means to separate one thing from another with difficulty. *His grip was so strong that I couldn't free my hand.*

contrasting words: **join, combine**

series   *noun*

a number of things or events arranged or happening in a certain order. *A **series** of unusual events led to the conviction of the suspect.*

sequence A **sequence** is a series of things following each other. *His work involved the same sequence of tasks every day.*

chain A **chain** can be a series of connected things. *A strange chain of events led me to the conclusion that she was the murderer.*

succession A **succession** can be a number of people or things following one another in order. *Mom had a succession of people coming to see her today at the office.*

course A **course** is a set series of things. *I'm having a course of injections for my illness.*

cycle A **cycle** is a series of events happening in a regular repeating order. *The seasons come and go in a cycle.*

sew   *verb*

to join with loops of thread, using a needle. *I am going to **sew** a pocket on my shirt.*

stitch To **stitch** is very similar to sew. You can often use either word. *He stitched some braid around the cuff of his jacket.*

embroider To **embroider** means to sew decorative patterns on something. *I embroidered a place mat for my mother.*

work To **work** can mean to sew or **embroider** something. *I worked a design of roses onto the handkerchief.*

darn To **darn** means to mend something with crossing rows of stitches. *I darned the hole in my sock.*

tack To **tack** means to sew loosely with large stitches. *Mysan tacked the hem before she tried on the dress.*

shadowy   *adjective*

seeming faint and unreal. *There was a **shadowy** outline of a painting behind the white curtain.*

nebulous   **Nebulous** means cloudy or vague. *His ideas of how he should be doing the job were very nebulous.*

ghostly   **Ghostly** means looking or appearing like a ghost. *The trees were ghostly shapes in the fog.*

ethereal   **Ethereal** means light, airy, or not solid. *The clouds made ethereal shapes in the sky.*

intangible   **Intangible** means not able to be touched or seen. *Happiness is the intangible reward for helping others.*

---

contrasting words: **actual**

---

shake   *verb*

to move backward and forward with short quick movements. *The branches of the trees **shook** as the wind blew.*

vibrate   To **vibrate** means to keep on moving quickly up and down or to and fro. *The hummingbird's wings vibrated as it drank the flower's nectar.*

tremble   To **tremble** means to shake or quiver, especially from cold, weakness, or fear. *Trevor's hands trembled as he tried to take off his snow-covered boots.*

shudder   To **shudder** means to shake suddenly from horror, cold, or fear. *Kate shuddered when she saw that the cars couldn't avoid a collision.*

quake   To **quake** means to shake or **tremble**. *The teller quaked with fear when he saw the robbers come into the bank.*

rock   To **rock** means to move from side to side or to and fro. *The boat was rocking on the waves.*

---

similar words: **sway**

---

shape   *noun*

the way something looks or appears from its outline. *The children made animal* **shapes** *out of the pastry.*

form A **form** is the shape or appearance of something. *The little boy had a birthday cake in the form of a space ship.*

design **Design** can mean the shape or outline of something. *I like the streamlined design of our new car.*

structure **Structure** can be the way something is put together and gets its shape. *Look at this model that shows the structure of an atom.*

build Your **build** is the way your body is shaped or structured. *The weightlifter had a muscular build.*

figure Your **figure** is the shape of your body. *The dancer has a graceful figure.*

share   *noun*

the part given to or owned by someone. *We each received a* **share** *of the prize money.*

quota A **quota** is the share that you are entitled to. *Each boy had a quota of work to do before he could go home.*

allocation An **allocation** is a part of something set apart for a special purpose. *The principal made an allocation of funds for the school library.*

allotment An **allotment** is something handed out or distributed. *We received our allotment of books in September.*

cut A **cut** can be a share of profits made. It is more suited to everyday language. *My cut from the sale of the homemade toys was $10.*

helping A **helping** is a share of food. *May I have a second helping of dessert, please?*

similar words: **part**

share *verb*

to distribute parts of something, with each person receiving a part. *The children shared the raisins.*

divide	To **divide** means to separate anything into parts. *I divided the books among the children.*
split	To **split** can mean to separate something into parts in any way. *After our lunch at the restaurant, we split the bill among the four of us.*
dole out	To **dole out** means to give something out in small quantities. *She doled out the pieces of fruit until we all had some.*
divvy up	To **divvy up** means to share something out. This is more suited to everyday language. *The thieves divvied up the stolen money.*

similar words: **distribute**

shine *verb*

to give out light. *The sun shone all day.*

beam	To **beam** means to send out rays of light. *The searchlight beamed over the ocean.*
glow	To **glow** can mean to shine like something very hot. *The forest was full of insects that glowed in the dark.*
burn	To **burn** can mean to shine brightly. *The lights in the house burned all night.*
blaze	To **blaze** can mean to shine brightly like a flame or fire. *The headlights of the car blazed into my eyes and I couldn't see anything.*
flare	To **flare** can mean to shine brightly and suddenly. *All was dark and then the lights flared.*

similar words: **sparkle**

shining *adjective*

giving out or reflecting bright light. *She looked at me with **shining** eyes when I told her the good news.*

gleaming   **Gleaming** means giving out flashes or beams of light. *The rooms of the castle were lit up by gleaming torches held by the soldiers.*

flaming   **Flaming** can mean shining very brightly. *We sat and watched the flaming logs in the fireplace.*

luminous   **Luminous** means giving off or reflecting light. *I am able to tell the time in the dark because the hands of my watch are luminous.*

incandescent   **Incandescent** means shining or white with heat. *The bar of iron was heated until it was incandescent and then began to melt.*

phosphorescent   **Phosphorescent** means giving out light with little or no heat. *A special substance called phosphorus is used to make a phosphorescent light.*

similar words: **shiny, bright**
contrasting words: **dull**

shiny *adjective*

having a bright shining surface. *She polished the table until it was **shiny**.*

glossy   **Glossy** is so similar to **shiny** that you can usually use either. *I like a book to have a glossy cover.*

lustrous   **Lustrous** can mean shiny or with a glistening sheen like silk. *She chose a lustrous material for her wedding dress.*

sleek   **Sleek** means shiny and smooth. *That dog has a very sleek coat of hair.*

satin   **Satin** means shiny and very smooth like the cloth called satin. *This paint has a satin finish.*

silky   **Silky** means shiny and soft like silk. *The manufacturer says you will have silky hair if you use this shampoo.*

similar words: **shining**
contrasting words: **dull**

shock *verb*

to strike someone with very great surprise, mixed with horror or disgust. *The number of burglaries these days **shocks** me.*

appall	To **appall** can mean to shock, displease, or dismay someone. *The fact that one of our students was involved in the vandalism appalled all the school.*
startle	To **startle** can mean to disturb or surprise someone suddenly. *The loud clap of thunder startled us.*
take aback	To **take aback** means to cause someone great surprise and confusion. *My best friend's cold attitude toward me certainly took me aback.*
bowl over	To **bowl over** means to surprise, upset, and confuse someone. It is only suited to everyday language. *I was bowled over when I heard the cost of the car repairs.*

similar words: **frighten**

shore *noun*

the land at the edge of an ocean, sea, lake, or other body of water. *There are trees all along the **shore** of this uninhabited lake.*

coast	A **coast** is the land at the edge of an ocean or sea. *The New England coast is very irregular and offers many natural harbors.*
beach	A **beach** is a stretch of shore that is flat and made up of sand or small stones or shells. *After our swim we built a sand castle on the beach.*
strand	A **strand** is a **beach**. It is usually used in a poetic way. *The castaway was washed up onto a lonely strand.*
seaside	**Seaside** is similar to **coast**. *Let's go down to the seaside and watch the sailboats.*
waterfront	A **waterfront** is the part of a city or town that borders on a body of water. *They tore down the old docks and warehouses and built a park along the waterfront.*

shorten   *verb*

to make something short or shorter. *Please **shorten** the discussion, because I'm getting bored.*

condense	To **condense** can mean to say or write something in fewer words. *He condensed his story into just a few pages.*
abbreviate	To **abbreviate** means to make a word, phrase, or story shorter by leaving out some letters or words. *We abbreviate "Mister" to "Mr." to save space.*
abridge	To **abridge** means to shorten a book, interview, and so on by leaving out some parts. *Sometimes a writer abridges a famous novel to make it easier for children to read.*
summarize	To **summarize** means to say or write something in a short clear way, giving the main points only. *The coach summarized the rules of the game for the new players.*
sum up	To **sum up** means to give only the main points of something that has already been said or done. *I will sum up all I have just said so that everyone understands our plan.*

contrasting words: **expand**

shout   *verb*

to call or cry out loudly. *He **shouted** with happiness when our team won the game.*

yell	To **yell** is so similar to shout that you can usually use either. *The man yelled to the boy crossing the road to watch out for the car.*
bellow	To **bellow** means to shout out angrily. *The sergeant bellowed at the troops when they disobeyed his order.*
roar	To **roar** means to make a loud deep sound such as a lion makes. *The man roared when he stubbed his toe.*
whoop	To **whoop** means to cry out loudly. *We all whooped with happiness when we were told about the upcoming holiday.*
bawl	To **bawl** means to cry noisily. It is more suited to everyday language. *The baby bawled for her bottle.*

similar words: **shriek**

show   *verb*

to cause or allow something to be seen. *He **showed** his drawing to his mother.*

display	To **display** means to show something so that it can be clearly seen. *He displayed his prize roses in a beautiful vase.*
exhibit	To **exhibit** means to show something in a place where the public can go to see it. *The young artist is going to exhibit her paintings in the town hall.*
demonstrate	To **demonstrate** means to show something clearly and plainly. *He demonstrated his skill at gymnastics before an astonished crowd.*
parade	To **parade** means to show by making something move or march in an orderly way. *The farmer paraded his cattle around the ring.*
flaunt	To **flaunt** means to show something off boldly. *He flaunted his trophy until we were sick of him.*

contrasting words: **hide**

show-off   *noun*

someone who says or does things to make people pay attention or give praise. *She's such a **show-off**; she wants everyone to watch her do her handstands.*

exhibitionist	An **exhibitionist** is someone who tries to attract other people's attention in an annoyingly showy way. It is more formal than show-off. *The exhibitionist practiced his dancing in the middle of the playground where everyone could see him.*
boaster	A **boaster** is someone who talks too much about how good or clever he or she is. *The boaster kept telling us that she would win the prize.*
braggart	A **braggart** is a **boaster**. *He was such a braggart; said no one could run as fast as he could.*
know-it-all	A **know-it-all** is someone who thinks he or she knows everything. *I grew tired of the know-it-all correcting me whenever I started to say something.*
smart alec	A **smart alec** is someone who likes to show everyone how much they know or how clever they are. It is more suited to everyday language. *Stop being such a smart alec and let me have a try!*

shrewd *adjective*

clever at making good judgments. *The **shrewd** antique dealer realized the chair was a fake.*

astute   **Astute** means able to understand things clearly and quickly. *The astute manufacturer saw how good my invention was.*

sharp   **Sharp** can mean mentally quick and alert. *The sharp young fellow saw the holdup and took the number of the getaway car.*

canny   **Canny** can mean shrewd or wise. *The canny businesswoman always bought her supplies from people she trusted.*

ingenious   **Ingenious** means having a very clever, and often surprising, way of doing something. *This new mousetrap is ingenious.*

---

similar words: **clever, sensible**
contrasting words: **silly**

---

shriek *verb*

to make a loud, sharp, high-pitched cry or noise. *The fans **shrieked** with delight when the rock star appeared on the stage.*

screech   To **screech** means to make a harsh high-pitched cry or noise. *The tires screeched on the wet road when the car stopped suddenly.*

squeal   To **squeal** means to make a sudden high-pitched cry. *The pigs squealed with delight as they rolled in the mud.*

yelp   To **yelp** means to give a quick sharp cry. *The dog yelped when it hurt its paw.*

scream   To **scream** means to make a loud piercing cry or sound. *The sirens screamed as the fire engines raced to the fire.*

squawk   To **squawk** means to make a loud unpleasant cry. *The chickens squawked when the fox chased them.*

---

similar words: **shout**

---

shrink *verb*

to become smaller. *Oh dear! Your woolen clothes have **shrunk** in the hot water.*

shrivel	To **shrivel** can mean to shrink and wrinkle. *The plant shriveled and died when it wasn't watered.*
wither	To **wither** can mean to dry up. It is very similar to **shrivel**. *You'd better water the ferns or they'll wither.*
atrophy	To **atrophy** means to lose size or strength. *Muscles atrophy if they aren't used.*
dwindle	To **dwindle** means to become smaller or fewer in number. *Enrollments in our local school dwindled last year.*
contract	To **contract** can mean to become smaller in size. *Metal contracts as it cools.*

similar words: **decrease**
contrasting words: **increase**

shy *adjective*

not feeling relaxed with other people. *The **shy** boy found it hard to talk to people at parties.*

bashful	**Bashful** means easily embarrassed. *He was bashful and knew people would look at him if he answered.*
modest	**Modest** means having a moderate opinion of yourself and your abilities. *She was modest about her success in the art competition.*
demure	**Demure** means shyly well-behaved. *We were surprised that the demure child was an aggressive athlete.*
diffident	**Diffident** means not confident or sure of yourself. *He is diffident about being in the school play.*
coy	**Coy** means pretending to be shy so that you can attract attention. *She gave the audience a coy smile as she crossed the stage.*

similar words: **reticent**
contrasting words: **bold**

sick *adjective*

having a disease or being unwell. *I was so **sick** my parents took me to the doctor.*

ill	**Ill** is so similar to sick that you can usually use either word. *"You are too ill to get out of bed," he said.*
ailing	**Ailing** means not being very well even though you may not have anything particular wrong with you. *I told him I had been ailing for a long time.*
indisposed	**Indisposed** means just slightly sick. *Jenny was indisposed with a cold but allowed out of bed.*
not yourself	**Not yourself** means not feeling or looking as healthy or energetic as usual. *I'm not myself today because I didn't sleep well last night.*
under the weather	**Under the weather** means in poor health. *This cold has left me feeling under the weather.*

contrasting words: **healthy**

side *noun*

one of the outer parts, edges, or lines of something, usually not the top, bottom, front, or back. *You run past the **side** of the house to get around to the back.*

flank	The **flank** can mean the side of anything. *The general made plans to defend the army's flank.*
wing	A **wing** can be a side part, especially a side building joined to a central building. *The board decided to add a new wing to the school.*
jamb	A **jamb** is the side part of a doorway, window, or other such opening. *We used pine to make the jambs for the windows and doors.*
profile	A **profile** is the outline of someone's face as seen from the side. *I'd rather be looking straight ahead for this photo, because I hate my profile.*

sign   *noun*

a mark, figure, or other indicator used to stand for a word, idea, or mathematical value. *The **signs** for addition (+) and subtraction (−) were first used in print only five hundred years ago.*

symbol A **symbol** is something that stands for or represents something else. *The dove is a symbol of peace.*

emblem An **emblem** is a badge or something that serves as a sign or **symbol**. *A bee is the emblem of the U.S. Navy's Seabees.*

token A **token** is a sign or **symbol** of something, usually given to someone. *A wedding ring is a token of love.*

totem A **totem** is something, often an animal, used as a **token** or **emblem** of a family or group. *The Haida carve their totems onto tall poles of wood.*

significant   *adjective*

important and likely to have great effect on something. *Your eighteenth birthday will be a **significant** event in your life.*

momentous **Momentous** means of great importance. *The Louisiana Purchase was a momentous development in U.S. history.*

memorable **Memorable** means worth remembering. *My sister's wedding was a memorable occasion.*

critical **Critical** can mean having to do with an important or dangerous time. *He had to make a critical decision.*

fateful **Fateful** means important because of the seriousness of the things that happened. *The world will always remember the fateful day when the atomic bomb was first dropped.*

serious **Serious** can mean important, weighty, or needing a lot of care. *I have brought you here to discuss a very serious matter.*

similar words: **main**
contrasting words: **insignificant, minor**

silly *adjective*

without sense. *He gave a **silly** answer.*

foolish	**Foolish** is so similar to silly that you can usually use either. *That was a foolish thing to do.*
senseless	**Senseless** means without good sense. It is similar to silly and **foolish**. *The plan they suggested was senseless.*
idiotic	**Idiotic** means extremely silly. *I won't listen to any more of your idiotic ideas.*
inane	**Inane** means silly or not intelligent. *I'm sick of your inane chatter.*
stupid	**Stupid** means not intelligent. *It would be stupid to climb that rusty old ladder.*

similar words: **ridiculous, irrational**
contrasting words: **sensible**

---

similar *adjective*

having a likeness, especially in a general or not specific way. *Tom and Edward drew **similar** pictures.*

alike	**Alike** means the same as similar but is used at the end of a sentence, rather than before the noun. *The sisters are very much alike.*
comparable	**Comparable** means similar enough for it to be sensible to compare them. *If Katharine can beat Clare, she can probably beat Jane, because Clare and Jane are comparable runners.*
akin	**Akin** means related or **alike**. *Ponies are akin to horses.*
corresponding	**Corresponding** means similar or matching. *She told a story corresponding to that of her friend's.*
synonymous	**Synonymous** means very similar or the same in meaning. *This thesaurus groups together synonymous words.*

similar words: **equal, related**
contrasting words: **various, unlike**

simple *adjective*

not having complicated or unnecessary, added parts. *We like **simple** home cooking best.*

plain	**Plain** can mean simple and not fussily decorated. *I bought some plain blue material to make a dress.*
natural	**Natural** can mean real and in its original state. *This is the natural look of wool before it is dyed.*
unadorned	**Unadorned** means not having been made more attractive by adding decorations or ornaments. *How bare the unadorned room looked after the party decorations had been taken down.*
unobtrusive	**Unobtrusive** means not making an effort to be noticed. *She looked very elegant in her simple black dress and unobtrusive gold jewelry.*
quiet	**Quiet** can mean toned down and not made for show. *The house was decorated in quiet tones of beige.*

contrasting words: **gaudy, spectacular**

simplify *verb*

to make something easier to understand, do, or use. *I will **simplify** the instructions for this test.*

streamline	To **streamline** means to simplify something so as to make it more efficient. *We will get the work done more quickly if we streamline the way we do it.*
sort out	To **sort out** can mean to simplify and understand something by separating it into parts and solving each one. *We'll soon sort out your problems.*
unravel	To **unravel** can mean to make something less complicated and easier to understand. *I eventually unraveled his explanation and understood what he was saying.*
disentangle	To **disentangle** can mean to work something out by simplifying it. It is very similar to **unravel**. *I think I've disentangled the mystery by talking to each person involved.*

contrasting words: **confuse**

singer　*noun*

someone who can make musical sounds with the voice, often someone who has been specially trained. *We have thirty **singers** in our choir.*

vocalist　A **vocalist** is a **singer**. You can usually choose either word. *My sister is the lead vocalist in a rock band.*

soloist　A **soloist** can be someone who sings alone. *The soloist sang a beautiful song at the wedding.*

crooner　A **crooner** is someone who sings in a soft and sentimental way. *The famous crooner Frank Sinatra performed at the benefit concert.*

minstrel　A **minstrel** was a musician in the Middle Ages who sang or said poetry while playing a musical instrument. *The lord's minstrel entertained the feasters in the castle.*

troubadour　A **troubadour** was a singer or songwriter, especially in medieval France. *The troubadour sang for the king in his castle.*

single　*adjective*

one alone. *My **single** reason for going to the farm is to see the new calves.*

only　**Only** means single or just one. *The only thing I haven't finished is my math homework.*

sole　**Sole** means single or **only**. *Peter is the sole member of the team who hasn't been injured.*

exclusive　**Exclusive** can mean single or **sole**. *The school bus was his exclusive means of getting to school.*

unique　**Unique** means different from all others or having no equal. *Each person's fingerprints are unique.*

contrasting words: **numerous, double**

skillful   *adjective*

very good or expert at doing something. *She was a **skillful** debater and rarely lost an argument.*

adept

Adept means extremely skillful. *My ski instructor is an adept skier and has won many competitions.*

deft

Deft means skillful, especially at doing something with your hands. *The plumber's deft fingers guided the pipe into place.*

dexterous

Dexterous is so similar to **deft** that you can usually use either. *You are so dexterous that you could be a surgeon one day.*

adroit

Adroit is very similar to **dexterous** and **deft**. *The musician's adroit fingers moved quickly over the keyboard.*

handy

Handy can mean skillful at constructing things. *If you're handy, you'll find it easy to build a trunk for your toys.*

similar words: **competent**
contrasting words: **clumsy, incompetent**

slander   *verb*

to make a false statement about someone that harms their good name. This is often a legal word. *The reporter **slandered** the company director when she spoke about him on the radio.*

defame

To **defame** means to damage someone's good name, especially when the person is well known. *The newspaper story defamed the politician.*

libel

To **libel** means to write or print a statement that damages someone's reputation. This is often a legal word. *The politician sued the newspaper that libeled her.*

malign

To **malign** means to speak unfavorably or badly of someone. *He maligned me when he said I lied.*

smear

To **smear** can mean to damage someone's good name, usually without any proof. *Your nasty stories smeared my reputation and I had to resign as leader.*

similar words: **insult**
contrasting words: **worship, praise**

sleep *verb*

to rest with your eyes closed and your mind unconscious. *How long did you **sleep** last night?*

slumber To **slumber** means to sleep deeply. *Please be quiet, because the baby is slumbering.*

doze To **doze** means to sleep lightly or off and on. *The cat is dozing in front of the fire.*

nap To **nap** means to sleep for a short time. *I think I will nap for half an hour or so.*

snooze To **snooze** means to sleep lightly for a short time. It is similar to **doze** and **nap**. *I like to snooze on the couch after a big meal.*

slight *adjective*

small and thin. *If you want to be a jockey, you must have a **slight** build.*

petite **Petite** means very small and slim. It is usually used to describe a woman or girl. *This store sells smaller-sized clothes specially designed for petite women.*

dainty **Dainty** can mean small and fine in appearance or movement. *We saw a collection of dainty china dolls.*

delicate **Delicate** can mean so small and fragile as to seem likely to be easily hurt or broken. *He was very delicate after his long illness.*

elfin **Elfin** means being so small and **dainty**, or having such a mischievous appearance, that you remind others of an elf. *Annie's elfin looks matched her saucy behavior.*

puny **Puny** can mean small and weak. *Most sea creatures are puny when compared with the blue whale.*

similar words: **thin, small**
contrasting words: **fat, heavy, stocky**

slope   *noun*

a direction or line that leans to one side rather than being flat or completely upright. *Roofs are usually built with a **slope** to let the rainwater run off.*

slant	**Slant** is so similar to slope that you can usually use either. *Fix these awnings so that they have a slight slant.*
tilt	A **tilt** is a slope or a leaning to one side. *That post has such a tilt that it will probably fall over.*
incline	An **incline** is a surface that has a slope. *We walked down the incline of the hill.*
gradient	The **gradient** is the amount of slope of something. *What is the gradient of this road?*
pitch	The **pitch** is the degree of slope. It is similar to **gradient**. *This roof has a steep pitch.*

slope   *verb*

to have a direction or line that is neither flat nor upright. *Our garden **slopes** down to a creek.*

slant	To **slant** is so similar to slope that you can usually use either. *Draw a line that slants to the left.*
lean	To **lean** means to be in a sloping position. *In the Italian town of Pisa, there is a famous tower that leans to one side.*
tilt	To **tilt** means to move into a sloping position. *The fence began to tilt as the boys climbed over it.*
tip	To **tip** means to fall to one side. *Be careful that your cup doesn't tip.*
list	To **list** means to lean to one side. It is usually used about ships. *The huge wave made the ship list to starboard.*

slow *adjective*

taking a long time or not moving or acting quickly. *It was such a **slow** trip we didn't arrive till after dark.*

leisurely   **Leisurely** means slow or without haste. *After lunch we went for a leisurely stroll by the river.*

unhurried   **Unhurried** means slow or without any rush. *We packed a picnic and had an unhurried meal by the river.*

plodding   **Plodding** means moving in a slow and heavy way. *I could tell that she was tired by her plodding steps.*

lazy   **Lazy** can mean slow-moving. *We spent a lazy afternoon reading by the fireplace.*

---

contrasting words: **fast**

---

small *adjective*

not very big or great. *The car was too **small** for everyone to fit into.*

little   **Little** means small in size. *These little puppies are only two weeks old.*

tiny   **Tiny** means very small or **little**. *We still have the tiny shoes you wore when you were a baby.*

minute   **Minute** means extremely small. *The insect was so minute we could hardly see it.*

miniature   **Miniature** means being a very small copy of something. *There were miniature astronauts in the toy space ship.*

short   **Short** can mean not very tall. *He was too short to see over the top of the fence.*

---

similar words: **slight**
contrasting words: **big, huge**

---

smell *noun*

the quality of something that you sense through your nose. *I like the **smell** of newly cut grass.*

odor
Odor is so similar to **smell** that you can usually use either. *There is a strange odor in this room.*

scent
A **scent** is a pleasant smell. *These flowers have a strong scent.*

fragrance
Fragrance is a sweet smell. It is similar to **scent**. *He could smell the fragrance of her perfume.*

aroma
An **aroma** is a special, usually pleasant, smell of something. *The kitchen was filled with the aroma of coffee.*

bouquet
A **bouquet** is an **aroma**. *The herbs gave the stew a beautiful bouquet.*

smelly *adjective*

giving out a strong or unpleasant smell. *Skunks are **smelly** animals.*

stinking
Stinking means very unpleasantly smelly. *There was a bag of stinking garbage in the pail.*

rank
Rank can mean having a strong unpleasant smell. *The streets were rank during the garbage strike.*

putrid
Putrid means having the smell of something rotting or going bad. *A bad egg has a putrid smell.*

high
High can mean bad-smelling and is similar to **putrid**. *This meat is high.*

fetid
Fetid means having a stale, sickening smell. *The room was filled with hot, fetid air.*

smile   *verb*

to show you are happy or amused by widening your mouth and turning it up at the corners. *I **smiled** when I thought about my birthday party.*

grin	To **grin** means to smile broadly. *I grinned at my friend across the classroom.*
smirk	To **smirk** means to smile in a smug way that annoys people. *He smirked when the teacher praised him.*
giggle	To **giggle** means to laugh in a silly way. *We giggled when he pulled a funny face.*
snicker	To **snicker** means to **giggle** in a rather rude way and try to hide it. *The villain snickered at the hero's misfortune.*
titter	To **titter** means to **giggle** in a foolish or nervous way. *A titter ran through the audience when the actor tripped on his robe.*

similar words: **laugh**
contrasting words: **frown**

smooth   *adjective*

feeling even and without bumps or lumps. *This pear has such a **smooth** skin.*

polished	**Polished** means made smooth and shiny by rubbing. *She slipped on the polished floor.*
slippery	**Slippery** means too smooth to get a hold on. *The slippery material slid through her fingers.*
silken	**Silken** means smooth and soft like silk. *She has silken hair.*
glassy	**Glassy** means feeling or looking smooth and transparent like glass. *We rowed across the glassy lake.*
creamy	**Creamy** can mean feeling rich and smooth like cream. *I spread the creamy lotion all over my sunburnt skin.*

similar words: **shiny**
contrasting words: **rough**

smooth *verb*

to make something even or level. *She **smoothed** her hair with her hand.*

iron	To **iron** means to press the creases out of clothes with a heated iron. *I must iron my wrinkled slacks before I wear them.*
level	To **level** means to make even or flatten. *They will have to level the ground before they build the house.*
sand	To **sand** means to smooth something by rubbing it with sandpaper. *The workers sanded our floor before polishing it.*
grind	To **grind** means to make something smooth by rubbing it with something rough. *The glassmaker ground the lens.*
plane	To **plane** means to smooth wood using a special tool called a plane. *The carpenter planed the pieces of wood before fitting them together.*

similar words: **polish**
contrasting words: **roughen**

soak *verb*

to wet something thoroughly, especially by leaving it in a liquid for a long time. *She **soaked** the clothes in the tub to loosen the dirt.*

drench	To **drench** means to make something very wet. *The rain drenched our hair and clothes.*
flood	To **flood** can mean to cover something with water as happens in a flood. *The river rose and flooded many houses along its banks.*
inundate	To **inundate** can be so similar to **flood** that you can usually use either word. *The tidal wave inundated the village on the island.*
swamp	To **swamp** can mean to cover something with water. It is similar to **flood**. *A wave swamped the boat and it nearly sank.*

similar words: **wet**

soft   *adjective*

easily cut or pressed out of shape and usually pleasant to touch. *I kneaded the dough until it was* **soft.** *My quilt is very* **soft.**

downy	**Downy** means fluffy and soft as fine hair or feathers are. *I let my head sink into the downy pillow.*
silky	**Silky** means smooth and shiny like silk. *She brushed her dog's silky hair.*
velvet	**Velvet** can mean soft and smooth like fur. *The kitten padded through the house on her velvet paws.*
spongy	**Spongy** means soft and squashy like a sponge. *We walked carefully over the spongy ground.*
tender	**Tender** means not tough or hard. *She made a salad from tender young lettuce leaves.*

contrasting words: **hard**

---

soften   *verb*

to make something easy to cut or press out of shape. *I* **softened** *the toffee in my mouth as I sucked it.*

thaw	To **thaw** means to make something that is frozen melt and become softer. *He took the strawberries out of the freezer and thawed them in hot water.*
mash	To **mash** means to crush or beat something until it is softer. *Please mash the potatoes.*
squash	To **squash** means to crush something into a soft mass. *I squashed the grape when I stepped on it.*
pulp	To **pulp** means to make into a soft wet mass. *Paper mills pulp wood, cloth, and other materials to make paper.*
tenderize	To **tenderize** means to make something less tough or hard. *We tenderized the meat with lemon before we cooked it.*

contrasting words: **harden**

solemn *adjective*

sincere or earnest. *I made a **solemn** promise.*

serious   **Serious** means solemn and really meaning what you say. *I will give you some serious advice.*

grave   **Grave** means solemn and without humor. *She listened to his story with a grave expression.*

sober   **Sober** can mean solemn and quiet. *The sad news put us in a sober mood.*

stern   **Stern** can mean solemn and severe. *He gave them a stern warning.*

dour   **Dour** can mean gloomily solemn, **stern,** or hard. *His dour manner was rather discouraging.*

---

contrasting words: **happy**

---

solve *verb*

to explain or find the answer to something. *He **solved** the mystery.*

work out   To **work out** can mean to solve something, using a great deal of effort. *It took me ages to work this problem out.*

crack   To **crack** can mean to find the answer to something. *They cracked the spy's code.*

decipher   To **decipher** means to untangle a coded message. *The war ended quickly once experts were able to decipher the enemy's secret code.*

figure out   To **figure out** means to solve or understand something. *I can't figure out the inscription on this monument.*

resolve   To **resolve** means to solve or settle something. *We resolved the problem by taking both cars.*

song   *noun*

a short musical composition with words. *Craig wrote the music and I made up the words for our new **song**.*

tune	A **tune** is a simple musical composition. *She played a merry little tune on her flute.*
anthem	An **anthem** is a song written for a country or organization and sung on special occasions. *Our national anthem was composed during the War of 1812.*
ballad	A **ballad** is a simple poem that tells a story and is often set to music and sung. *He sang a sad ballad about a ship that was lost at sea.*
dirge	A **dirge** is a song of mourning. *If you play that music any slower it will sound like a dirge.*
lullaby	A **lullaby** is a soft gentle song, sung to put a baby to sleep. *He finally fell asleep as his father rocked him and sang a lullaby.*

sorry   *adjective*

feeling sad because you have done something wrong. *I'm **sorry** I yelled at you.*

ashamed	**Ashamed** means feeling sorry or guilty for what you have done. *I was ashamed that I forgot to call my grandmother on her birthday.*
remorseful	**Remorseful** means feeling deeply sorry for your wrongdoing. *He was so remorseful that he couldn't sleep all night.*
repentant	**Repentant** means feeling sorrow and regret for what you have done. *They were repentant for all the times they had broken the rules.*
contrite	**Contrite** means feeling or showing that you are sorry or sad, especially from guilt. *We knew he was contrite when he let us join his secret club.*
penitent	**Penitent** means sorry for something you have done wrong and willing to put it right. *I will clean up the mess to show you that I really am penitent.*

contrasting words: **unashamed**

sour   *adjective*

having a sharp taste such as that of lemons. *These grapes are **sour** because they are not ripe.*

acid **Acid** means having a very sharp taste. It is similar to sour. *Vinegar has an acid taste.*

bitter **Bitter** means having an unpleasantly sharp taste. *This coffee is very bitter.*

tart **Tart** means sour or sharp in taste. *This applesauce is too tart.*

green **Green** can mean not ripe and therefore tasting sour. *These plums are too green for my taste.*

contrasting words: **sweet**

souvenir   *noun*

something you keep as a memory of a place or event. *I kept the concert program as a **souvenir** of Sarah's first piano recital.*

memento A **memento** is something that acts as a reminder of the past. *She gave them a book as a memento of her visit.*

keepsake A **keepsake** is something you keep in order to remember a person or event. *Glen gave Ingrid a beautiful shell as a keepsake of their picnic at the beach.*

remembrance A **remembrance** can be a **memento** or **keepsake**. *We compiled a scrapbook as a remembrance of our trip across the United States.*

trophy A **trophy** can be a souvenir of a victory. *This basketball trophy reminds us that team effort pays off.*

token A **token** is a sign or symbol of something you want to remember. *The bride and groom exchanged wedding rings as tokens of the vows they had made.*

spacious   *adjective*

ample or having a lot of space. *We will use this room for the assembly because it is* ***spacious****.*

roomy	**Roomy** is a more informal way of saying spacious. *They live in a big roomy house.*
commodious	**Commodious** means conveniently spacious. *I need a more commodious office.*
wide	**Wide** can mean having plenty of space from side to side. *The kindergarten room is big and wide.*
open	**Open** can mean not limited or blocked. *We had a lovely open view from the veranda.*
expansive	**Expansive** means **open** and widespread. *Their house has an expansive garden.*

contrasting words: **narrow**

sparkle   *verb*

to give out little flashes of light. *The raindrops* ***sparkled*** *in the sunshine.*

glitter	To **glitter** means to sparkle brightly, as gold or silver does. *Her dress glittered with jewels.*
shimmer	To **shimmer** means to give out a soft light that comes and goes. *The surface of the lake shimmered in the moonlight.*
glimmer	To **glimmer** means to give out a faint light that comes and goes. *The lamp glimmered in the distance.*
twinkle	To **twinkle** means to sparkle softly, as something a long way away does. *The stars twinkled brightly in the night sky.*
flicker	To **flicker** means to give out an unsteady light. *The candle flickered and then went out.*

similar words: **shine**

spectacular *adjective*

excitingly or impressively unusual and attracting people's notice. *The audience clapped and cheered the **spectacular** display of ice skating.*

eye-catching   **Eye-catching** means noticeable or attracting attention because of an unusual or attractive appearance. *The store manager put the most eye-catching clothes in the shop window.*

resplendent   **Resplendent** means splendidly bright and noticeable. *The mounted soldiers were resplendent in their white and gold uniforms as they paraded down the street.*

opulent   **Opulent** means spectacular and richly decorated with gold, jewels, and finery. *The opulent castle of King Ludwig is a great tourist attraction.*

ostentatious   **Ostentatious** means noticeable in an overdone and showy way. *I don't like that ostentatious diamond-studded bracelet.*

flamboyant   **Flamboyant** means dazzlingly bright and noticeable. *Rock stars often set new fashion trends with their flamboyant style of dress.*

---

similar words: **gaudy**
contrasting words: **simple, drab**

---

speed *verb*

to move very quickly. *She **sped** away on her bike as fast as she could go.*

race   To **race** can mean to run or move very quickly. *I raced to the station only to see the train pull out.*

hurtle   To **hurtle** means to rush noisily. *The rickety old train hurtled straight through the quiet stations.*

tear   To **tear** can mean to move with a great rush. *We tore out the door to see what the noise was.*

fly   To **fly** can mean to move swiftly. *We flew down the hill on our toboggan.*

streak   To **streak** can mean to move extremely quickly and suddenly. *Before I could stop him, the dog streaked across the road.*

---

similar words: **hurry, dart**
contrasting words: **dawdle, walk**

---

spin *verb*

to turn around and around. *Look how the top is **spinning**.*

gyrate	To **gyrate** means to move around in a circle. *The sails of the windmill gyrated slowly on their axle in the light breeze.*
whirl	To **whirl** means to turn around or spin rapidly. *We whirled faster and faster in time to the music.*
whirr	To **whirr** can mean to spin around quickly with a low buzzing noise. *The wheels whirred along the road as we pedaled harder.*
twirl	To **twirl** means to spin rapidly. *We twirled and twirled until we were so dizzy we fell over.*
swirl	To **swirl** means to move or turn around in a whirling way. *The water swirled around the rocks in the middle of the river.*

similar words: **turn**

spoil *verb*

to ruin something or make it go bad. *Leaving the milk out overnight has **spoiled** it.*

taint	To **taint** means to spoil something slightly. *The bad smell in the refrigerator tainted the cheese.*
contaminate	To **contaminate** means to make something dirty or impure. *Flies crawling over the meat contaminated it.*
pollute	To **pollute** means to spoil something by adding dirty or damaging things to it. *Smoke from the factories polluted the air over most of the city.*
foul	To **foul** means to make something dirty and unpleasant. *Mud from their boots fouled the entrance to the house.*
corrupt	To **corrupt** means to change something or someone from good to bad. *I hope you won't be corrupted by all the money you won.*

similar words: **damage**

star *noun*

someone who is excellent in something or who is famous in an art or profession. *The **star** of a television show signed autographs at our school.*

celebrity   A **celebrity** is a famous or well-known person. *The audience clapped and cheered when the celebrity finished her violin recital.*

idol   An **idol** is someone who is adored or admired excessively. *The football captain became the idol of the school when the team won for the third time in a row.*

hero   A **hero** is someone who has done something brave or outstanding. *He was the hero of the hour when he saved the little boy from drowning.*

household name   A **household name** is someone almost everybody has heard about. *Bobby Kennedy was once a household name in American politics.*

leading light   A **leading light** is someone who is well-known or outstanding in a particular area. This is more suited to everyday language. *The mayor of our town is also one of the leading lights of the musical society.*

similar words: **expert**

stare *verb*

to look at directly for a long time, usually with your eyes wide open. *I **stared** at the zebra the first time I saw one at the zoo.*

gaze   To **gaze** means to look long and steadily. *The artist gazed at the scene he was about to paint.*

gape   To **gape** means to stare with your mouth wide open. *They all gaped at the shattered window.*

ogle   To **ogle** means to stare with your eyes opened wide. *We ogled at the magician's amazing tricks.*

gawk   To **gawk** means to stare stupidly. It is more suited to everyday language. *We all gawked at the burning fence until someone shouted for a hose.*

start   *noun*

the first part of something. *Everyone was lined up for the **start** of the race.*

beginning	**Beginning** is so similar to start that you can usually use either word. *We arrived just in time to see the beginning of the play.*
commencement	**Commencement** is very similar to start and **beginning**. It is usually used in more formal language, such as in written reports. *The commencement of the festival was marked by a display of fireworks.*
outset	**Outset** means the very start of something. *From the outset of the game we knew our team would win.*
onset	**Onset** means the start of a particular thing. *The onset of the disease was sudden and violent.*
origin	An **origin** is the place where something starts or comes from. *The origin of the Olympic Games was in Ancient Greece.*

contrasting words: **end**

start   *verb*

to set moving or take the first step in something. *I **started** as soon as it was light enough to see.*

get going	To **get going** means to start or make haste. *Get going — you're holding everyone up!*
set out	To **set out** means to start on a journey. *He set out before the sun rose and the day became too hot.*
set up	To **set up** means to make the first arrangements. *He set up the chairs for the conference.*
fire away	To **fire away** means to start speaking, usually when someone tells you to. This is more suited to everyday language. *I'm listening, so fire away.*

similar words: **begin, initiate**
contrasting words: **end**

steadfast *adjective*

constant and unchanging. *The two sisters have a **steadfast** love for each other.*

staunch	**Staunch** means loyal and steadfast. *Ian and Stephen are staunch friends who have had many adventures together.*
firm	**Firm** can mean strong, definite, and unchanging. *They have been firm friends for many years.*
enduring	**Enduring** means lasting or permanent. *Their enduring friendship has not been spoiled by their occasional arguments.*
stout-hearted	**Stout-hearted** means brave and determined. *Our stout-hearted team didn't stop trying to win until the final whistle blew.*
true-blue	**True-blue** means unchanging. *She remained a true-blue supporter even though her party lost the election.*

similar words: **faithful, reliable**

steady *adjective*

firmly placed so that it won't move. *Make sure the ladder is **steady** before you climb it.*

stable	**Stable** means not likely to fall or move. *You need a stable foundation to build a house on.*
firm	**Firm** means steady or not likely to move or shake. *We made sure the rock was firm before we climbed onto it.*
secure	**Secure** means firmly fastened in place. *We checked that the boat's mooring was secure before we went ashore.*
well-balanced	**Well-balanced** means placed in a steady position or not likely to fall over. *Not even the strongest wind could blow down the well-balanced tree house.*
fixed	**Fixed** means so firmly or securely placed that it cannot move. *We set the ladder in a fixed position so we could always reach our attic.*

similar words: **still**
contrasting words: **moving**

398

steady   *verb*

to make something firm so that it won't move. ***Steady*** *the boat so it doesn't tip over while I'm getting in.*

secure   To **secure** means to make something firm, usually by tying or fastening it in some way. *We secured our bikes to the fence so they would be there when we got back.*

fix   To **fix** can mean to make something firm or to put it securely in place. *Fix the poles into the ground before you put up the tent.*

support   To **support** means to hold or steady someone or something to prevent a fall. *Get ready to support me when I do my handstand.*

stabilize   To **stabilize** means to make something firm or steady. *We stabilized the boat by changing the position of the sails.*

balance   To **balance** means to make something steady. *The seal balanced a ball on the tip of its nose.*

similar words: **strengthen**
contrasting words: **overturn**

steal   *verb*

to take something that does not belong to you. *I left my bike outside and someone **stole** it.*

pilfer   To **pilfer** means to steal things that are small or not worth much. *Stop pilfering cookies from the jar.*

cop   To **cop** means to steal or take something without asking. It is only suited to everyday language. *Did someone cop my ruler when I wasn't looking?*

rob   To **rob** means to steal from or take forcibly. *My apartment was robbed while I was on vacation.*

embezzle   To **embezzle** means to steal money entrusted to your care. *The dishonest banker was arrested for embezzling money from trust funds.*

similar words: **abduct, take**

still *adjective*

free from movement. *The mountains were reflected in the **still** waters of the lake.*

motionless   **Motionless** means not showing any movement. *The antelope was unaware of the motionless lioness as she crouched waiting to pounce.*

stationary   **Stationary** means standing still. *The car was stationary at the red light.*

immobile   **Immobile** means not moving or able to be moved. *This plaster cast will make sure the broken bones in your arm are immobile while they heal.*

sedentary   **Sedentary** can mean not often moving about, or joined to an object that cannot move. This is a scientific word used to describe some animals. *This sea anemone is sedentary and traps food with its sticky tentacles.*

stagnant   **Stagnant** means not running or flowing. It is used to describe water and air. *Mosquitoes breed in stagnant water.*

similar words: **steady**
contrasting words: **moving**

stocky *adjective*

short, solid, and strong in the way you are built. *The **stocky** football player was placed in the front line.*

thickset   **Thickset** means having a very thick and solid build. *Weightlifting has made him thickset and powerful.*

stout   **Stout** can mean tough and strongly built. *That stout old oak tree has withstood many storms.*

squat   **Squat** means short and thick. It can describe things as well as people. *The squat old buildings were left standing next to the new skyscraper.*

beefy   **Beefy** means solid and having plenty of muscles. *No one wanted to block the team's beefy left guard.*

burly   **Burly** means big and solidly built. *His burly figure was just right for a wrestler.*

similar words: **fat, heavy**
contrasting words: **thin, slight**

stone   *noun*

a piece of the hard substance that makes up part of the earth. *Please don't throw stones.*

rock	A **rock** is a large mass of stone. *We explored the rocks at the end of the beach.*
boulder	A **boulder** is a very large rounded **rock**. *We tried to move the boulder that was blocking the entrance to the cave.*
pebble	A **pebble** is a small rounded stone. *Our garden path is made of pebbles.*
cobble	A **cobble** is a specially shaped stone used in paving streets. *The horse's hooves clattered on the cobbles in the old town.*
gravel	**Gravel** is pieces of rocks and pebbles coarser than sand. *We ordered a load of gravel to surface the driveway.*

stop   *verb*

to end or finish. *Work **stopped** when the bell sounded.*

quit	To **quit** means to finish or give up. *I'm sick of playing this game — let's quit.*
halt	To **halt** means to stop for a while, especially when you are marching. *After walking five kilometers we halted and took a rest.*
pause	To **pause** means to stop or rest for a short time. *He paused to look out the window before he sat down to do his homework.*
stall	To **stall** means to stop, especially when you don't want to. *The car stalled at the lights.*
hesitate	To **hesitate** means to wait or **pause** as if you are not sure if you should go on. *She hesitated before she came into the room.*

similar words: **end, finish**
contrasting words: **start, begin, initiate**

store *verb*

to put something aside or away so it will be ready when you need it. *We **stored** our winter clothes and blankets during summer.*

save	To **save** can mean to keep something or to put it aside for when you need it. *I saved my money so I could buy a camera.*
stockpile	To **stockpile** means to save up large amounts of something for when you need it. *We stockpiled wood so we could burn it in winter.*
stow	To **stow** means to put something somewhere or to pack it away. *Stow your bags under your seats where no one can trip over them.*
hoard	To **hoard** means to save something up and hide it away where no one else can find it. *We hoarded cookies so we could have a midnight feast.*
bank	To **bank** can mean to put or deposit something in a bank where it will be kept safe until you need it. *I banked some money every week because I was saving up for a bike.*

similar words: **gather, keep**
contrasting words: **scatter, discard**

strange *adjective*

unusual or extraordinary. *We did not enjoy the movie because the story was rather **strange**.*

odd	**Odd** is so similar to strange that you can usually use either. *Everyone wondered whether he was feeling all right because his behavior was so odd.*
peculiar	**Peculiar** is so similar to strange and **odd** that you can usually use any of them. *We noticed a peculiar smell as we walked past the factory.*
abnormal	**Abnormal** means different from usual, often not in a desirable way. *The heat is abnormal for this time of the year.*
bizarre	**Bizarre** means very strange. *That multicolored car is bizarre.*
weird	**Weird** means surprisingly and alarmingly strange. *She wore weird clothes to the party.*

similar words: **unconventional, unusual**
contrasting words: **usual**

strengthen *verb*

to make something or someone stronger. *He used examples to* **strengthen** *his argument.*

reinforce
To **reinforce** means to strengthen something by adding to it. *Reinforce the poster by backing it with cardboard.*

brace
To **brace** can mean to make something stronger and firmly fixed in place. *He braced the ceiling with long pieces of wood.*

prop up
To **prop up** can mean to strengthen something by giving support to it. *They worked harder in order to prop up the failing business.*

shore up
To **shore up** means to strengthen something by supporting it with a post or beam. *The builder shored up the cracked wall.*

fortify
To **fortify** means to strengthen something against attack or damage. *They fortified the castle with a moat.*

---

similar words: **steady**
contrasting words: **weaken**

---

strict *adjective*

demanding that you behave well and obey the rules. *My parents are very* **strict**.

rigid
Rigid can mean strict and not changing from what you have decided is right. *They have very rigid rules that we must follow.*

firm
Firm can mean strong, definite, and unchanging in what you have decided, have agreed to, or believe. *Once they have made a rule, they are quite firm about it.*

straitlaced
Straitlaced means too strict and proper in the way you behave. *Sometimes we think they are too straitlaced and old-fashioned.*

austere
Austere can mean strict or severely simple, especially in the way you live or discipline yourself. *His grandmother was an austere person but seemed very serene.*

harsh
Harsh means strict in a cruel way. *Those are harsh words to use on a child who meant no harm.*

---

contrasting words: **broad-minded, lenient**

---

strong *adjective*

having great bodily power or energy. *You are **strong** because you have had so much exercise.*

robust	**Robust** means strongly or solidly built. *She is a robust little baby.*
hearty	**Hearty** means strong, healthy, and energetic. *My mother is a hearty woman who loves to hike in the mountains.*
brawny	**Brawny** means having well-developed muscles. *The lifeguard had a brawny build.*
husky	**Husky** can mean big and strong. *The husky lumberjack soon chopped down the tree.*
wiry	**Wiry** can mean thin and strong. *She looks weak but she is very wiry.*

similar words: **hardy**
contrasting words: **weak**

stubborn *adjective*

determined not to give way or change your mind. *We tried to talk her into wearing another dress but she was **stubborn** and wore the luminous pink one.*

obstinate	**Obstinate** means stubborn, even though you know you may be wrong. *She is obstinate and insists on doing everything her way.*
pig-headed	**Pig-headed** means stupidly stubborn. *It is no use trying to talk sense to a pig-headed person.*
adamant	**Adamant** means staying firm in what you decide. *He was adamant that he would not go.*
inflexible	**Inflexible** means not changing your mind under any circumstances. *We begged him to try another route but he was inflexible.*
uncompromising	**Uncompromising** means having your mind made up without taking notice of other people's opinions or trying to fit in with them. *"No" was his uncompromising answer.*

similar words: **persistent**

student   *noun*

someone who is learning something in a systematic way, usually in a school.
*There are thirty-four **students** in my sixth-grade class.*

pupil

A **pupil** is someone who is being taught by another person. It is very similar to student. *The pupils learned about geography and history from one teacher.*

apprentice

An **apprentice** is someone who is learning a trade or craft from someone who is already an expert. *My apprentice is going to be a carpenter by the summer.*

rookie

A **rookie** is a beginner at something. *The rookie on our team will be an excellent volleyball player with practice.*

disciple

A **disciple** is a follower of a teacher or leader. *The brilliant professor has many disciples who believe all of her theories.*

---

similar words: **scholar**

---

subdue   *verb*

to overcome someone or something, usually by force. *The invading army **subdued** the civilians who tried to resist them.*

overpower

To **overpower** means to subdue someone using your greater strength. *The ex-boxer overpowered the thug who attacked him on the street.*

repress

To **repress** means to keep something or someone under control by effort or force. *She repressed her anger with difficulty.*

dominate

To **dominate** means to control or rule someone or something. *Ahmed was strong-willed and dominated his younger brother.*

oppress

To **oppress** can mean to be cruel to someone in your power. *The soldiers oppressed their prisoners.*

persecute

To **persecute** means to constantly treat someone unfairly or cruelly, usually someone less powerful than you. *In some countries the governments persecute people because of their beliefs.*

---

similar words: **force**
contrasting words: **free**

---

submissive *adjective*

giving in obediently, without questioning. *The frightened animal was* **submissive** *when we approached it.*

subservient	**Subservient** means very submissive. *She was often subservient to her strong-minded, older sister.*
weak-willed	**Weak-willed** means giving in to others because you have a weak character. *He was so weak-willed he obeyed every unfair order.*
servile	**Servile** means weakly allowing others to control you. *I expect you to do what you are asked, but I do not expect you to be servile.*
downtrodden	**Downtrodden** means governed or treated so harshly that you are frightened not to obey. *The downtrodden people finally fought back.*

similar words: **obedient**
contrasting words: **defiant, argumentative, aggressive**

subordinate *adjective*

placed in or belonging to a lower order or rank. *He handed his work to a* **subordinate** *employee.*

junior	**Junior** can mean of a low rank. *His brother is a junior officer in the navy.*
subsidiary	**Subsidiary** means of a secondary order or rank. *She manages one of the subsidiary companies.*
common	**Common** can mean of the ordinary rank. *His wit and good timing showed he was no common comedian.*
lowly	**Lowly** means of very low or humble position or rank. *He was given the most lowly job in the factory.*

similar words: **insignificant, minor**

subtract   *verb*

to take away a part from a whole, or one number or quantity from another. *If you* **subtract** *2 from 7, you get 5.*

deduct	To **deduct** means to take away or subtract one quantity from another. *My father deducted $2 from my allowance because I broke a window.*
remove	To **remove** means to take something off or away. *Please remove your shoes before you walk on the new carpet.*
dock	To **dock** means to cut off or take away a part from something. *The boss docked Dad's wages when he was late for work.*
diminish	To **diminish** means to make something smaller. *The fact that I had read the book didn't diminish my enjoyment of the film.*
curtail	To **curtail** means to cut something short. *We curtailed our trip and came home two weeks early.*

similar words: **reduce, remove**
contrasting words: **add**

succeed   *verb*

to do or accomplish what you have attempted. *Anne* **succeeded** *in learning to play the violin.*

shine	To **shine** can mean to be very good at something. *Kris shines at spelling.*
steal the show	To **steal the show** means to achieve great success. *Mike stole the show with his beautiful singing.*
make the grade	To **make the grade** means to reach the standard that has been set. *Darion made the grade after very little practice.*
triumph	To **triumph** means to have a victory or success. *Kim triumphed as usual in her tennis match.*
win	To **win** means to gain a victory. *The competition was a hard one but Darka won.*

contrasting words: **fail**

sudden *adjective*

happening quickly and without warning. *We all jumped at the **sudden** noise.*

abrupt	**Abrupt** means sudden and unexpected. *His abrupt departure made us wonder what had happened.*
impulsive	**Impulsive** means acting on a sudden desire. *She reached out her hand in an impulsive gesture of friendship.*
snap	**Snap** means done quickly or suddenly. *She made a snap decision to go to town.*
impromptu	**Impromptu** means made up or done on the spur of the moment. *We surprised him with a farewell gift and he made an impromptu speech of thanks.*
meteoric	**Meteoric** can mean swift or happening quickly, like a meteor's path. *She is a brilliant architect and her progress in this career has been meteoric.*

sufficient *adjective*

having as much as is needed or wanted. *Julie bought **sufficient** material to make curtains for the living room and dining room.*

enough	**Enough** means the same as sufficient. You can usually use either. *There is only enough cake for one slice each.*
adequate	**Adequate** means **enough** or sufficient for the purpose. *I hope our clothes are adequate for the cold weather.*
satisfactory	**Satisfactory** means fulfilling all the requirements or demands. *Mom wouldn't pay for the car repairs until she was sure they were satisfactory.*
decent	**Decent** can mean sufficiently big to fulfill a particular need. *The hungry hikers had not had a decent meal in days.*

contrasting words: **abundant, extra**

suffocate   *verb*

to kill by stopping someone from breathing. *Don't ever put a plastic bag over your face, because it could **suffocate** you.*

choke To **choke** means to stop someone from breathing. *A long scarf could choke you if it became tangled in the ski tow.*

strangle To **strangle** can mean to kill someone by holding something tight around their neck. *This collar is so tight it is practically strangling me.*

smother To **smother** means to suffocate someone by blocking the supply of air to the nose and mouth. *There were so many blankets on me I felt like I was smothering.*

asphyxiate To **asphyxiate** means to suffocate. It is a more formal, medical word. *We heard on the news that the gas had asphyxiated ten people.*

stifle To **stifle** means to smother or prevent someone from breathing. *The air in this stuffy room is stifling.*

suggestion   *noun*

an idea brought to someone for them to consider and possibly do something about. *My **suggestion** to dress up made all the children happy.*

recommendation A **recommendation** can be a suggestion about what to do, or how to do something. *The council made several recommendations on how the shopping center should be designed.*

piece of advice A **piece of advice** is an opinion suggested, or offered, by someone who thinks it is worth following. *Let me give you a piece of advice — don't play at work and don't work at play.*

pointer A **pointer** can be a helpful suggestion. *The tennis coach gave me a few pointers on how to improve my backhand.*

tip A **tip** can be a piece of useful information. *My sister gave me a tip on how to solve a math problem.*

similar words: **offer**

suit *verb*

to be satisfactory or convenient. *Will tomorrow* **suit** *you for our meeting?*

serve
To **serve** can mean to be fit for a particular purpose. *The tree served as a shelter for the birds.*

suffice
To **suffice** means to be enough to be satisfactory. *I think twenty sausage rolls will suffice for the party.*

qualify
To **qualify** means to make or show yourself fit for something. *She qualified for the finals by winning the heat.*

fill the bill
To **fill the bill** means to be entirely suitable for a particular purpose. It is more suited to everyday language. *I think Sue will fill the bill as student council president.*

summary *noun*

a short statement in speech or writing giving the main points of something. *I gave the class a* **summary** *of the new rules.*

précis
A **précis** is a brief piece of writing containing the main points of a longer piece. *He wrote a précis of the article on whales.*

synopsis
A **synopsis** is a written **outline** or summary of a longer piece of writing. *She wrote a synopsis of the novel to persuade us to read it.*

outline
An **outline** is a short description of something giving only its most important points. *We were all given an outline of what had to be done.*

résumé
A **résumé** is a summary of a person's education and work experience. *I applied for the job by sending a letter and a copy of my résumé.*

plan
A **plan** can be a scheme for something that is to be done. *I jotted down a plan for my story before I began to write it.*

similar words: **report**

superior *adjective*

of higher grade than usual. *I am only interested in buying* **superior** *goods.*

high-class **High-class** is so similar to superior that you can usually use either. *High-class hotels are usually very expensive.*

quality **Quality** can mean excellent or of superior grade. *The stall had a sign saying "Quality produce sold here."*

deluxe **Deluxe** means of expensive and luxurious quality. *I would expect a deluxe hotel to have a restaurant service all through the night.*

prize **Prize** means so high in quality as to be greatly valued. *That gold pencil is his prize possession.*

similar words: **excellent, best, great**
contrasting words: **inferior**

support *noun*

someone or something that holds anything up. *This pole is one of the* **supports** *for the tent.*

base A **base** is the bottom part of anything, and gives support. *The statue stood on a strong base.*

foundation A **foundation** is the prepared or natural **base** on which something rests or stands. *The stone foundations of the old building had to be repaired.*

framework A **framework** is a structure designed to support or enclose something. *The framework of the ship was made of steel.*

skeleton A **skeleton** can mean a bare **framework** of something. *The devastating fire reduced the house to a blackened skeleton.*

sure   *adjective*

having no doubt about something. *I am **sure** of what I am saying.*

certain
: **Certain** is so similar to sure that you can usually use either. *I am certain my answer is correct.*

positive
: **Positive** can mean absolutely sure. *I am positive you are lying.*

confident
: **Confident** means having a strong belief about something. *She was confident that she had passed the test.*

clear
: **Clear** can mean not able to be doubted. *She achieved a clear win in the race.*

definite
: **Definite** means **clear** and **certain**. *It is a definite advantage to be able to run fast.*

---

contrasting words: **confused, uncertain**

---

surroundings   *noun*

everything that is around or near someone or something. *We are all affected by our **surroundings**.*

environment
: Your **environment** is the whole surroundings of your life. *He grew up in a city environment.*

habitat
: A **habitat** is the **environment** in which a particular plant or animal naturally grows or lives. *These plants need a very warm habitat.*

environs
: **Environs** are the surrounding districts of a place. *This is a map of Los Angeles and its environs.*

setting
: A **setting** is the surroundings in which something is placed or set. *The house had a pretty country setting.*

scene
: **Scene** can be the place or surroundings in which an event happens. *We need to look at the scene of the crime.*

swamp   *noun*

an area of soft wet ground. *Many water birds lived in the **swamp**.*

bog	A **bog** is an area of muddy ground. It is similar to swamp. *Be careful you don't wander into the bog.*
marsh	A **marsh** is an area of low-lying wet land. It is similar to both swamp and **bog**. *The marsh was full of reeds.*
mire	A **mire** is an area of deep mud. *The car sank in the mire.*
quagmire	A **quagmire** is a muddy patch of ground. *The rain has turned the backyard into a quagmire.*

sway   *verb*

to move or swing from side to side. *She **swayed** in time with the music.*

wave	To **wave** means to move loosely to and fro or up and down. *The pennants waved in the strong wind.*
wobble	To **wobble** means to move unsteadily from side to side. *When I first got on a bike, I wobbled all over the road.*
waddle	To **waddle** means to walk with short steps, swaying from side to side. *The duck waddled across to the pond followed by her ducklings.*
reel	To **reel** means to stagger or sway, especially from dizziness or a blow. *She was reeling when she got off the merry-go-round.*
lurch	To **lurch** means to move suddenly and unsteadily. *The boat lurched through the whitecaps.*

similar words: **shake**

sweet *adjective*

having a pleasant taste like that of sugar or honey. *Do you like **sweet** snacks or salted snacks better?*

sugary	**Sugary** means tasting too sweet because of having too much sugar. *I don't like this sugary drink.*
candied	**Candied** means cooked in sugar or having a crust of sugar. *The cake was decorated with pieces of candied orange peel.*
glacé	**Glacé** means cooked in or covered with sugar. It is similar to **candied**. *I gave them a box of glacé fruit.*

contrasting words: **sour**

swelter *verb*

to feel very hot and sweaty. *We **sweltered** all summer.*

boil	To **boil** can mean to feel very hot. *We were boiling because the air conditioner had broken down.*
roast	To **roast** can mean to be or become very hot, like food cooked in an oven or over a fire. *We roasted sitting in the hot car.*
burn	To **burn** can mean to feel very hot and as if on fire. *His forehead burned with the fever.*
scorch	To **scorch** can mean to **burn** and dry up. *The ground was scorched by the blistering sun.*

take   *verb*

to get, accept, or receive something. *Will you **take** a check instead of cash?*

confiscate	To **confiscate** means to take something and keep it. *The teacher confiscated my comic book.*
appropriate	To **appropriate** means to take something because you want to use it yourself. *She appropriated Tom's desk while he was away.*
annex	To **annex** means to obtain something and join it to what you already own. *The farmer annexed the neighboring land.*
borrow	To **borrow** means to take or get something on the understanding that you have to return it. *I borrowed three books from the library this week.*
adopt	To **adopt** means to take something or someone as your own. *They adopted the baby.*

similar words: **grab, steal, abduct**
contrasting words: **give**

talk   *noun*

an exchange of thoughts using spoken words, especially in a friendly or informal way. *We had a good **talk** after dinner.*

conversation	**Conversation** is so similar to talk that you can usually use either. *Don't interrupt our conversation.*
discussion	A **discussion** is a talk in which you consider something from all sides. *Our family had a discussion about where to go for our vacation.*
debate	A **debate** is an organized talk in which the things for and against something are considered. It is similar to **discussion**. *The debate in the Senate went on all through the night.*
interview	An **interview** is a talk in which someone is asked questions about something. *The actor gave an interview about his latest film.*
dialog	**Dialog** means a talk between two or more people, especially in a play or story. *The dialog in the first part of the play was not very interesting.*

talk *verb*

to speak together. *The girls **talked** all the way to school.*

converse	To **converse** means to talk with someone else. It is used in rather formal language. *We conversed about music.*
confer	To **confer** means to have a discussion about something. *I will have to confer with the other teachers about that.*
chat	To **chat** means to talk in a friendly way, not about a serious subject. *The children chatted about their holidays.*
gossip	To **gossip** means to talk in a silly way about other people's business. *All the neighbors gossiped about the newcomers.*
discuss	To **discuss** means to talk over. *We discussed the outcome of the upcoming elections.*

similar words: **rave**

talkative *adjective*

liking to talk a lot. *Garth finds it hard to keep quiet in class because he is very **talkative**.*

loquacious	**Loquacious** is similar to talkative. It is a rather formal word. *My mother is loquacious when she talks on the phone.*
voluble	**Voluble** means talking with a ready and continuous flow of words. *He is voluble if you get him talking about his favorite sport.*
communicative	**Communicative** means liking to share or pass on thoughts, opinions, or information by talking. *Jill is a friendly, communicative person.*
chatty	**Chatty** means liking to chat. *You can hear all the neighborhood gossip from the chatty man at the corner store.*
garrulous	**Garrulous** means very talkative, often in a silly way. *I think he is so garrulous because he is lonely.*

contrasting words: **reticent, abrupt**

tall   *adjective*

of more than average height. *He can reach the box on top of the cupboard because he is so **tall**.*

high	**High** can mean stretching a long way upward. *We have a high fence around our backyard to keep the dog in.*
lofty	**Lofty** means reaching high into the air. *The lofty mountains seemed to touch the clouds.*
towering	**Towering** means very tall or **lofty**. *The city was full of towering buildings.*
grand	**Grand** can mean of great or impressive size. *What a grand house you live in!*
elevated	**Elevated** means raised up, generally above the ground. *The stage was elevated so that the whole audience could see.*

task   *noun*

a piece of work you are expected to do. *We were each given our own **task** so we would be ready to leave on time.*

chore	A **chore** is a task you have to do that is not very exciting or that you don't like much. *I have to finish my chores before I can come and play.*
errand	An **errand** is a small task you are sent to do. *Dad sent me into town on an errand for him.*
assignment	An **assignment** is a particular task you are given to do. *Our assignment was to make a model of our solar system.*
duty	A **duty** is something you have to do because of your position. *It is your duty as captain to decide the batting order.*
mission	A **mission** is a special task someone is sent to carry out. *Your mission is to discover their secret hide-out.*

tasteless *adjective*

lacking in taste. *The food at that restaurant is **tasteless**.*

plain	**Plain** means not rich or strong in taste. *He believes in cooking old-fashioned, plain meals.*
bland	**Bland** means pleasant and easy to digest but lacking a strong or interesting taste. *The right spice can change a bland meal into a tasty meal.*
mild	**Mild** can mean not strong or sharp in taste and easy to digest. *He was put on a diet of mild food after his illness.*
insipid	**Insipid** means too tasteless to be pleasant. *The unseasoned soup was insipid.*
flat	**Flat** can mean disappointingly tasteless. *I used all the ingredients in the recipe but the meal was flat.*

contrasting words: **tasty**

tasty *adjective*

full of flavor. *This meat needs a **tasty** sauce.*

savory	**Savory** means having a delicious taste, usually not sweet. *There are many savory stews on the menu.*
spicy	**Spicy** means strong-tasting because of being flavored with a spice, such as pepper or cinnamon. *Do you like spicy Mexican food?*
sharp	**Sharp** can mean having a strong biting taste. *This aged cheese is too sharp for me.*
pungent	**Pungent** means having a biting taste. *This is a pungent grapefruit juice.*
piquant	**Piquant** means having a pleasantly strong, biting taste. *This lemon sauce should be more piquant.*

contrasting words: **tasteless**

teach   *verb*

to give a skill to someone, or to give knowledge of something. *She **teaches** our class. He **teaches** music.*

instruct	To **instruct** means to teach someone or tell someone something. *The dentist instructed us on how to care for our teeth.*
train	To **train** means to teach a person or animal to know or do something. *She trained us to speak loudly and clearly.*
drill	To **drill** can mean to **train** someone through repeated exercises. *She drilled us until we knew all our lines for the play.*
coach	To **coach** means to **train** or teach people in small groups or on their own. *She coached me in math so I could understand the new work.*
educate	To **educate** means to teach or **instruct** someone in order to increase the person's knowledge and skills. *She also educates her class in skills such as debating.*

contrasting words: **learn**

teacher   *noun*

someone who instructs other people. *The **teacher** showed us how to mix the paints to make a new color.*

tutor	A **tutor** is someone who is hired to teach people in small groups or on their own. *A tutor came to help him with his schoolwork while he was in the hospital.*
instructor	An **instructor** is a teacher. *His music instructor was pleased with his progress.*
lecturer	A **lecturer** teaches very large groups of people. *When the hall was full, the lecturer began telling us about her new discovery.*
coach	A **coach** is someone who teaches people privately to help them get ready for an exam, or someone who trains athletes. *Did the coach say we have to do a hundred push-ups?*
trainer	A **trainer** is someone who helps athletes stay fit and teaches them the skills they need for their sport. *Her trainer developed a program she had to follow to get ready for the big race.*

similar words: **adviser**

tear *verb*

to pull something apart leaving rough edges. *She **tore** the paper in two.*

rip   To **rip** means to tear something in a rough way. *He ripped his shirt on the barbed-wire fence.*

slash   To **slash** means to cut something violently and unevenly. *Vandals have slashed the train seats.*

slit   To **slit** means to make a long straight cut or opening in something. *He slit the envelope open and took out the letter.*

gash   To **gash** means to make a long deep cut in something. *She gashed her hand with the knife.*

lacerate   To **lacerate** means to cut or tear something roughly. *The broken glass lacerated his foot.*

similar words: **cut, scratch**

tease *verb*

to make fun of or pester someone in a lighthearted but embarrassing way. *We **teased** him about arriving too early for the dance.*

taunt   To **taunt** means to insult or tease someone in a cruel way. *It was cruel to taunt her for doing poorly on the test.*

rib   To **rib** can mean to tease, **ridicule,** or make fun of someone. It is more suited to everyday language. *We ribbed Andrew about always being late for lunch.*

heckle   To **heckle** means to torment and bother a speaker with annoying questions and comments. *The man in the audience heckled the politician at the election meeting.*

ridicule   To **ridicule** means to make fun of someone or something in a scornful way. *John ridiculed Robert's attempt to row the boat.*

similar words: **insult**

tell *verb*

to give someone an account or description of something. ***Tell** us the old tale of* The Hare and the Tortoise.

narrate   To **narrate** means to tell a particular story in speech or writing. *On my record of* Peter and the Wolf *a famous actor narrates the story.*

relate   To **relate** means to tell or **narrate** something, usually a story. *He related the story of how he had found the lost gold mine.*

recount   To **recount** means to tell about something, giving as much information as you can. *Recount everything that happened after I left you.*

describe   To **describe** means to tell about something or someone in a way that gives a very clear picture or idea. *She described the strawberry cream cake so well we could almost taste it.*

outline   To **outline** means to tell about something briefly, giving only the main points. *He outlined the plan for us again.*

---

similar words: **inform, explain**

---

temporary *adjective*

lasting for a short time. *Adam had a **temporary** job during vacation delivering newspapers.*

provisional   **Provisional** means temporary or just for the time being. *A provisional government was appointed only until a new election could be held.*

interim   **Interim** means temporary or lasting for a short time. *We had to obey the interim orders until a new plan was thought up.*

fill-in   **Fill-in** means temporary or used for only a short time. *I agreed to be a fill-in player until Ronnie came back.*

casual   **Casual** can mean employed occasionally. *The manager hired a casual typist when we were busy.*

part-time   **Part-time** means for part of the regular hours. *She has a part-time job delivering pizzas.*

---

similar words: **momentary**
contrasting words: **permanent**

---

test *noun*

a set of questions to answer or some other method of evaluation, designed to show how much you know about something or what your abilities are. *We had a math **test** on all the work we've learned this term.*

exam
An **exam** is a test of knowledge or skill that often has to be passed before the next stage of learning begins. *If I don't pass my exams at the end of the year, I will be upset.*

trial
A **trial** can be an experiment or test carried out in order to prove something. *The scientist ran several trials on the new cream to make sure that it was safe to use.*

audition
An **audition** is a special test or hearing to see how suitable an actor or performer is for a particular job. *Elsa is having an audition for a part in the new play.*

checkup
A **checkup** is a test designed to make sure that all is in order, especially your health. *She went to the doctor for her yearly checkup.*

test *verb*

to attempt to find out a particular thing about something or someone. *I **tested** the water to see how cold it was.*

try
To **try** can mean to test something, often by using it yourself. *I am going to try my new skis today.*

sample
To **sample** means to test or judge something by eating or using some of it. *The judges sampled all the cakes before they announced the winner of the competition.*

check
To **check** means to find out the correctness of something. *Dominic checked the car battery before we set off on our trip.*

screen
To **screen** means to examine or test a number of people or things. *Jasper screened the rock samples for signs of gold.*

similar words: **examine, investigate**

thanks   *noun*

an expressing of pleasure for a favor received. *We expressed our thanks to our aunt by sending her a note.*

gratitude
: **Gratitude** is the feeling of **appreciation** for a favor received. *We were filled with gratitude for her understanding attitude.*

thankfulness
: **Thankfulness** is so much like **gratitude** that you can usually use either one. *I can see your thankfulness in your face.*

appreciation
: **Appreciation** is generally any feeling of understanding for an act you like or approve of, but especially a feeling of **thankfulness**. *If you show your appreciation, people will do favors for you more often.*

thick   *adjective*

measuring rather a lot from one surface to another, or being of a closely packed material. *I have a lovely, **thick** blanket on my bed in winter.*

dense
: **Dense** means thick or closely packed. *The tropical rainforest was very dense and hard to walk through.*

heavy
: **Heavy** can mean thicker or greater than usual. *She drew a heavy line under the title of her story.*

solid
: **Solid** can mean thick or **dense**. *Solid fog filled the valley and progress was impossible.*

compact
: **Compact** means **dense** or firmly packed. *The wet snow was perfect for making heavy, compact snowballs.*

contrasting words: **thin, narrow**

thicken

thicken *verb*

to become thicker or more dense. *The recipe says to stir the egg and milk mixture until it **thickens**.*

clot — To **clot** means to thicken by forming solid lumps. *After you have been bleeding for a while, your blood clots and stops flowing.*

coagulate — To **coagulate** means to change from a liquid into thick lumps. *The gravy became cold and coagulated in the bottom of the pan.*

congeal — To **congeal** means to thicken by becoming solid. It is similar to **coagulate**. *Cooking fat congeals as it cools.*

curdle — To **curdle** means to get lumpy. It is used particularly about milk that has been treated with an acid or has not been refrigerated. *The milk curdled when it was left out in the sun.*

condense — To **condense** means to become thicker and less in volume. *The steam condensed and formed drops of water when it hit the cold windshield.*

thief *noun*

someone who steals. *A **thief** must have taken my school bag.*

robber — A **robber** is a thief, often one who uses force or violence. *A robber attacked the woman and stole her money.*

burglar — A **burglar** is someone who steals by breaking into a house or building. *Our house has an alarm to scare away burglars.*

shoplifter — A **shoplifter** is someone who steals from a store while pretending to be shopping. *Shoplifters will be reported to the police.*

pickpocket — A **pickpocket** is someone who steals from people's pockets or handbags while they are in public places. *My father's wallet was stolen by a pickpocket on the train.*

kleptomaniac — A **kleptomaniac** is someone who feels an uncontrollable urge to steal things, even though he or she does not need them. *So many things have been disappearing that I think there must be a kleptomaniac in the school.*

similar words: **bandit, criminal**

thin   *adjective*

measuring very little from one surface to the other. *I like nice, **thin** toast.*

slim	**Slim** means pleasantly thin. This can be used about people or things. *He was reading a slim volume of poetry.*
slender	**Slender** is so similar to **slim** you can usually choose either of them. *The furniture had graceful, slender proportions.*
skinny	**Skinny** means very thin. This is usually only used about people or animals. *The poor, skinny old horse was pulling a heavy cart.*
lean	**Lean** can mean thin, but usually also fit and strong. *The lean equestrian mounted the horse and galloped away.*
spindly	**Spindly** means long or tall and **slender**, but usually also weak or frail. *The spindly young shrubs needed plenty of care to make them grow strong and thick.*

similar words: **slight**
contrasting words: **thick, stocky**

think   *verb*

to form or have an idea of something in your mind. ***Think** about the different things you did on the weekend.*

suppose	To **suppose** can mean to think or believe something without having any actual knowledge. *Do you suppose he would mind if I borrowed his book?*
suspect	To **suspect** can mean to think that something is very likely to be true. *I suspect I would be too surprised to be able to say anything.*
reckon	To **reckon** can mean to think or **suppose**. It is more suited to everyday language. *I reckon she is the only one who knows about this.*
guess	To **guess** can mean to think or believe something. *I guess the old mariner would have some interesting stories to tell.*

similar words: **believe, conclude, ponder, imagine**

thorough *adjective*

complete, careful, or without missing anything. *We gave our cottage a **thorough** cleaning before we left.*

comprehensive   **Comprehensive** means including nearly everything. *The newspaper gave a comprehensive report of the opening of the school's new building.*

detailed   **Detailed** means looking at every little part of something. *The scientist made a detailed examination of the sample of blood.*

exhaustive   **Exhaustive** means dealing with something in detail. *The police made an exhaustive search for the missing man.*

intensive   **Intensive** means done with a lot of attention or work. *The nurses and doctors gave him intensive care after his accident.*

in-depth   **In-depth** means thorough or dealing with something completely. *They had an in-depth discussion about how to prevent vandalism.*

similar words: **whole, careful**
contrasting words: **incomplete**

thought *noun*

something that has come into your mind as a result of thinking. *I suddenly had the **thought** that a swim would make me cooler.*

idea   An **idea** is a thought or a picture in your mind. *Our idea grew clearer until we knew exactly what we should do.*

brainstorm   A **brainstorm** is a sudden brilliant thought. *His brainstorm gave us the solution to the whole problem.*

notion   A **notion** is an **idea**, often not very clear in your mind. *I have a notion of what traveling through space may be like.*

theory   A **theory** is an explanation based on thought or opinion. *I have a different theory about how the planets were formed.*

concept   A **concept** is a general **idea** or understanding of something. *I do not have a very clear concept of computer programming.*

thread   *noun*

a thin, slender string that has been spun from a material such as cotton, silk, nylon, and so on. *I pulled the loose **thread** and my button fell off.*

filament   A **filament** is a very slender thread, or something like it. *Under a microscope, a filament of wool from my sweater looked rough and jagged.*

fiber   A **fiber** is a **filament** of material that is used to make cloth or yarn. *Fibers of my white scarf are all over my black jacket.*

strand   A **strand** is one of the threads that a **cord**, rope, or cable is made from. *When a rope unravels, it splits up into strands.*

cord   A **cord** is a string made from many threads that have been twisted together. *This multicolored cord has red, blue, and green threads in it.*

tendril   A **tendril** is a threadlike part of a plant that wraps around something to support itself. *The tendrils of the vine clung to the bars of the railing.*

threaten   *verb*

to tell someone, using words or some other sign, that you intend to cause harm. *The leader of the gang **threatened** the bank teller.*

menace   To **menace** means to take a threatening attitude toward someone. *I felt menaced by the stranger, so I locked the front door.*

intimidate   To **intimidate** means to frighten someone in order to make that person do something. *The spy tried to intimidate the ambassador's secretary into revealing the secret code.*

warn   To **warn** means to give notice of possible danger. *The sign warned us to stay off the property.*

blackmail   To **blackmail** means to demand money from someone by threatening to reveal damaging secrets. *He was able to blackmail me because he knew about my criminal background.*

similar words: **frighten, force**

thrifty *adjective*
carefully managing or looking after your money or supplies. *The **thrifty** woman always kept a record of how she spent her money.*

frugal
> **Frugal** means being very careful not to waste anything. *We must be frugal with our supplies or we won't have enough for the whole journey.*

economical
> **Economical** means not wasting anything. *He found it was more economical to buy his groceries once a week.*

provident
> **Provident** means carefully managing things like money so that you are prepared for the future. *She was so provident that she had enough money for her retirement.*

stingy
> **Stingy** means saving money in an ungenerous way. *I hope you do not think I am stingy if I do not treat you to lunch.*

contrasting words: **generous**

thrive *verb*
to grow strong or to do well. *Our new business is **thriving**.*

prosper
> To **prosper** means to be successful. *The farmers have prospered this year because of the abundant crops.*

benefit
> To **benefit** means to get better or gain an advantage. *We will all benefit from a trip to the mountains.*

boom
> To **boom** means to do very well suddenly. *During the gold rush, business in western towns was booming.*

blossom
> To **blossom** can mean to develop or turn out well. *He has blossomed into a fine musician.*

bloom
> To **bloom** can mean to be healthy and full of life. *The animals bloomed under the expert care of the vet.*

similar words: **succeed, flourish**
contrasting words: **fail**

throb *verb*

to pound regularly and strongly. *The engine of the boat **throbbed** as we made our way up the river.*

beat	To **beat** can mean to throb. *Her heart beat wildly as she raced for the finish line.*
pulsate	To **pulsate** means to throb or **beat** like your heart does. *We could hear the drums pulsating in the distance.*
palpitate	To **palpitate** means to **beat** much faster than usual. *Our hearts palpitated at the eerie sounds of the forest.*
drum	To **drum** can mean to make a thumping sound like a drum. *The blood drummed in his ears as he ran up the steep hill.*
buzz	To **buzz** means to make a low humming sound. *His stream of words buzzed in my head.*

throw *verb*

to send something through the air. *Megan **threw** the ball to Amanda.*

toss	To **toss** means to throw something, often in a casual way. *She tossed her bag on the bed.*
fling	To **fling** means to throw something, usually forcefully or impatiently. *He flung the book angrily onto the table.*
hurl	To **hurl** means to throw something with great force or strength. *The Apache hunter hurled his spear at the buffalo.*
pitch	To **pitch** means to throw something, often taking careful aim. *Pitch the ball low so that the little girl can catch it.*
chuck	To **chuck** means to throw something carelessly. It is more suited to everyday language. *He chucked the garbage into the basket.*

tidy *adjective*

having everything in its right place. *If you have a **tidy** room, it is easy to find things.*

neat
Neat means tidy and well-ordered. *Her homework was neat and easy to read.*

trim
Trim means **neat** and tidy. *John was very trim in his new uniform.*

orderly
Orderly means arranged in a tidy manner. *The books were in orderly rows on the shelves.*

shipshape
Shipshape means **neat** and tidy. *We made the house shipshape before my cousins came to visit us.*

methodical
Methodical means acting or done in a careful, **orderly** way. *He was methodical in his habits and always hung up his clothes.*

contrasting words: **untidy, scruffy**

tire *verb*

to reduce someone's strength and make them sleepy or weak. *The long walk **tired** the children.*

fatigue
To **fatigue** means to tire someone's body or mind. *The climb up the steep hill fatigued us.*

weary
To **weary** is so similar to tire and **fatigue** that you can usually use any of these. *The constant noise and bustle of her office wearies Mom.*

exhaust
To **exhaust** means to tire or wear someone out to a great extent. *Digging in the garden exhausts me.*

tax
To **tax** means to burden or **exhaust** someone or something. *Commuting to work taxed him much more than he had expected.*

strain
To **strain** can mean to make too many demands upon something or someone. *Having all her relations staying with her at once has strained her resources.*

similar words: **weaken**

tired *adjective*

weak from effort or hard work and needing sleep. *The children were **tired** and ready for bed by the end of the busy day.*

weary
    Weary means tired out in your mind or body by hard work, or something similar. *We were very weary after our long hike in the country.*

worn
    Worn can mean made very tired. *My shoulders were stooped and worn after doing the gardening.*

exhausted
    Exhausted means greatly tired or drained of strength and energy. *The runners were all exhausted after the cross-country race.*

bushed
    Bushed means very tired or **exhausted**. It is usually used in rather informal language. *I was bushed by the time I finished my homework.*

fatigued
    Fatigued means very tired or drained of energy due to effort of your mind or body. *The student was fatigued after the three-hour examination.*

similar words: **lethargic, weak**
contrasting words: **energetic, lively**

toast *verb*

to brown something by heat or a flame. *We sat around the campfire and **toasted** marshmallows.*

grill
    To **grill** means to cook something under or on a grill. *For breakfast we grilled some sausages and eggs.*

barbecue
    To **barbecue** means to cook meat outdoors over an open fire in a specially built fireplace or metal frame. *In summer we barbecue hamburgers and wieners.*

bake
    To **bake** means to cook something in an oven. *Turn the oven on and bake the pie for forty minutes.*

roast
    To **roast** means to cook something over a fire or **bake** it in an oven. *When you roast a chicken the delicious smell spreads all through the house.*

similar words: **broil**

top *noun*

the highest point or surface of anything. *Sir Edmund Hillary climbed to the **top** of Mt. Everest in 1953.*

peak A **peak** is the pointed top of anything, usually a mountain. *Mount Elbert is the highest peak in the Colorado Rockies.*

pinnacle A **pinnacle** is the highest point of anything, usually a mountain. *No one has ever climbed that treacherous rocky pinnacle.*

summit A **summit** is the top or highest point of something. *We reached the summit of the hill after a steep climb.*

apex An **apex** is the tip, point, or highest part of anything. *Only one tree grew on the apex of the mountain.*

crest A **crest** is the very top of something. *The sunlight bounced off the crests of the waves.*

contrasting words: **bottom**

touch *verb*

to put your hand or finger on something. *I **touched** the book with dirty hands and left a mark on it.*

feel To **feel** means to examine something by touching. *I felt the grass to see how wet it was.*

handle To **handle** means to use your hands to examine or touch something. *The vet handled the injured puppy gently to find any broken bones.*

finger To **finger** means to touch something lightly. *She fingered the lucky charm in her pocket while waiting for the contest to start.*

stroke To **stroke** means to pass your hand gently over something. *The rider stroked the frightened horse to calm it.*

pat To **pat** means to **stroke** something lightly with your hand. *He patted the chair to show me where to sit.*

touchy *adjective*

irritable or easily offended. *He's so **touchy** you have to be careful what you say to him.*

thin-skinned **Thin-skinned** means touchy. *Some people are too thin-skinned to listen to any criticism of their work.*

moody **Moody** means changeable in mood or feelings. *If you are going to be moody, you might as well stay at home by yourself.*

prickly **Prickly** means easily made angry. *He's always prickly when he's tired.*

sensitive **Sensitive** means easily affected by something. *My friend has a sensitive nature and is easily hurt.*

similar words: **grumpy**

trace *noun*

a very small amount. *We found **traces** of gold in the sand from the riverbed.*

drop A **drop** can be a very small amount of something, especially a liquid. *Only a drop of water was left to ease their thirst.*

dash A **dash** can be a small unmeasured amount of something. It is often used in cooking. *Add just a dash of pepper to the stew.*

pinch A **pinch** can be the very small amount of something you can hold between your thumb and first finger. *The recipe says to add only a pinch of salt.*

hint A **hint** can be such a tiny amount of something that you can hardly tell it is there. *There was just a hint of warmth in the air.*

whisper A **whisper** can be a **hint** or suggestion. *There isn't a whisper of truth in that rumor.*

similar words: **piece**

tradition   *noun*

a belief or way of doing something that is handed down from generation to generation. *Our family has a **tradition** of getting together at my grandparents' house on the first day of summer every year.*

custom	A **custom** is a usual way of doing something. *Is it your custom to eat a large breakfast?*
habit	A **habit** is a usual manner of behavior, usually done without much thought. *He had a habit of taking his shoes off at the front door.*
practice	A **practice** can be so similar to a **custom** that you can usually use either. *My practice is to go for a run twice a week.*
usage	**Usage** is the customary way of using words in a particular language or dialect. *This book on English usage will explain the difference between a common noun and a proper noun.*

transparent   *adjective*

allowing light to pass through so that it can be seen through. *I traced the map using **transparent** paper.*

clear	**Clear** can mean transparent or able to be seen through. *I covered my book with clear plastic so that I could still see the title.*
sheer	**Sheer** means so thin that you can see through. *We could see our visitors through the sheer curtains.*
limpid	**Limpid** means transparent and **clear**. *We could see the shellfish on the sandy bottom of the limpid pools of water.*
translucent	**Translucent** means allowing some light to come through. *Soft light came through the translucent stained-glass window.*

contrasting words: **opaque**

travel *verb*

to go from one place to another. *We had only **traveled** a little way when we had a flat tire.*

journey	To **journey** means to travel, usually a long way. *We journeyed right across Texas.*
voyage	To **voyage** means to travel by sea or air, usually to somewhere quite far away. *I just read about Christopher Columbus's voyage to the New World.*
roam	To **roam** can mean to travel with no special purpose. *He spent his spare time roaming through the woods.*
wander	To **wander** means to go about with no special purpose or place in mind. *I wandered a long way from the farm, trying to decide where to go.*
rove	To **rove** is very similar to **roam** and **wander**. *She roved around the world visiting any place that sounded interesting.*

traveler *noun*

someone who goes about from place to place. *After they retired they became world **travelers** for a year.*

tourist	A **tourist** is someone who travels or tours for pleasure. *The tourists bought many souvenirs of their trip to Europe.*
sightseer	A **sightseer** is someone who travels to see places of interest or beauty. *Niagara Falls is a popular place for sightseers.*
wayfarer	A **wayfarer** is a traveler, especially one on foot. *There were rest stations set up where the wayfarer could stop along the way.*
pilgrim	A **pilgrim** is someone who travels to a holy place especially to carry out a religious duty. *Every Muslim hopes to be a pilgrim to Mecca at least once in a lifetime.*
commuter	A **commuter** is someone who travels regularly between the home and workplace. *The buses are filled with commuters every morning and evening.*

trick   *noun*

something done to deceive someone. *Let's play a **trick** on Mom and hide under the bed.*

hoax   A **hoax** is a trick or practical joke. *We didn't really mean it — it was only a hoax!*

prank   A **prank** is a playful trick. *She is full of pranks and mischief.*

ruse   A **ruse** is a dishonest trick or scheme. *Very carefully they planned a ruse to make everyone think they were still in bed.*

swindle   A **swindle** is a trick that cheats someone out of something that belongs to them. *The swindle was discovered when they found pieces of paper instead of money in the envelope.*

con   A **con** is a trick or a **swindle**. It is a shortened form of "confidence trick" and is more suited to everyday language. *We didn't know it was a con until we got home and found the bag was empty.*

---

similar words: **plot**

---

trick   *verb*

to outwit, deceive, or cheat someone. *We managed to **trick** Dad on April Fool's Day when we made him believe we had been given a holiday from school.*

fool   To **fool** means to trick someone or make them think or believe something that isn't true. *Chris fooled us by pretending to be asleep and then began reading under the blankets.*

bluff   To **bluff** means to trick someone by pretending to be very bold. *They bluffed the guards by walking straight past them talking and laughing.*

hoax   To **hoax** means to deceive someone by playing a trick on them. *Andrea even hoaxed her family with her clever disguise.*

kid   To **kid** can mean to trick or tease someone. *We bandaged Craig's arm and kidded his friends into believing he'd had an accident.*

---

similar words: **deceive, cheat, outwit**

---

trickery   *noun*

the tricking, cheating, or fooling of someone. *We were so used to Uncle Jack's* **trickery** *that we never knew when to believe him.*

subterfuge   Subterfuge means something, such as a trick or plan, aimed to hide or avoid something. *Our subterfuge worked when they followed the false trail down to the river.*

deceit   Deceit means something aimed at tricking or deceiving someone. *Because of their deceit, we were blamed and punished.*

cunning   Cunning means the use of a clever plan to trick or deceive someone. *His cunning was rewarded when he escaped without being seen.*

guile   Guile means cleverness or cunning in the way you deceive someone. *The wily fox used guile to trick the gingerbread man.*

monkey business   Monkey business is trickery or secret and crafty dealing. *It is so quiet I know they are up to some monkey business.*

trudge   *verb*

to tread or walk heavily and slowly. *We* **trudged** *through the mud in our rubber boots.*

tramp   To tramp means to tread or walk heavily and steadily. *Hour after hour the soldiers tramped through the jungle.*

plod   To plod means to walk or move in a slow, steady, and unexciting way. *We plodded through the heavy snow.*

toil   To toil can mean to walk or move with difficulty. *We toiled through thick mud and reeds before we finally reached the river.*

slog   To slog can mean to keep trudging along. *The weary hikers slogged up yet another long, steep hill.*

lumber   To lumber means to move clumsily or heavily, especially because of great size or weight. *The elephants lumbered along the road carrying their huge loads.*

similar words: **walk, march, limp**
contrasting words: **frisk, dart**

true *adjective*

full of truth or not false. *Her story about the bank robbery was **true**.*

right	**Right** can mean free from error or agreeing with the truth or the facts. *I'm sure your information about reptiles is right.*
correct	**Correct** means free from mistakes. *All the answers she gave were correct.*
accurate	**Accurate** can mean free from error. *The police said that her account of the accident was accurate.*
valid	**Valid** means made with good reasons. *The teacher thought that he had a valid reason for being late for school.*
certain	**Certain** can mean accepted as true or sure. *It is certain that he tried to be friends with you.*

similar words: **actual**
contrasting words: **incorrect**

turn *verb*

to make something move around or partly around in a circle. *Very slowly Rod **turned** the handle and peered through the doorway.*

rotate	To **rotate** means to turn something around in a circle. *Rotate the handle in a clockwise direction.*
wind	To **wind** means to tighten something, usually a spring, by turning it around. *You have to wind the music box before it will play.*
screw	To **screw** means to turn something, usually to tighten or seal it. *I poured myself a glass of lemonade, then screwed the lid back on the bottle.*
twist	To **twist** can mean to combine two or more things by **winding** them together. *Louise twisted pieces of string together to make a thick, strong rope.*
reel	To **reel** means to **wind** something on a reel or on a cylinder or wheel. *As soon as I felt a bite, I reeled in my fishing line.*

similar words: **spin, bend**

438

twisted *adjective*

curved or bent. *The **twisted** old tree was just right for climbing.*

coiled   **Coiled** means curled around into loops. *The snake was coiled and ready to strike.*

winding   **Winding** means turning first one way and then another. *We had to drive slowly along the winding mountain roads.*

squiggly   **Squiggly** means having many short twists and curves. *I thought the squiggly line looked like a snake.*

wavy   **Wavy** means curving first one way and then the other. *Jason has thick wavy hair.*

sinuous   **Sinuous** means **winding** or having many curves and bends. *We followed the sinuous path up and down and round about until we ended up where we started.*

tyrannical *adjective*

severely cruel or harsh. *The people hated their **tyrannical** king.*

oppressive   **Oppressive** means unjustly cruel. *The oppressive laws of the time allowed people to be exiled for committing only petty crimes.*

repressive   **Repressive** means forcefully keeping people under control. *Some repressive governments use armies to stop the people from standing up for their rights.*

domineering   **Domineering** means commanding or governing without considering the wishes of others. *The domineering general took no notice of the opinions of his advisers.*

despotic   **Despotic** means like a ruler who has total power, especially one who is cruel and unjust. *The despotic manager made the workers do overtime even if they didn't want to.*

totalitarian   **Totalitarian** means having to do with a government that has complete control and does not allow any opposition. *People who live in a totalitarian state have every aspect of their lives directed and find it difficult to leave if they want to.*

similar words: **bossy**
contrasting words: **submissive**

ugly *adjective*

unpleasant to look at. *I was frightened by the **ugly** monster mask.*

hideous	**Hideous** means extremely ugly. *The film was about a hideous monster.*
repulsive	**Repulsive** can mean so unpleasant to look at that you feel sick or disgusted. *Some people find spiders repulsive.*
grotesque	**Grotesque** means ugly in a way that is odd or unnatural. *A grotesque creature stepped out of the flying saucer.*
monstrous	**Monstrous** can mean very ugly. It is similar to **grotesque**. *I dreamed a monstrous two-headed bull was chasing me.*
foul	**Foul** can mean very ugly or nasty. This is rather an unusual way of using this word today. *The brave princess was not afraid of the foul dragon.*

similar words: **horrible, unpleasant**
contrasting words: **beautiful, pretty**

unashamed *adjective*

not feeling shame or sorrow. *She was **unashamed** of her support for the illegal aliens who were homeless.*

impenitent	**Impenitent** means not feeling sorry for doing wrong and unwilling to put things right. *The judge sentenced the impenitent criminal to ten years in jail.*
unrepentant	**Unrepentant** means not showing regret or sorrow for doing wrong. It is very similar to **impenitent**. *They were unrepentant in spite of the trouble their behavior caused for others.*
unremorseful	**Unremorseful** means not feeling any regret for doing wrong. *My parents were angry because I was unremorseful when I returned home late.*
unapologetic	**Unapologetic** means not wanting to say sorry. *The car accident was the fault of the other driver but he was quite unapologetic.*

similar words: **bold**
contrasting words: **sorry**

unbelievable   *adjective*

not able to be believed or accepted as true. *I find that what you say is*
unbelievable.

incredible	**Incredible** can be so similar to **unbelievable** that you can usually use either. *This book is full of incredible tales.*
unlikely	**Unlikely** means not likely to be true. *I'm not tricked by your unlikely story.*
improbable	**Improbable** means probably not true. It is very similar to **unlikely**. *I've never heard such an improbable excuse.*
implausible	**Implausible** means seeming not to be true or reasonable. It is similar to **unlikely** and **improbable**. *His explanation was implausible.*
farfetched	**Farfetched** means seeming to be too exaggerated to be true. *I prefer a story to be realistic rather than farfetched.*

similar words: **impossible**
contrasting words: **believable, possible, likely**

uncertain   *adjective*

not known for sure. *The time of the train's arrival is still **uncertain**.*

doubtful	**Doubtful** can mean causing doubt or uncertainty. *He gave a doubtful answer and I wondered if he had really read the book.*
dubious	**Dubious** means open to doubt or suspicion. *He told a dubious tale explaining the whereabouts of his sister.*
questionable	**Questionable** means open to doubt or argument. *It is questionable whether this is true.*
debatable	**Debatable** means open to argument. It is very similar to **questionable**. *Your explanation as to how the world began is debatable.*
open	**Open** can mean not completed or decided. *The question is still open and we will consider it again tomorrow.*

similar words: **vague**
contrasting words: **sure**

unconscious *adjective*

having fainted or lost consciousness. *He tumbled down the hill and was lying* ***unconscious*** *at the bottom.*

comatose	**Comatose** means in a coma or unconscious because of sickness or an injury. *After her accident she was comatose for two days.*
stunned	**Stunned** can mean being unconscious or unaware of your surroundings for a short time. *He was stunned for a moment by the blow to his head.*
dazed	**Dazed** means made confused or almost unconscious. *She was dazed by the crash and tried to remember how it had happened.*
drugged	**Drugged** means unconscious or only partly conscious because you have taken or been given drugs. *The patient couldn't stand or think clearly in his drugged state.*
out cold	**Out cold** means unconscious. This is more suited to everyday language. *The boxer was out cold after the heavy blow to his head.*

unconventional *adjective*

not according to usual or accepted ways of behavior. *Her wedding dress was* ***unconventional*** *because it was black.*

nonconformist	**Nonconformist** means refusing to accept the usual or expected ideas, customs, or ways of living. *My parents think I'm nonconformist because I want to leave school earlier than my brothers did.*
bohemian	**Bohemian** means living and acting without any interest in the usual or accepted ways of behavior. This word is often used to describe an artist or a writer. *The group of artists led a bohemian life in which their art was all they thought about.*
alternative	**Alternative** can mean offering the types of behavior or values of a smaller group within, but opposed to, an established society or community, particularly a Western society. *Some people who don't like city living lead alternative life-styles in the country and grow their own food.*
radical	**Radical** means being in favor of extreme social or political reforms. *The radical group demonstrated outside the Capitol.*

similar words: **strange**
contrasting words: **usual**

understand   *verb*

to take the idea of something into your mind. *I tried to* **understand** *his explanation.*

grasp
To **grasp** can mean to understand or take something into your mind. *She grasped the idea of the game very quickly.*

comprehend
To **comprehend** means to understand the meaning of something. *We tried hard to comprehend our parents' reasons for not wanting us to watch that TV program.*

perceive
To **perceive** can mean to understand or become aware of something with your mind. *The wise teacher perceived that John was unhappy about something.*

fathom
To **fathom** means to understand something completely. *I couldn't fathom the instructions for building the model until Maurice helped me.*

make out
To **make out** means to see or understand something. *I can't make out the handwriting on this note.*

similar words: **realize**

---

undertaking   *noun*

a task or piece of work you promise to do. *Moving all the books from the old library to the new one will be a huge* **undertaking**.

enterprise
An **enterprise** is something that requires effort or courage. *Running the school dance was quite an enterprise.*

venture
A **venture** is something you do that is risky or dangerous. *Both companies were involved in the oil exploration venture.*

job
A **job** is a piece of work you have to do. *Painting the house was a big job.*

project
A **project** is a plan or scheme for a piece of work. *This is a project that should make a lot of money.*

engagement
An **engagement** can mean something you are hired to do, especially only once. *The band had an engagement to play at the dance.*

uneven   *adjective*

not being equally balanced with something else. *The competition between the older and younger students was **uneven**.*

unequal	**Unequal** means not being of the same quantity, amount, quality, and so on. *The customers were upset when they were given unequal servings of dessert.*
unbalanced	**Unbalanced** means not equal or properly balanced. *The teams were unbalanced because two of our players were sick.*
lopsided	**Lopsided** means larger or heavier on one side than the other. *The cake was lopsided, so I had to put more icing on one side.*
irregular	**Irregular** means not even or regular. *The sick man's pulse was irregular.*

contrasting words: **equal**

unfair   *adjective*

showing favoritism or not treating everyone the same. *It was **unfair** of her to give Peter the best book.*

unjust	**Unjust** can mean unfair and is usually used to describe the actions of someone in authority. It is rather a formal word. *It was unjust of the judge not to listen to all the accused man's witnesses.*
inequitable	**Inequitable** means not fair or even-handed. *The crowd booed the referee for his inequitable treatment of the two teams.*
discriminatory	**Discriminatory** means treating one person or group unfairly. *The discriminatory laws of that country give special privileges to a few selected people.*
partial	**Partial** can mean showing unfair support for or favoritism toward someone. *We thought that the umpire was being partial toward the other team because his son played on it.*
prejudiced	**Prejudiced** means behaving unfairly because you have formed an opinion without good reason or evidence. *You should not be prejudiced against the new student because he came from another school.*

contrasting words: **fair, neutral**

unfaithful *adjective*

not staying true to someone or to what you have promised. *The knight was* ***unfaithful*** *to his vow to save the king.*

disloyal   **Disloyal** means not faithful or true. *It was disloyal of you not to take my side in the argument.*

false   **False** can mean not faithful or loyal. *He turned out to be a false friend.*

treacherous   **Treacherous** means **disloyal** or likely to betray someone who has trusted you. *The treacherous soldier gave information to the enemy.*

traitorous   **Traitorous** means betraying a person, a cause, or a country. *The traitorous spy plotted to overthrow the government of his country.*

slippery   **Slippery** can mean not to be depended on. This is a rather informal word. *He was such a slippery businessman that no one wanted to buy things from him.*

similar words: **fickle**
contrasting words: **faithful**

unfriendly *adjective*

not showing friendship or being kind. *The book was snatched from me in an* ***unfriendly*** *way.*

cold   **Cold** can mean lacking friendliness or interest. *His cold greeting showed he didn't like me.*

aloof   **Aloof** means not joining in with other people in a friendly way. *People think she is aloof, but I know she is only shy.*

standoffish   **Standoffish** means unfriendly or keeping your distance from other people. It is rather similar to **aloof**. *She is standoffish with people she doesn't know well.*

antisocial   **Antisocial** means not wanting to join in with other people. *He has been antisocial all his life.*

inhospitable   **Inhospitable** means not welcoming or showing people kindness, especially in your own home. *The family next door is quite inhospitable and never ask us over to swim in their pool.*

contrasting words: **friendly**

ungrateful *adjective*

not showing or feeling gratitude or thanks. *How can you be so **ungrateful** when I spent all afternoon cooking you this special dinner?*

unappreciative **Unappreciative** means not showing or feeling appreciation or gratitude. *The band was upset when the unappreciative audience left the concert before the end.*

thankless **Thankless** means not saying how grateful you are. *That's the last time I put myself out for a thankless person like him!*

grudging **Grudging** means unwillingly expressing appreciation or gratitude. *I'd rather have no thanks at all than her grudging thanks.*

heedless **Heedless** can mean not noticing or being aware of someone else's kindness. *She was quite heedless of our efforts to help her.*

similar words: **selfish**

---

unlike *adjective*

not the same, or without a likeness. *This dirt road is quite **unlike** the highway we were driving on before.*

different **Different** is similar to unlike. It is usually used with "from." *Apples are different from oranges in their color and taste.*

dissimilar **Dissimilar** means unlike. *You wouldn't know they are sisters, because their faces have such dissimilar features.*

contrasting **Contrasting** means greatly **different**. *The contrasting photographs showed the house in its run-down condition, and then after it had been painted.*

disparate **Disparate** means completely distinct and unlike. *You and I have disparate goals, so I'm not surprised that we disagree about how the project should be done.*

divergent **Divergent** means going in **different** directions. *Anna and I took divergent paths through the park, but we reached the playground at the same time.*

similar words: **various**
contrasting words: **similar, equal**

unlucky   *adjective*

ill-fated or not having good luck. *We were rather **unlucky** this month because we all caught chicken pox.*

unfortunate **Unfortunate** is so similar to unlucky that you can usually use either. *It was unfortunate that we couldn't get any tickets for the film we wanted to see.*

hapless **Hapless** means unlucky and without much hope. *The man sleeping in the park looked like a hapless fellow.*

wretched **Wretched** can mean very unlucky or miserable. *What a wretched thing to happen just when you were doing so well.*

cursed **Cursed** can mean so unlucky that it's as if someone has wished evil or misfortune to come to you. *I think that racehorse is cursed because it never wins a race.*

star-crossed **Star-crossed** means having a great deal of bad luck, once thought to be caused by the influence of the stars. *Romeo and Juliet were star-crossed lovers.*

contrasting words: **lucky**

unpleasant   *adjective*

unpleasant or disgusting. *We had an **unpleasant** experience last week.*

awful **Awful** means very bad or unpleasant. *We had an awful mess to clean up when the paint spilled.*

repulsive **Repulsive** means dreadful or disgusting. *The food was so repulsive it made her feel quite ill.*

revolting **Revolting** means disgusting or **repulsive.** *The milk tasted revolting because it had turned sour.*

vile **Vile** means disgustingly bad. *He used vile language when he shouted at us.*

gross **Gross** can mean disgusting or coarse. It is more suited to everyday language. *There is a gross smell of garbage in this room.*

similar words: **bad, horrible, ugly**
contrasting words: **nice, agreeable, good**

unrelated *adjective*

having no particular relationship or connection. *His question about space travel was quite **unrelated** to the road safety talk we listened to.*

irrelevant   **Irrelevant** means having nothing to do with the matter being discussed or thought about. *The speaker made so many irrelevant remarks it was hard to understand what he was trying to tell us.*

unconnected   **Unconnected** can mean not thought of as related or connected. *His hobby of stamp collecting is quite unconnected with his ambition to be a professional golfer.*

immaterial   **Immaterial** means unimportant, often especially to the matter being discussed. *Where the shoes were made was immaterial to him as long as they were comfortable.*

foreign   **Foreign** can mean unnatural or not familiar. *Getting up early seemed foreign to us after the summer vacation.*

independent   **Independent** can mean not depending on something else for its existence, working, and so on. *Your argument is independent of anything we have heard so far.*

contrasting words: **related**

untidy *adjective*

not tidy or neat. *Dad made us clean up our **untidy** rooms before we went to bed.*

messy   **Messy** means in an untidy and dirty state. *The kitchen was very messy when we finished cooking dinner.*

chaotic   **Chaotic** means in total disorder. *The house was chaotic when we were unpacking after our trip.*

disorganized   **Disorganized** means in confusion or disorder. *My desk was so disorganized I couldn't start my homework.*

haywire   **Haywire** can mean in disorder. *Everything was haywire in the house after the birthday party.*

slovenly   **Slovenly** means untidy and careless. *There is no excuse for your slovenly behavior at home.*

similar words: **scruffy**
contrasting words: **tidy**

unusual *adjective*

not usual, common, or ordinary. *She is generally a punctual person, so it is* ***unusual*** *for her to be late.*

uncommon	**Uncommon** means not likely to be found or encountered. *Seagulls are uncommon in Utah.*
extraordinary	**Extraordinary** means beyond what is ordinary. *He is a boy of extraordinary strength.*
rare	**Rare** means unusual, **uncommon**, or occurring infrequently. *This stamp is valuable because it is rare.*
remarkable	**Remarkable** means worthy of notice because it is so unusual. *Climbing Mount Everest was a remarkable achievement.*
singular	**Singular** means out of the ordinary or **remarkable**. *Her career as an actress has been a singular success.*

similar words: **strange, scarce**
contrasting words: **ordinary, usual**

unwilling *adjective*

not eager or not agreeing quite happily. *I am **unwilling** to spend a lot of money on a toy that could break so easily.*

reluctant	**Reluctant** means unwilling or not prepared. *The children are always eager to do crafts but often reluctant to clean up afterward.*
disinclined	**Disinclined** means not feeling a wish or inclination. *I'm disinclined to go cycling on such a hot day.*
hesitant	**Hesitant** means waiting or pausing because you are not sure what you should do. *Mom said she was hesitant about letting us go to the movie on our own.*
loath	**Loath** means unwilling or not inclined. *I am loath to go out into that freezing cold.*
averse	**Averse** means opposed or very unwilling. *Luckily for us, our teacher is averse to giving us homework every night.*

contrasting words: **enthusiastic**

upset *adjective*

feeling anxious or unhappy. *I was **upset** when I wasn't chosen for the team.*

agitated	**Agitated** means feeling anxious and unable to be still. *Mom was very agitated when they had not come home by dark.*
disturbed	**Disturbed** means feeling troubled or unsettled. *We were quite disturbed by the news reports about the earthquakes.*
flustered	**Flustered** means confused, usually because you are nervous. *Paul was flustered and forgot what to say when he stood up to give his speech.*
uptight	**Uptight** means anxious and unsettled. It is more suited to everyday language. *He was uptight about his piano exam.*
perturbed	**Perturbed** means very **disturbed** or troubled. *The perturbed pilot looked for a place to land the damaged plane.*

similar words: **nervous**
contrasting words: **calm**

upset *verb*

to make someone feel sad or disturbed. *His insults **upset** me.*

distress	To **distress** means to cause someone great pain, anxiety, or sorrow. *His plan to leave school before he graduated distressed his parents.*
hurt	To **hurt** can mean to harm someone or cause them to have painful feelings. *Her thoughtlessness hurt him, and he turned and walked away.*
worry	To **worry** can mean to make someone feel anxious or uneasy. *It worries our parents if we stay out late.*
trouble	To **trouble** means to disturb or bother someone. *It's a shame to trouble him when he's tired.*
sadden	To **sadden** means to make someone feel sad or upset. *The news of his illness saddened me.*

similar words: **annoy**
contrasting words: **comfort**

use   *verb*

to put something into action for some purpose. *Let's **use** our wagon to carry our toys home.*

employ   To **employ** means to use something. *I'd rather employ my spare time reading than watching television.*

ply   To **ply** means to use something, especially in a busy way. This is a rather old-fashioned use of the word. *Ply the oars, lads, and we'll soon be home.*

wield   To **wield** means to use something as a powerful tool. *She wields her influence with the parents to raise money for the school.*

exploit   To **exploit** can mean to put something to good use. *They exploited the land well, growing crops for food.*

utilize   To **utilize** means to put something into use. *Many people utilize the sun's energy to heat their homes.*

contrasting words: **discard**

useful   *adjective*

of use or service. *Don't throw away anything that might be **useful** at another time.*

handy   **Handy** can mean useful or convenient. *That brick made a handy hammer!*

helpful   **Helpful** means able or likely to help or be of use. *The dictionary is helpful when I'm not sure what something means.*

valuable   **Valuable** can mean of great use or service. *It would be a valuable help if you would return these books for me.*

beneficial **Beneficial** means **helpful** or of benefit. *After a long tiring hike we longed for the beneficial effects of a hot bath.*

advantageous **Advantageous** means **helpful** or of advantage to you. *It would be advantageous to get your tickets early so you don't miss out.*

similar words: **possible**
contrasting words: **useless**

useless   *adjective*

of no use or serving no purpose. *It is **useless** to try to plug that large hole with that small stopper.*

vain

Vain can have a meaning so similar to useless you can usually use either word. *He made a vain attempt to stop the runaway car before it crashed.*

futile

Futile means not able to produce any result. *The dog made futile leaps at the cat in the tree.*

ineffective

Ineffective means not producing or giving the expected result. *She made an ineffective attempt to mend the broken chair.*

ineffectual

Ineffectual means not able to produce an intended result. *He was an ineffectual spokesperson for us in our protest against the closing of the park.*

similar words: **impossible**
contrasting words: **useful, possible**

usual   *adjective*

most frequently occurring. *We went to school in the **usual** way, forgetting that today was a public holiday.*

normal

Normal means standard, common, or regular. *It is normal to have rain at this time of the year.*

conventional

Conventional means relating to standards or rules, often unwritten, that everyone accepts. *There is a conventional way to dress to play tennis.*

orthodox

Orthodox means accepted or approved. *At a formal occasion, the orthodox dress for a man is a suit.*

customary

Customary means according to custom or the usual way of acting or doing things. *Shaking hands when you meet someone is customary.*

traditional

Traditional means according to the beliefs, customs, and stories that have been handed down from one generation to another. *Eating turkey at Thanksgiving is traditional in our family.*

contrasting words: **unusual, unconventional, strange,**

vague *adjective*

not clear or certain. *We saw **vague** shapes in the mist. I had a **vague** feeling of fear.*

indefinite	**Indefinite** means doubtful or not definite. *He was indefinite about his future plans.*
hazy	**Hazy** can mean confused or not distinct. *As I was coming out of the anesthetic, everything was hazy.*
faint	**Faint** can mean not clear or distinct. *I have only a faint idea of how to get there.*
fuzzy	**Fuzzy** can mean not clear or firm. *That was very fuzzy thinking, so please try again.*
approximate	**Approximate** can mean rough or not exact. *I can't even give you an approximate answer.*

similar words: **uncertain**
contrasting words: **precise, clear**

various *adjective*

different from one another. *Simon earned pocket money doing **various** jobs during vacation.*

diverse	**Diverse** means of many different kinds or forms. *The castaways found that they had diverse abilities and soon built a shelter.*
mixed	**Mixed** can mean made up of different sorts. *I brought a plate of mixed sandwiches to the picnic.*
assorted	**Assorted** means made up of different kinds. It is similar to **mixed** and you can usually choose either word. *I asked for a box of assorted chocolates.*
miscellaneous	**Miscellaneous** means made up of a mixture of different things. *He had a miscellaneous collection of pencils, rubber bands, and paper clips.*
motley	**Motley** means made up of different types or kinds. *It was a motley group of people who answered the Red Cross appeal for help.*

similar words: **unlike**
contrasting words: **similar**

view *noun*

whatever you can see from a particular place. *We all looked at the spectacular* **view** *from the top of the skyscraper.*

landscape	A **landscape** is a view of country scenery. *The landscape consisted of a beautiful green valley with a river running through it.*
vista	A **vista** is a view, especially one seen through an opening or passage. *From the farmhouse veranda we gazed at the vista of rolling hills.*
outlook	An **outlook** is what you see when looking out from a place. *My bedroom has a pleasant outlook.*
scene	A **scene** can be a view, especially one in which something is happening. *The main street of our town was a colorful scene on New Year's Eve.*

violence *noun*

rough, powerful, or damaging force. *The* **violence** *of the earthquake destroyed the village.*

severity	**Severity** can mean violence or sharpness. *The severity of the pain caused him to cry out.*
fury	**Fury** can mean violence or fierceness. *The hurricane raged with such fury that roofs were ripped off houses.*
vehemence	**Vehemence** can mean violence or unusual force. *The door was slammed with such vehemence that all the glasses rattled.*
ferocity	**Ferocity** is savage or cruel violence. *The ferocity of the attack on the defenseless man stunned the bystanders.*
brutality	**Brutality** is savage cruelty. *The brutality of the storm was evident from all the debris strewn along the shore.*

similar words: **force**

violent *adjective*

powerful and causing damage. *The **violent** earthquake killed many people and wrecked all the buildings in the city.*

fierce	**Fierce** can mean violent in force or strength. *Fierce winds buffeted the ship.*
furious	**Furious** means strong and violent. *A furious storm damaged crops over a wide area of land.*
ferocious	**Ferocious** can mean cruel in a violent way. *The intruders were frightened away by the ferocious guard dog.*
wild	**Wild** can mean violent or **fierce**. *Wild fighting broke out between the rebels and the government forces.*
forceful	**Forceful** can mean full of strength or power. *The forceful blow of the sledgehammer shattered the concrete.*

similar words: **intense, cruel**
contrasting words: **peaceful**

virtue *noun*

goodness or moral excellence. *The help she gave us is another sign of her **virtue**.*

decency	**Decency** is good or proper behavior. *They showed their decency by turning in the wallet full of money to the police.*
rectitude	**Rectitude** is good or honest behavior. It is a rather formal word. *She was made a judge because of her rectitude.*
character	**Character** can be goodness or integrity. *Your kind actions show that you are a person of character.*
principle	A **principle** can be a rule on which good behavior is based. *It is my principle not to lose my temper with a friend.*

visible *adjective*

able to be seen. *The lighthouse was **visible** a long way out to sea.*

noticeable **Noticeable** means able to be seen easily. *His scar was noticeable when he first came out of the hospital, but it soon faded.*

conspicuous **Conspicuous** means very **noticeable**. *She was conspicuous in her red dress.*

prominent **Prominent** means standing out. *Their house was so prominent because it was the only one in the street with two stories.*

exposed **Exposed** can mean open to view or not hidden. *I tried to hide the present, but I left one end exposed and my sister found it.*

overt **Overt** means not concealed. *He wore many gold chains and other expensive jewelry in an overt display of wealth.*

similar words: **obvious**
contrasting words: **invisible**

visit *verb*

to go to see someone or something. *I'm coming to **visit** on Sunday.*

call To **call** can mean to make a short visit. *We called at Daisy's house on our way home from school.*

drop in To **drop in** means to visit someone in an informal or casual way. *We dropped in to see why you didn't come to football practice.*

stop by To **stop by** means to visit somewhere on your way to another place. *We drove from Washington to Boston and stopped by to see our cousins in New York.*

blow in To **blow in** means to make an unexpected visit. This is only used in everyday language. *My friend blew into town.*

look in To **look in** means to come or go in for a short visit. *I decided to look in when I heard you were sick.*

vulgar *adjective*

ill-mannered, rude, and badly behaved. *He apologized for his **vulgar** manners during the concert.*

common **Common** can mean vulgar or impolite. *His common manners surprised and shocked his new boss.*

uncouth **Uncouth** means behaving in an ill-mannered or rough way. *I wish those uncouth commuters wouldn't push past us like that.*

tasteless **Tasteless** can mean not showing any sense of what is accepted as polite or correct behavior. *That is a tasteless way to talk about another person's sorrow.*

crude **Crude** can mean rude or in such bad taste that some people might be upset. *Nobody laughed at the crude joke.*

coarse **Coarse** can mean offensive or so rude that it disgusts you. *Such coarse behavior does not belong in the classroom.*

similar words: **rude**
contrasting words: **polite**

vulnerable *adjective*

likely or able to be hurt or wounded. *The injured bird was **vulnerable** to attack from other animals because it couldn't fly away.*

insecure **Insecure** can mean not safe from danger. *I'm in an insecure position at the top of this ladder.*

exposed **Exposed** means **open** to danger, attack, or injury. *We were in an exposed position on the cliff face and the winds howled around us.*

susceptible **Susceptible** means easily affected by something, especially something dangerous or harmful. *Because Mark was so weak after his long illness, he was very susceptible to colds.*

open **Open** can mean likely to be affected by danger or harm. *The goal was left open when the goalie left to chase the puck.*

contrasting words: **safe**

walk *verb*

to go by moving one foot after the other. *I missed the bus so I had to **walk** to school.*

amble   To **amble** means to walk at a relaxed, comfortable pace. *It was still early, so we ambled along.*

saunter   To **saunter** means to walk in an unhurried, carefree way. *I sauntered down to the beach munching an apple.*

stroll   To **stroll** means to walk in a slow, enjoyable way. *We strolled along the path listening to the birds and crickets.*

pad   To **pad** means to walk very softly. *I padded around in my bare feet so I wouldn't wake anyone.*

pace   To **pace** means to walk with regular steps. *The lion paced up and down inside its cage.*

---

similar words: **march, limp, trudge**
contrasting words: **frisk, dart, hurry, speed**

---

want *verb*

to wish for or have need of something. *I **want** money to buy my lunch.*

desire   To **desire** means to wish for something very much. This is a rather formal word. *After the long walk they desired nothing more than a comfortable bed.*

long for   To **long for** means to have a strong wish for something. *He longed for a canoe.*

crave   To **crave** means to want or need something desperately. *The day was so hot he craved a cool drink.*

covet   To **covet** means to want to have something very much, especially something that belongs to someone else. *She covets that car of yours.*

warlike   *adjective*

being ready or eager for fighting or conflict. *The Hurons were gentle, not **warlike**, people.*

martial   **Martial** means having to do with fighting or war. *Some people learn martial arts as a form of exercise.*

militant   **Militant** means fighting or ready to fight, especially for a cause. *The militant marchers were carefully briefed by their leaders.*

bellicose   **Bellicose** means warlike or ready to fight. *The bellicose settlers began fighting at the slightest dispute over their property rights.*

bloodthirsty   **Bloodthirsty** means wanting to kill. *The bloodthirsty pirates made all the prisoners walk the plank.*

hawkish   **Hawkish** means favoring a militant attitude toward other nations. It is mostly used about politicians. *We were worried by the diplomat's hawkish attitude at the summit conference.*

similar words: **aggressive**

warn   *verb*

to tell someone or to signal to someone that there may be danger ahead. *They **warned** us that the road was icy.*

caution   To **caution** is so similar to warn that you can usually use either word. *Dad cautioned us not to get into cars with strangers.*

forewarn   To **forewarn** means to warn beforehand. *The weather bureau forewarned us about the approaching tornado.*

alert   To **alert** means to warn someone of a possible attack or danger. *The scout alerted the general about the planned raid on the camp.*

alarm   To **alarm** can mean to give someone notice of danger to them. *The sentries alarmed the camp when they saw the approaching enemy.*

tip off   To **tip off** can mean to warn someone about trouble they are likely to have. This is more suited to everyday language. *The dishonest police officer tipped off the illegal gamblers about the police raid.*

similar words: **advise, predict**

wary *adjective*

on your guard against danger or trouble. *I was **wary** of the ice on the sidewalk.*

watchful   **Watchful** means looking out carefully for danger or trouble. *I was rescued by the watchful lifeguard.*

cautious   **Cautious** means being very wary when there is danger. *Be cautious when you cross a busy street.*

careful   **Careful** means taking care to avoid risks. *A careful driver never causes accidents.*

deliberate   **Deliberate** means carefully thought out. *My deliberate movements calmed the frightened horse.*

discreet   **Discreet** means taking trouble not to upset people. *Her discreet behavior made people trust her.*

---

similar words: **alert**
contrasting words: **rash**

waste *verb*

to spend or use up something without much result. *Don't **waste** your time being silly when you should be doing your homework.*

squander   To **squander** means to spend or use something wastefully. *The man had squandered all his money on gambling.*

fritter away   To **fritter away** means to waste something gradually. *She fritters away her money on useless things.*

blow   To **blow** can mean to waste something or **squander** it, usually all at one time. It is more suited to everyday language. *He blew all his money at the races and didn't have enough to catch the train home.*

splurge   To **splurge** means to spend money extravagantly or wastefully. *I splurged by taking my friends out to dinner.*

weak   *adjective*

not strong or healthy. *She is still very **weak** from her illness.*

frail	**Frail** means weak and delicate. *He helped the frail man up the stairs.*
feeble	**Feeble** means weak in body or mind. *Grandma became so feeble she had to use a walking stick.*
invalid	**Invalid** means weak and sick. *She has to look after her invalid father.*
helpless	**Helpless** means so weak that you are unable to do anything. *Pam felt helpless as she looked at all her homework assignments.*
debilitated	**Debilitated** means having a weakened body. *Many people were debilitated because of the long famine.*

contrasting words: **strong, hardy, energetic**

weaken   *verb*

to make someone or something weaker. *The lack of food and water had **weakened** him.*

sap	To **sap** means to weaken or destroy something gradually. *Worry has sapped his health.*
disable	To **disable** means to make someone unfit or unable to use part of his or her body. *A car accident disabled him.*
incapacitate	To **incapacitate** is so similar to **disable** that you can usually use either. *Illness has incapacitated many people.*
cripple	To **cripple** means to make someone unable to use one or more of his or her limbs. *A fall from a ladder crippled her when she was only five.*
paralyze	To **paralyze** means to make part of your body unable to move. *The stroke paralyzed her left side.*

similar words: **tire**
contrasting words: **strengthen**

wealth   *noun*

a large store of money and property. *Her **wealth** comes from her successful business ventures.*

money	**Money** can mean a person's wealth. *He made his money by inventing a robot to do the housework.*
fortune	A **fortune** is a great amount of **money** or property. *Anyone who invented a robot to do homework would make a fortune.*
riches	**Riches** means wealth or many and valuable possessions. *We stared at all the king's riches displayed before us.*
treasure	**Treasure** means a store of wealth or **riches,** especially precious metals or money. *We found the stolen treasure hidden in a cave.*
capital	**Capital** means the amount of money owned by a business or person. *They used nearly all their capital to buy the apartment building.*

contrasting words: **poverty**

wealthy   *adjective*

having a lot of money and valuable belongings. *My friends are **wealthy** enough to live in a large house and travel overseas every year.*

rich	**Rich** means having a lot of money. *The rich woman could buy expensive sports cars.*
prosperous	**Prosperous** means successful and wealthy. *The prosperous businessman worked hard to make his company grow.*
well-off	**Well-off** can mean wealthy enough to live a comfortable life. It is usually used in less formal language. *Most of the well-off people in our town have large homes near the water.*
affluent	**Affluent** means wealthy and **prosperous.** It can describe things as well as people. *The United States is an affluent country.*
loaded	**Loaded** can mean very wealthy. It is only suited to everyday language. *They were so loaded that they had their own private jet.*

contrasting words: **broke, poor**

weight   *noun*

a heavy object or mass. *I put a **weight** on the pile of papers so that they wouldn't blow away.*

burden
A **burden** can be something that is carried. *He lifted his heavy burden onto his back.*

load
A **load** is something carried on a cart or something similar. *She carted the load of paper into her office.*

ballast
Ballast is the heavy material carried by a ship to keep it steady, or by a balloon to control its height. *The cargo of iron bars acted as ballast for the ship.*

encumbrance
An **encumbrance** is a **burden** or something useless that weighs you down. *Please don't bring all those books, because they'll just be an encumbrance.*

well-behaved   *adjective*

behaving properly. *All her children are **well-behaved**.*

good
Good is so similar to well-behaved that you can usually use either. *Please be good when the visitors arrive.*

as good as gold
As good as gold means being as well-behaved as possible. It is more suited to everyday language. *It was an enjoyable outing because all the children were as good as gold.*

well-mannered
Well-mannered means polite or courteous. *Show that you are well-mannered by giving your seat to that elderly man.*

considerate
Considerate means behaving properly and thinking about other people's feelings. *It was considerate of you to let me have first choice.*

cooperative
Cooperative means behaving well and being helpful. *The cooperative children worked well together.*

similar words: **obedient, polite**
contrasting words: **naughty, disobedient**

wet   *adjective*

soaked with water or some other liquid. *My clothes were* **wet** *because I couldn't find shelter from the rain.*

damp	**Damp** means slightly wet. *We took the damp clothes off the line before the rain started.*
moist	**Moist** is so similar to **damp** you can usually choose either word. *His face was moist with perspiration.*
dank	**Dank** means unpleasantly **moist** or **damp**. *The back of the cave was dank from lack of sun and fresh air.*
soggy	**Soggy** means soaked or thoroughly wet. *The ground was soggy after a week of heavy rain.*
sodden	**Sodden** means completely soaked with liquid. *Our shoes were sodden after walking in the rain.*

contrasting words: **dry**

wet   *verb*

to soak something with water, or something similar. *We* **wet** *the ground thoroughly before planting the rosebush.*

dampen	To **dampen** means to make something slightly wet. *I dampened my handkerchief with water and rubbed the dirty mark from my cheek.*
moisten	To **moisten** means to make something moderately wet. *Moisten the sticker before you apply it to the window.*
water	To **water** means to pour water on something. *We water our garden every evening during the summer.*
irrigate	To **irrigate** means to supply water to something using a system of canals and pipes. *The farmers irrigated their crops from the river running through the town.*

similar words: **soak**

whisper *noun*

a very soft, quietly spoken sound. *We spoke in a **whisper** so that no one else would hear us.*

murmur A **murmur** is a whispered conversation or whispering sound. *As the curtain rose at the start of the play, you could still hear the murmur of the audience.*

sigh A **sigh** is the soft sound you make when you let your breath out slowly, usually when you're tired, sad, or relieved about something. *We all gave a sigh of relief when we heard that they had landed safely.*

tinkle A **tinkle** is a short, light, ringing sound. *We heard the tinkle of the wind chimes hanging on the veranda.*

undertone An **undertone** can be a low quiet sound when it refers to speech. *He was hard to hear because he spoke in an undertone.*

rustle A **rustle** is the very soft sound made when leaves, papers, or something similar rub gently together. *We heard a rustle among the leaves and a skunk appeared.*

contrasting words: **noise**

white *adjective*

having a color like milk. *Some soft, **white** clouds drifted across the blue summer sky.*

cream **Cream** means of a yellowish-white color. *We chose white for the ceiling and a rich, cream paint for the walls.*

pale **Pale** means having a whitish or colorless appearance. *There was no color in her pale face after her long illness.*

lily-white **Lily-white** means as white as the flower of the same name. *A little bleach made the shirts lily-white again.*

ivory **Ivory** means of a creamy white color. *All we could see were huge, ivory teeth as the shark opened its mouth wide.*

snowy **Snowy** means white like snow. *The old man stroked his snowy beard.*

whole   *adjective*

making up the maximum or proper quantity, number, or amount of anything. *She gave me the **whole** box of chocolates.*

complete	**Complete** means having all its parts. *She has a complete set of those stamps.*
full	**Full** can mean whole or **complete**. *We will probably never know the full story of what happened.*
entire	**Entire** means whole or without a break. *We played cards the entire evening.*
total	**Total** means making up or having to do with the whole of something. *They all put in enough money to pay the total cost of the farewell gift.*

similar words: **thorough**
contrasting words: **incomplete**

wide   *adjective*

having a large size from side to side. ***Wide** roads are much safer for motorists to drive on.*

broad	**Broad** means very wide. *The river is broad when it gets nearer the lake.*
extensive	**Extensive** means large in size. *They own an extensive piece of land in Texas.*
deep	**Deep** can mean going far in or back. *The cupboard was so deep that all our dishes fitted in it.*
outspread	**Outspread** means stretched out wide. *She stood to welcome us with outspread arms.*

contrasting words: **narrow**

winner   *noun*

someone who wins something or gains a victory. *She was the **winner** of the prize for the best painting.*

victor	A **victor** can be the winner in any game, fight, and so on. *Julie was the victor in the tennis match against Andrea.*
champion	A **champion** is someone who holds first place in a sport or contest. *He is the school's chess champion.*
master	A **master** can be someone who has a special skill at a game, like chess or bridge, and has won a certain number of formal competitions. *He is a golf master and competes in international tournaments.*
hit	A **hit** can be a great success. *She has been a hit at parties since she learned to play the guitar.*

wintry   *adjective*

cold and stormy like the season of winter. *It was a **wintry** day with lots of snow left on the mountains.*

chilly	**Chilly** means causing you to shiver or feel cold. *The water was chilly when we first dove in.*
arctic	**Arctic** means extremely cold, like the icy regions north of the Arctic Circle. *We had to dress very warmly to protect ourselves from the arctic winds of February.*
raw	**Raw** can mean damp and cold. *The air was raw as we climbed higher.*
bleak	**Bleak** means cold or harsh. *It was a bleak, gray day outside.*
glacial	**Glacial** means icy or as cold as ice. *The glacial weather and blizzards made a rescue mission impossible.*

similar words: **cold**
contrasting words: **fine, hot**

wipe   *verb*

to rub lightly in order to dry or clean. *Please **wipe** off the chalkboard for me.*

mop   To **mop** means to remove, clean, or rub something with a mop. *I mopped the water I had spilled on the floor.*

blot   To **blot** means to dry or soak something up. *He blotted the spilled juice with a cloth.*

sponge   To **sponge** means to wash or wipe something with a sponge, or something similar. *She sponged her little boy's dirty hands and face before lunch.*

swab   To **swab** means to clean or wipe with a large mop, or a piece of sponge, cloth, or cotton batting. *Go and swab the deck! The nurse swabbed the deep cut in my leg before putting a bandage on it.*

towel   To **towel** means to dry or wipe something with a towel. *I toweled my soaking hair until water stopped dripping down my neck.*

wisecrack   *noun*

a smart or amusing remark. *Her **wisecracks** are sometimes hurtful.*

quip   A **quip** is a clever or sarcastic remark. *I laughed at his quip that my room looked as though a hurricane had hit it.*

gibe   A **gibe** is a taunting or sarcastic remark. *He made a cruel gibe about my new shirt.*

in joke   An **in joke** is a joke that only the people who are involved in a particular situation can understand. *Every family has its in jokes.*

pun   A **pun** is a play on words that sound alike but are different in meaning. *The baker who was short of money made a pun when he said he would need some dough.*

witticism   A **witticism** is a joke or witty remark. *If you have to make a speech, try to include a few witticisms so people don't get bored.*

similar words: **joke**

wish   *noun*

something that you long for. *It is my **wish** to finish school and become a plumber.*

desire
A **desire** is a strong wish or need for something. *Her main desire in life is to help others less lucky than herself.*

craving
A **craving** is an eager or urgent **desire**. *Mountain climbers usually have a craving for excitement in their lives.*

will
Your **will** can be your wish or **desire**. *He was forced to sell his house against his will.*

yen
A **yen** is a strong wish or longing. *Many immigrants have a yen to return to their homelands for a visit.*

inclination
Inclination means a preference or tendency for something. *My inclination was to go to the beach rather than the farm for our vacation.*

wonderful   *adjective*

causing surprise and excitement. *It was a **wonderful** sight to see the rocket taking off.*

marvelous
Marvelous means wonderful and surprising. *It was marvelous to see the pictures of Earth taken from space.*

fabulous
Fabulous means wonderful and very pleasing. It is more suited to everyday language. *We had a fabulous time looking over the space museum.*

incredible
Incredible means hard to believe because it is so surprising. *It is incredible to think that people have walked on the moon.*

extraordinary
Extraordinary means unusual or remarkable. *Sending spacecraft into space is an extraordinary achievement.*

phenomenal
Phenomenal is very similar to **extraordinary** and means beyond what is ordinary or everyday. *What a phenomenal feeling it would be to travel through space!*

similar words: **astonishing, excellent, great**

work   *noun*

something that needs to be done using your muscles or mind. *Farming is hard work.*

labor	**Labor** is hard, tiring work. *The people were sweating after their labor in the fields.*
drudgery	**Drudgery** is hard, boring work. *He hated the drudgery of scrubbing the floors.*
effort	**Effort** is the use of physical strength. *He put a lot of effort into building the wall.*
exertion	**Exertion** is similar to **effort** and you can often use either word. *The exertion of her long swim tired her.*
industry	**Industry** is hard, careful, conscientious work. *His success on the test was due to his industry.*

contrasting words: **rest**

work   *verb*

to do something that needs an effort of your body or mind. *You should work when you're in class.*

labor	To **labor** means to do hard or tiring work. *They labored for four months building the house.*
toil	To **toil** means to work hard for a long time. *Each day the people toiled in the fields.*
slave	To **slave** means to work very hard, like a slave. *The farmer slaved to get his crops planted before sunset.*
slog	To **slog** means to work very hard. *We slogged through the mud until we reached the road.*
pull your weight	To **pull your weight** means to do your full share of the work. *You must pull your weight on this project or we won't finish on time.*

contrasting words: **rest, laze**

worry *verb*

to feel anxious or uneasy. *I **worry** when I am running late for school.*

bother To **bother** means to worry or give yourself trouble. *Don't bother about making your bed this morning.*

fret To **fret** means to be worried or annoyed. *Don't fret, I'll show you how to fix it!*

fuss To **fuss** means to worry or be anxious about unnecessary things. *That's too silly to fuss about.*

stew To **stew** means to worry constantly about something. *I knew you would stew for days about losing your wallet.*

sweat To **sweat** means to feel worried or impatient about something. This is more suited to everyday language. *We sweated about the results of the test.*

similar words: **fear**

worship *verb*

to feel love, esteem, and veneration for someone or something, sometimes in a religious way. *The children **worshiped** their granny. Many religions **worship** a Supreme Being.*

revere To **revere** means to feel deep admiration or a high regard for someone. *Jews revere Moses and all their prophets.*

respect To **respect** means to hold someone or something in high regard. *Navaho children are taught to respect their tribal elders.*

honor To **honor** means to show admiration or esteem for someone or something. *We honor the founders of our community by holding a parade every year.*

venerate To **venerate** means to pay honor to someone or something that you respect very much. *The people venerated their leader and organized a celebration when she retired.*

idolize To **idolize** means to worship someone or regard them with devotion, despite their faults. *She idolized her children and often didn't correct them when they were naughty.*

similar words: **love**
contrasting words: **insult, slander, hate**

471

write *verb*

to form letters or words with a pen, pencil, or similar thing. *Karen said she would* ***write*** *the results on the chalkboard.*

print	To **print** means to write something in separate letters rather than in cursive writing. *I printed the names of the towns on my map.*
scribble	To **scribble** means to write something hastily or carelessly. *I scribbled a note to Lisa to remind her to buy the comics, but she couldn't read my writing.*
scrawl	To **scrawl** means to write something untidily. *He scrawled his name in my autograph book.*
doodle	To **doodle** means to draw something or **scribble** while you are thinking about something else. *I doodled a pattern of triangles and circles while waiting for the lesson to begin.*
jot	To **jot** means to write or note something quickly. *I'll just jot down the directions to your place.*

yard *noun*

a piece of ground that surrounds or is close to a building such as a house or school. *I looked out my window and saw my friends waiting in the* ***yard***.

lawn	A **lawn** is a yard that is open and covered in grass that is cut short. *We water our front lawn late in the afternoon.*
enclosure	An **enclosure** is a piece of ground surrounded by a fence or some other barrier. *Behind the factory was an enclosure where the equipment was locked up.*
pen	A **pen** can be an **enclosure** built especially to keep animals. *The sick calf was put in a pen by itself.*
courtyard	A **courtyard** is a fairly small, open piece of land surrounded by walls or buildings. *At the center of the museum there is a courtyard where visitors can sit in the sun.*

yellow *adjective*
having a bright color like butter. *The sun was like a big, **yellow** ball in the sky.*

lemon — **Lemon** means having a clear light yellow color. *My favorite roses are the lemon ones.*

canary — **Canary** can mean having a very bright, clear yellow color. *You can see my sister's new canary car from a long way off.*

tawny — **Tawny** means having a yellowish-brown color. *I would love to stroke the lion's rich, tawny coat.*

buff — **Buff** means having a light yellow color. *Pass me the buff folder, please.*

blond — **Blond** means having a light yellow color. It is commonly used to refer to hair or furniture. *His blond hair turns even lighter in the summer sun.*

young *adjective*
being in the early stage of life or growth. *A **young** wolf is called a cub.*

juvenile — **Juvenile** can be very similar to **young**. It is usually used in more formal language. *Juvenile offenders are treated with compassion by the courts.*

adolescent — **Adolescent** means being older than a child but not yet an adult. *We spend most of our adolescent years at high school.*

junior — **Junior** means younger. *Heats for the junior club members will be held first.*

youthful — **Youthful** means being young, or looking or behaving as you did when you were young. *Their youthful high spirits led them into a lot of trouble.*

childish — **Childish** means belonging to or like a child. *Throwing a tantrum if you do not get your way is childish behavior.*

contrasting words: **adult**

Appendixes

Collective nouns for animals

Mammals

A *shrewdness* of apes
A *sloth* of bears
A *clowder* of cats
A *drove* of cattle
A *rag* of colts
A *herd* of elephants
A *skulk* of foxes
A *trip* of goats
A *drift* of hogs
A *team* of horses (while pulling)
A *troop* of kangaroos
A *leap* of leopards
A *pride* of lions
A *nest* of mice
A *labor* of moles
A *troop* of monkeys
A *string* of ponies
A *litter* of pups
A *warren* of rabbits
A *crash* of rhinoceroses
A *flock* of sheep
A *pod* of whales
A *pack* of wolves

Reptiles/Amphibians

A *knot* of toads
A *bed* of snakes
A *nest* of vipers

Birds

A *peep* of chickens
A *murder* of crows
A *paddling* of ducks (while swimming)
A *team* of ducks (while flying)
A *charm* of finches
A *gaggle* of geese (while standing)
A *skein* of geese (while flying)
A *brood* of hens
A *siege* of herons
A *parliament* of owls
A *company* of parrots
A *muster* of peacocks
A *colony* of penguins
A *host* of sparrows
A *rafter* of turkeys
A *wedge* of swans

Fish

A *school* of fish
A *smack* of jellyfish

Insects

A *colony* of ants
A *swarm* of bees
An *army* of caterpillars
A *cluster* of grasshoppers
A *plague* of locusts

Animal similes

Busy as a bee
Free as a bird
Quick as a bunny
Nervous as a colt
Sly as a fox
Sharp as a hawk
Gentle as a lamb

Happy as a lark
Quiet as a mouse
Stubborn as a mule
Wise as an owl
Strong as an ox
Proud as a peacock
Slow as a turtle

A sampling of U.S. wildlife

Mammals

badger
bat
beaver
bighorn sheep
black bear
bobcat
brown bear
buffalo (bison)
caribou
chipmunk
cougar (mountain lion, puma)
coyote
deer
elk
ermine
fisher
fox
gopher
grizzly bear
groundhog (woodchuck)
hare
kodiak bear
lynx
marten
mink
mole
moose
mountain goat
mouse
musk-ox
muskrat
otter
polar bear
porcupine
prairie dog
rabbit
raccoon
rat
sea lion
seal
shrew
skunk
squirrel
vole
walrus
weasel
whale
wolf
wolverine

Food fishes in native waters

albacore
bass
bonito
brook trout
carp
catfish
Chinook salmon
cod
coho salmon
Dolly Varden
eel
flounder
haddock
halibut
herring
mackerel
mahi mahi
muskellunge
perch
pickerel
pike
pompano (butterfish)
rainbow trout
shad
smelt
sole
sturgeon
walleye pike
whitefish

Birds

bald eagle
blackbird
blue jay
bobolink
bobwhite
bunting
buzzard
California condor
Canada goose
cardinal
chickadee
chicken hawk
cowbird
crane
crow
dove
duck
finch
flamingo
flicker
gannet
golden eagle
golden plover
goldfinch
gooney bird
grackle
grebe
grosbeak
grouse
guillemot
gull
hawk
heron
hummingbird
kingfisher
kite
kittiwake
loon
mallard
meadowlark
merganser
nene
nuthatch
oriole
osprey
owl
partridge
pelican
petrel
pheasant
pigeon
ptarmigan
purple martin
quail
robin
sandpiper
sapsucker
snow goose
sparrow
starling
swallow
swan
swift
tanager
teal
tern
thrush
towhee
turnstone
vireo
vulture
whippoorwill
woodcock
wood duck
woodpecker
wren

Snakes

brown snake
bull snake
coachwhip
coral snake

garter snake
green snake
king snake
racer
rat snake
rattlesnake
ringneck snake
water moccasin (cottonmouth)

Lizards

alligator lizard
beaded lizard
California legless lizard
gecko
Gila monster
horny toad
night lizard
skink

Ancient creatures

Meat-eating dinosaurs

Albertosaurus
Allosaurus
Ceratosaurus
Compsognathus
Tyrannosaurus

Plant-eating dinosaurs

Ankylosaurus
Apatosaurus
Brachiosaurus
Centrosaurus
Diplodocus
Edmontosaurus
Iguanadon
Protoceratops
Stegosaurus
Styracosaurus
Triceratops

Reptiles that lived in the sea

Ichthyosaurus
Mesasaurus
Plesiosaurus

Flying reptiles

Pteranodon
Pterodactyl
Rhamphorhynchus

Birds

Ichthyornis
Teratornis

Mammals

giant ground sloth
giant wombat
mammoth
mastodon
sabre-toothed tiger

Computer terms

backup
boot
buffer
chip
CPU
cursor
database
desktop computer
desktop publishing
disk
disk drive
DOS
dot-matrix printer
draft mode
file
floppy disk
graphics program
hard disk
hardware
interface
joystick

keyboard
laptop computer
laser printer
letter quality
menu
modem
monitor
mouse
network
port
printer
program
RAM
ROM
scanner
shareware
sheet feeder
software
spreadsheet
tractor feed
word processor

Space

Selected terms

asteroid
black hole
comet
constellation
dwarf star
galaxy
meteor
meteorite
Milky Way
moon
nebula
nova
planet
pulsar
quasar
red giant

satellite
star
sun
supernova
white dwarf

Our solar system — known planets, principal satellites

Mercury
Venus
Earth (moon)
Mars (Phobos, Deimos)
Jupiter (Io, Europa, Callisto, Ganymede)
Saturn (Titan, Rhea, Iapetus)
Uranus (Titania, Oberon)
Neptune (Triton)
Pluto (Charon)

World geography

Continents
Africa
Antarctica
Asia
Australia
Europe
North America
South America

Oceans
Arctic
Atlantic
Indian
Pacific

Major mountain ranges
Alps
Andes
Himalayas
Pyrenees
Rockies
Urals

Largest islands
Baffin Island
Borneo
Great Britain
Greenland
Honshu
Madagascar
New Guinea
Sulawesi
Sumatra
Victoria Island

Largest mountains
Communist Peak
Dhaulagiri
Everest
Godwin Austen (K2)

Kamet
Kanchenjunga
Makalu
Minya Konka
Nanga Parbat

Largest seas
Andaman Sea
Bering Sea
Caribbean Sea
East China Sea
Gulf of Mexico
Hudson Bay
Mediterranean Sea
North Sea
Sea of Japan
Sea of Okhotsk

Largest fresh-water lakes
Baikal
Erie
Great Bear
Great Slave
Huron
Malawi
Michigan
Superior
Tanganyika
Victoria

Principal rivers
Amazon
Amur
Congo
Huang-Ho
Lena
Mekong
Missouri-Mississippi
Nile
Ob-Irtysh
Yangtze

U.S. geography

States and their nicknames

Alabama	Cotton State	Texas	Lone Star State
Alaska	Last Frontier	Utah	Beehive State
Arizona	Grand Canyon State	Vermont	Green Mountain State
Arkansas	Wonder State	Virginia	Old Dominion
California	Golden State	Washington	Evergreen State
Colorado	Centennial State	West Virginia	Mountain State
Connecticut	Constitution State	Wisconsin	Badger State
Delaware	Diamond State	Wyoming	Equality State
Florida	Sunshine State		
Georgia	Cracker State		
Hawaii	The Aloha State		
Idaho	Gem State		
Illinois	Prairie State		
Indiana	Hoosier State		
Iowa	Hawkeye State		
Kansas	Sunflower State		
Kentucky	Bluegrass State		
Louisiana	Pelican State		
Maine	Pine Tree State		
Maryland	Old Line State		
Massachusetts	Bay State		
Michigan	Wolverine State		
Minnesota	Gopher State		
Mississippi	Magnolia State		
Missouri	Show-Me State		
Montana	Treasure State		
Nebraska	Cornhusker State		
Nevada	Silver State		
New Hampshire	Granite State		
New Jersey	Garden State		
New Mexico	Land of Enchantment		
New York	Empire State		
North Carolina	Tar Heel State		
North Dakota	Flickertail State		
Ohio	Buckeye State		
Oklahoma	Sooner State		
Oregon	Beaver State		
Pennsylvania	Keystone State		
Rhode Island	Little Rhody		
South Carolina	Palmetto State		
South Dakota	Coyote State		
Tennessee	Volunteer State		

Largest lakes

Erie
Great Salt Lake
Huron
Michigan
Okeechobee
Ontario
St. Claire
Superior

Principal rivers

Missouri
Mississippi
St. Lawrence
Rio Grande
Arkansas
Colorado
Columbia
Snake
Red
Ohio

Tallest mountains

Mt. McKinley, Alaska
Mt. Foraker, Alaska
Mt. Whitney, California
Mt. Elbert, Colorado
Mt. Harvard, Colorado
Mt. Massive, Colorado
Mt. Rainier, Washington
Mt. Williamson, California
Blanca Peak, Colorado
Uncompahgre Peak, Colorado

U.S. government terms

Judicial branch

Supreme Court
Chief Justice
Associate Justices
U.S. District Courts
U.S. District Attorney

Legislative branch

Senate
House of Representatives
Senator
Congressman (Representative)
President Pro tempore of the Senate
Speaker of the House

Executive branch

President   Cabinet
Vice-President   Ambassador

State and local Government

Governor
Lieutenant Governor
State Senator
Assemblyman
State Attorney
Mayor
City Manager
Alderman
City Councilman

Music

Wind instruments

bagpipes
bassoon
clarinet
contrabassoon
English horn
fife
flute
harmonica
kazoo
oboe
panpipe
piccolo
recorder
saxophone
tin whistle

Brass instruments

bugle
cornet
euphonium
flugelhorn
French horn
mellophone

sousaphone
trombone
trumpet
tuba

String instruments

cello
double bass
viola
viola da gamba
violin

Percussion instruments

Drums

bongo
conga
kettledrum
snare drum
tabor
tambourine
timbal
timpani
tom-tom

Bells and gongs

carillon
cowbell
cymbal
triangle

Chimes

celesta
glockenspiel
marimba
vibraphone (vibes)
xylophone

Other percussion instruments

castanet
maraca
song sticks (claves)

Keyboard instruments

clavichord
harmonium
harpsichord
organ
piano (pianoforte)
piano accordion
synthesizer

Guitars and harps

balalaika
banjo
bass
bouzouki
dulcimer
guitar
harp
koto
lute
lyre
mandolin
samisen
sitar
ukelele
zither

Sweet sounds

concordant
dulcet
harmonious
in tune
lyrical
melodious
musical
rhythmic
tonal
tuneful

Harsh sounds

atonal
discordant
dissonant
flat
grating
jarring
off-key
off-pitch
out of tune
sharp

Some musical terms

beat
harmony
key
melody
note
pitch
rest
rhythm
scale
tempo
time
tone
volume

Feelings . . .

affection	gratitude
amusement	grief
anger	happiness
annoyance	hate
anxiety	hope
bliss	humility
boredom	insecurity
composure	jealousy
confidence	joy
courage	kindness
curiosity	loneliness
depression	love
despair	nastiness
disliking	pity
distress	pride
ecstasy	rage
envy	regret
excitement	sadness
fear	tolerance
friendship	wonder
glee	worry

. . . and how we show them

cower	shout
cry	shriek
cuddle	shrug
dance	sigh
embrace	sing
frown	smile
giggle	smirk
grimace	squeal
grin	squint
gulp	squirm
hug	strut
jump	sulk
kiss	titter
laugh	whine
pout	whistle
scowl	wiggle
scream	wink

Environmental phenomena

acid rain

avalanche

blizzard

drought

earthquake

fault

flood

fog

hail

hurricane

northern lights

lightning

rain

rainbow

sleet

smog

snow

storm

tornado

thunder

tidal wave

volcano

Index

Guide to the index

What do you do when you want to describe a recent holiday and the only word you can think of is "nice"?

. . . Simple! Start at the INDEX, the back section of the book. The Index lists all the words in the thesaurus in alphabetical order. At the top of the page you will find the first and last words on that page.

Look at the sample of the index below. You will find "nice" listed twice. These two entries direct you to two different meanings of this word.

The first time "nice" is listed it is printed in bold (darker) type, along with its part of speech and the page it is on. The bold type tells you that **nice** is a keyword. This means that it is the first word in a word group that has the overall meaning "nice." This word group can be found on page 276 and includes the other adjectives *pleasant, enjoyable, lovely, acceptable, welcome.* "Pleasant" and "enjoyable" would probably be better words than "nice" to describe your holiday.

The second time "nice" is listed it is printed in normal type, along with its part of speech, the keyword **kind** in bold type, and its page number. Obviously, you would not want to describe your holiday as "kind," so you would not bother to look up this word group to find other useful words. However, if you wanted to describe a nice person you met on your holiday, you could look up **kind** on page 231. Here you will find other words with the overall meaning "kind." These are *thoughtful, considerate, unselfish, well-meaning.* Any one of these words could be used to describe your friend.

So, when you look up a word in the index, it guides you to the right meaning of the word as well as to the page on which you will find it.

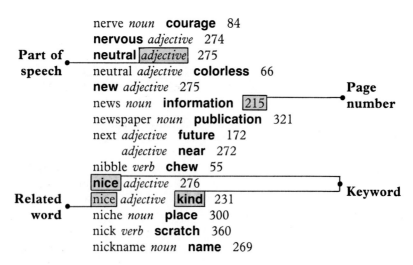

490

Aa

abandon *verb* **quit** 325
abate *verb* **decrease** 97
abbreviate *verb* **shorten** 373
abduct *verb* 1
abhor *verb* **hate** 190
able *adjective* **competent** 70
abnormal *adjective* **strange** 402
abode *noun* **home** 198
abolish *verb* **cancel** 49
abominable *adjective* **bad** 26
abominate *verb* **hate** 190
abridge *verb* **shorten** 373
abridged *adjective* **brief** 42
abrupt *adjective* 1
abrupt *adjective* **sudden** 408
abscond *verb* **flee** 157
absent-minded
  adjective **dreamy** 120
absorb *verb* **learn** 237
absurd *adjective* **ridiculous** 347
abundant *adjective* 2
abuse *verb* **maltreat** 251
abysmal *adjective* **bad** 26
accentuate *verb* **emphasize** 126
accept *verb* **believe** 32
acceptable *adjective* **nice** 276
accident *noun* **misfortune** 262
accidental *adjective* 2
accident-prone *adjective* **clumsy** 63
acclaim *verb* 3
accommodating *adjective* **helpful** 193
accompanist *noun* **musician** 268
accompany *verb* 3
accomplish *verb* 4
accomplishment
  noun **achievement** 5
accumulate *verb* **gather** 173
  verb **increase** 209
accurate *adjective* **precise** 310
  adjective **true** 438
accuse *verb* 4

ace *noun* **expert** 141
ache *noun* **pain** 290
achieve *verb* **accomplish** 4
achievement *noun* 5
acid *adjective* **sour** 392
acknowledge *verb* **admit** 6
acknowledgment *noun* **reaction** 328
acquaintance *noun* **friend** 167
acquire *verb* **get** 175
acquittal *noun* **pardon** 290
acquit yourself *verb* **behave** 31
act *noun* **deed** 98
action *noun* **deed** 98
active *adjective* **busy** 46
actor *adjective* **entertainer** 132
actual *adjective* 5
adage *noun* **saying** 357
adamant *adjective* **stubborn** 404
adapt *verb* **change** 53
add *verb* 6
add up *verb* **count** 82
additional *adjective* **extra** 143
adept *adjective* **skillful** 382
adequate *adjective* **sufficient** 408
adhesive *noun* **glue** 178
adjacent *adjective* **near** 272
adjourn *verb* **defer** 100
adjudicate *verb* **judge** 228
administrator *noun* **manager** 252
admit *verb* 6
admonish *verb* **scold** 359
adolescent *adjective* **young** 473
adopt *verb* **take** 415
adore *verb* **love** 247
adroit *adjective* **skillful** 382
adult *adjective* 7
advance *verb* 7
  verb **go** 179
advance *verb* **further** 171
advantageous *adjective* **useful** 451
adversary *noun* **enemy** 130
advertise *verb* **publish** 321
advise *verb* 8
advise *verb* **inform** 214
advise against *verb* **discourage** 112

adviser *noun* 8
advocate *noun* **lawyer** 235
    verb **advise** 8
    verb **approve** 17
affected *adjective* **pompous** 304
affectionate *adjective* **loving** 248
affluent *adjective* **wealthy** 462
affront *verb* **insult** 220
afraid *adjective* **frightened** 168
agent *noun* **clerk** 59
aggravate *verb* **annoy** 14
aggressive *adjective* 9
agile *adjective* 9
agitated *adjective* **upset** 450
agrarian *adjective* **country** 83
agree *verb* 10
agreeable *adjective* 10
aid *noun* **help** 192
    verb **help** 192
aide *noun* **helper** 193
ailing *adjective* **sick** 377
air *noun* **appearance** 17
air-condition *verb* **cool** 79
akin *adjective* **similar** 379
alarm *verb* **frighten** 168
    verb **warn** 459
alarmed *adjective* **frightened** 168
alert *adjective* 11
alert *verb* **warn** 459
alias *noun* **name** 269
alien *adjective* **foreign** 163
alight *verb* **land** 233
alike *adjective* **similar** 379
allege *verb* **accuse** 4
alleviate *verb* **comfort** 68
allied *adjective* **related** 334
allocate *verb* **distribute** 118
allocation *noun* **share** 369
allot *verb* **distribute** 118
allotment *noun* **share** 369
allow *verb* 11
allowance *noun* **gift** 176
all right *adjective* **good** 179
all thumbs *adjective* **clumsy** 63
allude to *verb* **hint** 196

alone *adjective* **lonely** 246
aloof *adjective* **unfriendly** 445
alter *verb* **change** 53
altercation *noun* **argument** 18
alternative
    adjective **unconventional** 442
    noun **choice** 56
amalgamate *verb* **combine** 67
amass *verb* **gather** 173
amateur *adjective* **inexperienced** 212
amateurish
    adjective **incompetent** 208
amazed *adjective* **astonished** 21
amazing *adjective* **astonishing** 22
amber *adjective* **orange** 285
ambiguous *adjective* **confusing** 77
ambivalent *adjective* **confused** 77
amble *verb* **walk** 458
ambush *noun* **attack** 22
    verb **catch** 51
amend *verb* **correct** 81
amiable *adjective* **agreeable** 10
amnesty *noun* **pardon** 290
ample *adjective* **abundant** 2
    adjective **big** 34
amplify *verb* **enlarge** 131
    verb **expand** 139
amusing *adjective* **funny** 171
analyse *verb* **examine** 135
analysis *noun* **inquiry** 216
ancestor *noun* 12
ancient *adjective* **old** 282
anger *noun* 12
anger *verb* 13
angry *adjective* 13
anguish *noun* **misery** 261
animated *adjective* **energetic** 131
animosity *noun* **dislike** 113
annex *verb* **take** 415
annihilate *verb* **destroy** 105
announce *verb* **inform** 214
annoy *verb* 14
annoyed *adjective* 14
annoying *adjective* 15
annul *verb* **cancel** 49

answer *verb* 15
answer *noun* **reaction** 328
antagonist *noun* **enemy** 130
antagonistic *adjective* **defiant** 101
antecedents *noun* **ancestor** 12
anthem *noun* **song** 391
anthology *noun* **book** 38
anticipate *verb* **expect** 140
anticlimax *noun* **disappointment** 109
antipathy *noun* **dislike** 113
antiquated *adjective* **old-fashioned** 282
antique *adjective* **old** 282
antisocial *adjective* **unfriendly** 445
antithetical *adjective* **opposite** 284
anxious *adjective* **enthusiastic** 132
    adjective **nervous** 274
apathetic *adjective* 16
ape *verb* **mimic** 259
aperture *noun* **hole** 197
apex *noun* **top** 432
appall *verb* **shock** 372
apparel *noun* **clothing** 61
apparent *adjective* **obvious** 280
apparition *noun* **ghost** 175
appeal to *verb* **please** 301
appear *verb* 16
appearance *noun* 17
appease *verb* **pacify** 289
append *verb* **add** 6
appetizing *adjective* **delicious** 102
applaud *verb* **acclaim** 3
appointment *noun* **meeting** 256
    noun **position** 306
appraise *verb* **judge** 228
appreciate *verb* **like** 241
appreciation *noun* **thanks** 423
appreciative *adjective* **grateful** 182
apprehend *verb* **capture** 49
apprehensive *adjective* **nervous** 274
apprentice *noun* **student** 405
apprenticeship *noun* **profession** 316
approach *noun* **method** 258
appropriate *verb* **take** 415
approval *noun* **permission** 296

approve *verb* 17
approximate *adjective* **vague** 453
apt *adjective* **likely** 242
aqua *adjective* **blue** 36
arbitrary *adjective* **irrational** 224
arbitrate *verb* **negotiate** 274
archaic *adjective* **old-fashioned** 282
arctic *adjective* **winter** 467
arduous *adjective* **difficult** 106
argue *verb* 18
argument *noun* 18
argumentative *adjective* 19
arid *adjective* **dry** 122
arise *verb* **happen** 187
aristocratic
    adjective **distinguished** 117
aroma *noun* **smell** 386
arrange *verb* 19
arrange *verb* **plan** 301
arrangement *noun* **deal** 96
arrest *verb* **capture** 49
arrive *verb* **come** 67
arrogant *adjective* **proud** 319
artful *adjective* **cunning** 90
articulate *adjective* **fluent** 160
    verb **pronounce** 317
ascend *verb* **climb** 60
ascertain *verb* **realize** 329
as good as gold
    adjective **well-behaved** 463
ashamed *adjective* **sorry** 391
ask *verb* 20
aspect *noun* **appearance** 17
asphyxiate *verb* **suffocate** 409
assassinate *verb* **kill** 230
assault *noun* **attack** 22
    verb **attack** 23
assemble *verb* 20
assemble *verb* **combine** 67
assembly *noun* **club** 62
assent *verb* **agree** 10
assess *verb* **examine** 135
assets *noun* **property** 318
assignation *noun* **meeting** 256
assignment *noun* **task** 417

assimilate *verb* **learn** 237
assist *verb* **help** 192
assistance *noun* **help** 192
assistant *noun* **helper** 193
associate *noun* 21
associated *adjective* **related** 334
associate with *verb* **accompany** 3
association *noun* **club** 62
assorted *adjective* **various** 453
assortment *noun* **mixture** 264
assume *verb* **believe** 32
astonished *adjective* 21
astonishing *adjective* 22
astounded *adjective* **astonished** 21
astounding *adjective* **astonishing** 22
astute *adjective* **shrewd** 375
asylum *noun* **refuge** 333
athletic *adjective* **agile** 9
atonal *adjective* **discordant** 111
atrocious *adjective* **bad** 26
atrophy *verb* **shrink** 376
attach *verb* **add** 6
attack *noun* 22
attack *verb* 23
attack *verb* **attempt** 24
attain *verb* **accomplish** 4
attempt *noun* 23
attempt *verb* 24
attendant *noun* **helper** 193
attend to *verb* **concentrate** 73
attentive *adjective* **alert** 11
          adjective **careful** 50
attire *noun* **clothing** 61
attitude *noun* **manner** 252
         noun **opinion** 283
attorney *noun* **lawyer** 235
attract *verb* 24
attract *verb* **please** 301
attractive *adjective* 25
attractive *adjective* **pretty** 312
auction *verb* **sell** 364
audition *noun* **test** 422
augment *verb* **enlarge** 131
auspicious *adjective* **lucky** 248
austere *adjective* **strict** 403

authentic *adjective* **genuine** 174
authoritarian *adjective* **bossy** 40
authority *noun* **expert** 141
authorize *verb* **allow** 11
authorized *adjective* **legal** 238
autocratic *adjective* **bossy** 40
autonomous
    adjective **independent** 210
available *adjective* **ready** 329
avant-garde *adjective* **new** 275
avaricious *adjective* **greedy** 183
average *adjective* **ordinary** 286
averse *adjective* **unwilling** 449
aversion *noun* **dislike** 113
avid *adjective* **enthusiastic** 132
avoid *verb* 25
awake *adjective* **alert** 11
award *noun* **prize** 315
       verb **give** 176
awareness *noun* **feeling** 151
awful *adjective* **unpleasant** 447
awkward *adjective* **clumsy** 63
azure *adjective* **blue** 36

Bb

babble *verb* **rave** 327
back *verb* **reverse** 346
backing *noun* **help** 192
backlog *noun* **excess** 137
bad *adjective* 26
badly behaved *adjective* **naughty** 271
baffle *verb* **puzzle** 324
bake *verb* **toast** 431
balance *verb* **steady** 399
bald *adjective* **bare** 28
ball *noun* 26
ballad *noun* **song** 391
ballast *noun* **weight** 463
balmy *adjective* **fine** 155
bamboozle *verb* **confuse** 76
ban *verb* 27
banal *adjective* **mediocre** 255

band *noun* **group** 185
bandit *noun* 27
bang *verb* **beat** 29
banish *verb* **expel** 140
bank *verb* **store** 402
bankrupt *adjective* **broke** 44
bar *verb* **ban** 27
    verb **block** 36
barbaric *adjective* **cruel** 89
barbecue *verb* **toast** 431
bare *adjective* 28
bargain *noun* **deal** 96
bargain for *verb* **expect** 140
barge in *verb* **intrude** 222
barricade *verb* **block** 36
barrier *noun* **obstacle** 280
base *noun* **bottom** 41
    noun **support** 411
bashful *adjective* **shy** 376
basin *noun* **lake** 233
bat *verb* **hit** 196
battle *noun* **fight** 153
bawl *verb* **cry** 90
    verb **shout** 373
bay *noun* 28
be *verb* **live** 245
beach *noun* **shore** 372
beam *verb* **shine** 370
bear *verb* **produce** 315
bearing *noun* **manner** 252
bear out *verb* **prove** 320
beat *verb* 29
beat *noun* **rhythm** 346
    verb **defeat** 99
    verb **pass** 291
    verb **throb** 429
beat up *verb* **attack** 23
beautiful *adjective* 29
bed *noun* **bottom** 41
bedraggled *adjective* **scruffy** 361
beefy *adjective* **stocky** 400
beeline *noun* **course** 84
befriend *verb* 30
befuddle *verb* **confuse** 76
beg *verb* **ask** 20

begin *verb* 30
beginning *noun* **start** 397
beguile *verb* **charm** 53
behave *verb* 31
behavior *noun* 31
beholden *adjective* **grateful** 182
beige *adjective* **brown** 44
belabor *verb* **emphasize** 126
belief *noun* **religion** 335
believable *adjective* 32
believe *verb* 32
belittle *verb* **insult** 220
bellicose *adjective* **warlike** 459
belligerent *adjective* **aggressive** 9
bellow *verb* **shout** 373
belly *noun* **inside** 218
belongings *noun* **property** 318
be lost in thought
    verb **daydream** 95
bemused *adjective* **dreamy** 120
bend *verb* 33
beneficial *adjective* **useful** 451
benefit *verb* **thrive** 428
bent *adjective* **crooked** 87
beseech *verb* **ask** 20
best *adjective* 33
betray *verb* 34
better *verb* **improve** 206
bewilder *verb* **puzzle** 324
bewildering *adjective* **confusing** 77
bewitch *verb* **charm** 53
bias *verb* **influence** 213
biased *adjective* **narrow-minded** 270
bicker *verb* **disagree** 108
bid *noun* **offer** 281
big *adjective* 34
big-headed *adjective* **conceited** 73
bight *noun* **bay** 28
bigoted
    adjective **narrow-minded** 270
billow *verb* **protrude** 319
bistro *noun* **restaurant** 343
bitter *adjective* **resentful** 340
    adjective **sour** 392
bizarre *adjective* **strange** 402

blab *verb* 35
black *adjective* 35
blackmail *verb* **threaten** 427
bland *adjective* **tasteless** 418
blank *adjective* **empty** 127
blanket *verb* **cover** 84
blaring *adjective* **loud** 247
blasé *adjective* **bored** 39
blaze *verb* **shine** 370
blazing *adjective* **hot** 200
bleached *adjective* **colorless** 66
bleak *adjective* **dreary** 120
　　　adjective **wintry** 467
blend *verb* **combine** 67
bless *verb* **approve** 17
blessed *adjective* **holy** 198
blissful *adjective* **joyful** 228
blithe *adjective* **happy** 188
blitz *noun* **attack** 22
block *verb* 36
blockade *verb* **block** 36
blond *adjective* **yellow** 473
bloodshot *adjective* **rosy** 348
bloodthirsty *adjective* **warlike** 459
bloom *verb* **flourish** 158
　　　verb **thrive** 428
blossom *verb* **flourish** 158
　　　verb **thrive** 428
blot *verb* **wipe** 468
blow *noun* **disappointment** 109
　　　noun **misfortune** 262
　　　verb **gasp** 172
　　　verb **waste** 460
blow hot and cold
　verb **fluctuate** 159
blow in *verb* **visit** 456
blow your own horn *verb* **boast** 37
blue *adjective* 36
blue *adjective* **miserable** 261
　　　noun **mistake** 263
bluff *verb* **trick** 436
blunder *noun* **mistake** 263
blunt *adjective* **abrupt** 1
blurt out *verb* **admit** 6
bluster *verb* **boast** 37

board *noun* **council** 81
　　　verb **reside** 341
boast *verb* 37
boaster *noun* **show-off** 374
bog *noun* **swamp** 413
bogus *adjective* **fake** 145
bohemian
　adjective **unconventional** 442
boil *verb* 37
boil *verb* **swelter** 414
bold *adjective* 38
bold *adjective* **brave** 41
bonus *noun* **profit** 316
book *noun* 38
book *verb* **accuse** 4
bookkeeper *noun* **clerk** 59
boom *verb* **thrive** 428
boost *verb* **enlarge** 131
booty *noun* **loot** 246
border *noun* **edge** 125
bored *adjective* 39
boring *adjective* 39
borrow *verb* **take** 415
boss *noun* 40
bossy *adjective* 40
botch *verb* **bungle** 45
bother *verb* **worry** 471
bottom *noun* 41
boulder *noun* **stone** 401
bounce back *verb* **recover** 331
bouncy *adjective* **elastic** 126
bound *verb* **jump** 229
boundary *noun* **outskirts** 287
bountiful *adjective* **abundant** 2
bouquet *noun* **smell** 386
bowl over *verb* **overturn** 288
　　　verb **shock** 372
box in *verb* **enclose** 127
boy *noun* **male** 250
boycott *verb* **ban** 27
brace *verb* **strengthen** 403
brag *verb* **boast** 37
braggart *noun* **show-off** 374
brainstorm *noun* **thought** 426
brainwash *verb* **influence** 213

brainy *adjective* **clever** 60
braise *verb* **boil** 37
brand *verb* **label** 232
brave *adjective* 41
bravery *noun* **courage** 84
brawl *noun* **fight** 153
brawny *adjective* **strong** 404
brazen *adjective* **bold** 38
break *noun* 42
break *noun* **rest** 342
breakable *adjective* **fragile** 165
break off *verb* **cancel** 49
        verb **separate** 366
break up *verb* **laugh** 234
breathe *verb* **live** 245
breathe your last *verb* **die** 106
breathtaking *adjective* **exciting** 138
breed *verb* **produce** 315
bridge *verb* **cross** 88
brief *adjective* 42
brief *adjective* **momentary** 265
        noun **report** 340
brigand *noun* **bandit** 27
bright *adjective* 43
bright *adjective* **clever** 60
        adjective **colorful** 66
brighten *verb* **recover** 331
brilliant *adjective* **bright** 43
        adjective **clever** 60
brim *noun* **edge** 125
bring off *verb* **accomplish** 4
brink *noun* **edge** 125
bristly *adjective* **rough** 349
brittle *adjective* **fragile** 165
broad *adjective* **wide** 466
broadcast *verb* **publish** 321
broad-minded *adjective* 43
broke *adjective* 44
broker *noun* **seller** 364
brood *verb* **grieve** 184
brown *adjective* 44
browse through *verb* **read** 328
brunette *adjective* **brown** 44
brusque *adjective* **abrupt** 1
brutal *adjective* **cruel** 89

brutality *noun* **violence** 454
buccaneer *noun* **bandit** 27
buckled *adjective* **crooked** 87
budge *verb* **move** 266
buff *adjective* **yellow** 473
        verb **polish** 303
bug *verb* **irritate** 224
build *verb* 45
build *noun* **shape** 369
bulge *verb* **protrude** 319
bulky *adjective* **big** 34
bulldoze *verb* **force** 162
bulletin *noun* **report** 340
bully *verb* **force** 162
bump into *verb* **meet** 256
bumpy *adjective* **rough** 349
bunch *noun* **group** 185
bungle *verb* 45
buoyant *adjective* **optimistic** 284
burden *noun* **weight** 463
burglar *noun* **thief** 424
burly *adjective* **stocky** 400
burn *verb* **shine** 370
        verb **swelter** 414
burnish *verb* **polish** 303
bursting *adjective* **full** 170
bushed *adjective* **tired** 431
business *noun* **job** 226
busy *adjective* 46
butter up *verb* **flatter** 156
butt in *verb* **intrude** 222
buy *verb* 46
buyer *noun* 47
buzz *verb* **throb** 429
bygone *adjective* **past** 292

Cc

cackle *verb* **laugh** 234
cacophonous
        adjective **discordant** 111
café *noun* **restaurant** 343
cafeteria *noun* **restaurant** 343

cagey *adjective* **secretive** 362
cajole *verb* **flatter** 156
calamity *noun* **disaster** 110
calculate *verb* 47
call *verb* **name** 269
   verb **visit** 456
calling *noun* **profession** 316
callous *adjective* 48
callow *adjective* **inexperienced** 212
calm *adjective* 48
calm *verb* **pacify** 289
camouflage *verb* **hide** 194
canary *adjective* **yellow** 473
cancel *verb* 49
candid *adjective* **frank** 165
candied *adjective* **sweet** 414
canny *adjective* **shrewd** 375
cantankerous
   adjective **argumentative** 19
capable *adjective* **competent** 70
caper *verb* **frisk** 169
capital *noun* **city** 57
   noun **wealth** 462
capitulate *verb* **give in** 177
capricious *adjective* **fickle** 152
captive *noun* **prisoner** 314
capture *verb* 49
carcinogenic
   adjective **poisonous** 303
career *noun* **job** 226
care for *verb* **love** 247
careful *adjective* 50
careful *adjective* **wary** 460
careless *adjective* 50
caricature *verb* **mimic** 259
carriage *noun* **manner** 252
carry *verb* 51
carry through *verb* **accomplish** 4
carry yourself *verb* **behave** 31
casual *adjective* **careless** 50
   adjective **informal** 214
   adjective **temporary** 421
catastrophe *noun* **disaster** 110
catch *verb* 51
catch on *verb* **realize** 329

caucus *noun* **council** 81
cause *verb* 52
caution *verb* **warn** 459
cautious *adjective* **wary** 460
cease *verb* **end** 129
celebrate *verb* **rejoice** 334
celebrated *adjective* **famous** 147
celebrity *noun* **star** 396
cell *noun* **room** 348
cement *noun* **glue** 178
censor *verb* **ban** 27
censure *verb* **fault** 150
center *noun* 52
ceremonial *adjective* **formal** 164
cerise *adjective* **purple** 323
certain *adjective* **sure** 412
   adjective **true** 438
chafe *verb* **roughen** 350
chain *noun* **series** 367
chamber *noun* **room** 348
champion *noun* **winner** 467
   verb **befriend** 30
championship *noun* **competition** 71
chance *adjective* **accidental** 2
   noun **fate** 149
change *verb* 53
changeable *adjective* **fickle** 152
change your tune *verb* **fluctuate** 159
channel *noun* **groove** 185
chaotic *adjective* **untidy** 448
chap *verb* **roughen** 350
chaperone *verb* **accompany** 3
character *noun* **virtue** 455
charcoal *adjective* **gray** 182
charge *noun* **price** 313
   verb **accuse** 4
   verb **attack** 23
charisma *noun* **influence** 213
charismatic *adjective* **attractive** 25
charitable *adjective* **generous** 174
charity *noun* **help** 192
charm *verb* 53
charm *verb* **please** 301
charming *adjective* **agreeable** 10
chase *verb* **follow** 161

chastise *verb* **punish** 322
chat *verb* **talk** 416
chatty *adjective* **talkative** 416
cheap *adjective* 54
cheat *verb* 54
cheat *noun* **crook** 87
check *verb* **test** 422
checkup *noun* **test** 422
cheeky *adjective* **rude** 351
cheer *verb* **acclaim** 3
cheerful *adjective* **happy** 188
cheerless *adjective* **dreary** 120
cherish *verb* **love** 247
chew *verb* 55
chic *adjective* 55
chicken out *verb* **cower** 85
chief *adjective* **main** 249
        noun **boss** 40
childish *adjective* **young** 473
chill *verb* **cool** 79
chilly *adjective* **wintry** 467
chime *verb* **ring** 347
chink *noun* **hole** 197
chivalrous *adjective* **polite** 304
choice *noun* 56
choke *verb* **suffocate** 409
chomp *verb* **chew** 55
choose *verb* 56
choose *verb* **intend** 220
chore *noun* **task** 417
chortle *verb* **laugh** 234
chubby *adjective* **fat** 148
chuck *verb* **throw** 429
chuckle *verb* **laugh** 234
circumvent *verb* **outwit** 288
citified *adjective* **civic** 57
city *noun* 57
civic *adjective* 57
claim *noun* **demand** 102
clamber up *verb* **climb** 60
clap *verb* **acclaim** 3
clarify *verb* **explain** 142
clash *noun* **conflict** 76
        verb **argue** 18
clasp *verb* **hold** 197

class *noun* **grade** 181
        noun **lesson** 239
classified *adjective* **secret** 361
classify *verb* **arrange** 19
classy *adjective* **distinguished** 117
clay *noun* **earth** 123
clean *adjective* 58
clean *verb* 58
cleanse *verb* **clean** 58
clear *adjective* 59
clear *adjective* **obvious** 280
        adjective **sure** 412
        adjective **transparent** 434
        verb **forgive** 164
clearance *noun* **permission** 296
clerk *noun* 59
clever *adjective* 60
climb *verb* 60
climb down *verb* **descend** 104
cling to *verb* **hold** 197
clip *verb* **cut** 91
        verb **hit** 196
close *adjective* **humid** 202
        adjective **narrow** 270
        adjective **near** 272
        noun **end** 128
        verb **block** 36
        verb **finish** 155
clot *verb* **thicken** 424
cloth *noun* 61
clothing *noun* 61
cloudy *adjective* 62
cloudy *adjective* **opaque** 283
clout *noun* **influence** 213
club *noun* 62
clue *noun* **indicator** 211
clumsy *adjective* 63
clutch *verb* **hold** 197
clutter *noun* **mess** 257
coach *noun* **teacher** 419
        verb **teach** 419
coagulate *verb* **thicken** 424
coarse *adjective* **rough** 349
        adjective **vulgar** 457
coarsen *verb* **roughen** 350

coast *noun* **shore** 372
    verb **descend** 104
    verb **sail** 354
coat *verb* 63
coating *noun* 64
coax *verb* **persuade** 298
cobble *noun* **stone** 401
coddle *verb* **boil** 37
coerce *verb* **force** 162
coherent *adjective* **sane** 355
coil *noun* 64
coiled *adjective* **twisted** 439
coin *verb* **invent** 222
coincidental *adjective* **accidental** 2
cold *adjective* 65
cold *adjective* **unfriendly** 445
cold-blooded *adjective* **callous** 48
collaborate *verb* **cooperate** 79
collaborator *noun* **associate** 21
collapse *verb* **fail** 143
    verb **sag** 354
colleague *noun* **associate** 21
collect *verb* **gather** 173
collection *noun* **mixture** 264
collective *adjective* **public** 320
collude *verb* **plot** 302
colonize *verb* **inhabit** 215
colossal *adjective* **huge** 201
color *verb* 65
colorful *adjective* 66
colorless *adjective* 66
comatose *adjective* **unconscious** 442
combat *noun* **fight** 153
combative *adjective* **aggressive** 9
combine *verb* 67
combine *verb* **cooperate** 79
come *verb* 67
come *verb* **appear** 16
come about *verb* **happen** 187
come across *verb* **meet** 256
comedian *noun* **entertainer** 132
come to blows *verb* **fight** 154
comfort *noun* 68
comfort *verb* 68
comfortable *adjective* **satisfied** 356

comical *adjective* **funny** 171
command *noun* **order** 285
    verb **rule** 352
commence *verb* **begin** 30
commencement *noun* **start** 397
commend *verb* **praise** 310
commendable *adjective* **good** 179
comment *noun* 69
commission *noun* **pay** 293
commissioner *noun* **manager** 252
commodious *adjective* **spacious** 393
common *adjective* **public** 320
    adjective **subordinate** 406
    adjective **vulgar** 457
commotion *noun* 69
communal *adjective* **public** 320
communicative
    adjective **talkative** 416
communiqué *noun* **message** 257
commuter *noun* **traveler** 435
compact *adjective* **thick** 423
companion *noun* **friend** 167
company *noun* **organization** 286
comparable *adjective* **similar** 379
compartment *noun* **room** 348
compassion *noun* **pity** 299
compassionate
    adjective **lenient** 239
compel *verb* **force** 162
compensate *verb* **repay** 338
compete *verb* 70
competent *adjective* 70
competition *noun* 71
complacent *adjective* **satisfied** 356
complain *verb* 71
complete *adjective* **perfect** 295
    adjective **whole** 466
    verb **finish** 155
complex *adjective* **complicated** 72
    adjective **difficult** 106
    noun **obsession** 279
complexion *noun* **appearance** 17
compliant *adjective* **obedient** 278
complicated *adjective* 72
compliment *verb* **praise** 310

comply with *verb* **obey** 279
compose *verb* 72
compose *verb* **create** 86
composed *adjective* **calm** 48
compound *noun* **prison** 314
comprehend *verb* **understand** 443
comprehensive
   adjective **thorough** 426
compress *verb* **press** 312
comprise *verb* **include** 207
compromise *verb* **endanger** 129
compute *verb* **calculate** 47
comrade *noun* **associate** 21
con *noun* **trick** 436
conceal *verb* **hide** 194
concealed *adjective* **invisible** 223
concede *verb* **admit** 6
conceited *adjective* 73
conceivable *adjective* **believable** 32
conceive *verb* **invent** 222
concentrate *verb* 73
concept *noun* **thought** 426
concert *noun* 74
concise *adjective* **brief** 42
conclude *verb* 74
conclude *verb* **finish** 155
conclusion *noun* **end** 128
      noun **result** 344
concoct *verb* 75
concrete *adjective* **actual** 5
concrete jungle *noun* **city** 57
concur *verb* **agree** 10
condemn *verb* **fault** 150
condense *verb* **shorten** 373
      verb **thicken** 424
condensed *adjective* **brief** 42
condition *verb* **influence** 213
conduct *noun* **behavior** 31
conduct yourself *verb* **behave** 31
confer *verb* **give** 176
     verb **talk** 416
confess *verb* **admit** 6
confident *adjective* **optimistic** 284
     adjective **sure** 412
confidential *adjective* **secret** 361

confine *verb* 75
confine *verb* **enclose** 127
confined *adjective* **narrow** 270
confirm *verb* **prove** 320
confiscate *verb* **take** 415
conflict *noun* 76
conflict *verb* **argue** 18
conflicting *adjective* **opposite** 284
confound *verb* **puzzle** 324
confuse *verb* 76
confused *adjective* 77
confusing *adjective* 77
congeal *verb* **thicken** 424
congratulate *verb* **praise** 310
congregate *verb* **assemble** 20
congress *noun* **council** 81
connect *verb* **join** 226
connected *adjective* **related** 334
connive *verb* **plot** 302
conquer *verb* **defeat** 99
conscientious *adjective* **careful** 50
        adjective **reliable** 335
consent *noun* **permission** 296
     verb **allow** 11
consequence *noun* **result** 344
conservative
   adjective **narrow-minded** 270
consider *verb* **concentrate** 73
considerate
   adjective **kind** 231
   adjective **well-behaved** 463
consolation *noun* **comfort** 68
conspicuous *adjective* **visible** 456
conspiracy *noun* **plot** 302
conspire *verb* **plot** 302
constant *adjective* **continuous** 78
     adjective **faithful** 145
construct *verb* **build** 45
consultant *noun* **expert** 141
consume *verb* **eat** 124
consumer *noun* **buyer** 47
contaminate *verb* **spoil** 395
contemplate *verb* **ponder** 305
contemporary *adjective* **modern** 265
contempt *noun* **scorn** 360

contemptible *adjective* **mean** 254
content *adjective* **satisfied** 356
contentious
   adjective **argumentative** 19
contents *noun* **inside** 218
contest *verb* **compete** 70
continue *verb* 78
continuous *adjective* 78
contraband *adjective* **illegal** 204
contract *noun* **deal** 96
contract *verb* **shrink** 376
contradict *verb* **disprove** 116
contradictory *adjective* **opposite** 284
contrary *adjective* **argumentative** 19
         adjective **opposite** 284
contrasting *adjective* **unlike** 446
contribution *noun* **gift** 176
contrite *adjective* **sorry** 391
contrive *verb* **concoct** 75
control *verb* **limit** 242
        verb **manage** 251
controversy *noun* **argument** 18
convalesce *verb* **recover** 331
convention *noun* **rule** 351
conventional *adjective* **usual** 452
conversation *noun* **talk** 415
converse *adjective* **opposite** 284
         verb **talk** 416
convert *verb* **change** 53
convey *verb* **carry** 51
convict *noun* **prisoner** 314
conviction *noun* **opinion** 283
convince *verb* **persuade** 298
convoluted *adjective* **complicated** 72
cook up *verb* **concoct** 75
cool *verb* 79
cool *adjective* **calm** 48
cooperate *verb* 79
cooperative
   adjective **helpful** 193
   adjective **well-behaved** 463
coop up *verb* **enclose** 127
cop *verb* **steal** 399
copious *adjective* **abundant** 2
copy *noun* 80

copy *verb* 80
cord *noun* **thread** 427
core *noun* **center** 52
corporation *noun* **organization** 286
correct *verb* 81
correct *adjective* **true** 438
        verb **punish** 322
correspondent *noun* **messenger** 258
corresponding *adjective* **similar** 379
corroborate *verb* **prove** 320
corrupt *adjective* **indecent** 210
        verb **spoil** 395
cost *noun* **price** 313
costly *adjective* **expensive** 141
council *noun* 81
counsel *noun* **lawyer** 235
counselor *noun* **adviser** 8
count *verb* 82
counter *verb* **resist** 341
counterfeit *adjective* **fake** 145
countless *adjective* 82
count on *verb* **expect** 140
country *adjective* 83
country *noun* 83
countryside *noun* **country** 83
coup *noun* **rebellion** 330
couple *verb* **join** 226
courage *noun* 84
courageous *adjective* **brave** 41
courier *noun* **messenger** 258
course *noun* 84
course *noun* **lesson** 239
        noun **series** 367
courteous *adjective* **polite** 304
courtyard *noun* **yard** 472
cove *noun* **bay** 28
cover *verb* 85
cover *verb* **hide** 194
       verb **include** 207
covet *verb* **want** 458
covetous *adjective* **jealous** 225
cow *verb* **threaten** 427
cowardly *adjective* **fearful** 151
cower *verb* 85
coy *adjective* **shy** 376

crack *noun* **attempt** 23
   noun **break** 42
   noun **joke** 227
   verb **solve** 390
cradle *verb* **hug** 200
craft *noun* **profession** 316
crafty *adjective* **cunning** 90
crammed *adjective* **full** 170
cramp *noun* **pain** 290
cramped *adjective* **narrow** 270
cranky *adjective* **annoyed** 14
crave *verb* **want** 458
craving *noun* **wish** 469
craze *noun* **fashion** 147
crazy *adjective* **mad** 249
cream *adjective* **white** 465
creamy *adjective* **smooth** 387
create *verb* 86
credible *adjective* **believable** 32
creepy *adjective* **frightening** 169
crest *noun* **top** 432
crevice *noun* **break** 42
criminal *noun* 86
criminal *adjective* **illegal** 204
crimson *adjective* **red** 332
cripple *verb* **weaken** 461
critical *adjective* **significant** 378
criticize *verb* **fault** 150
crook *noun* 87
crooked *adjective* 87
crooked *adjective* **dishonest** 113
crooner *noun* **singer** 381
cross *verb* 88
cross *adjective* **grumpy** 186
   verb **extend** 142
crotchety *adjective* **grumpy** 186
crow *verb* **boast** 37
crowd *noun* 88
crowded *adjective* **full** 170
crucial *adjective* **necessary** 273
crude *adjective* **vulgar** 457
cruel *adjective* 89
cruise *verb* **sail** 354
crumble *verb* **crush** 89
crumbling *adjective* **decrepit** 98

crummy *adjective* **inferior** 212
crush *verb* 89
crust *noun* **coating** 64
cry *verb* 90
cubicle *noun* **room** 348
cuddle *verb* **hug** 200
cuisine *noun* **food** 161
cultivated *adjective* **educated** 125
cunning *adjective* 90
cunning *noun* **trickery** 437
curb *verb* **limit** 242
curdle *verb* **thicken** 424
curiosity *noun* **miracle** 260
curious *adjective* **inquisitive** 217
curl *noun* **coil** 64
   verb **bend** 33
current *adjective* **modern** 265
cursed *adjective* **unlucky** 447
curt *adjective* **abrupt** 1
curtail *verb* **subtract** 407
curve *verb* **bend** 33
custom *noun* **tradition** 434
customary *adjective* **usual** 452
customer *noun* **buyer** 47
cut *noun* 91
cut *verb* 91
cut *noun* **share** 369
cut off *verb* **interrupt** 221
cycle *noun* **series** 367

Dd

dainty *adjective* **slight** 383
dally *verb* **dawdle** 94
dam *noun* **lake** 233
damage *verb* 92
damn *verb* **fault** 150
damp *adjective* **wet** 464
dampen *verb* **wet** 464
dance *verb* **frisk** 169
dangerous *adjective* 92
dank *adjective* **wet** 464
dapper *adjective* **chic** 55

dark *adjective* 93
dark *adjective* **black** 35
darken *verb* 93
darn *verb* **sew** 367
dart *verb* 94
dash *noun* **trace** 433
   verb **hurry** 202
dash off *verb* **compose** 72
data *noun* **information** 215
date *noun* **meeting** 256
dated *adjective* **old-fashioned** 282
daub *verb* **coat** 63
dawdle *verb* 94
daydream *verb* 95
dazed *adjective* **unconscious** 442
dazzling *adjective* **bright** 43
dead *adjective* 95
deadlock *noun* **halt** 186
deadly *adjective* **fatal** 149
deafening *adjective* **loud** 247
dealer *noun* **seller** 364
deal *noun* 96
dearth *noun* **lack** 232
debacle *noun* **disaster** 110
debatable *adjective* **uncertain** 441
debate *noun* **talk** 415
debilitated *adjective* **weak** 461
debris *noun* **rubbish** 350
decay *verb* **rot** 349
deceased *adjective* **dead** 95
deceit *noun* **trickery** 437
deceitful *adjective* **dishonest** 113
deceive *verb* 96
decency *noun* **virtue** 455
decent *adjective* 97
decent *adjective* **sufficient** 408
decide *verb* **choose** 56
   verb **negotiate** 274
decipher *verb* **solve** 390
declare *verb* **publish** 321
decline *verb* **deteriorate** 105
   verb **refuse** 333
decompose *verb* **rot** 349
decrease *verb* 97
decree *noun* **order** 285

decrepit *adjective* 98
deduce *verb* **conclude** 74
deduct *verb* **subtract** 407
deed *noun* 98
deep *adjective* **wide** 466
defame *verb* **slander** 382
defeat *verb* 99
defective *adjective* 99
defend *verb* **befriend** 30
   verb **protect** 318
defense *noun* 100
defer *verb* 100
defiant *adjective* 101
deficiency *noun* **lack** 232
deficient *adjective* **incomplete** 208
   adjective **insufficient** 219
deficit *noun* **lack** 232
definite *adjective* **precise** 310
   adjective **sure** 412
deflect *verb* **bend** 33
defraud *verb* **cheat** 54
deft *adjective* **skillful** 382
defuse *verb* **pacify** 289
defy *verb* **disobey** 114
   verb **resist** 341
degenerate *adjective* **indecent** 210
   verb **deteriorate** 105
dehydrated *adjective* **dry** 122
delay *verb* **dawdle** 94
   verb **defer** 100
delete *verb* **exclude** 139
deliberate *adjective* 101
deliberate *adjective* **wary** 460
delicate *adjective* **fragile** 165
   adjective **slight** 383
delicious *adjective* 102
delight *verb* **please** 301
delighted *adjective* **glad** 177
delinquent
   adjective **disobedient** 114
deliver *verb* **carry** 51
   verb **free** 166
delude *verb* **deceive** 96
deluxe *adjective* **superior** 411
delve into *verb* **investigate** 223

demand *noun* 102
demand *verb* 103
demanding *adjective* **difficult** 106
dematerialize *verb* **disappear** 109
demeanor *noun* **behavior** 31
demolish *verb* **destroy** 105
       verb **disprove** 116
demonstrate *verb* **show** 374
demonstration *noun* **display** 115
demure *adjective* **shy** 376
den *noun* **room** 348
denomination *noun* **religion** 335
denounce *verb* **accuse** 4
dense *adjective* **opaque** 283
      adjective **thick** 423
depart *verb* **leave** 237
      verb **go** 179
departed *adjective* **dead** 95
dependable *adjective* **reliable** 335
dependant *noun* 103
depict *verb* **describe** 104
deportment *noun* **behavior** 31
deposit *noun* **layer** 235
      verb **place** 300
depraved *adjective* **indecent** 210
depressed *adjective* **miserable** 261
depressing *adjective* **dreary** 120
      adjective **pessimistic** 298
depression *noun* **misery** 261
deprivation *noun* **poverty** 307
deputy *noun* **helper** 193
derision *noun* **scorn** 360
derive *verb* **calculate** 47
descend *verb* 104
descendant *noun* **offspring** 281
describe *verb* 104
describe *verb* **tell** 421
desert *verb* **quit** 325
deserted *adjective* **empty** 127
desiccated *adjective* **dry** 122
design *noun* **shape** 369
      verb **create** 86
desire *noun* **wish** 469
      verb **want** 458
despicable *adjective* **mean** 254

despise *verb* **hate** 190
despondent *adjective* **miserable** 261
despotic *adjective* **tyrannical** 439
destiny *noun* **fate** 149
destitute *adjective* **broke** 44
destitution *noun* **poverty** 307
destroy *verb* 105
detach *verb* **separate** 366
detached *adjective* **neutral** 275
detailed *adjective* **thorough** 426
detect *verb* **find** 154
deter *verb* **discourage** 112
deteriorate *verb* 105
determined *adjective* **persistent** 297
detest *verb* **hate** 190
develop *verb* **create** 86
      verb **expand** 139
devious *adjective* **cunning** 90
devise *verb* **invent** 222
devoted *adjective* **faithful** 145
      adjective **loving** 248
devotion *noun* **respect** 342
devour *verb* **eat** 124
devout *adjective* **religious** 336
dextrous *adjective* **skillful** 382
dialect *noun* **language** 234
dialog *noun* **talk** 415
diary *noun* **book** 38
dictatorial *adjective* **bossy** 40
die *verb* 106
differ *verb* **disagree** 108
difference *noun* **argument** 18
different *adjective* **unlike** 446
difficult *adjective* 106
diffident *adjective* **shy** 376
dig *verb* 107
digest *verb* **learn** 237
digit *noun* **number** 277
dignified *adjective* **grand** 181
digress *verb* **ramble** 326
diligent *adjective* **careful** 50
dim *adjective* **dark** 93
      verb **darken** 93
diminish *verb* **decrease** 97
      verb **subtract** 407

din *noun* **noise** 276
diner *noun* **restaurant** 343
dingy *adjective* **drab** 119
dip *verb* **drop** 122
direct *adjective* **frank** 165
    verb **manage** 251
director *noun* **manager** 252
dirge *noun* **song** 391
dirt *noun* **earth** 123
dirt-cheap *adjective* **cheap** 54
dirty *adjective* 107
dirty *verb* 108
disable *verb* **weaken** 461
disadvantaged *adjective* **poor** 305
disagree *verb* 108
disagreeable *adjective* **nasty** 271
disagreement *noun* **conflict** 76
disappear *verb* 109
disappointment *noun* 109
disapprove of *verb* 110
disaster *noun* 110
disaster *noun* **failure** 144
disbelieve *verb* **doubt** 119
discard *verb* 111
disciple *noun* **student** 405
discipline *verb* **punish** 322
disclose *verb* **reveal** 345
disconnect *verb* **interrupt** 221
    verb **separate** 366
discontented
  adjective **dissatisfied** 116
discordant *adjective* 111
discount *adjective* **cheap** 54
discourage *verb* 112
discouraging
  adjective **pessimistic** 298
discover *verb* **find** 154
    verb **realize** 329
discreet *adjective* **wary** 460
discriminatory *adjective* **unfair** 444
discuss *verb* **talk** 416
discussion *noun* **talk** 415
disdain *noun* **scorn** 360
disembark *verb* **land** 233
disentangle *verb* **simplify** 380

disgruntled *adjective* **dissatisfied** 116
disguise *verb* **hide** 194
disgust *verb* 112
disheartening
  adjective **pessimistic** 298
disheveled *adjective* **scruffy** 361
dishonest *adjective* 113
disinclined *adjective* **unwilling** 449
disinterested *adjective* **neutral** 275
disjointed *adjective* **inarticulate** 207
dislike *noun* 113
dislodge *verb* **remove** 337
disloyal *adjective* **unfaithful** 445
dismal *adjective* **dreary** 120
  adjective **pathetic** 292
dismount *verb* **land** 233
disobedient *adjective* 114
disobey *verb* 114
disobey *verb* **rebel** 330
disorganize *verb* 115
disorganized *adjective* **untidy** 448
disparate *adjective* **unlike** 446
dispatch *noun* **message** 257
  verb **send** 365
dispel *verb* **repel** 339
dispensable
  adjective **insignificant** 218
dispensation *noun* **permission** 296
dispense *verb* **distribute** 118
disperse *verb* **scatter** 358
display *noun* 115
display *verb* **show** 374
displeased *adjective* **dissatisfied** 116
disprove *verb* 116
dispute *noun* **argument** 18
  verb **disagree** 108
disqualify *verb* **ban** 27
disregard *verb* **neglect** 273
disrespect *noun* **scorn** 360
disrupt *verb* **disorganize** 115
dissatisfied *adjective* 116
dissent *verb* **disagree** 108
dissident *adjective* **defiant** 101
dissimilar *adjective* **unlike** 446
dissipate *verb* **scatter** 358

dissolve *verb* **cancel** 49
    verb **disappear** 109
dissonant *adjective* **discordant** 111
dissuade *verb* **discourage** 112
distant *adjective* 117
distinct *adjective* **obvious** 280
distinguished *adjective* 117
distort *verb* **misrepresent** 262
distorted *adjective* **crooked** 87
distract *verb* **confuse** 76
distress *noun* **poverty** 307
    verb **upset** 450
distribute *verb* 118
distribute *verb* **scatter** 358
district attorney *noun* **lawyer** 235
distrust *verb* **doubt** 119
disturb *verb* **disorganize** 115
    verb **interrupt** 221
disturbed *adjective* **mad** 249
    adjective **upset** 450
ditch *noun* **groove** 185
    verb **discard** 111
dive *verb* **dart** 94
diverge *verb* **ramble** 326
divergent *adjective* **unlike** 446
diverse *adjective* **various** 453
divide *verb* **separate** 366
    verb **share** 370
dividend *noun* **profit** 316
divine *verb* **predict** 311
divvy up *verb* **share** 370
docile *adjective* **obedient** 278
dock *verb* **subtract** 407
document *noun* **report** 340
dogged *adjective* **persistent** 297
dole out *verb* **share** 370
dominant *adjective* **powerful** 308
dominate *verb* **rule** 352
    verb **subdue** 405
domineering
  adjective **tyrannical** 439
donate *verb* **give** 176
donation *noun* **gift** 176
doodle *verb* **write** 472
dossier *noun* **report** 340

dote on *verb* **love** 247
double *adjective* 118
double-cross *verb* **betray** 34
doubt *verb* 119
doubtful *adjective* **uncertain** 441
dour *adjective* **solemn** 390
do without *verb* **sacrifice** 352
down-to-earth *adjective* **practical** 309
downtrodden
  adjective **submissive** 406
downy *adjective* **soft** 389
doze *verb* **sleep** 383
drab *adjective* 119
draft *verb* **compose** 72
drag *verb* **pull** 322
draw *verb* **attract** 24
    verb **pull** 322
drawback *noun* **obstacle** 280
dreadful *adjective* **horrible** 199
dream *verb* **imagine** 205
dreamy *adjective* 120
dreary *adjective* 120
drench *verb* **soak** 388
dress *noun* **clothing** 61
dribble *verb* **drip** 121
drift *noun* **meaning** 254
drill *noun* **practice** 309
    verb **teach** 419
drink *verb* 121
drip *verb* 121
drive *verb* **force** 162
    verb **push** 323
drive someone up the wall
    verb **anger** 13
drivel *noun* **nonsense** 277
drizzle *verb* **rain** 326
droll *adjective* **funny** 171
droop *verb* **sag** 354
drop *verb* 122
drop *noun* **trace** 433
    verb **descend** 104
    verb **exclude** 139
drop in *verb* **visit** 456
drowse *verb* **sleep** 383
drudgery *noun* **work** 470

drugged *adjective* **unconscious** 442
drum *verb* **throb** 429
dry *adjective* 122
dual *adjective* **double** 118
dub *verb* **name** 269
dubious *adjective* **uncertain** 441
dud *adjective* **inferior** 212
   noun **failure** 144
dull *adjective* 123
dull *adjective* **boring** 39
   adjective **cloudy** 62
dumb *adjective* **stupid** 405
dump *verb* **discard** 111
dupe *verb* **deceive** 96
duplicate *adjective* **double** 118
   noun **copy** 80
   verb **copy** 80
durable *adjective* **hardy** 189
dutiful *adjective* **obedient** 278
   adjective **reliable** 335
duty *noun* **task** 417
dwell *verb* **reside** 341
dwelling *noun* **home** 198
dwindle *verb* **shrink** 376
dye *verb* **color** 65
dynamic *adjective* **energetic** 131
   adjective **moving** 266

Ee

eager *adjective* **enthusiastic** 132
earth *noun* 123
ease *noun* **comfort** 68
   verb **comfort** 68
   verb **further** 171
   verb **insert** 217
easy *adjective* 124
easygoing *adjective* **informal** 214
eat *verb* 124
ebb *verb* **reverse** 346
ebony *adjective* **black** 35
eclipse *verb* **darken** 93
economical *adjective* **thrifty** 428

ecstatic *adjective* **joyful** 228
edge *noun* 125
edgy *adjective* **nervous** 274
educate *verb* **teach** 419
educated *adjective* 125
effect *noun* **result** 344
effigy *noun* **copy** 80
effort *noun* **achievement** 5
   noun **attempt** 23
   noun **work** 470
effortless *adjective* **easy** 124
egotistic *adjective* **conceited** 73
eject *verb* **expel** 140
elaborate *adjective* **complicated** 72
elastic *adjective* 126
elated *adjective* **joyful** 228
elect *verb* **prefer** 311
elective *noun* **choice** 56
elegant *adjective* **chic** 55
elevate *verb* **lift** 240
elevated *adjective* **tall** 417
elfin *adjective* **slight** 383
elope *verb* **flee** 157
eloquent *adjective* **fluent** 160
elucidate *verb* **explain** 142
elude *verb* **avoid** 25
emancipate *verb* **free** 166
embark on *verb* **begin** 30
embellish *verb* **expand** 139
embezzle *verb* **steal** 399
emblem *noun* **sign** 378
embrace *verb* **hug** 200
   verb **include** 207
embroider *verb* **expand** 139
   verb **sew** 367
emerald *adjective* **green** 184
emerge *verb* **appear** 16
emigrate *verb* **leave** 237
eminent *adjective* **important** 205
emphasize *verb* 126
employ *verb* **use** 451
empty *adjective* 127
emulsify *verb* **mix** 263
encircle *verb* **enclose** 127
enclose *verb* 127

enclose *verb* **insert** 217
enclosure *noun* **yard** 472
encounter *verb* **meet** 256
encourage *verb* 128
encumbrance *noun* **weight** 463
end *noun* 128
end *verb* 129
end *verb* **finish** 155
endanger *verb* 129
endeavor *noun* **attempt** 23
endless *adjective* **continuous** 78
  adjective **countless** 82
endorse *verb* **approve** 17
endurance *noun* **persistence** 297
endure *verb* 130
endure *verb* **continue** 78
enduring *adjective* **steadfast** 398
enemy *noun* 130
energetic *adjective* 131
engagement *noun* **undertaking** 443
engineer *verb* **plan** 301
engulf *verb* **flood** 158
enhance *verb* **improve** 206
enjoy *verb* **like** 241
enjoyable *adjective* **nice** 276
enlarge *verb* 131
enormous *adjective* **huge** 201
enough *adjective* **sufficient** 408
enrage *verb* **anger** 13
enrich *verb* **improve** 206
enter *verb* **record** 331
enterprise *noun* **undertaking** 443
entertainer *noun* 132
enthusiastic *adjective* 132
entice *verb* **charm** 53
entire *adjective* **whole** 466
entreat *verb* **ask** 20
enumerate *verb* **list** 244
enunciate *verb* **pronounce** 317
envelop *verb* **cover** 85
envious *adjective* **jealous** 225
environment *noun* **surroundings** 412
environs *noun* **surroundings** 412
envoy *noun* **messenger** 258
ephemeral *adjective* **momentary** 265

epigram *noun* **saying** 357
equal *adjective* 133
equipped *adjective* **ready** 329
equivalent *adjective* **equal** 133
eradicate *verb* **destroy** 105
erase *verb* **remove** 337
erect *verb* **build** 45
err *verb* 133
errand *noun* **task** 417
erratic *adjective* 134
erroneous *adjective* **incorrect** 209
error *noun* **mistake** 263
erudite *adjective* **educated** 125
escape *verb* **flee** 157
escapee *noun* 134
escort *verb* **accompany** 3
essence *noun* **meaning** 254
essential *adjective* **necessary** 273
establish *verb* **initiate** 216
  verb **position** 306
established *adjective* **formal** 164
esteem *noun* **respect** 342
estimate *verb* **measure** 255
estuary *noun* **bay** 28
eternal *adjective* **permanent** 295
ethereal *adjective* **shadowy** 368
ethical *adjective* **decent** 97
ethnic *adjective* **foreign** 163
evacuate *verb* **quit** 325
evade *verb* **avoid** 25
evaluate *verb* **judge** 228
even *adjective* **equal** 133
  adjective **flat** 156
even-handed *adjective* **neutral** 275
everlasting *adjective* **permanent** 295
evict *verb* **expel** 140
evident *adjective* **clear** 59
  adjective **obvious** 280
evil *adjective* 135
evil *noun* **misfortune** 262
evoke *verb* **cause** 52
exact *adjective* **precise** 310
exaggerate *verb* **misrepresent** 262
exam *noun* **test** 422
examination *noun* **inquiry** 216

examine *verb* 135
example *noun* 136
exasperate *verb* **annoy** 14
exasperating *adjective* **annoying** 15
excavate *verb* **dig** 107
excellent *adjective* 136
exceptional *adjective* **excellent** 136
excess *noun* 137
excessive *adjective* **extra** 143
exchange *verb* 137
excise *verb* **remove** 337
excited *adjective* 138
exciting *adjective* 138
exclamation *noun* **comment** 69
exclude *verb* 139
exclusive *adjective* **single** 381
excursion *noun* **journey** 227
excuse *verb* **forgive** 164
        verb **justify** 229
execute *verb* **kill** 230
exertion *noun* **work** 470
exhaust *verb* **tire** 430
exhausted *adjective* **tired** 431
exhaustive *adjective* **thorough** 426
exhibit *verb* **show** 374
exhibition *noun* **display** 115
exhibitionist *noun* **show-off** 374
exhilarated *adjective* **excited** 138
exhilarating *adjective* **exciting** 138
exile *verb* **expel** 140
exist *verb* **live** 245
exorbitant *adjective* **expensive** 141
exotic *adjective* **foreign** 163
expand *verb* 139
expand *verb* **enlarge** 131
        verb **increase** 209
expansive *adjective* **spacious** 393
expect *verb* 140
expected *adjective* **likely** 242
expedition *noun* **journey** 227
expel *verb* 140
expend *verb* **pay** 294
expendable
    adjective **insignificant** 218
expense *noun* **price** 313

expensive *adjective* 141
experience *verb* **sense** 365
expert *noun* 141
expert *adjective* **competent** 70
expire *verb* **die** 106
        verb **end** 129
explain *verb* 142
explain *verb* **justify** 229
explicit *adjective* **clear** 59
exploit *noun* **deed** 98
        verb **use** 451
explore *verb* **investigate** 223
expose *verb* **endanger** 129
        verb **reveal** 345
exposed *adjective* **bare** 28
        adjective **visible** 456
        adjective **vulnerable** 457
express *adjective* **fast** 148
        verb **describe** 104
exquisite *adjective* **beautiful** 29
extend *verb* 142
extensive *adjective* **wide** 466
exterior *noun* **outside** 287
exterminate *verb* **destroy** 105
extra *adjective* 143
extract *verb* **remove** 337
extraordinary
    adjective **unusual** 449
    adjective **wonderful** 469
exult *verb* **rejoice** 334
eye-catching
    adjective **spectacular** 394

Ff

fabric *noun* **cloth** 61
fabulous *adjective* **wonderful** 469
facade *noun* **outside** 287
face *noun* **outside** 287
facilitate *verb* **further** 171
factual *adjective* **genuine** 174
fad *noun* **fashion** 147
fade *verb* **disappear** 109

faded *adjective* **colorless** 66
fail *verb* 143
failure *noun* 144
faint *adjective* **quiet** 325
　　adjective **vague** 453
fair *adjective* 144
fair *adjective* **fine** 155
　　adjective **ordinary** 286
　　adjective **pretty** 312
faith *noun* **religion** 335
faithful *adjective* 145
faithful *adjective* **religious** 336
fake *adjective* 145
fall *verb* 146
fall *verb* **happen** 187
fall apart *verb* **deteriorate** 105
fallen *adjective* **dead** 95
fall through *verb* **fail** 143
false *adjective* **fake** 145
　　adjective **incorrect** 209
　　adjective **unfaithful** 445
falsetto *adjective* **high-pitched** 195
falsify *verb* **misrepresent** 262
faltering *adjective* **inarticulate** 207
family *noun* 146
famous *adjective* 147
fan *verb* **cool** 79
fanciful *adjective* **imaginary** 204
fancy *verb* **imagine** 205
fantasize *verb* **daydream** 95
fantastic *adjective* **excellent** 136
　　adjective **imaginary** 204
faraway *adjective* **distant** 117
farcical *adjective* **ridiculous** 347
fare *noun* **food** 161
farfetched
　　adjective **unbelievable** 441
fascinate *verb* **charm** 53
fashion *noun* 147
fashion *verb* **build** 45
fashionable *adjective* **chic** 55
fast *adjective* 148
fat *adjective* 148
fatal *adjective* 149
fate *noun* 149

fateful *adjective* **significant** 378
fathom *verb* **understand** 443
fatigue *verb* **tire** 430
fatigued *adjective* **tired** 431
fault *verb* 150
faultless *adjective* **perfect** 295
faulty *adjective* **defective** 99
faux pas *noun* **mistake** 263
favor *verb* **prefer** 311
fawn *adjective* **brown** 44
fear *verb* 150
fearful *adjective* 151
fearless *adjective* **brave** 41
feasible *adjective* **possible** 307
feast *noun* **meal** 253
feat *noun* **achievement** 5
feathery *adjective* **light** 241
fed up *adjective* **annoyed** 14
　　adjective **bored** 39
fee *noun* **pay** 293
feeble *adjective* **powerless** 308
　　adjective **weak** 461
feedback *noun* **reaction** 328
feel *verb* **sense** 365
　　verb **touch** 432
feeling *noun* 151
feign *verb* **imagine** 205
felon *noun* **criminal** 86
felonious *adjective* **illegal** 204
female *noun* 152
ferocious *adjective* **violent** 455
ferocity *noun* **violence** 454
fester *verb* **rot** 349
fetid *adjective* **smelly** 386
fetish *noun* **obsession** 279
feud *noun* **conflict** 76
fiasco *noun* **failure** 144
fiber *noun* **thread** 427
fickle *adjective* 152
fictitious *adjective* **imaginary** 204
fidget *verb* 153
fierce *adjective* **violent** 455
fiery *adjective* **hot** 200
fight *noun* 153
fight *verb* 154

figure *noun* **number** 277
    noun **shape** 369
    verb **calculate** 47
figure out *verb* **solve** 390
filament *noun* **thread** 427
file *noun* **line** 243
  verb **arrange** 19
fill-in *adjective* **temporary** 421
fill the bill *verb* **suit** 410
film *noun* **coating** 64
filthy *adjective* **dirty** 107
finale *noun* **end** 128
find *verb* 154
fine *adjective* 155
fine *adjective* **good** 179
  adjective **healthy** 190
  adjective **light** 241
finger *verb* **touch** 432
finish *verb* 155
finish *noun* **end** 128
  verb **end** 129
finished *adjective* **empty** 127
fire away *verb* **start** 397
firm *adjective* **hard** 188
  adjective **steadfast** 398
  adjective **steady** 398
  adjective **strict** 403
  noun **organization** 286
first-rate *adjective* **great** 183
fissure *noun* **break** 42
fit *adjective* **healthy** 190
  adjective **ready** 329
fitful *adjective* **erratic** 134
fix *verb* **choose** 56
  verb **repair** 338
  verb **steady** 399
fixed *adjective* **steady** 398
fizzle out *verb* **fail** 143
flabbergasted *adjective* **astonished** 21
flamboyant *adjective* **spectacular** 394
flaming *adjective* **shining** 371
flank *noun* **side** 377
flap *verb* **fly** 160
flare *verb* **shine** 370
flashy *adjective* **gaudy** 173

flat *adjective* 156
flat *adjective* **discordant** 111
  adjective **dull** 123
  adjective **tasteless** 418
flatter *verb* 156
flaunt *verb* **show** 374
flee *verb* 157
fleece *verb* **cheat** 54
fleeting *adjective* **momentary** 265
flesh and blood *noun* **family** 146
flex *verb* **bend** 33
flexible *adjective* 157
flicker *verb* **sparkle** 393
flighty *adjective* **fickle** 152
flimsy *adjective* **light** 241
flinch *verb* **cower** 85
fling *verb* **throw** 429
flip *verb* **overturn** 288
flit *verb* **fly** 160
float *verb* **sail** 354
flock *noun* **crowd** 88
flood *verb* 158
flood *verb* **soak** 388
  verb **rain** 326
floor *noun* **bottom** 41
flop *noun* **failure** 144
floppy *adjective* **flexible** 157
florid *adjective* **rosy** 348
flourish *verb* 158
flout *verb* **disobey** 114
flow *verb* 159
flower *verb* **flourish** 158
fluctuate *verb* 159
fluent *adjective* 160
fluff *verb* **bungle** 45
fluid *adjective* **liquid** 244
fluky *adjective* **accidental** 2
flunk *verb* **fail** 143
flushed *adjective* **rosy** 348
fluster *verb* **confuse** 76
flustered *adjective* **upset** 450
flutter *verb* **fly** 160
fly *verb* 160
fly *verb* **speed** 394
focus *noun* **center** 52

focus on *verb* **concentrate** 73
foe *noun* **enemy** 130
fog *verb* **darken** 93
foggy *adjective* **cloudy** 62
foil *verb* **outwit** 288
fold *verb* **mix** 263
follow *verb* 161
follow *verb* **obey** 279
fond *adjective* **loving** 248
food *noun* 161
fool *verb* **trick** 436
foolhardy *adjective* **rash** 327
foolish *adjective* **silly** 379
foolproof *adjective* **easy** 124
foot *noun* **bottom** 41
foray *noun* **attack** 22
forbid *verb* **prevent** 313
forbidding *adjective* **frightening** 169
force *noun* 162
force *verb* 162
forceful *adjective* **powerful** 308
   adjective **violent** 455
ford *verb* **cross** 88
forebear *noun* **ancestor** 12
forecast *noun* 163
forecast *verb* **predict** 311
forefather *noun* **ancestor** 12
forego *verb* **sacrifice** 352
foreign *adjective* 163
foreign *adjective* **unrelated** 448
foreman *noun* **boss** 40
foresee *verb* **expect** 140
   verb **predict** 311
forewarn *verb* **warn** 459
forge ahead *verb* **advance** 7
forget *verb* **neglect** 273
foretell *verb* **predict** 311
forgive *verb* 164
forlorn *adjective* **miserable** 261
form *noun* **shape** 369
   verb **make** 250
formal *adjective* 164
former *adjective* **past** 292
formula *noun* **rule** 351
forsake *verb* **quit** 325

forthright *adjective* **frank** 165
fortify *verb* **strengthen** 403
fortunate *adjective* **lucky** 248
fortune *noun* **fate** 149
   noun **wealth** 462
forward *adjective* **bold** 38
   verb **send** 365
foul *adjective* **ugly** 440
   verb **spoil** 395
found *verb* **initiate** 216
foundation *noun* **support** 411
fraction *noun* **number** 277
   noun **part** 291
fragile *adjective* 165
fragment *noun* **piece** 299
fragmentary *adjective* **incomplete** 208
fragrance *noun* **smell** 386
frail *adjective* **fragile** 165
   adjective **weak** 461
frame *verb* **accuse** 4
framework *noun* **support** 411
frank *adjective* 165
fraud *noun* **crook** 87
fraudulent *adjective* **illegal** 204
fray *noun* **fight** 153
freak out *verb* **fear** 150
free *adjective* 166
free *verb* 166
free *verb* **separate** 366
freelance *adjective* **independent** 210
freeze *verb* **cool** 79
   verb **harden** 189
freezing *adjective* **cold** 65
frenzied *adjective* **excited** 138
frequent *adjective* **repeated** 339
fresh *adjective* **bold** 38
   adjective **new** 275
fret *verb* **worry** 471
friend *noun* 167
friendly *adjective* 167
frighten *verb* 168
frightened *adjective* 168
frightening *adjective* 169
frightful *adjective* **horrible** 199
frigid *adjective* **cold** 65

frisk *verb* 169
frisky *adjective* **lively** 245
fritter away *verb* **waste** 460
frolicsome *adjective* **lively** 245
frontier *noun* **outskirts** 287
frosty *adjective* **cold** 65
frown *verb* 170
frown on *verb* **disapprove of** 110
frugal *adjective* **thrifty** 428
frustrate *verb* **hinder** 195
frustration *noun* **disappointment** 109
fugitive *noun* **escapee** 134
fulfill *verb* **accomplish** 4
full *adjective* 170
full *adjective* **whole** 466
full-grown *adjective* **adult** 7
fumble *verb* **bungle** 45
fumbling *adjective* **incompetent** 208
fundamental *adjective* **main** 249
funny *adjective* 171
furbish *verb* **polish** 303
furious *adjective* **angry** 13
　　　adjective **violent** 455
furrow *noun* **groove** 185
further *verb* 171
furtive *adjective* **secretive** 362
fury *noun* **anger** 12
　　　noun **violence** 454
fuse *verb* **combine** 67
fuss *noun* **commotion** 69
　　　verb **worry** 471
fussy *adjective* **careful** 50
futile *adjective* **useless** 452
future *adjective* 172

Gg

gag *noun* **joke** 227
gain *verb* **get** 175
gallant *adjective* **polite** 304
gambol *verb* **frisk** 169
game *noun* **competition** 71
gang *noun* **group** 185

gangling *adjective* **clumsy** 63
gangster *noun* **criminal** 86
gap *noun* **hole** 197
gape *verb* **stare** 396
garb *noun* **clothing** 61
garbage *noun* **rubbish** 350
garish *adjective* **colorful** 66
garrulous *adjective* **talkative** 416
gash *noun* **cut** 91
　　　verb **tear** 420
gasp *verb* 172
gather *verb* 173
gather *verb* **assemble** 20
　　　verb **conclude** 74
gaudy *adjective* 173
gauge *verb* **measure** 255
gawk *verb* **stare** 396
gaze *verb* **stare** 396
gear *noun* **property** 318
general *adjective* **public** 320
generous *adjective* 174
generous *adjective* **big** 34
genial *adjective* **friendly** 167
genius *noun* **scholar** 359
genteel *adjective* **distinguished** 117
gentle *adjective* **lenient** 239
　　　adjective **peaceful** 294
gentleman *noun* **male** 250
genuine *adjective* 174
genuine *adjective* **frank** 165
germinate *verb* **flourish** 158
get *verb* 175
get a move on *verb* **hurry** 202
get even *verb* **retaliate** 344
get going *verb* **start** 397
get on someone's nerves
　　　verb **annoy** 14
get the better of *verb* **outwit** 288
ghost *noun* 175
ghostly *adjective* **shadowy** 368
gibberish *noun* **nonsense** 277
gibe *noun* **wisecrack** 468
gift *noun* 176
gigantic *adjective* **huge** 201
giggle *verb* **smile** 387

gilt *adjective* **orange** 285
ginger *adjective* **orange** 285
girl *noun* **female** 152
gist *noun* **meaning** 254
give *verb* 176
give away *verb* **blab** 35
give in *verb* 177
give way *verb* **move** 266
glacé *adjective* **sweet** 414
glacial *adjective* **wintry** 467
glad *adjective* 177
glare *verb* **frown** 170
glaring *adjective* **bright** 43
glassy *adjective* **smooth** 387
glaze *noun* **coating** 64
gleaming *adjective* **shining** 371
glean *verb* **realize** 329
glee *noun* **happiness** 187
gleeful *adjective* **happy** 188
glide *verb* **sail** 354
glimmer *verb* **sparkle** 393
glitter *verb* **sparkle** 393
globe *noun* **ball** 26
globule *noun* **ball** 26
gloom *noun* **misery** 261
gloomy *adjective* **drab** 119
    adjective **glum** 178
    adjective **pessimistic** 298
glorify *verb* **praise** 310
glossy *adjective* **shiny** 371
glow *verb* **shine** 370
glower *verb* **frown** 170
glue *noun* 178
glum *adjective* 178
glut *noun* **excess** 137
gnarled *adjective* **rough** 349
gnaw *verb* **chew** 55
goad *verb* **irritate** 224
gobble *verb* **eat** 124
go *verb* 179
go crazy *verb* **rejoice** 334
goggle *verb* **stare** 396
good *adjective* 179
good *adjective* **well-behaved** 463
good at *adjective* **competent** 70

good-looking *adjective* **pretty** 312
good-natured *adjective* **agreeable** 10
gorgeous *adjective* **beautiful** 29
gossip *noun* 180
gossip *verb* **talk** 416
gouge *verb* **dig** 107
govern *verb* **manage** 251
go wrong *verb* **err** 133
grab *verb* 180
gracious *adjective* **polite** 304
grade *noun* 181
grade *verb* **arrange** 19
gradient *noun* **slope** 384
grand *adjective* 181
grand *adjective* **tall** 417
grant *verb* **give** 176
grapple *verb* **fight** 154
grasp *verb* **hold** 197
    verb **understand** 443
grasping *adjective* **greedy** 183
grateful *adjective* 182
gratitude *noun* **thanks** 423
grave *adjective* **solemn** 390
gravel *noun* **stone** 401
gray *adjective* 182
gray *adjective* **dreary** 120
graze *verb* **scratch** 360
great *adjective* 183
great *adjective* **important** 205
greedy *adjective* 183
green *adjective* 184
green *adjective* **inexperienced** 212
    adjective **sour** 392
grieve *verb* 184
grill *verb* **toast** 431
grim *adjective* **frightening** 169
grimy *adjective* **dirty** 107
grin *verb* **smile** 387
grind *verb* **crush** 89
    verb **smooth** 388
grip *verb* **hold** 197
gripe *verb* **complain** 71
grit *noun* **persistence** 297
groove *noun* 185
gross *adjective* **unpleasant** 447

grotesque *adjective* **ugly** 440
ground *noun* **earth** 123
groundless *adjective* **irrational** 224
group *noun* 185
group *verb* **arrange** 19
grow *verb* **increase** 209
　　　verb **produce** 315
grubby *adjective* **dirty** 107
grudging *adjective* **ungrateful** 446
grumble *verb* **complain** 71
grumpy *adjective* 186
grungy *adjective* **dirty** 107
guard *verb* **protect** 318
guess *verb* **think** 425
guffaw *verb* **laugh** 234
guide *noun* **adviser** 8
　　　noun **example** 136
　　　noun **indicator** 211
　　　verb **advise** 8
guile *noun* **trickery** 437
gulf *noun* **bay** 28
gullible *adjective* **naive** 268
gulp *verb* **eat** 124
guru *noun* **adviser** 8
gush *verb* **flow** 159
gutless *adjective* **fearful** 151
guzzle *verb* **drink** 121
gyrate *verb* **spin** 395

Hh

habit *noun* **tradition** 434
habitat *noun* **surroundings** 412
hairy *adjective* **frightening** 169
half-asleep *adjective* **dreamy** 120
half-hearted *adjective* **apathetic** 16
hallowed *adjective* **holy** 198
halt *noun* 186
halt *verb* **stop** 401
hammer *verb* **beat** 29
hamper *verb* **hinder** 195
handicap *noun* **obstacle** 280

handle *verb* **touch** 432
handsome *adjective* **pretty** 312
handy *adjective* **skillful** 382
　　　adjective **useful** 451
hang around with
　　　verb **accompany** 3
hanger-on *noun* **dependant** 103
hang in *verb* **persist** 296
hang-up *noun* **obsession** 279
haphazard *adjective* **accidental** 2
hapless *adjective* **unlucky** 447
happen *verb* 187
happiness *noun* 187
happy *adjective* 188
happy *adjective* **lucky** 248
happy-go-lucky
　　　adjective **optimistic** 284
hard *adjective* 188
hard *adjective* **difficult** 106
harden *verb* 189
hard-hearted *adjective* **callous** 48
hardship *noun* **misfortune** 262
hard up *adjective* **poor** 305
hardworking *adjective* **busy** 46
hardy *adjective* 189
harebrained *adjective* **rash** 327
harm *verb* **hurt** 203
harmonious *adjective* **peaceful** 294
harsh *adjective* **strict** 403
hassle *verb* **annoy** 14
hasten *verb* **hurry** 202
hasty *adjective* **rash** 327
hatch *verb* **concoct** 75
hate *verb* 190
hatred *noun* **dislike** 113
haul *verb* **pull** 322
have all to yourself *verb* **own** 289
have in mind *verb* **intend** 220
have it out *verb* **argue** 18
haven *noun* **refuge** 333
hawk *verb* **sell** 364
hawkish *adjective* **warlike** 459
haywire *adjective* **untidy** 448
hazardous *adjective* **dangerous** 92
hazel *adjective* **green** 184

hazy *adjective* **cloudy** 62
   adjective **vague** 453
head *adjective* **best** 33
   noun **boss** 40
headstrong *adjective* **disobedient** 114
healthy *adjective* 190
heap *noun* 191
hearsay *noun* **gossip** 180
heart *noun* **center** 52
heartbroken *adjective* **miserable** 261
hearty *adjective* **strong** 404
heave *verb* **gasp** 172
heavy *adjective* 191
heavy *adjective* **thick** 423
heavy-duty *adjective* **hardy** 189
heavy-handed *adjective* **clumsy** 63
heckle *verb* **tease** 420
hectic *adjective* **busy** 46
heed *verb* **obey** 279
heedless *adjective* **ungrateful** 446
hefty *adjective* **heavy** 191
heinous *adjective* **evil** 135
help *noun* 192
help *verb* 192
helper *noun* 193
helpful *adjective* 193
helpful *adjective* **useful** 451
helping *noun* **share** 369
helpless *adjective* **weak** 461
herd *noun* **crowd** 88
hermit *noun* 194
hero *noun* **star** 396
heroic *adjective* **brave** 41
hesitant *adjective* **inarticulate** 207
   adjective **unwilling** 449
hesitate *verb* **stop** 401
hidden *adjective* **invisible** 223
hide *verb* 194
hideous *adjective* **ugly** 440
high *adjective* **high-pitched** 195
   adjective **tall** 417
high-class *adjective* **superior** 411
highlight *verb* **color** 65
   verb **emphasize** 126
high-pitched *adjective* 195

high spirits *noun* **happiness** 187
highwayman *noun* **bandit** 27
hijack *verb* **capture** 49
hilarious *adjective* **funny** 171
hinder *verb* 195
hindrance *noun* **obstacle** 280
hint *verb* 196
hint *noun* **trace** 433
hit *verb* 196
hit *noun* **winner** 467
hitch *noun* **obstacle** 280
hoard *verb* **store** 402
hoax *noun* **trick** 436
   verb **trick** 436
hobble *verb* **limp** 243
hodgepodge *noun* **mixture** 264
hoist *verb* **lift** 240
hold *verb* 197
hold *noun* **influence** 213
   verb **own** 289
hold on *verb* **continue** 78
hold with *verb* **approve** 17
hole *noun* 197
hollow out *verb* **dig** 107
holy *adjective* 198
home *noun* 198
homesick *adjective* **sad** 353
honest *adjective* 199
honor *noun* **respect** 342
   verb **acclaim** 3
   verb **worship** 471
honorable *adjective* **honest** 199
hood *noun* **criminal** 86
hoodwink *verb* **deceive** 96
hop *verb* **jump** 229
hopeful *adjective* **optimistic** 284
hopeless *adjective* **impossible** 206
horizontal *adjective* **flat** 156
horrendous *adjective* **horrible** 199
horrible *adjective* 199
horrify *verb* **disgust** 112
hospitable *adjective* **generous** 174
hostile *adjective* **aggressive** 9
hostility *noun* **dislike** 113
hot *adjective* 200

Ii

improbable
adjective **unbelievable** 441
impromptu *adjective* **sudden** 408
improve *verb* 206
improvise *verb* **create** 86
impudent *adjective* **rude** 351
impulsive *adjective* **sudden** 408
inaccurate *adjective* **incorrect** 209
inadequate *adjective* **insufficient** 219
inane *adjective* **silly** 379
inarticulate *adjective* 207
inattentive *adjective* **dreamy** 120
incandescent *adjective* **shining** 371
incapacitate *verb* **weaken** 461
incapacitated *adjective* **powerless** 308
incense *verb* **anger** 13
incision *noun* **cut** 91
inclination *noun* **wish** 469
incline *noun* **slope** 384
include *verb* 207
income *noun* **pay** 293
incompetent *adjective* 208
incomplete *adjective* 208
inconceivable
adjective **impossible** 206
inconsiderate *adjective* **selfish** 363
inconsistent *adjective* **irrational** 224
inconspicuous *adjective* **invisible** 223
incorporate *verb* **include** 207
incorrect *adjective* 209
incorrigible *adjective* **naughty** 271
increase *verb* 209
increase *verb* **enlarge** 131
incredible *adjective* **unbelievable** 441
adjective **wonderful** 469
indebted *adjective* **grateful** 182
indecent *adjective* 210
indefinite *adjective* **vague** 453
independent *adjective* 210
independent *adjective* **unrelated** 448
in-depth *adjective* **thorough** 426
index *verb* **list** 244
indicator *noun* 211
indifferent *adjective* **apathetic** 16
adjective **mediocre** 255

indignant *adjective* **annoyed** 14
indigo *adjective* **purple** 323
indisposed *adjective* **sick** 377
indistinct *adjective* **quiet** 325
indolent *adjective* **lazy** 236
induce *verb* **cause** 52
verb **persuade** 298
indulgent *adjective* **broad-minded** 43
industrious *adjective* **busy** 46
industry *noun* **work** 470
inedible *adjective* 211
ineffective *adjective* **useless** 452
ineffectual *adjective* **useless** 452
inept *adjective* **incompetent** 208
inequitable *adjective* **unfair** 444
inert *adjective* **lethargic** 240
inexpensive *adjective* **cheap** 54
inexperienced *adjective* 212
infer *verb* **conclude** 74
inferior *adjective* 212
infinite *adjective* **countless** 82
infirm *adjective* **decrepit** 98
inflamed *adjective* **rosy** 348
inflexible *adjective* **stubborn** 404
influence *noun* 213
influence *verb* 213
inform *verb* 214
informal *adjective* 214
information *noun* 215
infrequent *adjective* **scarce** 358
infringe *verb* **disobey** 114
infuriate *verb* **anger** 13
infuriated *adjective* **angry** 13
infuriating *adjective* **annoying** 15
ingenious *adjective* **shrewd** 375
inhabit *verb* 215
inhibit *verb* **hinder** 195
verb **limit** 242
inhospitable
adjective **unfriendly** 445
initiate *verb* 216
in-joke *noun* **wisecrack** 468
injure *verb* **hurt** 203
inky *adjective* **black** 35
inlet *noun* **bay** 28

inmate *noun* **prisoner** 314
innards *noun* **inside** 218
innocent *adjective* **naive** 268
innovate *verb* **invent** 222
innovative *adjective* **new** 275
innumerable
    adjective **numerous** 278
inquire *verb* **question** 324
inquiring *adjective* **inquisitive** 217
inquiry *noun* 216
inquisitive *adjective* 217
insane *adjective* **mad** 249
insatiable *adjective* **greedy** 183
insecure *adjective* **vulnerable** 457
insensitive *adjective* **callous** 48
insert *verb* 217
inside *noun* 218
insignificant *adjective* 218
insinuate *verb* **hint** 196
        verb **insert** 217
insipid *adjective* **tasteless** 418
insist *verb* **demand** 103
insolent *adjective* **rude** 351
insolvent *adjective* **broke** 44
inspect *verb* 219
inspire *verb* **cause** 52
        verb **encourage** 128
install *verb* **position** 306
institute *verb* **initiate** 216
instruct *verb* **inform** 214
        verb **teach** 419
instructions *noun* **order** 285
instructor *noun* **teacher** 419
instrumentalist *noun* **musician** 268
insubordinate
    adjective **disobedient** 114
insufficiency *noun* **lack** 232
insufficient *adjective* 219
insult *verb* 220
insulting *adjective* **rude** 351
intangible *adjective* **shadowy** 368
integer *noun* **number** 277
intellectual *noun* **scholar** 359
intelligence *noun* **information** 215
intelligent *adjective* **clever** 60

intend *verb* 220
intense *adjective* 221
intensive *adjective* **thorough** 426
intentional *adjective* **deliberate** 101
intercede *verb* **negotiate** 274
interfere *verb* **intrude** 222
interim *adjective* **temporary** 421
interior *noun* **inside** 218
interject *verb* **intrude** 222
interjection *noun* **comment** 69
interminable
    adjective **continuous** 78
intermittent *adjective* **erratic** 134
intern *verb* **confine** 75
internee *noun* **prisoner** 314
interpret *verb* **explain** 142
interrogate *verb* **question** 324
interrupt *verb* 221
intervene *verb* **negotiate** 274
interview *noun* **talk** 415
        verb **question** 324
intimidate *verb* **threaten** 427
intolerant
    adjective **narrow-minded** 270
intricate *adjective* **complicated** 72
intrigue *noun* **plot** 302
        verb **plot** 302
introduce *verb* **insert** 217
introvert *noun* **hermit** 194
intrude *verb* 222
inundate *verb* **flood** 158
        verb **soak** 388
invalid *adjective* **weak** 461
invalidate *verb* **disprove** 116
invent *verb* 222
invert *verb* **overturn** 288
invest *verb* **pay** 294
investigate *verb* 223
investigation *noun* **inquiry** 216
invigorate *verb* **refresh** 332
invisible *adjective* 223
involve *verb* **include** 207
involved *adjective* **complicated** 72
in your prime *adjective* **adult** 7
irate *adjective* **angry** 13

ire *noun* **anger** 12
iron *verb* **smooth** 388
irrational *adjective* 224
irregular *adjective* **erratic** 134
    adjective **uneven** 444
irrelevant *adjective* **unrelated** 448
irresistible *adjective* **attractive** 25
irresponsible *adjective* **careless** 50
irrigate *verb* **wet** 464
irritable *adjective* **grumpy** 186
irritate *verb* 224
irritating *adjective* **annoying** 15
isolate *verb* 225
isolated *adjective* **distant** 117
issue *noun* **offspring** 281
    verb **distribute** 118
itemize *verb* **list** 244
ivory *adjective* **white** 465

Jj

jabber *verb* **rave** 327
jack up *verb* **lift** 240
jail *noun* **prison** 314
    verb **confine** 75
jam *verb* **press** 312
jamb *noun* **side** 377
jam session *noun* **concert** 74
jargon *noun* **language** 234
jaunt *noun* **journey** 227
jaunty *adjective* **lively** 245
jealous *adjective* 225
jeopardize *verb* **endanger** 129
jest *noun* **joke** 227
jester *noun* **entertainer** 132
jet-black *adjective* **black** 35
jettison *verb* **discard** 111
jittery *adjective* **nervous** 274
job *noun* 226
job *noun* **undertaking** 443
join *verb* 226
join up with *verb* **meet** 256

joke *noun* 227
jolly *adjective* **happy** 188
jot *verb* **write** 472
journal *noun* **publication** 321
journey *noun* 227
journey *verb* **travel** 435
joy *noun* **happiness** 187
joyful *adjective* 228
jubilant *adjective* **joyful** 228
judge *verb* 228
jumble *noun* **mixture** 264
    noun **mess** 257
jump *verb* 229
jumpy *adjective* **nervous** 274
junior *adjective* **subordinate** 406
    adjective **young** 473
junk *noun* **rubbish** 350
just *adjective* **fair** 144
justify *verb* 229
jut *verb* **protrude** 319
juvenile *adjective* **young** 473

Kk

keen *adjective* **enthusiastic** 132
keep *verb* 230
keepsake *noun* **souvenir** 392
key *adjective* **main** 249
kid *verb* **trick** 436
kidnap *verb* **abduct** 1
kill *verb* 230
kin *noun* **family** 146
kind *adjective* 231
kinetic *adjective* **moving** 266
kleptomaniac *noun* **thief** 424
knave *noun* **crook** 87
knell *verb* **ring** 347
knit *verb* **join** 226
knock *verb* **hit** 196
know-it-all *noun* **show-off** 374
knowledgeable
    adjective **educated** 125

LI

label *noun* 231
label *verb* 232
labor *noun* **work** 470
    verb **work** 470
lacerate *verb* **tear** 420
lack *noun* 232
lacking *adjective* **insufficient** 219
lackluster *adjective* **dull** 123
laconic *adjective* **reticent** 345
laden *adjective* **full** 170
lady *noun* **female** 152
lagoon *noun* **lake** 233
lake *noun* 233
lament *verb* **grieve** 184
lance *verb* **scratch** 360
land *verb* 233
land, the *noun* **country** 83
landscape *noun* **view** 454
language *noun* 234
languid *adjective* **lethargic** 240
lap *verb* **pass** 291
large *adjective* **big** 34
last *verb* **continue** 78
last the distance *verb* **persist** 296
late *adjective* **dead** 95
    adjective **modern** 265
    adjective **past** 292
laugh *verb* 234
laugh *noun* **joke** 227
laugh off *verb* **minimize** 259
launch *verb* **initiate** 216
lavish *adjective* **generous** 174
law *noun* **rule** 351
law-abiding *adjective* **obedient** 278
lawful *adjective* **legal** 238
lawn *noun* **yard** 472
lawyer *noun* 235
lax *adjective* **careless** 50
layer *noun* 235
laze *verb* 236
lazy *adjective* 236
lazy *adjective* **slow** 385

leaden *adjective* **heavy** 191
leading *adjective* **best** 33
leading light *noun* **star** 396
leaf through *verb* **read** 328
lean *adjective* **thin** 425
    verb **slope** 384
leap *verb* **jump** 229
learn *verb* 237
learn *verb* **realize** 329
learned *adjective* **educated** 125
lease *verb* **buy** 46
leave *verb* 237
    verb **go** 179
leave *noun* **permission** 296
leave out *verb* **exclude** 139
    verb **neglect** 273
leavings *noun* **remains** 336
lecture *noun* **lesson** 239
lecturer *noun* **teacher** 419
leftovers *noun* **remains** 336
legacy *noun* **gift** 176
legal *adjective* 238
legion *adjective* **numerous** 278
legitimate *adjective* **genuine** 174
    adjective **legal** 238
leisure *noun* **rest** 342
leisurely *adjective* **slow** 385
lemon *adjective* **yellow** 473
lengthy *adjective* 238
lenient *adjective* 239
lessen *verb* **minimize** 259
lesson *noun* 239
let down *verb* **drop** 122
letdown *noun* **disappointment** 109
lethal *adjective* **fatal** 149
lethargic *adjective* 240
let off *verb* **forgive** 164
let on *verb* **blab** 35
let out *verb* **blab** 35
let slip *verb* **blab** 35
letter *noun* **message** 257
letter carrier *noun* **messenger** 258
let your thoughts wander
    verb **daydream** 95
levee *noun* **heap** 191

level *adjective* **flat** 156
   noun **grade** 181
   verb **smooth** 388
level-headed *adjective* **sensible** 366
lever *verb* **lift** 240
levy *noun* **demand** 102
liable *adjective* **likely** 242
libel *verb* **slander** 382
liberal *adjective* **broad-minded** 43
   adjective **generous** 174
liberate *verb* **free** 166
license *verb* **allow** 11
lifeless *adjective* **dead** 95
   adjective **dull** 123
lift *verb* 240
light *adjective* 241
light *adjective* **agile** 9
   adjective **bright** 43
lighten *verb* **comfort** 68
likable *adjective* **agreeable** 10
like *verb* 241
likely *adjective* 242
likeness *noun* **copy** 80
lilac *adjective* **purple** 323
lily-white *adjective* **white** 465
lime *adjective* **green** 184
limit *verb* 242
limit *noun* **outskirts** 287
limp *verb* 243
limpid *adjective* **transparent** 434
line *noun* 243
linger *verb* **dawdle** 94
link *verb* **join** 226
liquid *adjective* 244
lisp *verb* **mumble** 267
list *verb* 244
list *verb* **slope** 384
listless *adjective* **lethargic** 240
litter *noun* **mess** 257
little *adjective* **small** 385
live *verb* 245
live *verb* **reside** 341
lively *adjective* 245
lively *adjective* **energetic** 131
livid *adjective* **angry** 13

load *noun* **weight** 463
loaded *adjective* **wealthy** 462
loaf *verb* **laze** 236
loam *noun* **earth** 123
loath *adjective* **unwilling** 449
loathe *verb* **hate** 190
lobby *noun* **club** 62
   verb **persuade** 298
locate *verb* **find** 154
   verb **position** 306
location *noun* **place** 300
lock up *verb* **confine** 75
lockup *noun* **prison** 314
lofty *adjective* **grand** 181
   adjective **tall** 417
log *verb* **record** 331
logical *adjective* **sane** 355
loiter *verb* **dawdle** 94
loll *verb* **laze** 236
   verb **sag** 354
lone *adjective* **lonely** 246
lonely *adjective* 246
loner *noun* **hermit** 194
long for *verb* **want** 458
long-suffering *adjective* **patient** 293
long-winded *adjective* **lengthy** 238
look down on *verb* **disapprove of** 110
look forward to *verb* **expect** 140
look in *verb* **visit** 456
look over *verb* **inspect** 219
loom *verb* **appear** 16
loop *noun* **coil** 64
   verb **bend** 33
loot *noun* 246
lopsided *adjective* **uneven** 444
loquacious *adjective* **talkative** 416
lose *verb* **pass** 291
loser *noun* **failure** 144
lose your nerve *verb* **fear** 150
loud *adjective* 247
loud *adjective* **gaudy** 173
lounge *verb* **laze** 236
love *verb* 247
lovely *adjective* **beautiful** 29
   adjective **nice** 276

loving *adjective* 248
low *adjective* **quiet** 325
    adjective **sad** 353
lower *verb* **drop** 122
lowly *adjective* **humble** 201
    adjective **subordinate** 406
loyal *adjective* **faithful** 145
luck *noun* **fate** 149
lucky *adjective* 248
ludicrous *adjective* **ridiculous** 347
lug *verb* **pull** 322
lukewarm *adjective* **apathetic** 16
lullaby *noun* **song** 391
lumber *verb* **trudge** 437
luminous *adjective* **shining** 371
lurch *verb* **sway** 413
lure *verb* **attract** 24
luscious *adjective* **delicious** 102
lustrous *adjective* **shiny** 371
lyrical *adjective* **musical** 267

Mm

mad *adjective* 249
maddening *adjective* **annoying** 15
made-up *adjective* **imaginary** 204
magazine *noun* **publication** 321
magenta *adjective* **purple** 323
magnanimous
   adjective **generous** 174
magnetic *adjective* **attractive** 25
magnetize *verb* **attract** 24
magnificent *adjective* **grand** 181
magnify *verb* **emphasize** 126
maim *verb* **hurt** 203
main *adjective* 249
maintain *verb* **keep** 230
majestic *adjective* **grand** 181
major *adjective* **main** 249
make *verb* 250
make a slip *verb* **err** 133
make believe *verb* **imagine** 205

make headway *verb* **advance** 7
make light of *verb* **minimize** 259
make out *verb* **understand** 443
make the grade *verb* **succeed** 407
make up *verb* **concoct** 75
male *noun* 250
malevolent *adjective* **evil** 135
malicious *adjective* **nasty** 271
      adjective **resentful** 340
malign *verb* **slander** 382
malignant *adjective* **fatal** 149
malleable *adjective* **flexible** 157
maltreat *verb* 251
man *noun* **male** 250
manage *verb* 251
manager *noun* 252
maniacal *adjective* **mad** 249
manipulate *verb* **influence** 213
manner *noun* 252
manners *noun* **behavior** 31
maneuvrable *adjective* **moving** 266
manual *noun* **book** 38
manufacture *verb* **make** 250
mar *verb* **damage** 92
march *verb* 253
margin *noun* **edge** 125
marine *noun* **sailor** 355
mariner *noun* **sailor** 355
maritime *adjective* **nautical** 272
mark *verb* **label** 232
marker *noun* **indicator** 211
maroon *adjective* **red** 332
marsh *noun* **swamp** 413
martial *adjective* **warlike** 459
marvel *noun* **miracle** 260
marvelous *adjective* **wonderful** 469
mash *verb* **mix** 263
    verb **soften** 389
mask *verb* **hide** 194
massive *adjective* **heavy** 191
master *noun* **winner** 467
mastermind *noun* **scholar** 359
     verb **plan** 301
masticate *verb* **chew** 55
mat *adjective* **dull** 123

match *noun* **competition** 71

     verb **copy** 80

mate *noun* **sailor** 355

material *adjective* **actual** 5

     noun **cloth** 61

materialize *verb* **appear** 16

matter-of-fact

  adjective **practical** 309

mature *adjective* **adult** 7

mauve *adjective* **purple** 323

maxim *noun* **saying** 357

meager *adjective* **scant** 357

meal *noun* 253

mean *adjective* 254

mean *verb* **intend** 220

meaning *noun* 254

means *noun* **method** 258

measly *adjective* **scant** 357

measure *verb* 255

medal *noun* **prize** 315

meddle *verb* **intrude** 222

mediate *verb* **negotiate** 274

mediocre *adjective* 255

meditate on *verb* **ponder** 305

medley *noun* **mixture** 264

meek *adjective* **humble** 201

meet *verb* 256

meet *verb* **assemble** 20

meeting *noun* 256

melancholy *noun* **misery** 261

mellow *adjective* **musical** 267

melodious *adjective* **musical** 267

melt *verb* **disappear** 109

memento *noun* **souvenir** 392

memo *noun* **message** 257

memorable *adjective* **significant** 378

memorize *verb* **learn** 237

menace *verb* **threaten** 427

mend *verb* **repair** 338

mentor *noun* **adviser** 8

merchant *noun* **seller** 364

merciful *adjective* **lenient** 239

mercurial *adjective* **fickle** 152

mercy *noun* **pity** 299

merge *verb* **combine** 67

merriment *noun* **happiness** 187

merry *adjective* **happy** 188

mesmerize *verb* **charm** 53

mess *noun* 257

message *noun* 257

messenger *noun* 258

mess up *verb* **disorganize** 115

     verb **bungle** 45

messy *adjective* **untidy** 448

meteoric *adjective* **sudden** 408

method *noun* 258

methodical *adjective* **tidy** 430

metropolis *noun* **city** 57

metropolitan *adjective* **civic** 57

middle-of-the-road

  adjective **moderate** 264

middling *adjective* **mediocre** 255

might *noun* **force** 162

mighty *adjective* **powerful** 308

mild *adjective* **fine** 155

  adjective **lenient** 239

  adjective **tasteless** 418

militant *adjective* **defiant** 101

  adjective **warlike** 459

mill *verb* **crush** 89

mimic *verb* 259

mind *verb* **concentrate** 73

mine *verb* **dig** 107

miniature *adjective* **small** 385

minimize *verb* 259

minor *adjective* 260

minstrel *noun* **singer** 381

minute *adjective* **small** 385

miracle *noun* 260

mire *noun* **swamp** 413

mirth *noun* **happiness** 187

miscalculate *verb* **err** 133

miscarry *verb* **fail** 143

miscellaneous

  adjective **various** 453

mischievous *adjective* **naughty** 271

miserable *adjective* 261

miserable *adjective* **pathetic** 292

misery *noun* 261

misfortune *noun* 262

mishap *noun* **misfortune** 262
mislead *verb* **deceive** 96
misrepresent *verb* 262
miss *verb* **avoid** 25
mission *noun* **task** 417
mistake *noun* 263
mistake *verb* **err** 133
misty *adjective* **cloudy** 62
misunderstanding
  noun **mistake** 263
mix *verb* 263
mixed *adjective* **various** 453
mixture *noun* 264
mix up *verb* **disorganize** 115
mob *noun* **crowd** 88
mobile *adjective* **moving** 266
mock *verb* **mimic** 259
model *noun* **copy** 80
  noun **example** 136
moderate *adjective* 264
moderate *verb* **decrease** 97
modern *adjective* 265
modest *adjective* **humble** 201
  adjective **moderate** 264
  adjective **shy** 376
moist *adjective* **wet** 464
moisten *verb* **wet** 464
mollify *verb* **pacify** 289
molten *adjective* **liquid** 244
momentary *adjective* 265
momentous
  adjective **significant** 378
money *noun* **wealth** 462
monk *noun* **hermit** 194
monkey business *noun* **trickery** 437
monopolize *verb* **own** 281
monotonous *adjective* **boring** 39
monstrous *adjective* **bad** 26
  adjective **ugly** 440
moody *adjective* **glum** 178
  adjective **touchy** 433
mop *verb* **wipe** 468
mope *verb* **grieve** 184
mop up *verb* **clean** 58
moral *adjective* **decent** 97

morose *adjective* **glum** 178
morsel *noun* **piece** 299
mortar *noun* **glue** 178
moth-eaten *adjective* **decrepit** 98
motionless *adjective* **still** 400
motivate *verb* **encourage** 128
motley *adjective* **various** 453
motto *noun* **saying** 357
mound *noun* **heap** 191
mount *verb* **climb** 60
  verb **increase** 209
mourn *verb* **grieve** 184
mousy *adjective* **drab** 119
mouth-watering
  adjective **delicious** 102
move *verb* 266
move *noun* **deed** 98
moving *adjective* 266
mow *verb* **cut** 91
muddle *verb* **confuse** 76
muddy *adjective* **opaque** 283
muff *verb* **bungle** 45
muffled *adjective* **quiet** 325
mug *verb* **attack** 23
muggy *adjective* **humid** 202
multiple *adjective* **numerous** 278
multiply *verb* **increase** 209
multitudinous
  adjective **numerous** 278
mumble *verb* 267
mumbo jumbo *noun* **nonsense** 277
munch *verb* **chew** 55
mundane *adjective* **mediocre** 255
murder *verb* **kill** 230
murky *adjective* **dark** 93
murmur *noun* **whisper** 465
  verb **mumble** 267
muscle *noun* **force** 162
muse *verb* **daydream** 95
musical *adjective* 267
musician *noun* 268
mutilate *verb* **hurt** 203
mutiny *noun* **rebellion** 330
  verb **rebel** 330
mutter *verb* **mumble** 267

myriad *adjective* **countless** 82

mysterious *adjective* **confusing** 77

mystified *adjective* **confused** 77

mystify *verb* **puzzle** 324

mythical *adjective* **imaginary** 204

Nn

nab *verb* **grab** 180

nag *verb* **complain** 71

nail *verb* **grab** 180

naive *adjective* 268

naked *adjective* **bare** 28

name *noun* 269

name *verb* 269

nap *verb* **sleep** 383

narcissistic *adjective* **conceited** 73

narrate *verb* **tell** 421

narrow *adjective* 270

narrow-minded *adjective* 270

nasty *adjective* 271

nation *noun* **country** 83

natural *adjective* **simple** 380

naughty *adjective* 271

nauseate *verb* **disgust** 112

nautical *adjective* 272

naval *adjective* **nautical** 272

navy *adjective* **blue** 36

near *adjective* 272

neat *adjective* **good** 179

    adjective **tidy** 430

nebulous *adjective* **shadowy** 368

necessary *adjective* 273

need *noun* **poverty** 307

needy *adjective* **poor** 305

neglect *verb* 273

negligent *adjective* **careless** 50

negotiate *verb* 274

neighboring *adjective* **near** 272

neighborly *adjective* **friendly** 167

nerve *noun* **courage** 84

nervous *adjective* 274

neutral *adjective* 275

neutral *adjective* **colorless** 66

new *adjective* 275

news *noun* **information** 215

newspaper *noun* **publication** 321

next *adjective* **future** 172

    adjective **near** 272

nibble *verb* **chew** 55

nice *adjective* 276

nice *adjective* **kind** 231

niche *noun* **place** 300

nick *verb* **scratch** 360

nickname *noun* **name** 269

nimble *adjective* **agile** 9

nippy *adjective* **cold** 65

noble *adjective* **distinguished** 117

no-frills *adjective* **cheap** 54

noise *noun* 276

noncommital *adjective* **neutral** 275

nonconformist

    adjective **unconventional** 442

nondescript *adjective* **ordinary** 286

nonplussed *adjective* **confused** 77

nonsense *noun* 277

nonsensical

    adjective **ridiculous** 347

normal *adjective* **usual** 452

nosey *adjective* **inquisitive** 217

notable *adjective* **famous** 147

notch *noun* **cut** 91

note *noun* **message** 257

    verb **record** 331

noted *adjective* **famous** 147

notice *verb* **see** 362

noticeable *adjective* **visible** 456

notify *verb* **inform** 214

notion *noun* **thought** 426

notorious *adjective* **famous** 147

not pull your weight *verb* **laze** 236

not yourself *adjective* **sick** 377

nourishment *noun* **food** 161

novel *adjective* **new** 275

noxious *adjective* **poisonous** 303

nucleus *noun* **center** 52

nude *adjective* **bare** 28

number *noun* 277
number *verb* **count** 82
numeral *noun* **number** 277
numerous *adjective* 278
nurse *verb* **help** 192
nutty *adjective* **mad** 249

Oo

oath *noun* **promise** 317
obedient *adjective* 278
obese *adjective* **fat** 148
obey *verb* 279
objective *adjective* **fair** 144
obligatory *adjective* **necessary** 273
oblige *verb* **help** 192
obliged *adjective* **grateful** 182
obliging *adjective* **helpful** 193
obscure *adjective* **dark** 93
　　verb **darken** 93
observant *adjective* **alert** 11
observation *noun* **comment** 69
observe *verb* **obey** 279
　　verb **see** 362
obsession *noun* 279
obsolete *adjective* **old-fashioned** 282
obstacle *noun* 280
obstinate *adjective* **stubborn** 404
obstruct *verb* **block** 36
　　verb **resist** 341
obvious *adjective* 280
obvious *adjective* **clear** 59
occasional *adjective* **scarce** 358
occupation *noun* **job** 226
occupy *verb* **inhabit** 215
　　verb **own** 289
occur *verb* **happen** 187
odd *adjective* **strange** 402
odds and ends *noun* **remains** 336
odor *noun* **smell** 386
off base *adjective* **incorrect** 209

offend *verb* **disgust** 112
offended *adjective* **angry** 13
offender *noun* **criminal** 86
offer *noun* 281
office *noun* **position** 306
official *adjective* **formal** 164
　　noun **manager** 252
officiate *verb* **rule** 352
offspring *noun* 281
old *adjective* 282
old-fashioned *adjective* 282
olive *adjective* **green** 184
omen *noun* **forecast** 163
omit *verb* **neglect** 273
only *adjective* **single** 381
onset *noun* **start** 397
onslaught *noun* **attack** 22
ooze *verb* **drip** 121
opaque *adjective* 283
open *adjective* **free** 166
　　adjective **spacious** 393
　　adjective **uncertain** 441
　　adjective **vulnerable** 457
　　verb **begin** 30
opinion *noun* 283
opponent *noun* **enemy** 130
oppose *verb* **prevent** 313
　　verb **resist** 341
opposite *adjective* 284
oppress *verb* **subdue** 405
oppressive *adjective* **humid** 202
　　adjective **tyrannical** 439
opt for *verb* **prefer** 311
optimistic *adjective* 284
option *noun* **choice** 56
opulent *adjective* **spectacular** 394
orange *adjective* 285
orb *noun* **ball** 26
orbit *noun* **course** 84
order *noun* 285
order *verb* **demand** 103
orderly *adjective* **tidy** 430
ordinary *adjective* 286
organization *noun* 286
organize *verb* **plan** 301

origin *noun* **start** 397
original *adjective* **new** 275
originate *verb* **invent** 222
orthodox *adjective* **usual** 452
oscillate *verb* **fluctuate** 159
ostentatious
  adjective **spectacular** 394
ostracize *verb* **isolate** 225
out cold
  adjective **unconscious** 442
outcome *noun* **result** 344
outdoors, the *noun* **country** 83
outfit *noun* **organization** 286
outgoing *adjective* **friendly** 167
outlaw *noun* **criminal** 86
    verb **ban** 27
outlay *noun* **price** 313
    verb **pay** 294
outline *noun* **summary** 410
    verb **tell** 421
outlook *noun* **opinion** 283
    noun **view** 454
outlying *adjective* **distant** 117
out-of-date
  adjective **old-fashioned** 282
outset *noun* **start** 397
outside *noun* 287
outskirts *noun* 287
outspread *adjective* **wide** 466
outstanding
  adjective **excellent** 136
outstrip *verb* **pass** 291
outwit *verb* 288
overbearing *adjective* **bossy** 40
overcast *adjective* **cloudy** 62
overlook *verb* **neglect** 273
overpower *verb* **subdue** 405
overseer *noun* **boss** 40
oversupply *noun* **excess** 137
overt *adjective* **visible** 456
overtake *verb* **pass** 291
overturn *verb* 288
overweight *adjective* **fat** 148
overwhelm *verb* **flood** 158
own *verb* 289

Pp

pace *verb* **walk** 458
pacify *verb* 289
pack *noun* **crowd** 88
packed *adjective* **full** 170
pact *noun* **promise** 317
pad *verb* **expand** 139
  verb **walk** 458
pageant *noun* **display** 115
pain *noun* 290
painless *adjective* **easy** 124
paint *verb* **color** 65
pal *noun* **friend** 167
pale *adjective* **colorless** 66
  adjective **white** 465
palpitate *verb* **throb** 429
paltry *adjective* **scant** 357
pamphlet *noun* **publication** 321
pandemonium *noun* **noise** 276
panic *verb* **fear** 150
panicky *adjective* **frightened** 168
pant *verb* **gasp** 172
parade *noun* **display** 115
    verb **march** 253
    verb **show** 374
paralegal *noun* **lawyer** 235
paralyze *verb* **weaken** 461
paraphernalia *noun* **property** 318
parasite *noun* **dependant** 103
parched *adjective* **dry** 122
pardon *noun* 290
pardon *verb* **forgive** 164
park *verb* **place** 300
parliament *noun* **council** 81
part *noun* 291
partial *adjective* **incomplete** 208
    adjective **unfair** 444
particle *noun* **piece** 299
partner *noun* **associate** 21
part-time *adjective* **temporary** 421
pass *verb* 291
pass away *verb* **die** 106
passing *adjective* **momentary** 265

passionate *adjective* **intense** 221
passive *adjective* **apathetic** 16
pass on *verb* **send** 365
past *adjective* 292
paste *noun* **glue** 178
pastel *adjective* **colorless** 66
pastoral *adjective* **country** 83
pat *verb* **touch** 432
patch up *verb* **repair** 338
path *noun* **course** 84
pathetic *adjective* 292
pathetic *adjective* **powerless** 308
patient *adjective* 293
patron *noun* **buyer** 47
pattern *noun* **example** 136
pause *noun* **rest** 342
    verb **stop** 401
pave *verb* **coat** 63
pay *noun* 293
pay *verb* 294
peaceful *adjective* 294
peach *adjective* **orange** 285
peak *noun* **top** 432
peal *verb* **ring** 347
pebble *noun* **stone** 401
peculiar *adjective* **strange** 402
peddle *verb* **sell** 364
pen *noun* **yard** 472
    verb **compose** 72
penalize *verb* **punish** 322
penitent *adjective* **sorry** 391
penitentiary *noun* **prison** 314
pen name *noun* **name** 269
pennant *noun* **prize** 315
perceive *verb* **sense** 365
    verb **understand** 443
perception *noun* **feeling** 151
perennial *adjective* **permanent** 295
perfect *adjective* 295
perfect *verb* **improve** 206
perforation *noun* **hole** 197
perform *verb* **behave** 31
performance *noun* **concert** 74
performer *noun* **entertainer** 132
perilous *adjective* **dangerous** 92

perimeter *noun* **outskirts** 287
periodic *adjective* **repeated** 339
peripheral *adjective* **insignificant** 218
periphery *noun* **outskirts** 287
perish *verb* **die** 106
permanent *adjective* 295
permissible *adjective* **legal** 238
permission *noun* 296
permissive
  adjective **broad-minded** 43
permit *verb* **allow** 11
perpetual *adjective* **permanent** 295
perplex *verb* **puzzle** 324
perplexing *adjective* **confusing** 77
persecute *verb* **subdue** 405
perseverance *noun* **persistence** 297
persevere *verb* **persist** 296
persevering *adjective* **patient** 293
persist *verb* 296
persist *verb* **continue** 78
persistence *noun* 297
persistent *adjective* 297
persistent *adjective* **continuous** 78
    adjective **patient** 293
persuade *verb* 298
pert *adjective* **bold** 38
perturbed *adjective* **upset** 450
perverse *adjective* **naughty** 271
perverted *adjective* **indecent** 210
pessimistic *adjective* 298
pester *verb* **annoy** 14
petite *adjective* **slight** 383
petrified *adjective* **frightened** 168
petrify *verb* **frighten** 168
    verb **harden** 189
petty *adjective* **minor** 260
petulant *adjective* **grumpy** 186
phantom *noun* **ghost** 175
phenomenal *adjective* **wonderful** 469
philosopher *noun* **scholar** 359
phobia *noun* **obsession** 279
phony *adjective* **fake** 145
phosphorescent *adjective* **shining** 371
photocopy *verb* **copy** 80
physical *adjective* **actual** 5

pick *verb* **choose** 56
pick apart *verb* **fault** 150
pickings *noun* **loot** 246
pickpocket *noun* **thief** 424
pick up *verb* **capture** 49
piece *noun* 299
piecemeal *adjective* **incomplete** 208
piece of advice *noun* **suggestion** 409
piffle *noun* **nonsense** 277
pig-headed *adjective* **stubborn** 404
pile *noun* **heap** 191
pile up *verb* **gather** 173
pilfer *verb* **steal** 399
pilgrim *noun* **traveler** 435
pinch *noun* **trace** 433
pine away *verb* **grieve** 184
pink *adjective* **red** 332
pinnacle *noun* **top** 432
pioneer *verb* **initiate** 216
pious *adjective* **religious** 336
piquant *adjective* **tasty** 418
pique *verb* **irritate** 224
pirate *noun* **bandit** 27
pitch *noun* **slope** 384
   verb **throw** 429
pitch-black *adjective* **black** 35
pitch-dark *adjective* **dark** 93
pitch forward *verb* **fall** 146
pitiful *adjective* **pathetic** 292
pity *noun* 299
place *noun* 300
place *verb* 300
place *verb* **remember** 337
placid *adjective* **calm** 48
plain *adjective* **clear** 59
   adjective **obvious** 280
   adjective **simple** 380
   adjective **tasteless** 418
plan *verb* 301
plan *noun* **summary** 410
   verb **intend** 220
plane *verb* **smooth** 388
planned *adjective* **deliberate** 101
plaster *verb* **coat** 63
plausible *adjective* **believable** 32

play down *verb* **minimize** 259
player *noun* **entertainer** 132
playful *adjective* **lively** 245
playmate *noun* **friend** 167
pleasant *adjective* **nice** 276
please *verb* 301
pleased *adjective* **glad** 177
pledge *noun* **promise** 317
plentiful *adjective* **abundant** 2
pliable *adjective* **flexible** 157
plod *verb* **trudge** 437
plodding *adjective* **slow** 385
plot *noun* 302
plot *verb* 302
plump *adjective* **fat** 148
plunder *noun* **loot** 246
ply *verb* **use** 451
poach *verb* **abduct** 1
   verb **boil** 37
pointer *noun* **indicator** 211
   noun **suggestion** 409
poised *adjective* **calm** 48
poisonous *adjective* 303
polish *verb* 303
polished *adjective* **smooth** 387
polite *adjective* 304
poll *noun* **inquiry** 216
pollute *verb* **spoil** 395
polluted *adjective* **dirty** 107
pompous *adjective* 304
pond *noun* **lake** 233
ponder *verb* 305
ponderous *adjective* **heavy** 191
poor *adjective* 305
poor *adjective* **inferior** 212
popular *adjective* **public** 320
populate *verb* **inhabit** 215
pore over *verb* **ponder** 305
portion *noun* **part** 291
portray *verb* **describe** 104
position *noun* 306
position *verb* 306
position *noun* **place** 300
positive *adjective* **optimistic** 284
   adjective **sure** 412

possess *verb* **own** 289
possessions *noun* **property** 318
possessive *adjective* **jealous** 225
        adjective **selfish** 363
possible *adjective* 307
possible *adjective* **believable** 32
post *noun* **position** 306
postpone *verb* **defer** 100
posture *noun* **manner** 252
potent *adjective* **powerful** 308
pound *verb* **crush** 89
pour *verb* **rain** 326
pout *verb* **frown** 170
poverty *noun* 307
power *noun* **force** 162
    noun **influence** 213
powerful *adjective* 308
powerless *adjective* 308
practicable *adjective* **possible** 307
practical *adjective* 309
practice *noun* 309
practice *noun* **tradition** 434
pragmatic *adjective* **practical** 309
praise *verb* 310
prance *verb* **frisk** 169
prank *noun* **trick** 436
prattle *verb* **rave** 327
precarious *adjective* **dangerous** 92
precept *noun* **rule** 351
précis *noun* **summary** 410
precise *adjective* 310
preclude *verb* **exclude** 139
predecessor *noun* **ancestor** 12
predict *verb* 311
prediction *noun* **forecast** 163
pre-eminent
   adjective **important** 205
prefer *verb* 311
preference *noun* **choice** 56
prehistoric *adjective* **old** 282
prejudice *verb* **influence** 213
prejudiced
   adjective **narrow-minded** 270
   adjective **unfair** 444
premeditated *adjective* **deliberate** 101

preoccupied *adjective* **dreamy** 120
prepare *verb* **make** 250
prepared *adjective* **ready** 329
preposterous
   adjective **ridiculous** 347
presence *noun* **appearance** 17
present *noun* **gift** 176
     verb **give** 176
preserve *verb* **keep** 230
     verb **save** 356
preside *verb* **rule** 352
press *verb* 312
press *verb* **hug** 200
prestigious *adjective* **important** 205
pretend *verb* **imagine** 205
pretentious *adjective* **pompous** 304
pretty *adjective* 312
prevent *verb* 313
preview *noun* **display** 115
previous *adjective* **past** 292
price *noun* 313
pricey *adjective* **expensive** 141
prickly *adjective* **touchy** 433
primary *adjective* **main** 249
principal *adjective* **best** 33
principle *noun* **virtue** 455
print *verb* **write** 472
prison *noun* 314
prisoner *noun* 314
private *adjective* **secret** 361
prize *noun* 315
prize *adjective* **superior** 411
probable *adjective* **believable** 32
     adjective **likely** 242
probe *verb* **investigate** 223
procedure *noun* **method** 258
proceed *verb* **advance** 7
     verb **go** 179
proceeds *noun* **profit** 316
proclaim *verb* **publish** 321
procure *verb* **get** 175
prodigy *noun* **expert** 141
produce *verb* 315
produce *verb* **cause** 52
     verb **make** 250

profession *noun* 316
proficient *adjective* **competent** 70
profile *noun* **side** 377
profit *noun* 316
profound *adjective* **intense** 221
progeny *noun* **offspring** 281
prognosis *noun* **forecast** 163
progress *verb* **advance** 7
prohibit *verb* **prevent** 313
project *noun* **undertaking** 443
    verb **protrude** 319
prolific *adjective* **abundant** 2
prolong *verb* **keep** 230
prominent *adjective* **important** 205
    adjective **visible** 456
promise *noun* 317
promising *adjective* **lucky** 248
promote *verb* **further** 171
pronounce *verb* 317
propaganda *noun* **information** 215
propel *verb* **push** 323
proper *adjective* **decent** 97
    adjective **legal** 238
property *noun* 318
prophecy *noun* **forecast** 163
prophesy *verb* **predict** 311
proportion *noun* **part** 291
proposal *noun* **offer** 281
propose *verb* **advise** 8
proposition *noun* **offer** 281
prop up *verb* **strengthen** 403
prospective *adjective* **future** 172
prosper *verb* **thrive** 428
prosperous *adjective* **wealthy** 462
protect *verb* 318
protected *adjective* **safe** 353
protection *noun* **defense** 100
protégé *noun* **dependant** 103
protest *verb* **complain** 71
protrude *verb* 319
proud *adjective* 319
prove *verb* 320
proven *adjective* **genuine** 174
proverb *noun* **saying** 357
providence *noun* **fate** 149

provident *adjective* **thrifty** 428
provisional
    adjective **temporary** 421
provisions *noun* **food** 161
provoke *verb* **cause** 52
    verb **irritate** 224
prudent *adjective* **sensible** 366
pseudonym *noun* **name** 269
public *adjective* 320
publication *noun* 321
publish *verb* 321
puff *verb* **gasp** 172
pugnacious *adjective* **aggressive** 9
pull *verb* 322
pull a fast one *verb* **outwit** 288
pull in *verb* **attract** 24
pull your weight *verb* **work** 470
pulp *verb* **soften** 389
pulsate *verb* **throb** 429
pulverize *verb* **crush** 89
pun *noun* **wisecrack** 468
punch *verb* **beat** 29
punctuate *verb* **interrupt** 221
pungent *adjective* **tasty** 418
punish *verb* 322
puny *adjective* **slight** 383
pupil *noun* **student** 405
puppet *noun* **slave** 382
purchase *verb* **buy** 46
purchaser *noun* **buyer** 47
pure *adjective* **clean** 58
purple *adjective* 323
purposeful *adjective* **deliberate** 101
pursue *verb* **follow** 161
    verb **seek** 363
push *verb* 323
push on *verb* **advance** 7
put a damper on
    verb **discourage** 112
put at risk *verb* **endanger** 129
put in the picture
    verb **inform** 214
putrefy *verb* **rot** 349
putrid *adjective* **smelly** 386
put up *verb* **build** 45

put up with *verb* **endure** 130
put your feet up *verb* **rest** 343
puzzle *verb* 324
puzzled *adjective* **confused** 77
puzzling *adjective* **confusing** 77

Qq

quaff *verb* **drink** 121
quagmire *noun* **swamp** 413
quail *verb* **cower** 85
quake *verb* **shake** 368
qualify *verb* **suit** 410
quality *adjective* **superior** 411
quarantine *verb* **isolate** 225
quarrel *noun* **argument** 18
   verb **argue** 18
quarrelsome
   adjective **argumentative** 19
quavering
   adjective **inarticulate** 207
querulous
   adjective **dissatisfied** 116
query *verb* **doubt** 119
quest after *verb* **seek** 363
question *verb* 324
question *verb* **doubt** 119
questionable
   adjective **uncertain** 441
questioning
   adjective **inquisitive** 217
quick *adjective* **fast** 148
quiet *adjective* 325
quiet *adjective* **peaceful** 294
   adjective **reticent** 345
   adjective **simple** 380
quieten *verb* **pacify** 289
quip *noun* **wisecrack** 468
quit *verb* 325
quit *verb* **stop** 401
quiz *verb* **question** 324
quota *noun* **share** 369

Rr

race *noun* **competition** 71
   verb **compete** 70
   verb **speed** 394
racket *noun* **noise** 276
radical *adjective* **unconventional** 442
rage *noun* **anger** 12
raid *verb* **attack** 23
rain *verb* 326
raise *verb* **lift** 240
rake in *verb* **gather** 173
rally *verb* **assemble** 20
   verb **recover** 331
ram *verb* **push** 323
ramble *verb* 326
rambling *adjective* **lengthy** 238
rancid *adjective* **inedible** 211
random *adjective* **accidental** 2
rank *adjective* **smelly** 386
   noun **grade** 181
   noun **line** 243
rapacious *adjective* **greedy** 183
rapid *adjective* **fast** 148
rapturous *adjective* **joyful** 228
rare *adjective* **scarce** 358
   adjective **unusual** 449
rash *adjective* 327
rasp *verb* **roughen** 350
rate *noun* **price** 313
   verb **measure** 255
ration *verb* **distribute** 118
rat on *verb* **betray** 34
raucous *adjective* **loud** 247
rave *verb* 327
raw *adjective* **inexperienced** 212
   adjective **wintry** 467
reach *verb* **come** 67
   verb **extend** 142
react *verb* **answer** 15
reaction *noun* 328
read *verb* 328
ready *adjective* 329
real *adjective* **actual** 5

realistic *adjective* **practical** 309
realize *verb* 329
reason *verb* **conclude** 74
reasonable *adjective* **moderate** 264
    adjective **sensible** 366
rebel *verb* 330
rebellion *noun* 330
rebellious *adjective* **defiant** 101
rebound *verb* **reverse** 346
rebuff *verb* **refuse** 333
    verb **repel** 339
rebuke *verb* **scold** 359
rebut *verb* **disprove** 116
recalcitrant *adjective* **defiant** 101
recall *verb* **remember** 337
recede *verb* **reverse** 346
receive *verb* **get** 175
recent *adjective* **modern** 265
recess *noun* **rest** 342
reciprocate *verb* **retaliate** 344
recital *noun* **concert** 74
reckless *adjective* **rash** 327
reckon *verb* **calculate** 47
    verb **think** 425
recluse *noun* **hermit** 194
reclusive *adjective* **lonely** 246
recognize *verb* **remember** 337
    verb **sense** 365
recollect *verb* **remember** 337
recommend *verb* **advise** 8
recommendation
    noun **suggestion** 409
recompense *verb* **repay** 338
reconnoiter *verb* **inspect** 219
record *verb* 331
recount *verb* **tell** 421
recover *verb* 331
rectify *verb* **correct** 81
rectitude *noun* **virtue** 455
recuperate *verb* **recover** 331
recurrent *adjective* **repeated** 339
red *adjective* 332
redeem *verb* **buy** 46
reduced *adjective* **cheap** 54
redundant *adjective* **extra** 143

reel *verb* **sway** 413
    verb **turn** 438
refined *adjective* **distinguished** 117
reflect on *verb* **ponder** 305
reform *verb* **correct** 81
refresh *verb* 332
refrigerate *verb* **cool** 79
refuge *noun* 333
refugee *noun* **escapee** 134
refund *verb* **repay** 338
refuse *verb* 333
refuse *noun* **rubbish** 350
refute *verb* **disprove** 116
regard *noun* **respect** 342
register *verb* **record** 331
regular *adjective* **repeated** 339
regulation *noun* **rule** 351
rehearsal *noun* **practice** 309
reign *verb* **rule** 352
reimburse *verb* **repay** 338
reinforce *verb* **strengthen** 403
reject *verb* **refuse** 333
rejoice *verb* 334
relate *verb* **tell** 421
related *adjective* 334
relations *noun* **family** 146
relatives *noun* **family** 146
relax *verb* **rest** 343
relaxed *adjective* **calm** 48
    adjective **informal** 214
relay *verb* **send** 365
release *noun* **pardon** 290
    verb **free** 166
relevant *adjective* **related** 334
reliable *adjective* 335
relief *noun* **comfort** 68
    noun **help** 192
relieve *verb* **comfort** 68
religion *noun* 335
religious *adjective* 336
relinquish *verb* **sacrifice** 352
relish *verb* **like** 241
reluctant *adjective* **unwilling** 449
remain *verb* **live** 245
remains *noun* 336

remark *noun* **comment** 69
remarkable
  adjective **astonishing** 22
  adjective **unusual** 449
remedy *verb* **correct** 81
remember *verb* 337
remembrance *noun* **souvenir** 392
remnants *noun* **remains** 336
remorseful *adjective* **sorry** 391
remote *adjective* **distant** 117
remove *verb* 337
remove *verb* **subtract** 407
rendezvous *noun* **meeting** 256
renew *verb* **refresh** 332
renounce *verb* **refuse** 333
renovate *verb* **repair** 338
renowned *adjective* **famous** 147
rent *verb* **buy** 46
repair *verb* 338
repast *noun* **meal** 253
repay *verb* 338
repeal *verb* **cancel** 49
repeated *adjective* 339
repel *verb* 339
repentant *adjective* **sorry** 391
replace *verb* **exchange** 137
replica *noun* **copy** 80
reply *noun* **reaction** 328
  verb **answer** 15
report *noun* 340
report *verb* **betray** 34
  verb **publish** 321
represent *verb* **describe** 104
repress *verb* **subdue** 405
repressive *adjective* **tyrannical** 439
reprimand *verb* **scold** 359
reproduce *verb* **copy** 80
reprove *verb* **scold** 359
republic *noun* **country** 83
repulse *verb* **repel** 339
repulsive *adjective* **unpleasant** 447
    adjective **ugly** 440
request *verb* **ask** 20
require *verb* **demand** 103
requisition *noun* **demand** 102

rescue *verb* **free** 166
  verb **save** 356
research *verb* **investigate** 223
resentful *adjective* 340
reserved *adjective* **reticent** 345
reservoir *noun* **lake** 233
reside *verb* 341
residence *noun* **home** 198
residue *noun* **remains** 336
resign *verb* **sacrifice** 352
resilient *adjective* **elastic** 126
resist *verb* 341
resolve *verb* **solve** 390
resonant *adjective* **loud** 247
respect *noun* 342
respect *verb* **worship** 471
respectable *adjective* **decent** 97
resplendent
  adjective **spectacular** 394
respond *verb* **answer** 15
response *noun* **reaction** 328
responsible *adjective* **reliable** 335
rest *noun* 342
rest *verb* 343
rest *verb* **place** 300
restaurant *noun* 343
restless *adjective* **excited** 138
restore *verb* **repair** 338
restrain *verb* **confine** 75
restrained *adjective* **moderate** 264
restrict *verb* **limit** 242
result *noun* 344
résumé *noun* **summary** 410
retail *verb* **sell** 364
retailer *noun* **seller** 364
retain *verb* **keep** 230
retaliate *verb* 344
retard *verb* **hinder** 195
reticent *adjective* 345
retire *verb* **leave** 237
retort *verb* **answer** 15
retreat *noun* **refuge** 333
  verb **leave** 237
return *noun* **profit** 316
  verb **answer** 15

reveal *verb* 345
revel *verb* **rejoice** 334
revere *verb* **worship** 471
reverent *adjective* **religious** 336
reverse *verb* 346
review *verb* **examine** 135
revise *verb* **correct** 81
revive *verb* **refresh** 332
revolt *noun* **rebellion** 330
    verb **disgust** 112
    verb **rebel** 330
revolting *adjective* **unpleasant** 447
revolution *noun* **rebellion** 330
reward *verb* **repay** 338
rhythm *noun* 346
rhythmical
  adjective **repeated** 339
rib *verb* **tease** 420
rich *adjective* **colorful** 66
  adjective **wealthy** 462
riches *noun* **wealth** 462
ridicule *noun* **scorn** 360
  verb **tease** 420
ridiculous *adjective* 347
rift *noun* **break** 42
right *adjective* **decent** 97
  adjective **fair** 144
  adjective **true** 438
rigid *adjective* **hard** 188
  adjective **strict** 403
rim *noun* **edge** 125
ring *verb* 347
riot *noun* **commotion** 69
rip *verb* **tear** 420
rip off *verb* **cheat** 54
rise up *verb* **rebel** 330
risky *adjective* **dangerous** 92
ritual *adjective* **formal** 164
rival *noun* **enemy** 130
roam *verb* **travel** 435
roar *verb* **shout** 373
roast *verb* **swelter** 414
  verb **toast** 431
rob *verb* **steal** 399
robber *noun* **thief** 424

robust *adjective* **healthy** 190
  adjective **strong** 404
rock *noun* **stone** 401
  verb **shake** 368
rogue *noun* **crook** 87
rookie *noun* **student** 405
room *noun* 348
roomy *adjective* **spacious** 393
rosy *adjective* 348
rot *noun* 349
rotate *verb* **turn** 438
rotten *adjective* **bad** 26
  adjective **inedible** 211
rough *adjective* 349
roughen *verb* 350
rousing *adjective* **exciting** 138
route *noun* **course** 84
rove *verb* **travel** 435
row *noun* **line** 243
royalty *noun* **profit** 316
rubbery *adjective* **elastic** 126
rubbish *noun* 350
rubbish *noun* **nonsense** 277
ruby *adjective* **red** 332
ruddy *adjective* **rosy** 348
rude *adjective* 351
ruffle *verb* **roughen** 350
rugged *adjective* **hardy** 189
ruin *verb* **damage** 92
ruined *adjective* **broke** 44
rule *noun* 351
rule *verb* 352
rumor *noun* **gossip** 180
run *verb* **compete** 70
  verb **extend** 142
  verb **manage** 251
runaway *noun* **escapee** 134
run into *verb* **meet** 256
runny *adjective* **liquid** 244
run riot *verb* **rebel** 330
run-through *noun* **practice** 309
rural *adjective* **country** 83
ruse *noun* **plot** 302
  noun **trick** 436
rush *verb* **hurry** 202

rustic *adjective* **country** 83
rustle *noun* **whisper** 465
    verb **abduct** 1
rut *noun* **groove** 185
ruthless *adjective* **cruel** 89

Ss

sabotage *verb* **damage** 92
sacred *adjective* **holy** 198
sacrifice *verb* 352
sad *adjective* 353
sadden *verb* **upset** 450
safe *adjective* 353
safeguard *noun* **defense** 100
    verb **save** 356
sag *verb* 354
sage *adjective* **sensible** 366
    noun **scholar** 359
sail *verb* 354
sailor *noun* 355
saintly *adjective* **holy** 198
salary *noun* **pay** 293
salvage *verb* **save** 356
sample *noun* **example** 136
    verb **test** 422
sanction *verb* **approve** 17
sanctuary *noun* **refuge** 333
sand *verb* **smooth** 388
sane *adjective* 355
sap *verb* **weaken** 461
sapphire *adjective* **blue** 36
satellite *noun* **dependant** 103
satiated *adjective* **satisfied** 356
satin *adjective* **shiny** 371
satisfactory *adjective* **good** 179
    adjective **sufficient** 408
satisfied *adjective* 356
satisfy *verb* **please** 301
saucy *adjective* **bold** 38
saunter *verb* **walk** 458
savage *adjective* **cruel** 89
save *verb* 356

save *verb* **store** 402
savory *adjective* **tasty** 418
saying *noun* 357
scale *verb* **climb** 60
scamper *verb* **dart** 94
scan *verb* **inspect** 219
scant *adjective* 357
scarce *adjective* 358
scare *verb* **frighten** 168
scared *adjective* **frightened** 168
scare off *verb* **repel** 339
scarlet *adjective* **red** 332
scary *adjective* **frightening** 169
scatter *verb* 358
scene *noun* **surroundings** 412
    noun **view** 454
scent *noun* **smell** 386
schedule *verb* **plan** 301
scheme *noun* **plot** 302
    verb **plot** 302
scholar *noun* 359
scold *verb* 359
scoop *verb* **dig** 107
scoot *verb* **dart** 94
scorch *verb* **swelter** 414
score *noun* **cut** 91
    verb **scratch** 360
scorn *noun* 360
scowl *verb* **frown** 170
scramble *verb* **dart** 94
scrap *noun* **piece** 299
    verb **discard** 111
scratch *verb* 360
scrawl *verb* **write** 472
scream *verb* **shriek** 375
screech *verb* **shriek** 375
screen *verb* **protect** 318
    verb **test** 422
screw *verb* **turn** 438
scribble *verb* **write** 472
scrub *verb* **clean** 58
scruffy *adjective* 361
scrumptious *adjective* **delicious** 102
scrupulous *adjective* **honest** 199
scrutinize *verb* **investigate** 223

scuffle *verb* **fight** 154

scurry *verb* **dart** 94

seafarer *noun* **sailor** 355

seafaring *adjective* **nautical** 272

seagoing *adjective* **nautical** 272

seam *noun* **layer** 235

search *verb* **inspect** 219

search for *verb* **seek** 363

seaside *noun* **shore** 372

seasoned *adjective* **adult** 7

seaworthy *adjective* **nautical** 272

secondary *adjective* **minor** 260

second-rate *adjective* **mediocre** 255

secret *adjective* 361

secretary *noun* **clerk** 59

secretive *adjective* 362

secretive *adjective* **reticent** 345

section *noun* **part** 291

secure *adjective* **safe** 353

    adjective **steady** 398

    verb **protect** 318

    verb **steady** 399

security *noun* **defense** 100

sedentary *adjective* **still** 400

seductive *adjective* **attractive** 25

see *verb* 362

see eye to eye *verb* **agree** 10

seek *verb* 363

seep *verb* **drip** 121

segment *noun* **part** 291

segregate *verb* **isolate** 225

seize *verb* **grab** 180

select *verb* **choose** 56

selection *noun* **choice** 56

self-centered *adjective* **selfish** 363

self-confident *adjective* **proud** 319

self-effacing *adjective* **humble** 201

selfish *adjective* 363

self-reliant *adjective* **proud** 319

self-sufficient

  adjective **independent** 210

sell *verb* 364

seller *noun* 364

sell out *verb* **betray** 34

seminar *noun* **lesson** 239

senate *noun* **council** 81

send *verb* 365

sensation *noun* **feeling** 151

    noun **miracle** 260

sensational *adjective* **excellent** 136

sense *verb* 365

sense *noun* **feeling** 151

    noun **meaning** 254

senseless *adjective* **silly** 379

sensible *adjective* 366

sensitive *adjective* **touchy** 433

separate *verb* 366

separate *adjective* **independent** 210

sepia *adjective* **brown** 44

sequel *noun* **result** 344

sequence *noun* **series** 367

serene *adjective* **peaceful** 294

series *noun* 367

serious *adjective* **significant** 378

    adjective **solemn** 390

serve *verb* **suit** 410

servile *adjective* **submissive** 406

set *verb* **harden** 189

    verb **place** 300

set about *verb* **begin** 30

set an example for

  verb **encourage** 128

setback *noun* **disappointment** 109

set down *verb* **compose** 72

set out *verb* **start** 397

set up *verb* **start** 397

setting *noun* **surroundings** 412

settle *verb* **inhabit** 215

settle a score *verb* **retaliate** 344

set up *verb* **start** 397

severe *adjective* **intense** 221

severity *noun* **violence** 454

sew *verb* 367

shabby *adjective* **mean** 254

    adjective **scruffy** 361

shade *verb* **darken** 93

shadow *verb* **follow** 161

shadowy *adjective* 368

shadowy *adjective* **dark** 93

shady *adjective* **dishonest** 113

shaggy *adjective* **rough** 349
shake *verb* 368
shake a leg *verb* **hurry** 202
shake hands *verb* **agree** 10
sham *adjective* **fake** 145
shambles *noun* **mess** 257
shape *noun* 369
shape *verb* **build** 45
share *noun* 369
share *verb* 370
shark *noun* **crook** 87
sharp *adjective* **cold** 65
   adjective **discordant** 111
   adjective **shrewd** 375
   adjective **tasty** 418
shear *verb* **cut** 91
shed *verb* **discard** 111
sheer *adjective* **transparent** 434
shelter *noun* **refuge** 333
sheltered *adjective* **safe** 353
shelve *verb* **defer** 100
shield *noun* **defense** 100
   verb **protect** 318
shift *verb* **move** 266
shifty *adjective* **dishonest** 113
shimmer *verb* **sparkle** 393
shine *verb* 370
shine *verb* **polish** 303
   verb **succeed** 407
shining *adjective* 371
shinny up *verb* **climb** 60
shiny *adjective* 371
shipshape *adjective* **tidy** 430
shirk *verb* **avoid** 25
shock *verb* 372
shoddy *adjective* **defective** 99
   adjective **inferior** 212
shoplifter *noun* **thief** 424
shopper *noun* **buyer** 47
shore *noun* 372
shore up *verb* **strengthen** 403
short *adjective* **abrupt** 1
   adjective **brief** 42
   adjective **insufficient** 219
   adjective **small** 385

shortage *noun* **lack** 232
shorten *verb* 373
shout *verb* 373
shove *verb* **push** 323
show *verb* 374
show *noun* **concert** 74
   verb **reveal** 345
show-off *noun* 374
show up *verb* **appear** 16
   verb **come** 67
showy *adjective* **gaudy** 173
shrewd *adjective* 375
shriek *verb* 375
shrill *adjective* **high-pitched** 195
   adjective **loud** 247
shrink *verb* 376
shrivel *verb* **shrink** 376
shroud *verb* **cover** 85
shudder *verb* **fear** 150
   verb **shake** 368
shuffle *verb* **limp** 243
shut away *verb* **isolate** 225
shy *adjective* 376
sick *adjective* 377
sicken *verb* **disgust** 112
sick of *adjective* **bored** 39
side *noun* 377
side with *verb* **befriend** 30
sigh *noun* **whisper** 465
sightseer *noun* **traveler** 435
sign *noun* 378
sign *noun* **indicator** 211
significance *noun* **meaning** 254
significant *adjective* 378
silken *adjective* **smooth** 387
silky *adjective* **shiny** 371
   adjective **soft** 389
silly *adjective* 379
silver *adjective* **gray** 182
silver-tongued *adjective* **fluent** 160
similar *adjective* 379
simmer *verb* **boil** 37
simple *adjective* 380
simple *adjective* **easy** 124
   adjective **naive** 268

simplify *verb* 380
sincere *adjective* **honest** 199
sinful *adjective* **evil** 135
singer *noun* 381
single *adjective* 381
single-minded *adjective* **persistent** 297
single out *verb* **prefer** 311
sing someone's praises
   verb **praise** 310
singular *adjective* **unusual** 449
sink *verb* **descend** 104
   verb **drop** 122
sinuous *adjective* **twisted** 439
sip *verb* **drink** 121
site *noun* **place** 300
   verb **position** 306
situation *noun* **position** 306
size up *verb* **judge** 228
skeleton *noun* **support** 411
skillful *adjective* 382
skim *verb* **read** 328
   verb **sail** 354
skimpy *adjective* **scant** 357
skin *noun* **coating** 64
skinny *adjective* **thin** 425
skip *verb* **exclude** 139
   verb **frisk** 169
skirmish *noun* **fight** 153
slack *adjective* **lazy** 236
slander *verb* 382
slang *noun* **language** 234
slant *noun* **slope** 384
   verb **misrepresent** 262
   verb **slope** 384
slash *verb* **tear** 420
slate *adjective* **gray** 182
slave *verb* **work** 470
slay *verb* **kill** 230
sleek *adjective* **shiny** 371
sleep *verb* 383
slender *adjective* **thin** 425
slick *adjective* **fluent** 160
slight *adjective* 383
slight *adjective* **minor** 260
   verb **insult** 220

slim *adjective* **thin** 425
slip *noun* **mistake** 263
   verb **fall** 146
   verb **insert** 217
slippery *adjective* **smooth** 387
   adjective **unfaithful** 445
slit *noun* **cut** 91
   noun **hole** 197
   verb **tear** 420
sliver *noun* **piece** 299
slog *verb* **trudge** 437
   verb **work** 470
slope *noun* 384
slope *verb* 384
sloppy *adjective* **liquid** 244
   adjective **scruffy** 361
slothful *adjective* **lazy** 236
slouch *verb* **sag** 354
slovenly *adjective* **untidy** 448
slow *adjective* 385
sluggish *adjective* **lethargic** 240
slumber *verb* **sleep** 383
slump *verb* **sag** 354
sly *adjective* **cunning** 90
smack *verb* **beat** 29
small *adjective* 385
small *adjective* **narrow** 270
small-time *adjective* **insignificant** 218
smart *adjective* **chic** 55
   adjective **clever** 60
smart alec *noun* **show-off** 374
smear *verb* **coat** 63
   verb **dirty** 108
   verb **slander** 382
smell *noun* 386
smelly *adjective* 386
smile *verb* 387
smirk *verb* **smile** 387
smooth *adjective* 387
smooth *verb* 388
smooth *adjective* **flat** 156
   adjective **fluent** 160
smother *verb* **flood** 158
   verb **suffocate** 409
smudge *verb* **dirty** 108

smug *adjective* **proud** 319
snack *noun* **meal** 253
snack bar *noun* **restaurant** 343
snap *adjective* **sudden** 408
snappy *adjective* **grumpy** 186
snap up *verb* **grab** 180
snare *verb* **catch** 51
snatch *verb* **grab** 180
snicker *verb* **smile** 387
snip *verb* **cut** 91
snobbish *adjective* **pompous** 304
snoopy *adjective* **inquisitive** 217
snooty *adjective* **pompous** 304
snooze *verb* **sleep** 383
snowy *adjective* **white** 465
snub *verb* **insult** 220
soak *verb* 388
soar *verb* **fly** 160
sob *verb* **cry** 90
sober *adjective* **solemn** 390
sociable *adjective* **friendly** 167
sodden *adjective* **wet** 464
soft *adjective* 389
soft *adjective* **quiet** 325
soften *verb* 389
soft-soap *verb* **flatter** 156
soggy *adjective* **wet** 464
soil *noun* **earth** 123
    verb **dirty** 108
solace *noun* **comfort** 68
sole *adjective* **single** 381
solemn *adjective* 390
solid *adjective* **heavy** 191
    adjective **thick** 423
solidify *verb* **harden** 189
solitary *adjective* **lonely** 246
soloist *noun* **musician** 268
    noun **singer** 381
solve *verb* 390
somber *adjective* **drab** 119
sometime *adjective* **past** 292
song *noun* 391
soothe *verb* **comfort** 68
soprano *adjective* **high-pitched** 195
sorrow *noun* **misery** 261

sorry *adjective* 391
sort *verb* **arrange** 19
sort out *verb* **simplify** 380
so-so *adjective* **ordinary** 286
sound *adjective* **healthy** 190
    adjective **sane** 355
    verb **measure** 255
    verb **pronounce** 317
sour *adjective* 392
souvenir *noun* 392
spacious *adjective* 393
span *verb* **cross** 88
spare *adjective* **extra** 143
    verb **forgive** 164
sparkle *verb* 393
sparse *adjective* **scant** 357
spasm *noun* **pain** 290
spat *noun* **disagreement** 76
speak well of *verb* **praise** 310
specialist *noun* **expert** 141
specific *adjective* **precise** 310
specimen *noun* **example** 136
spectacular *adjective* 394
specter *noun* **ghost** 175
speed *verb* 394
speedy *adjective* **fast** 148
spell out *verb* **explain** 142
spend *verb* **pay** 294
sphere *noun* **ball** 26
spick-and-span *adjective* **clean** 58
spicy *adjective* **tasty** 418
spiffy *adjective* **chic** 55
spin *verb* 395
spindly *adjective* **thin** 425
spineless *adjective* **fearful** 151
spiral *noun* **coil** 64
spirit away *verb* **abduct** 1
spirited *adjective* **energetic** 131
spiteful *adjective* **nasty** 271
    adjective **resentful** 340
splendid *adjective* **great** 183
split *noun* **break** 42
    verb **share** 370
splurge *verb* **waste** 460
splutter *verb* **mumble** 267

spoil *verb* 395

spoiled *adjective* **selfish** 363

spoils *noun* **loot** 246

sponge *verb* **wipe** 468

spongy *adjective* **soft** 389

spontaneous *adjective* **free** 166

spook *noun* **ghost** 175

sporadic *adjective* **erratic** 134

    adjective **scarce** 358

spot *noun* **place** 300

    verb **dirty** 108

spotless *adjective* **clean** 58

spread *noun* **meal** 253

    verb **coat** 63

    verb **extend** 142

    verb **scatter** 358

sprightly *adjective* **agile** 9

spring *verb* **jump** 229

springy *adjective* **elastic** 126

sprinkle *verb* **rain** 326

sprout *verb* **flourish** 158

spry *adjective* **agile** 9

spunk *noun* **courage** 84

spurn *verb* **repel** 339

spurt *verb* **flow** 159

squabble *verb* **argue** 18

squander *verb* **waste** 460

squash *verb* **press** 312

    verb **soften** 389

squat *adjective* **stocky** 400

    verb **reside** 341

squawk *verb* **shriek** 375

squeal *verb* **shriek** 375

squeeze *verb* **press** 312

squiggly *adjective* **twisted** 439

squirm *verb* **fidget** 153

stab *noun* **attempt** 23

stabilize *verb* **steady** 399

stable *adjective* **steady** 398

stack *noun* **heap** 191

stage *noun* **grade** 181

stagger *verb* **limp** 243

staggering *adjective* **astonishing** 22

stagnant *adjective* **still** 400

stain *verb* **color** 65

stale *adjective* **boring** 39

    adjective **inedible** 211

stalemate *noun* **halt** 186

stall *verb* **stop** 401

stamina *noun* **persistence** 297

stammer *verb* **mumble** 267

stance *noun* **manner** 252

stand *noun* **opinion** 283

standard *adjective* **ordinary** 286

stand by *verb* **befriend** 30

stand in for *verb* **exchange** 137

standoffish *adjective* **unfriendly** 445

standstill *noun* **halt** 186

star *noun* 396

star *adjective* **best** 33

star-crossed *adjective* **unlucky** 447

stare *verb* 396

start *noun* 397

start *verb* 397

start *verb* **begin** 30

startle *verb* **shock** 372

state *noun* **country** 83

state attorney *noun* **lawyer** 235

stately *adjective* **grand** 181

statement *noun* **report** 340

station *noun* **position** 306

    verb **position** 306

stationary *adjective* **still** 400

staunch *adjective* **steadfast** 398

stay *noun* **pardon** 290

    verb **reside** 341

steadfast *adjective* 398

steady *adjective* 398

steady *verb* 399

steady *adjective* **continuous** 78

steal *verb* 399

steal the show *verb* **succeed** 407

stealthy *adjective* **secretive** 362

steel *adjective* **gray** 182

steer clear of *verb* **avoid** 25

step *noun* **grade** 181

sterilize *verb* **clean** 58

stern *adjective* **solemn** 390

stew *verb* **boil** 37

    verb **worry** 471

stick *verb* **place** 300
sticker *noun* **label** 231
stick out *verb* **endure** 130
stick to your guns *verb* **persist** 296
stick up for *verb* **befriend** 30
stiff *adjective* **hard** 188
stiffen *verb* **harden** 189
stifle *verb* **limit** 242
    verb **suffocate** 409
still *adjective* 400
stimulate *verb* **refresh** 332
stimulating *adjective* **exciting** 138
stingy *adjective* **thrifty** 428
stinking *adjective* **smelly** 386
stipulate *verb* **demand** 103
stir *verb* **mix** 263
    verb **move** 266
stitch *noun* **pain** 290
    verb **sew** 367
stockpile *verb* **store** 402
stocky *adjective* 400
stoical *adjective* **patient** 293
stone *noun* 401
stony *adjective* **callous** 48
stop *verb* 401
stop *verb* **end** 129
    verb **prevent** 313
stop by *verb* **visit** 456
stoppage *noun* **halt** 186
store *verb* 402
storm *verb* **rain** 326
stout *adjective* **fat** 148
    adjective **stocky** 400
stout-hearted *adjective* **steadfast** 398
stow *verb* **store** 402
straightforward *adjective* **clear** 59
    adjective **frank** 165
strain *verb* **tire** 430
straitlaced *adjective* **strict** 403
strand *noun* **shore** 372
    noun **thread** 427
strange *adjective* 402
strangle *verb* **suffocate** 409
stratagem *noun* **plot** 302
stratum *noun* **layer** 235

stray *verb* **ramble** 326
streak *verb* **speed** 394
stream *verb* **flow** 159
streamline *verb* **simplify** 380
strength *noun* **force** 162
strengthen *verb* 403
stress *verb* **emphasize** 126
stretch *verb* **extend** 142
stretchy *adjective* **elastic** 126
strew *verb* **scatter** 358
strict *adjective* 403
stride *verb* **march** 253
strike *verb* **hit** 196
string *noun* **line** 243
strive for *verb* **seek** 363
stroke *verb* **touch** 432
stroll *verb* **walk** 458
strong *adjective* 404
strong *adjective* **powerful** 308
structure *noun* **shape** 369
struggle *verb* **fight** 154
strut *verb* **march** 253
stubborn *adjective* 404
stuck-up *adjective* **conceited** 73
student *noun* 405
study *verb* **examine** 135
    verb **read** 328
stuff *noun* **cloth** 61
stumble *verb* **fall** 146
stunned *adjective* **astonished** 21
    adjective **unconscious** 442
stunning *adjective* **beautiful** 29
stupendous *adjective* **astonishing** 22
stupid *adjective* **silly** 379
sturdy *adjective* **hardy** 189
style *noun* **fashion** 147
subdue *verb* 405
submerge *verb* **drop** 122
submission *noun* **offer** 281
submissive *adjective* 406
submit *verb* **give in** 177
subordinate *adjective* 406
subordinate *noun* **clerk** 59
subservient *adjective* **submissive** 406
subsidiary *adjective* **subordinate** 406

substandard *adjective* **defective** 99
substantial *adjective* **big** 34
substantiate *verb* **prove** 320
substitute *verb* **exchange** 137
subterfuge *noun* **trickery** 437
subtract *verb* 407
suburb *noun* **city** 57
suburban *adjective* **civic** 57
succeed *verb* 407
success *noun* **achievement** 5
succession *noun* **series** 367
succumb *verb* **give in** 177
sudden *adjective* 408
suffer *verb* **endure** 130
suffice *verb* **suit** 410
sufficient *adjective* 408
suffocate *verb* 409
sugary *adjective* **sweet** 414
suggest *verb* **advise** 8
      verb **hint** 196
suggestion *noun* 409
suit *verb* 410
sullen *adjective* **glum** 178
sultry *adjective* **humid** 202
summarize *verb* **shorten** 373
summary *noun* 410
summit *noun* **top** 432
summons *noun* **order** 285
sum up *verb* **shorten** 373
sunny *adjective* **fine** 155
super *adjective* **great** 183
superb *adjective* **great** 183
superfluity *noun* **excess** 137
superfluous *adjective* **extra** 143
superintendent *noun* **manager** 252
superior *adjective* 411
superior *noun* **boss** 40
supervise *verb* **manage** 251
supervisor *noun* **boss** 40
supple *adjective* **flexible** 157
supplement *verb* **add** 6
support *noun* 411
support *verb* **help** 192
      verb **steady** 399
supporter *noun* **helper** 193

supportive *adjective* **helpful** 193
suppose *verb* **think** 425
suppress *verb* **prevent** 313
sure *adjective* 412
surface *noun* **outside** 287
surge *verb* **flow** 159
surly *adjective* **glum** 179
surplus *noun* **excess** 137
surprised *adjective* **astonished** 21
surrender *verb* **give in** 177
surreptitious *adjective* **secretive** 362
surround *verb* **enclose** 127
surroundings *noun* 412
survey *noun* **inquiry** 216
      verb **inspect** 219
      verb **measure** 255
survive *verb* **continue** 78
      verb **live** 245
susceptible *adjective* **vulnerable** 457
suspect *verb* **think** 425
suspend *verb* **defer** 100
sustain *verb* **keep** 230
swab *verb* **wipe** 468
swagger *verb* **march** 253
swallow *verb* **drink** 121
swamp *noun* 413
swamp *verb* **flood** 158
      verb **soak** 388
swap *verb* **exchange** 137
sway *verb* 413
sway *noun* **influence** 213
sweat *verb* **worry** 471
sweet *adjective* 414
sweet *adjective* **musical** 267
sweet-talk *verb* **flatter** 156
swell *verb* **protrude** 319
swelter *verb* 414
sweltering *adjective* **hot** 200
swift *adjective* **fast** 148
swindle *noun* **trick** 436
      verb **cheat** 54
swing *noun* **rhythm** 346
swirl *verb* **spin** 395
symbol *noun* **sign** 378
symmetrical *adjective* **equal** 133

sympathy *noun* **pity** 299
syndicate *noun* **organization** 286
synonymous *adjective* **similar** 379
synopsis *noun* **summary** 410

Tt

tab *noun* **label** 231
tabulate *verb* **list** 244
taciturn *adjective* **reticent** 345
tack *verb* **sew** 367
tackle *verb* **attempt** 24
tack on *verb* **add** 6
tacky *adjective* **gaudy** 173
tag *noun* **label** 231
   verb **label** 232
   verb **name** 269
tag along *verb* **follow** 161
taint *verb* **spoil** 395
take *verb* **415**
take *verb* **choose** 56
take aback *verb* **shock** 372
take a dim view of
  verb **disapprove of** 110
take by surprise *verb* **catch** 51
take exception to
  verb **disapprove of** 110
take for a ride *verb* **deceive** 96
take for granted *verb* **believe** 32
take in *verb* **learn** 237
take it easy *verb* **rest** 343
take notice of *verb* **concentrate** 73
take off *verb* **flee** 157
take revenge *verb* **retaliate** 344
take to your heels *verb* **flee** 157
take with a grain of salt
  verb **doubt** 119
talk *noun* **415**
talk *verb* **416**
talk *noun* **gossip** 180
talkative *adjective* **416**
talk big *verb* **boast** 37

talk into *verb* **persuade** 298
talk nonsense *verb* **rave** 327
talk out of *verb* **discourage** 112
tall *adjective* **417**
tally *verb* **count** 82
tan *adjective* **brown** 44
tangible *adjective* **actual** 5
tap *verb* **hit** 196
tarry *verb* **dawdle** 94
tart *adjective* **sour** 392
task *noun* **417**
taste *verb* **eat** 124
tasteless *adjective* **418**
tasteless *adjective* **vulgar** 457
tasty *adjective* **418**
taunt *verb* **tease** 420
tawdry *adjective* **gaudy** 173
tawny *adjective* **yellow** 473
tax *verb* **tire** 430
teach *verb* **419**
teacher *noun* **419**
teammate *noun* **friend** 167
team up *verb* **cooperate** 79
tear *verb* **420**
tear *verb* **speed** 394
tease *verb* **420**
technique *noun* **method** 258
tedious *adjective* **boring** 39
        adjective **lengthy** 238
tell *verb* **421**
temper *noun* **anger** 12
temperamental *adjective* **fickle** 152
temperate *adjective* **fine** 155
        adjective **moderate** 264
tempo *noun* **rhythm** 346
temporary *adjective* **421**
tempting *adjective* **attractive** 25
tenacious *adjective* **persistent** 297
tenacity *noun* **persistence** 297
tender *adjective* **loving** 248
        adjective **soft** 389
tenderize *verb* **soften** 389
tenderness *noun* **pity** 299
tendril *noun* **thread** 427
tepid *adjective* **hot** 200

term *verb* **name** 269
terminal *adjective* **fatal** 149
terminate *verb* **end** 129
       verb **finish** 155
termination *noun* **end** 128
terracotta *adjective* **orange** 285
terrible *adjective* **horrible** 199
terrific *adjective* **excellent** 136
terrify *verb* **frighten** 168
terrorize *verb* **frighten** 168
terse *adjective* **abrupt** 1
test *noun* 422
test *verb* 422
textbook *noun* **book** 38
textile *noun* **cloth** 61
thankful *adjective* **grateful** 182
thankfulness *noun* **thanks** 423
thankless *adjective* **ungrateful** 446
thanks *noun* 423
thaw *verb* **soften** 389
theology *noun* **religion** 335
theory *noun* **thought** 426
thick *adjective* 423
thick *adjective* **opaque** 283
thicken *verb* 424
thickset *adjective* **stocky** 400
thief *noun* 424
thieve *verb* **steal** 399
thin *adjective* 425
thin *adjective* **light** 241
think *verb* 425
thin-skinned *adjective* **touchy** 433
thorough *adjective* 426
thought *noun* 426
thoughtful *adjective* **kind** 231
thoughtless *adjective* **careless** 50
thread *noun* 427
threadbare *adjective* **decrepit** 98
threaten *verb* 427
threaten *verb* **endanger** 129
thrifty *adjective* 428
thrilled *adjective* **excited** 138
     adjective **glad** 177
thrilling *adjective* **exciting** 138
thrive *verb* 428

throb *verb* 429
throng *noun* **crowd** 88
throw *verb* 429
throw in *verb* **add** 6
throw out *verb* **expel** 140
thrust *verb* **push** 323
thump *verb* **beat** 29
ticket *noun* **label** 231
tickled pink *adjective* **glad** 177
tidy *adjective* 430
tight *adjective* **narrow** 270
tilt *noun* **slope** 384
     verb **slope** 384
time *noun* **rhythm** 346
timeworn *adjective* **decrepit** 98
timid *adjective* **fearful** 151
tinkle *noun* **whisper** 465
tint *verb* **color** 65
tiny *adjective* **small** 385
tip *noun* **forecast** 163
     noun **suggestion** 409
     verb **slope** 384
tip off *verb* **warn** 459
tip over *verb* **overturn** 288
tire *verb* 430
tired *adjective* 431
tired of *adjective* **bored** 39
title *noun* **name** 269
     verb **name** 269
titter *verb* **smile** 387
toast *verb* 431
toast *verb* **acclaim** 3
toddle *verb* **limp** 243
toil *verb* **trudge** 437
     verb **work** 470
token *noun* **sign** 378
     noun **souvenir** 392
tolerant *adjective* **broad-minded** 43
     adjective **patient** 293
tolerate *verb* **allow** 11
     verb **endure** 130
toll *verb* **ring** 347
tongue *noun* **language** 234
tongue-tied *adjective* **inarticulate** 207
top *noun* 432

top *adjective* **best** 33
topple *verb* **fall** 146
torment *verb* **maltreat** 251
torture *verb* **maltreat** 251
toss *verb* **throw** 429
toss and turn *verb* **fidget** 153
total *adjective* **whole** 466
    verb **count** 82
totalitarian *adjective* **tyrannical** 439
totem *noun* **sign** 378
totter *verb* **limp** 243
touch *verb* 432
touch down *verb* **land** 233
touchy *adjective* 433
tough *adjective* **difficult** 106
    adjective **hard** 188
    adjective **hardy** 189
tour *noun* **journey** 227
tourist *noun* **traveler** 435
tournament *noun* **competition** 71
tow *verb* **pull** 322
towel *verb* **wipe** 468
towering *adjective* **tall** 417
town *noun* **city** 57
toxic *adjective* **poisonous** 303
trace *noun* 433
trace *verb* **copy** 80
    verb **find** 154
track *noun* **course** 84
    verb **follow** 161
tractable *adjective* **obedient** 278
trade *noun* **deal** 96
    noun **profession** 316
tradition *noun* 434
traditional *adjective* **usual** 452
tragedy *noun* **disaster** 110
train *verb* **teach** 419
trainer *noun* **teacher** 419
training *noun* **practice** 309
traitorous *adjective* **unfaithful** 445
tramp *verb* **trudge** 437
trample *verb* **press** 312
tranquil *adjective* **peaceful** 294
transaction *noun* **deal** 96
transfer *verb* **carry** 51

transform *verb* **change** 53
transgress *verb* **disobey** 114
transitory *adjective* **momentary** 265
translucent *adjective* **transparent** 434
transmit *verb* **send** 365
transparent *adjective* 434
transpire *verb* **happen** 187
transport *verb* **carry** 51
transpose *verb* **exchange** 137
trap *verb* **capture** 49
    verb **catch** 51
trash *noun* **rubbish** 350
travel *verb* 435
traveler *noun* 435
traverse *verb* **cross** 88
treacherous *adjective* **unfaithful** 445
treasure *noun* **wealth** 462
treble *adjective* **high-pitched** 195
tremble *verb* **fear** 150
    verb **shake** 368
tremendous *adjective* **huge** 201
trench *noun* **groove** 185
trend *noun* **fashion** 147
trial *noun* **test** 422
trick *noun* 436
trick *verb* 436
trickery *noun* 437
trickle *verb* **drip** 121
trifling *adjective* **minor** 260
trim *adjective* **tidy** 430
    verb **cut** 91
trip *noun* **journey** 227
    verb **fall** 146
trip up *verb* **err** 133
triumph *verb* **succeed** 407
trivial *adjective* **minor** 260
trivialize *verb* **minimize** 259
troop *noun* **group** 185
trophy *noun* **prize** 315
    noun **souvenir** 392
troubadour *noun* **singer** 381
trouble *verb* **upset** 450
trounce *verb* **defeat** 99
truant *noun* **escapee** 134
trudge *verb* 437

true *adjective* 438
true blue *adjective* **steadfast** 398
trust *verb* **believe** 32
trustworthy *adjective* **faithful** 145
trusty *adjective* **faithful** 145
truthful *adjective* **honest** 199
try *verb* **attempt** 24
   verb **test** 422
trying *adjective* **annoying** 15
tryst *noun* **meeting** 256
tumult *noun* **commotion** 69
tune *noun* **song** 391
tuneful *adjective* **musical** 267
turbid *adjective* **opaque** 283
turmoil *noun* **commotion** 69
turn *verb* 438
turn down *verb* **refuse** 333
turn out *verb* **assemble** 20
turn up *verb* **come** 67
turquoise *adjective* **green** 184
tussle *verb* **fight** 154
tutor *noun* **teacher** 419
twin *adjective* **double** 118
twinge *noun* **pain** 290
twinkle *verb* **sparkle** 393
twirl *verb* **spin** 395
twist *noun* **coil** 64
   verb **misrepresent** 262
   verb **turn** 438
twisted *adjective* 439
twisted *adjective* **crooked** 87
two-piece *adjective* **double** 118
tyrannical *adjective* 439

Uu

ugly *adjective* 440
ultimatum *noun* **demand** 102
umpteen *adjective* **countless** 82
unadorned *adjective* **simple** 380
unapologetic
   adjective **unashamed** 440

unappreciative
   adjective **ungrateful** 446
unashamed *adjective* 440
unattached
   adjective **independent** 210
unattainable *adjective* **impossible** 206
unbalanced *adjective* **uneven** 444
unbelievable *adjective* 441
unburden oneself *verb* **admit** 6
uncertain *adjective* 441
uncommon *adjective* **unusual** 449
uncomplicated *adjective* **easy** 124
uncompromising
   adjective **stubborn** 404
unconnected *adjective* **unrelated** 448
unconscious *adjective* 442
unconventional *adjective* 442
unconventional *adjective* **free** 166
uncooperative *adjective* **naughty** 271
uncouth *adjective* **vulgar** 457
undecided *adjective* **confused** 77
underhanded *adjective* **secretive** 362
understand *verb* 443
undertake *verb* **attempt** 24
undertaking *noun* 443
under the weather *adjective* **sick** 377
undertone *noun* **whisper** 465
unearth *verb* **find** 154
uneducated *adjective* **ignorant** 203
unequal *adjective* **uneven** 444
uneven *adjective* 444
unfair *adjective* 444
unfaithful *adjective* 445
unfeeling *adjective* **callous** 48
unfinished *adjective* **incomplete** 208
unflagging *adjective* **persistent** 297
unfold *verb* **reveal** 345
unfortunate *adjective* **unlucky** 447
unfriendly *adjective* 445
ungrateful *adjective* 446
unhappy *adjective* **sad** 353
unhurried *adjective* **slow** 385
uniform *adjective* **equal** 133
unimportant
   adjective **insignificant** 218

uninformed *adjective* **ignorant** 203
uninhibited *adjective* **free** 166
union *noun* **club** 62
unique *adjective* **single** 381
unite *verb* **cooperate** 79
    verb **join** 226
unjust *adjective* **unfair** 444
unkempt *adjective* **scruffy** 361
unkind *adjective* **mean** 254
unlike *adjective* 446
unlikely *adjective* **unbelievable** 441
unlucky *adjective* 447
unobtrusive *adjective* **simple** 380
unofficial *adjective* **informal** 214
unpalatable *adjective* **inedible** 211
unpleasant *adjective* 447
unravel *verb* **simplify** 380
unreasonable *adjective* **irrational** 224
unrelated *adjective* 448
unremorseful
    adjective **unashamed** 440
unrepentant
    adjective **unashamed** 440
unruly *adjective* **disobedient** 114
unsafe *adjective* **dangerous** 92
unseen *adjective* **invisible** 223
unselfish *adjective* **kind** 231
unskillful *adjective* **incompetent** 208
unsophisticated *adjective* **naive** 268
unsound *adjective* **defective** 99
unsteady *adjective* **erratic** 134
unthinkable *adjective* **impossible** 206
untidy *adjective* 448
untold *adjective* **countless** 82
untrained *adjective* **inexperienced** 212
untrue *adjective* **incorrect** 209
unusual *adjective* 449
unwilling *adjective* 449
unworldly *adjective* **naive** 268
upgrade *verb* **improve** 206
uppity *adjective* **pompous** 304
upright *adjective* **honest** 199
uprising *noun* **rebellion** 330
uproar *noun* **noise** 276
upset *adjective* 450

upset *verb* 450
upset *adjective* **sad** 353
    verb **disorganize** 115
    verb **overturn** 288
uptight *adjective* **upset** 450
up-to-date *adjective* **modern** 265
urban *adjective* **civic** 57
urge *verb* **encourage** 128
usage *noun* **tradtion** 434
use *verb* 451
useful *adjective* 451
useful *adjective* **helpful** 193
useless *adjective* 452
usual *adjective* 452
utilize *verb* **use** 451
utter *verb* **pronounce** 317

Vv

vacant *adjective* **empty** 127
vacate *verb* **quit** 325
vacillate *verb* **fluctuate** 159
vague *adjective* 453
vain *adjective* **conceited** 73
    adjective **useless** 452
valiant *adjective* **brave** 41
valid *adjective* **true** 438
valor *noun* **courage** 84
valuable *adjective* **expensive** 141
    adjective **useful** 451
value *verb* **judge** 228
vandalize *verb* **damage** 92
vanish *verb* **disappear** 109
vanquish *verb* **defeat** 99
various *adjective* 453
vary *verb* **change** 53
vast *adjective* **huge** 201
vault *verb* **jump** 229
vehemence *noun* **violence** 454
vein *noun* **layer** 235
velvet *adjective* **soft** 389
vendor *noun* **seller** 364
veneer *noun* **coating** 64

venerate *verb* **worship** 471
veneration *noun* **respect** 342
vengeful *adjective* **resentful** 340
venomous *adjective* **poisonous** 303
venture *noun* **undertaking** 443
verbose *adjective* **lengthy** 238
verify *verb* **prove** 320
vex *verb* **irritate** 224
vexed *adjective* **annoyed** 14
viable *adjective* **possible** 307
vibrate *verb* **shake** 368
vicious *adjective* **cruel** 89
victimize *verb* **maltreat** 251
victor *noun* **winner** 467
victuals *noun* **food** 161
vie *verb* **compete** 70
view *noun* 454
view *verb* **see** 362
viewpoint *noun* **opinion** 283
vigor *noun* **force** 162
vigorous *adjective* **energetic** 131
vile *adjective* **unpleasant** 447
villainous *adjective* **evil** 135
vindicate *verb* **justify** 229
vindictive *adjective* **resentful** 340
vintage *adjective* **old** 282
violate *verb* **disobey** 114
violence *noun* 454
violent *adjective* 455
violent *adjective* **intense** 221
virtue *noun* 455
virtuoso *noun* **musician** 268
visible *adjective* 456
visit *verb* 456
vista *noun* **view** 454
vital *adjective* **necessary** 273
vivacious *adjective* **lively** 245
vivid *adjective* **colorful** 66
　　adjective **intense** 221
vocalist *noun* **singer** 381
vocation *noun* **job** 226
vogue *noun* **fashion** 147
voice *verb* **pronounce** 317
void *adjective* **empty** 127
voluble *adjective* **talkative** 416

volume *noun* **book** 38
voracious *adjective* **greedy** 183
vow *noun* **promise** 317
　　verb **intend** 220
voyage *verb* **travel** 435
vulgar *adjective* 457
vulnerable *adjective* 457

Ww

waddle *verb* **sway** 413
wade through *verb* **read** 328
wage *noun* **pay** 293
wail *verb* **cry** 90
walk *verb* 458
wander *verb* **ramble** 326
　　verb **travel** 435
wane *verb* **decrease** 97
want *verb* 458
want *noun* **poverty** 307
ward *noun* **dependant** 103
wardrooube *noun* **clothing** 61
warlike *adjective* 459
warm *adjective* **friendly** 167
　　adjective **hot** 200
　　adjective **near** 272
warm-up *noun* **practice** 309
warn *verb* 459
warn *verb* **threaten** 427
warped *adjective* **crooked** 87
warrant *noun* **order** 285
　　verb **justify** 229
wary *adjective* 460
wash *verb* **clean** 58
　　verb **flow** 159
waste *verb* 460
waste away *verb* **deteriorate** 105
watch *verb* **see** 362
watchful *adjective* **alert** 11
　　adjective **wary** 460
water *verb* **wet** 464
waterfront *noun* **shore** 372
wave *verb* **sway** 413

waver *verb* **cower** 85
    verb **fluctuate** 159
wavy *adjective* **twisted** 439
wax *verb* **polish** 303
wayfarer *noun* **traveler** 435
waylay *verb* **catch** 51
weak *adjective* 461
weak *adjective* **powerless** 308
weaken *verb* 461
weak-willed
  adjective **submissive** 406
wealth *noun* 462
wealthy *adjective* 462
weary *adjective* **tired** 431
    verb **tire** 430
weep *verb* **cry** 90
weigh *verb* **ponder** 305
weight *noun* 463
weird *adjective* **strange** 402
welcome *adjective* **nice** 276
    verb **like** 241
well *adjective* **healthy** 190
well-balanced *adjective* **sane** 355
    adjective **steady** 398
well-behaved *adjective* 463
well-informed
  adjective **educated** 125
well-mannered *adjective* **well-behaved** 463
well-meaning *adjective* **kind** 231
well-off *adjective* **wealthy** 462
wet *adjective* 464
wet *verb* 464
wheeze *verb* **gasp** 172
whimper *verb* **cry** 90
whine *verb* **complain** 71
whip up *verb* **make** 250
whirl *verb* **spin** 395
whirr *verb* **spin** 395
whisper *noun* 465
whisper *noun* **gossip** 180
    noun **trace** 433
white *adjective* 465
whole *adjective* 466
wholesale *verb* **sell** 364

whoop *verb* **shout** 373
whoop it up *verb* **rejoice** 334
wicked *adjective* **evil** 135
wide *adjective* 466
wide *adjective* **spacious** 393
wield *verb* **use** 451
wild *adjective* **free** 166
  adjective **violent** 455
will *noun* **wish** 469
willful *adjective* **disobedient** 114
willing *adjective* **enthusiastic** 132
wily *adjective* **cunning** 90
win *verb* **get** 175
    verb **succeed** 407
wind *verb* **turn** 438
wind down *verb* **rest** 343
winding *adjective* **twisted** 439
wing *noun* **side** 377
winner *noun* 467
wintry *adjective* 467
wipe *verb* 468
wipe out *verb* **destroy** 105
wiry *adjective* **strong** 404
wise *adjective* **sensible** 366
wisecrack *noun* 468
wish *noun* 469
withdraw *verb* **leave** 237
    verb **remove** 337
wither *verb* **shrink** 376
withstand *verb* **resist** 341
witness *verb* **see** 362
witticism *noun* **wisecrack** 468
wobble *verb* **sway** 413
woeful *adjective* **pathetic** 292
woman *noun* **female** 152
wonder *noun* **miracle** 260
wonderful *adjective* 469
wooly *adjective* **vague** 453
word *noun* **promise** 317
wordy *adjective* **lengthy** 238
work *noun* 470
work *verb* 470
work *noun* **job** 226
    verb **sew** 367
workable *adjective* **possible** 307

work out *verb* **solve** 390
work toward *verb* **attempt** 24
worn *adjective* **tired** 431
worry *verb* 471
worry *verb* **upset** 450
worsen *verb* **deteriorate** 105
worship *verb* 471
worthless *adjective* **inferior** 212
wound *verb* **hurt** 203
wraith *noun* **ghost** 175
wrangle *verb* **disagree** 108
wrap *verb* **cover** 85
wrath *noun* **anger** 12
wreathe *verb* **cover** 85
wreck *verb* **damage** 92
wretched *adjective* **pathetic** 292
     adjective **unlucky** 447
wriggle *verb* **fidget** 153
write *verb* 472
write *verb* **compose** 72

writhe *verb* **fidget** 153
wrought up *adjective* **excited** 138

#

yard *noun* 472
yell *verb* **shout** 373
yellow *adjective* 473
yelp *verb* **shriek** 375
yen *noun* **wish** 469
yield *verb* **give in** 177
    verb **produce** 315
young *adjective* 473
young *noun* **offspring** 281
young man *noun* **male** 250
young woman *noun* **female** 152
youthful *adjective* **young** 473
yummy *adjective* **delicious** 102